WASHINGTON DC

PATRICIA NEVINS KIME

The Magia Ayesha's Restaurant Presidential Mural by Karlisima/www.Karlisima.com

Contents

Maps

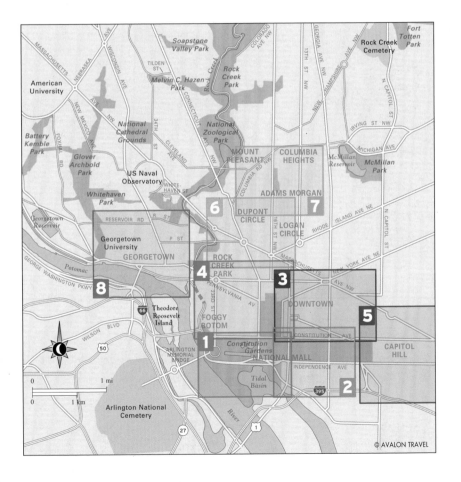

SEE MAP 4

CONSTITUTION AVE NW

CONSTITUTION AVE NW

CONSTITUTION AVE NW

23RD ST NW

22ND ST NW

21ST ST NW

20TH ST NW

HENRY BACON DR NW

Constitution
Gardens ✪2

1 ✪
Vietnam Veterans
National Memorial

Constitution
Gardens
Pond

LINCOLN MEMORIAL CIR

NATIONAL MALL WEST

✪3
Lincoln
Memorial

Reflecting Pool

23RD ST SW

DANIEL C FRENCH DR SW

Korean War
Veterans Memorial
6

INDEPENDENCE AVE SW

INDEPENDENCE AVE SW

INDEPENDENCE AVE SW

**Martin Luther King Jr.
National Memorial 8** ✪

West Potomac Park

Ⓐ
7

OHIO DR SW

WEST BASIN DR SW

Franklin Delano Roosevelt
Memorial

9

HAINS PT SW

✪ SIGHTS

1 VIETNAM VETERANS
   NATIONAL
   MEMORIAL
2 CONSTITUTION
   GARDENS
3 **⊂ LINCOLN MEMORIAL**
4 NATIONAL WORLD
   WAR II MEMORIAL
5 **⊂ WASHINGTON
   MONUMENT**
6 KOREAN WAR
   VETERANS
   MEMORIAL

8 MARTIN LUTHER
   KING JR. NATIONAL
   MEMORIAL
9 FRANKLIN DELANO
   ROOSEVELT
   MEMORIAL
10 TIDAL BASIN
11 U.S. HOLOCAUST
   MEMORIAL MUSEUM
12 U.S. BUREAU OF
   ENGRAVING AND
   PRINTING
13 **⊂ JEFFERSON
   MEMORIAL**

Ⓐ ARTS AND LEISURE

7 WEST POTOMAC
   PARK

Potomac

River

0   100 yds

0   100 m

DISTANCE ACROSS MAP
Approximate: 1.1 mi or 1.8 km

ELLIPSE RD NW

NW

19TH ST

15TH ST NW

14TH ST NW

CONSTITUTION AVE NW

VIA AVE NW

17TH ST NW

Constitution
Gardens
Pond

13TH ST NW

MADISON DR NW

National
World War II
Memorial

Washington
Monument   5

4

JEFFERSON DR SW

SEE MAP 2

INDEPENDENCE AVE SW

INDEPENDENCE AVE SW

INDEPENDENCE AVE SW

11
U.S. Holocaust
Memorial Museum

RAOUL WALLENBERG PL SW

MAINE AVE SW

MAINE AVE SW

Tidal Basin
10

12
U.S. Bureau of
Engraving and
Printing

14TH ST SW

Tidal Basin

EAST BASIN DR SW

14TH ST SW

14TH ST SW

OHIO DR SW

13   Jefferson
Memorial

Ronald
Reagan
Building

SIGHTS

1	NATIONAL MUSEUM OF AMERICAN HISTORY	13	THE SMITHSONIAN INSTITUTION
2	NATIONAL MUSEUM OF NATURAL HISTORY	18	NATIONAL AIR AND SPACE MUSEUM
3	NATIONAL ARCHIVES	20	NATIONAL MUSEUM OF THE AMERICAN INDIAN
6	NATIONAL GALLERY OF ART		

RESTAURANTS

4	PAVILION CAFÉ	21	MITSITAM NATIVE FOODS
7	GARDEN CAFÉ	22	CITYZEN
9	ESPRESSO AND GELATO BAR	23	SOU'WESTER
14	CASTLE CAFÉ		

ARTS AND LEISURE

5	SCULPTURE GARDEN ICE RINK	15	SMITHSONIAN GARDENS
10	CAPITAL BIKESHARE	16	THE NATIONAL MUSEUM OF AFRICAN ART
11	THE FREER GALLERY OF ART AND ARTHUR M. SACKLER GALLERY	17	THE HIRSHHORN MUSEUM AND SCULPTURE GARDEN
12	DISCOVERY THEATRE	19	SMITHSONIAN IMAX THEATERS

SHOPS

| 8 | THE NATIONAL GALLERY OF ART |

HOTELS

| 24 | MANDARIN ORIENTAL | 25 | L'ENFANT PLAZA HOTEL |

CONSTITUTION AVE NW

CONSTITUTIO

National Museum
of Natural Histor

National Museum
of American History

MADISON DR NW

JEFFERSON DR SW

The Smithson
Institution

Smithsonian

INDEPENDENCE AVE SW

INDEPENDENCE AVE S

SEE MAP 1

15TH ST SW

14TH ST SW

MAINE AVE SW

C ST SW

13TH ST SW

D ST SW

MARYLAND AVE SW

L'ENFANT PROMENADE SW

12TH ST SW

MAINE AVE SW

14TH ST SW

22,23 24

0   100 yds
0   100 m

DISTANCE ACROSS MAP
Approximate: 1.1 mi or 1.8 km

© AVALON TRAVEL

SEE MAP 3

D ST

D ST NW

INDIANA AVE NW

6TH ST NW

C ST NW

3RD ST NW

PENNSYLVANIA AVE NW

M

Archives-Navy
Memorial

9TH ST NW

National
Archives

★ 3

R 4

A 5

7TH ST NW

CONSTITUTION AVE NW

★ R S
6 7 8

National Gallery
of Art

4TH ST NW

R 9

DR NW

MADISON DR NW

NATIONAL MALL EAST

3RD ST SW

SEE MAP 5

20 ◆ R 21

National Museum of
the American Indian

The Hirshhorn
Museum and
Sculpture Garden

A 17

7TH ST SW

National Air and
Space Museum

18 ◆ A 19

MARYLAND AVE SW

MARYLAND AVE SW

6TH ST SW

C ST SW

9TH ST SW

C ST SW

Federal
Center
SW

3RD ST SW

VIRGINIA AVE SW

M

D ST SW

D ST SW

M

L'Enfant
Plaza

7TH ST SW

VIRGINIA AVE SW

SCHOOL ST SW

4TH ST SW

3RD ST SW

E ST SW

E ST SW

FRONTAGE RD SW

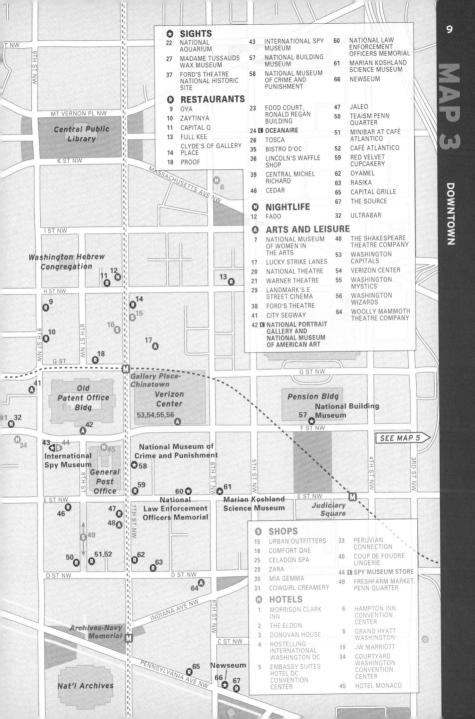

SIGHTS
22 NATIONAL AQUARIUM
27 MADAME TUSSAUDS WAX MUSEUM
37 FORD'S THEATRE NATIONAL HISTORIC SITE

43 INTERNATIONAL SPY MUSEUM
57 NATIONAL BUILDING MUSEUM
58 NATIONAL MUSEUM OF CRIME AND PUNISHMENT

60 NATIONAL LAW ENFORCEMENT OFFICERS MEMORIAL
61 MARIAN KOSHLAND SCIENCE MUSEUM
66 NEWSEUM

RESTAURANTS
9 OYA
10 ZAYTINYA
11 CAPITAL Q
13 FULL KEE
14 CLYDE'S OF GALLERY PLACE
18 PROOF

23 FOOD COURT, RONALD REGAN BUILDING
24 OCEANAIRE
26 TOSCA
35 BISTRO D'OC
36 LINCOLN'S WAFFLE SHOP
39 CENTRAL MICHEL RICHARD
46 CEDAR

47 JALEO
50 TEAISM PENN QUARTER
51 MINIBAR AT CAFÉ ATLANTICO
52 CAFÉ ATLÁNTICO
59 RED VELVET CUPCAKERY
62 OYAMEL
63 RASIKA
65 CAPITAL GRILLE
67 THE SOURCE

NIGHTLIFE
12 FADO

32 ULTRABAR

ARTS AND LEISURE
7 NATIONAL MUSEUM OF WOMEN IN THE ARTS
17 LUCKY STRIKE LANES
20 NATIONAL THEATRE
21 WARNER THEATRE
29 LANDMARK'S E STREET CINEMA
38 FORD'S THEATRE
41 CITY SEGWAY
42 NATIONAL PORTRAIT GALLERY AND NATIONAL MUSEUM OF AMERICAN ART

48 THE SHAKESPEARE THEATRE COMPANY
53 WASHINGTON CAPITALS
54 VERIZON CENTER
55 WASHINGTON MYSTICS
56 WASHINGTON WIZARDS
64 WOOLLY MAMMOTH THEATRE COMPANY

ST NW

9TH ST NW

MT VERNON PL NW

Central Public Library

K ST NW

MASSACHUSETTS AVE NW

H 6

I ST NW

Washington Hebrew Congregation

11 R 12 N

13 R

H ST NW

R 9

8TH ST NW

R 10

14 R

S 15

16 S

17 A

9TH ST NW

18 R

G ST

A 41

Old Patent Office Bldg

M Gallery Place-Chinatown
Verizon Center
53,54,55,56 A

G ST NW

Pension Bldg
National Building Museum
57 A Museum

F ST NW

SEE MAP 5

1 32
N

A 42

H 34

43 44
A B

International Spy Museum

H 45

8TH ST

General Post Office

59

National Museum of Crime and Punishment
58

60

6TH ST NW

61

5TH ST NW

F ST NW

4TH ST NW

3RD ST NW

E ST NW

M

Judiciary Square

E ST NW

46 R

National Law Enforcement Officers Memorial

Marian Koshland Science Museum

47 R
48 A

7TH ST NW

S 49

50 R

51,52 R

62 R

63 R

D ST NW

D ST NW

64 A

INDIANA AVE NW

6TH ST NW

Archives-Navy Memorial M

C ST NW

PENNSYLVANIA AVE NW

65 R

Newseum

66 67 R

Nat'l Archives

SHOPS
15 URBAN OUTFITTERS
16 COMFORT ONE
25 CELADON SPA
28 ZARA
30 MIA GEMMA
31 COWGIRL CREAMERY

33 PERUVIAN CONNECTION
40 COUP DE FOUDRE LINGERIE
44 SPY MUSEUM STORE
49 FRESHFARM MARKET, PENN QUARTER

HOTELS
1 MORRISON CLARK INN
2 THE ELDON
3 DONOVAN HOUSE
4 HOSTELLING INTERNATIONAL WASHINGTON DC
5 EMBASSY SUITES HOTEL DC CONVENTION CENTER

6 HAMPTON INN CONVENTION CENTER
8 GRAND HYATT WASHINGTON
19 JW MARRIOTT
34 COURTYARD WASHINGTON CONVENTION CENTER
45 HOTEL MONACO

MAP 4

FOGGY BOTTOM

1 National Postal Museum

Union Station

5 6 7-10
11-14

2
3
4
15 16

17 18 19,20

Lower Senate Park

21
22

23
24

National Japanese American Memorial 25

26

Sewall-Belmont House 27

28

CONSTITUTION AVE NW

CONSTITUTION AVE NE

The Supreme Court of the United States 32

United States Capitol 31
30 The U.S. Capitol Grounds

NATIONAL MALL

33 Library of Congress

34 35
Folger Shakespeare Library

36

U.S. Botanic Gardens 29

SEE MAP 2

INDEPENDENCE AVE SW

INDEPENDENCE AVE SE

38
39
42
40 41

The Spirit of Justice Park

Capitol South

43
44

54

SEE MAP 3

© AVALON TRAVEL

0   200 yds
0   200 m

DISTANCE ACROSS MAP
Approximate: 1.7 mi or 2.8 km

SIGHTS

1 NATIONAL POSTAL MUSEUM
5 UNION STATION
25 NATIONAL JAPANESE AMERICAN MEMORIAL
27 SEWALL-BELMONT HOUSE
29 U.S. BOTANIC GARDENS
30 UNITED STATES CAPITOL
31 ◖ THE U.S. CAPITOL GROUNDS
32 THE SUPREME COURT OF THE UNITED STATES
33 LIBRARY OF CONGRESS
34 FOLGER SHAKESPEARE LIBRARY
37 LINCOLN PARK
60 MARINE BARRACKS WASHINGTON

RESTAURANTS

3 DUBLINER PUB
6 UNION STATION FOOD COURT
15 BISTRO BIS
19 JOHNNY'S HALF SHELL
20 TAQUERIA NACIONAL
21 CAFÉ BERLIN
22 ◖ THE MONOCLE
23 BAGELS & BAGUETTES
26 ◖ CHARLIE PALMER STEAK
36 JIMMY T'S
39 GOOD STUFF EATERY
43 TORTILLA COAST
46 AQUA AL 2
47 TUNNICLIFF'S TAVERN
50 MONTMARTRE
51 MARKET LUNCH
53 LA PLAZA
55 TRATTORIA ALBERTO
56 MATCHBOX

NIGHTLIFE

2 KELLY'S IRISH TIMES
24 LOUNGE 201
38 SONOMA
40 THE POUR HOUSE
41 ◖ TUNE INN
44 BULLFEATHERS
58 PHASE 1

ARTS AND LEISURE

7 BIKE AND ROLL
8 DC DUCKS
9 OLD TOWN TROLLEY TOURS
10 OPEN TOP TOURS, GRAY LINE
35 FOLGER THEATRE
45 WILLIAM H. RUMSEY AQUATICS CENTER
54 RESULTS THE GYM
57 THE FRIDGE DC

SHOPS

11 AMERICA!
12 APPALACHIAN SPRING
13 JOS. A. BANK CLOTHIERS
14 UNION STATION
48 CAPITOL HILL BOOKS
49 WOVEN HISTORY & ◖ SILK ROAD
52 EASTERN MARKET
59 HOMEBODY

HOTELS

4 PHOENIX PARK HOTEL
16 ◖ HOTEL GEORGE
17 HYATT REGENCY WASHINGTON ON CAPITOL HILL
18 LIAISON CAPITOL HILL
28 APPLE TREE INN
42 CAPITOL HILL SUITES

E ST NE
MARYLAND AVE NE
D ST NE
ST NE
C ST NE
MASSACHUSETTS AVE NW
CONSTITUTION AVE NE
9TH ST SE
10TH ST NE
11TH ST NE
12TH ST NE
EAST CAPITOL ST
Lincoln Park
37
EAST CAPITOL ST
CAPITOL HILL
7TH ST SE
8TH ST SE
NORTH CAROLINA AVE SE
46
45
47
C ST
48
49
50
51
53
Eastern Market
M
D ST SE
D ST SE
12TH ST SE
13TH ST SE
14TH ST SE
KENTUCKY AVE SE
E ST SE
55
56
57
58
7TH ST SE
9TH ST SE
10TH ST SE
11TH ST SE
G ST SE
59
MARINE BARRACKS
Marine Barracks Washington
60
Potomac Ave
M
L ST SE

MAP 6

DUPONT CIRCLE

WYOMING AVE NW

TRACY PL NW

SHERIDAN-KALORAMA

23RD ST NW

CALIFORNIA ST NW

PHELPS PL NW

LEROY PL NW

BANCROFT PL NW

BANCROFT PL NW

KALORAMA TRIANGLE

VERNON ST NW

CONNECTICUT AVE

T ST NW

FLORIDA AVE NW

20TH ST NW

19TH ST NW

18TH ST NW

S ST NW

S ST NW

CONNECTICUT AVE NW

RIGGS PL NW

Textile Museum
Woodrow Wilson House

DECATUR PL NW

MASSACHUSETTS AVE NW

R ST NW

Sheridan Circle Park

SHERIDAN CIR

FLORIDA AVE NW

HILLYER CT NW

DUPONT CIRCLE

Embassy Row

Dumbarton Bridge

SEE MAP 8

GEORGETOWN

Q ST NW

Anderson House

MASSACHUSETTS AVE NW

21ST ST NW

20TH ST NW

19TH ST NW

NEW HAMPSHIRE AVE NW

NEW HAMPSHIRE AVE NW

DUPONT CIR

Dupont Circle

M

Dupont Circle

DUPONT CIR

P ST NW

23RD ST NW

Codman Carriage House

Rock Creek & Potomac Parkway

NEWPORT PL NW

O ST NW

SUNDERLAND PL NW

N ST NW

CONNECTICUT AVE NW

18TH ST NW

M ST NW

24TH ST NW

25TH ST NW

0   100 yds
0   100 m

DISTANCE ACROSS MAP
Approximate: 1.2 mi or 1.9 km

© AVALON TRAVEL

1 2 3 4 5 6 7 9 10 11 13 14 15 16 17 18 19 20 21 22 23 24 25 26 27 28 29 30 31 32 33, 34 35 36 37 38 40

MAP 6 DUPONT CIRCLE

SIGHTS
- 5 WOODROW WILSON HOUSE
- 6 TEXTILE MUSEUM
- 18 EMBASSY ROW
- 19 ANDERSON HOUSE
- 51 CATHEDRAL OF ST. MATTHEW THE APOSTLE
- 53 NATIONAL GEOGRAPHIC MUSEUM
- 59 MARY MCLEOD BETHUNE COUNCIL HOUSE NATIONAL HISTORIC SITE

RESTAURANTS
- 9 BISTROT DU COIN
- 16 RESTAURANT NORA
- 22 OBELISK
- 27 ZORBA'S CAFÉ
- 29 RAKU
- 30 KRAMERBOOKS & AFTERWORDS CAFÉ
- 32 BGR THE BURGER JOINT
- 36 LUNA GRILL
- 41 HANK'S OYSTER BAR
- 44 MR. YOGATO
- 45 KOMI
- 46 TABARD INN

NIGHTLIFE
- 3 RUSSIA HOUSE
- 4 VERITAS
- 12 COBALT
- 35 CAFÉ CITRON
- 39 LUCKY BAR
- 40 18TH STREET LOUNGE
- 43 JR'S BAR AND GRILL
- 57 CHURCHKEY

ARTS AND LEISURE
- 7 DC BY FOOT
- 13 STUDIO GALLERY
- 14 ALEX GALLERY AND GALLERY A
- 15 HILLYER ART SPACE
- 17 PHILLIPS COLLECTION
- 21 BURTON MARINKOVICH FINE ART
- 42 THEATER J
- 50 NATIONAL CAPITAL AREA YMCA
- 55 STUDIO THEATER
- 56 IRVINE CONTEMPORARY

SHOPS
- 10 GINZA
- 11 SECONDI
- 23 SECOND STORY BOOKS
- 25 MELODY RECORD SHOP
- 26 BLUE MERCURY
- 31 KRAMERBOOKS & AFTERWORDS
- 33 BEAUTY 360
- 34 PROPER TOPPER
- 37 KID'S CLOSET
- 38 BETSY FISHER
- 54 UNIVERSAL GEAR

HOTELS
- 1 THE NORMANDY
- 2 WASHINGTON HILTON
- 8 CARLYLE SUITES HOTEL
- 20 HOTEL PALOMAR WASHINGTON
- 24 MANSION AT O
- 28 THE DUPONT AT THE CIRCLE
- 47 HOTEL TABARD INN
- 48 THE TOPAZ
- 49 HOTEL ROUGE
- 52 THE JEFFERSON
- 58 HOTEL HELIX

SEE MAP 7

STRIVERS' SECTION

NEW HAMPSHIRE AVE NW

17TH ST NW

U ST NW

ILLARD ST

ST NW

S ST NW

RIGGS PL NW

R ST NW

CORCORAN ST NW

CHURCH ST NW

P ST NW

Q ST NW

MASSACHUSETTS AVENUE

GREATER 14TH STREET

St. Luke's Church

LOGAN CIRCLE

Grace Reformed Church

The Braxton

Mary McLeod Bethune Council House National Historic Site

Scott Circle

University of California Washington Center

Luther Place Mem. Church

Nat'l City Christian Church

Cathedral of St. Matthew the Apostle

National Geographic Museum

SEE MAP 4

Metropolitan A.M.E. Church

Thomas Circle

M ST NW

N ST NW

MASSACHUSETTS AVE NW

RHODE ISLAND AVE NW

VERMONT AVE NW

KINGMAN PL NW

ONTARIO RD NW

QUARRY RD NW

GIRARD ST NW

MOUNT PLEASANT

ONTARIO PL NW

FULLER ST NW

FAIRMONT

Engine Co. #21 &
Truck Co. #9 **N** 1

MOZART PL NW

LANIER PL NW

EUCLID ST

UNIVERSITY PL NW

ADAMS MILL RD NW

COLUMBIA RD NW

EUCLID ST NW

CLIFTO

17TH ST NW

ADAMS
MORGAN

N 3

Meridian
Hall

CHAPIN ST NW

Merid

4 **R**
7 **R**

5 **R** **N** 6

A 2

Merid#
Manc

8 **N** **A**
10

R 9

Meridian
Mansions

KALORAMA
TRIANGLE

KALORAMA RD NW

CRESCENT PL NW

Meridian
Hill
Park

BELMONT ST

18TH ST NW

CHAMPLAIN ST NW

ONTARIO RD NW

R 11

BELMONT RD NW

S 12

Meridian
House

BELMONT PL NW

KALORAMA RD NW

BEEKMAN PL NW

WYOMING AVE NW

FLORIDA AVE NW

SCHOOL PL NW

OLD MORGAN RD NW

13 **S**

V ST NW

14 **S**

CALIFORNIA ST NW

SEATON ST NW

VERNON ST NW

18TH ST NW

U ST NW

20 **H**

U ST NW

19 **S**

N 21

23,24 **S** **S** 25

26 **N** **S**

STRIVERS'
SECTION

WILLARD ST NW

17TH ST NW

NEW HAMPSHIRE AVE NW

CAROLINE ST NW

15TH ST NW

19TH ST NW

S 15

T ST NW

R 16

22 **H**

SIXTEENTH
STREET

T ST NW

S 17

SWANN ST NW

SWANN ST NW

N 18

S ST NW

JOHNSON AVE NW

0   200 yds

0   200 m

RIGGS PL NW

DISTANCE ACROSS MAP
Approximate: 1.2 mi or 2 km

DUPONT
CIRCLE

○ SIGHTS
38	AFRICAN AMERICAN CIVIL WAR MUSEUM AND MEMORIAL	43	HOWARD UNIVERSITY

® RESTAURANTS
4	PERRY'S	7	CASHION'S EAT PLACE	28	FAST GOURMET
5	JULIA'S EMPANADAS	9	THE DINER	29	BUSBOYS AND POETS
6	TRYST	11	JUMBO SLICE	34	BEN'S CHILI BOWL
		16	LAURIOL PLAZA	39	ETETE

ℕ NIGHTLIFE
3	MADAM'S ORGAN	32	PATTY BOOM BOOM	41	9:30 CLUB
8	THE REEF	35	U-STREET MUSIC HALL	42	TOWN DANCEBOUTIQUE
21	CHI-CHA LOUNGE	36	VINOTECA	44	GATE 54 AT CAFÉ SAINT-EX
26	U-TOPIA	37	BOHEMIAN CAVERNS	47	BLACK CAT
30	THE GIBSON	40	NELLIE'S SPORTS BAR	51	CORK
31	MARVIN				

○ ARTS AND LEISURE
2	MERIDIAN HILL PARK	10	DISTRICT OF COLUMBIA ARTS CENTER	33	LINCOLN THEATER

⑤ SHOPS
12	THE BRASS KNOB	15	RED ONION RECORDS & BOOKS	25	CAKELOVE
13	CROOKED BEAT RECORDS	17	DOGGIE STYLE	27	GOODWOOD
14	MEEPS AND AUNT NEENSIES VINTAGE FASHIONETTE	19	THE WRITTEN WORD	45	MULEH
		23	MILLENNIUM DECORATIVE ARTS	46	VASTU
		24	NANA	48	HOME RULE
				49	RUE 14
				50	PULP

ℍ HOTELS
1	ADAM'S INN	20	BED AND BREAKFAST ON U STREET	22	WINDSOR INN
18	SWANN HOUSE				

SEE MAP 6

© AVALON TRAVEL

0   200 yds
0   200 m

DISTANCE ACROSS MAP
Approximate: 1.4 mi or 2.3 km

T ST NW
S ST NW
R ST NW
39TH ST NW
38TH ST NW
37TH ST NW
36TH ST NW
35TH ST NW
35TH ST NW

RESERVOIR RD NW

WINFIELD LN NW

Q ST NW

VOLTA PL NW

P ST NW

34TH ST NW

Georgetown University

P ST NW

37TH ST NW

36TH ST NW

35TH ST NW

25 ⚬
Georgetown University

26,27 ⓡ

PROSPECT ST NW

CANAL RD NW

28 Ⓐ

29 Ⓐ

FRANCIS SCOTT KEY BRG NW

⚬ **SIGHTS**

7	OAK HILL CEMETERY	25	GEORGETOWN UNIVERSITY	46	OLD STONE HOUSE
8	DUMBARTON HOUSE				

ⓡ **RESTAURANTS**

2	CAFÉ DIVAN	37	GEORGETOWN CUPCAKE	45	MOBY DICK'S HOUSE OF KABOB
26	THE TOMBS	38	TACKLE BOX	50	CITRONELLE
27 Ⓒ	1789	39	HOOK	53	CAFÉ TU-O-TU
31	BANGKOK BISTRO	40 Ⓒ	OLD GLORY BAR-B-QUE	54	BOURBON STEAK
34 Ⓒ	PIZZERIA PARADISO	43	BISTRO FRANÇAIS	55	SEASONS
35	DEAN AND DELUCA			60	BAKED AND WIRED
				64 Ⓒ	SEQUOIA

Ⓝ **NIGHTLIFE**

3 Ⓒ	BISTROT LEPIC	32	RHINO BAR AND PUMPHOUSE	65	SEQUOIA
24	BILLY MARTIN'S TAVERN	44 Ⓒ	BLUES ALLEY		

Ⓐ **ARTS AND LEISURE**

4 Ⓒ	DUMBARTON OAKS	29	JACK'S BOATHOUSE	62	LOEWS GEORGETOWN 14
5	DUMBARTON OAKS PARK	30	GOVINDA GALLERY	63	GEORGETOWN WATERFRONT PARK AND WASHINGTON HARBOR
6	MONTROSE PARK	58	CHESAPEAKE AND OHIO CANAL NATIONAL HISTORIC PARK AND TOWPATH		
9	ADDISON/RIPLEY FINE ART			67	THOMPSON BOAT CENTER
28 Ⓒ	CAPITAL CRESCENT TRAIL	59	CHESAPEAKE & OHIO CANAL TOWPATH		

Ⓢ **SHOPS**

1	GEORGETOWN FLEA MARKET	16	BEADAZZLED	33	CADY'S ALLEY
10	A MANO	17	SECONDHAND ROSE	36	DEAN & DELUCA
11	MARSTON LUCE	18	THE PHOENIX	41	OLD PRINT GALLERY
12	SASSANOVA	19	CHRIST CHILD SOCIETY OPPORTUNITY SHOP	42	WINK
13	URBAN CHIC			47	BETSEY JOHNSON
14	THE DOG SHOP	20 Ⓒ	L'ENFANT GALLERY	48	THE PAPER SOURCE
15	PICCOLO PIGGIES	21 Ⓒ	SUSQUEHANNA	49	HU'S SHOES
		23	RANDOM HARVEST	52	BARTLEBY'S BOOKS

Ⓗ **HOTELS**

22	GEORGETOWN INN	56 Ⓒ	THE FOUR SEASONS	61	THE RITZ-CARLTON GEORGETOWN
51	LATHAM HOTEL	57	HOTEL MONTICELLO	66	GEORGETOWN SUITES

R 2

S ST NW

N 3

WISCONSIN AVE NW

32ND ST NW

N 4

5
A

R ST NW

31ST ST NW

6
A

7 Oak Hill
Cemetery

28TH ST NW A

9 A
RESERVOIR RD NW
S 10

DENT PL NW

S 11
S 12

13 S

S 14

Dumbarton
House 8

Q ST NW

DENT PL NW

AVON LN NW

CAMBRIDGE PL NW

32ND ST NW

26TH ST NW

Q ST NW

Q ST NW

S 15

VOLTA PL NW

S 16

WEST LANE KYS NW

P ST NW

30TH ST NW

POPLAR ST NW

OLIVE ST NW

17 S
18

19
S

GEORGETOWN

Q ST NW

20 S

33RD ST NW

POTOMAC ST NW

O ST NW

DUMBARTON ST NW

28TH ST NW

27TH ST NW

SEE MAP 6

S 21

22 H

S 23

N ST NW

24 N

29TH ST NW

OLIVE ST NW

M ST NW

30 A

NW PROSPECT ST

31 R

41
S

Old Stone
House

47
46 S

48 49
S S

52
S

53 R H

31ST ST NW

32 N

37 R
38 39
R R

40
S

42
S

M ST NW

54,55

56

PENNSYLVANIA AVE NW

26TH ST NW

M ST NW

33

POTOMAC ST NW

34 35 36

R

43 45
44 R
N

BLUES ALLEY

50 R H
51

57

A 58,59

WISCONSIN AVE

29TH ST NW

THOMAS JEFFERSON ST NW

WATER ST NW

33RD ST NW

GRACE ST NW

CECIL PL NW

60 R

SOUTH ST NW

30TH ST NW

H 66

N 61

62 N

K ST NW

I-66

63 A

64 R N 65

K ST NW

VIRGINIA AVE NW

NW 1ST ST

A 67

MASSACHUSETTS AVE

WATERSIDE DR NW

ROCK CREEK & POTOMAC P NW

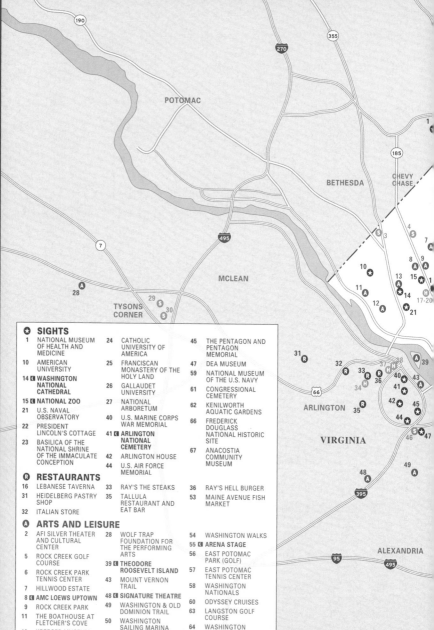

POTOMAC

BETHESDA

CHEVY CHASE

MCLEAN

TYSONS CORNER

ARLINGTON

VIRGINIA

ALEXANDRIA

⊙ SIGHTS

1	NATIONAL MUSEUM OF HEALTH AND MEDICINE
10	AMERICAN UNIVERSITY
14 ◖	**WASHINGTON NATIONAL CATHEDRAL**
15 ◖	**NATIONAL ZOO**
21	U.S. NAVAL OBSERVATORY
22	PRESIDENT LINCOLN'S COTTAGE
23	BASILICA OF THE NATIONAL SHRINE OF THE IMMACULATE CONCEPTION
24	CATHOLIC UNIVERSITY OF AMERICA
25	FRANCISCAN MONASTERY OF THE HOLY LAND
26	GALLAUDET UNIVERSITY
27	NATIONAL ARBORETUM
40	U.S. MARINE CORPS WAR MEMORIAL
41 ◖	**ARLINGTON NATIONAL CEMETERY**
42	ARLINGTON HOUSE
44	U.S. AIR FORCE MEMORIAL
45	THE PENTAGON AND PENTAGON MEMORIAL
47	DEA MUSEUM
59	NATIONAL MUSEUM OF THE U.S. NAVY
61	CONGRESSIONAL CEMETERY
62	KENILWORTH AQUATIC GARDENS
66	FREDERICK DOUGLASS NATIONAL HISTORIC SITE
67	ANACOSTIA COMMUNITY MUSEUM

ⓡ RESTAURANTS

16	LEBANESE TAVERNA
31	HEIDELBERG PASTRY SHOP
32	ITALIAN STORE
33	RAY'S THE STEAKS
35	TALLULA RESTAURANT AND EAT BAR
36	RAY'S HELL BURGER
53	MAINE AVENUE FISH MARKET

ⓐ ARTS AND LEISURE

2	AFI SILVER THEATER AND CULTURAL CENTER
5	ROCK CREEK GOLF COURSE
6	ROCK CREEK PARK TENNIS CENTER
7	HILLWOOD ESTATE
8 ◖	**AMC LOEWS UPTOWN**
9	ROCK CREEK PARK
11	THE BOATHOUSE AT FLETCHER'S COVE
12	KREEGER MUSEUM
13	OLMSTED WOODS AND THE BISHOP'S GARDENS
28	WOLF TRAP FOUNDATION FOR THE PERFORMING ARTS
39 ◖	**THEODORE ROOSEVELT ISLAND**
43	MOUNT VERNON TRAIL
48 ◖	**SIGNATURE THEATRE**
49	WASHINGTON & OLD DOMINION TRAIL
50	WASHINGTON SAILING MARINA
51	EAST POTOMAC PARK
52	WASHINGTON MARINA
54	WASHINGTON WALKS
55 ◖	**ARENA STAGE**
56	EAST POTOMAC PARK (GOLF)
57	EAST POTOMAC TENNIS CENTER
58	WASHINGTON NATIONALS
60	ODYSSEY CRUISES
63	LANGSTON GOLF COURSE
64	WASHINGTON REDSKINS
65	DC UNITED

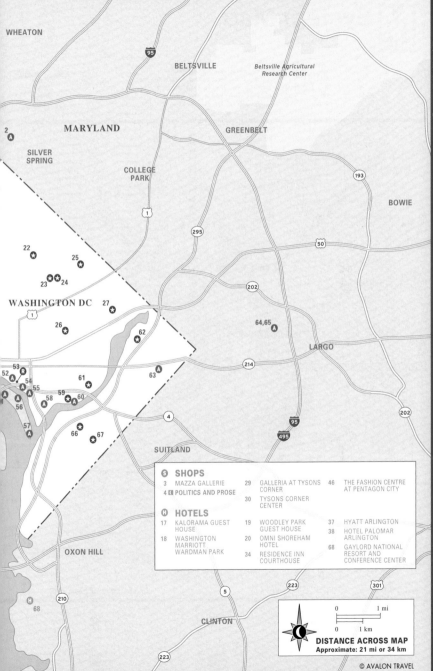

M metro® System Map

N

Legend
● Red Line • Glenmont to Shady Grove
● Orange Line • New Carrollton to Vienna/Fairfax-GMU
● Blue Line • Franconia-Springfield to Largo Town Center
● Green Line • Branch Avenue to Greenbelt
● Yellow Line • Huntington to Fort Totten

Station in
Service

Commuter Rail

Virginia
Railway
Express MARC

Bus to Airport   Transfer
                        Station

Parking

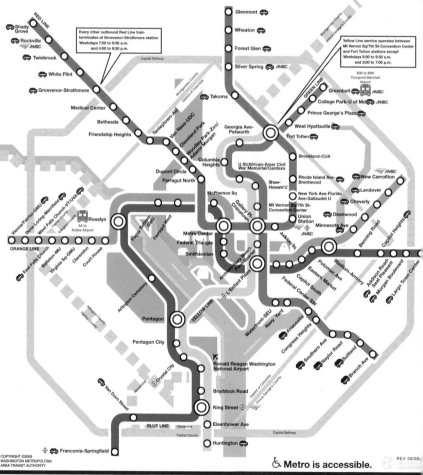

Every other outbound Red Line train
terminates at Grosvenor-Strathmore station
Weekdays 7:00 to 9:30 a.m.
and 4:00 to 6:30 p.m.

Yellow Line service operates between
Mt Vernon Sq/7th St-Convention Center
and Fort Totten stations except
Weekdays 5:00 to 9:30 a.m.
and 3:00 to 7:00 p.m.

&. Metro is accessible.

REV 09/08

No
Smoking

No Animals
(except service animals)

No Litter
or Spitting

No Eating
or Drinking

No Audio
(without earphones)

No Dangerous or
Flammable Items

COPYRIGHT ©2008
WASHINGTON METROPOLITAN
AREA TRANSIT AUTHORITY

Discover Washington DC

Washington DC is a city that has survived the ebbs of fire, war, and economic turmoil and ridden great flows of growth, wealth, and power to achieve what namesake George Washington originally intended: a cultural, economic, and political powerhouse on par with Europe's finest cities. The city's distinctive horizontal skyline, broad streets, tree-lined walks, and classical architecture give it an open, welcoming air, an approachable, walkable city of squares with the National Mall at its heart. Despite its southern locale, Washington is a multicultural municipality, with residents from an amalgam of backgrounds, the majority of whom hail from somewhere else. In Washington, much of the population rotates with changes in administrations, diplomatic postings, and military assignments, making for a lively mix. All days of the week, DC buzzes with an energy that emanates from its people, the very essence of type A. In this work-hard, play-hard environment, mornings start with a scour of the headlines, and the day doesn't end until well after late-night airings of *The Daily Show* and *The Colbert Report*. Washington DC has matured in the past two decades into a sophisticated destination boasting world-class museums and performing arts venues, fine dining, and exciting nightlife. It may be an infant city on the world stage, but it is one of the finest – a city for every American and beacon of democracy.

Planning Your Trip

▶ WHERE TO GO

National Mall West

Containing the country's most famous memorials as well as the city's famed cherry trees, the National Mall's western half, including West Potomac Park and the Tidal Basin, stirs the soul. From the spot at the Lincoln Memorial where Martin Luther King Jr. delivered his "I Have a Dream" speech to the somber wall bearing the names of 58,267 service members who died in the Vietnam War, each marker, architectural detail, statue, or hidden garden reflects the hard work and sacrifice of thousands. Built on land reclaimed from the Potomac River, this part of the city is verdant and extremely walkable.

interior dome, U.S. Capitol

National Mall East

The National Mall and its adjacent buildings form the heart of Washington's "Federal City" and are the city's top destination for visitors, a national town green that contains the city's tallest landmark, the Washington Monument, and the country's longest stretch of free museums. The mall itself is a well-beaten swath of lawn hemmed with pea-gravel paths and enormous American elms, running from the U.S. Capitol past the Washington Monument. It is used daily for picnicking and pickup sports as well as planned events like demonstrations and festivals.

Downtown

A lively urban area that has emerged in the past decade as the city's prime destination for spectator sports, headliner concerts, hip restaurants, fine-dining clubs, and off-the-Mall museums like Madame Tussauds and the International Spy Museum, Washington's downtown, bordered roughly by 6th Street, M Street, 21st Street, and Pennsylvania Avenue, contains government and private offices, condominiums, hotels, and nightspots as well as the Verizon Center, home to several professional sports teams.

Foggy Bottom

The country's most famous residence, the White House, sits on the verge of Foggy Bottom, a business district peculiarly named for its history as a low-lying area once clouded by fog that drifted from the river and the soot of 19th century factories. Today, Foggy Bottom contains the U.S. State Department, George Washington University, the infamous Watergate condominium complex, and the law and lobbying firms of K Street. A number of the city's most reputable restaurants can be found here as well as the city's premier performing arts venue, the Kennedy Center.

Capitol Hill

Much of what defines "official" Washington is found in the streets near the U.S. Capitol. But Capitol Hill is also home to one of the city's top residential neighborhoods, a lattice of tree-lined alleys and historic row houses, cozy restaurants, and lively watering holes. If two square miles could capture the timbre of life in DC, it is Capitol Hill, from busy Union Station and Independence and Pennsylvania Avenues to the side streets of an urban village with Federal and Victorian architecture, parks, pubs, and the city's oldest public market, Eastern Market.

Dupont Circle

DC's version of Greenwich Village, Dupont Circle is Washington's antidote to the button-down. It's a domain for bohos, gays, hipsters, the young, the homeless, office workers, and everything in between, studded with stylish boutiques, lively restaurants, vintage shops, and the immense park with a traffic circle, named for Civil War hero Adm. Samuel Du Pont. Dupont Circle is DC's historic gay village, home to the city's first rainbow shops and host to such events as the Halloween High Heel Drag Race and the city's Gay Pride Parade. Dupont Circle hops, drawing visitors to its galleries, including the country's first modern art museum, the Phillips Collection, as well as outdoor dining, bookstores, and coffeehouses.

Adams Morgan and U Street

A terminus for the DC party train, Adams Morgan, at the nexus of 18th Street and Columbia Road NW, is an ethnically diverse neighborhood known mainly for its nightlife. Brightly painted buildings hint at this neighborhood's eclectic roots, forged as the result of school desegregation and later serving as a gateway for Latino immigrants in the 1960s; African, Asian, and Caribbean newcomers in the 1970s; and with widespread gentrification in the 1980s, a magnet for music lovers, dancers, and barflies. East of Adams Morgan lies U Street, a dining and nightlife hotspot with a decidedly chill vibe. A historic hub for African American entertainment and jazz music, this neighborhood crumbled in the wake of riots following the death of Martin Luther King Jr. in 1968, but its soul has been revived, with new music clubs and bars to suit every taste.

Georgetown

A neighborhood that thrived as a tobacco port before Washington was founded, Georgetown is DC's old-school locale for the young, preppy, fashionable, and well-heeled, a top social destination that is home to a stunning array of historic homes, restaurants, boutiques, and pubs. Its hub lies at the intersection of M Street and Wisconsin Avenue, with shops, bars, and restaurants lining both thoroughfares and bustling day and night. Back streets and green spaces beg for daytime meandering, with stunning

Georgetown

the National Zoo

architecture and quiet walking spots like the Chesapeake and Ohio Canal towpath and the lush campus of Georgetown University.

Greater Washington DC

Many Washington landmarks lie outside the city center's tidy boxes. In fact, two of the most recognizable—the Pentagon and Arlington National Cemetery—are actually in Virginia, in areas once part of the city before Virginia asked for their return in 1846. Scattered across this great map are the colossal (the Pentagon is the world's largest office building), the spiritual (the Washington National Cathedral and the Basilica of the National Shrine of the Immaculate Conception), the somber (the Pentagon's September 11 Memorial), the inspirational (Frederick Douglass National Historic Site), and the animal (the National Zoo).

▶ WHEN TO GO

Washington has distinct seasons, with chilly temperatures and chance snowstorms in the winter and sultry, humid summer days. The best time to visit is spring and fall, which tend to be drier with a comfortable temperature range. From late March through May, the city's landscape explodes with color, led by its famous cherry blossoms, which usually peak around the first week of April but are highly dependent on conditions. Fading cherries give way to native dogwood and redbud as well as azaleas and other garden species. Along with great beauty, however, comes huge crowds: Early March through the end of July is peak tourism season. Fall is ideal for its crisp, exhilarating temperatures, changing autumn hues, and fewer crowds.

Summer, which can begin before Memorial Day, is hot, sticky, and for some, simply unbearable. Washington is very much a southern city in terms of humidity. But if you can bear the heat, you'll beat the hordes, especially in August when locals go on vacation. Winter is also peaceful, except during the two weeks spanning Christmas and New Year's Day, which tend to be nearly as popular as the spring.

Explore Washington DC

► THE FIVE-DAY BEST OF WASHINGTON DC

Day 1

Grab breakfast downtown or on Capitol Hill at the homespun Lincoln's Waffle Shop across from Ford's Theatre or Teaism Penn Quarter for healthier fare like Irish oatmeal and muesli.

Hit the National Archives at opening for a look at the Declaration of Independence, the Constitution, and the Bill of Rights, as well as a 1297 copy of the Magna Carta. These precious documents are faded, but their legacy endures.

Head eastward on Pennsylvania Avenue to the U.S. Capitol to tour the historic building or, if you haven't secured a timed ticket, to see the platform that held Lincoln's casket and other interesting artifacts on display in the Capitol Visitors Center.

At lunchtime, grab takeout at Taqueria Nacional or stop by the city's best museum cafeteria, Mitsitam, in the National Museum of the American Indian for indigenous cuisine like board-roasted salmon and pumpkin soup.

Next, it's decision time. What museum suits your interests? The 1903 Wright Flyer that soared at Kitty Hawk, North Carolina, holds a place of honor in the National Air and Space Museum. If you prefer art, check out Raphael's *Alba Madonna* and Monet's *Rouen Cathedral* at the National Gallery of Art. Or head to the National Museum of Natural History to see a *Tyrannosaurus rex* fossil, the Hope Diamond, rare butterfly species, meteorites, a coral reef, and more.

With preordered, timed ticket in hand, board the Washington Monument's elevator for a ride to a spectacular view, nearly 555 feet above the ground.

Continue your tour heading north for a White House photo op. Drop in for a drink and nosh at the Old Ebbitt Grill or a mint julep at Willard Hotel's Round Robin Bar, a historic spot where Mark Twain, Walt Whitman, and Ulysses S. Grant once relaxed.

the National Archives

CULTURAL CAPITAL: DC ART AND FOOD TOUR

For nearly 150 years after its founding, DC was considered a cultural backwater, a place where politics and intellect thrived but the arts, in all their forms, were an expense ill-afforded by the federal government, which managed the city. The opening of the city's first art museum, the privately owned Corcoran, in 1869, demonstrated that Washingtonians yearned to expand their city's cultural appeal. Now, more than 130 years later, it has happened: in 2010, *Travel + Leisure* magazine ranked the city second only to New York for its culture. If the transformation in the visual and performing arts was slow, the expansion of gastronomic choices in the city moved at an even slower pace, picking up, fortunately, in the past two decades. Some of the world's finest chefs have arrived and thankfully stayed in Washington, attracted by the city's diverse, adventurous, and affluent clientele as well as its vibrancy and locale not far from rural food sources. Today, Washington teems with choices, full-course and à la carte.

THE MODERN

For a glimpse of contemporary style in the DC area, start south of the city in Fairfax County, Virginia, at the area's only public Frank Lloyd Wright home, the **Pope-Leighey House,** a masterpiece of efficient design that was moved to the grounds of a Washington-era plantation when it was threatened with demolition. This mini-mod home is one of Wright's Usonian designs, a family residence furnished to the exacting architect's standards.

Return to Washington for lunch at **The Source,** Wolfgang Puck's Asian-fusion eatery in the oh-so-modern Newseum, serving some of the city's most flavorful, unique takes on Chinese cuisine.

Stroll to the **National Gallery of Art East Building,** an I. M. Pei-designed exhibit hall that showcases much of the museum's modern and contemporary art, including works by Picasso, Pollock, Miró, and Calder.

Dine at **Restaurant Nora** for dinner, enjoying a menu focused heavily on locally sourced ingredients, and catch a show you won't see elsewhere at **Woolly Mammoth Theatre Company,** staging the edgy, adventurous, or quirky in a new minimal theater space that manages to be chill and intimate all at once.

THE DECADENT

Take your eggs Benedict or lemon ricotta pancakes at **Seasons in the Four Seasons** and browse the hotel's lobby and hallways, featuring much of the property's 1,600-piece art collection, including an Andy Warhol *Indian Head Nickel* screen print, before heading to the woodland neighborhood of Northwest DC to tour **Hillwood,** Marjorie Merriweather Post's former estate, containing one of the finest collections of Russian imperial art outside Russia.

Grab a quick bite from the District's favorite food truck, **Red Hook Lobster Truck,** featuring buttery rolls stuffed with Maine's finest crustacean or plump shrimp. (The truck moves daily; find its location on Twitter.) Then enjoy Renoir's enormous and captivating *Luncheon of the Boating Party* and other fine works,

Plan to catch a free show—music, dance, or theater—at 6 P.M. nightly at Millennium Stage in the Kennedy Center's splendid Grand Foyer, with its adjacent terrace overlooking the Potomac River.

After dinner, venture to see the spectacularly lit monuments through one of the companies that offers a "hop-on, hop-off" tour, or better yet, a private for-hire car for a really special evening.

Day 2

Grab a quick breakfast sandwich or savory crepe at Café Tu-O-Tu in Georgetown or savor breakfast at pricey Seasons at the Four Seasons Hotel, an airy, elegant dining room favored by Washington diplomats.

Head toward the river and rent a bike or a kayak at Thompson Boat Center or catch a cab to enjoy a short, beautiful hike around Roosevelt Island. Cyclists can head north including those of William Merritt Chase and Winslow Homer, on display in the rooms of the **Phillips Collection.**

If you've thought well ahead and made reservations at precisely 10 A.M. a month to the day before you want to attend, enjoy your dining experience at **MiniBar,** a six-seat restaurant where guests enjoy a 30-plate chef's tasting menu from those under the tutelage of José Andrés. Didn't press redial fast enough? Reserve a table at **Café Atlántico,** Andrés's New Latin-Latin fusion restaurant that contains MiniBar.

AROUND-THE-WORLD

Start the day with a cheesy, gooey Croque and Dagger or more traditional breakfast fare amid an eclectic crowd at **The Diner** in Adams Morgan, and then head to the National Mall to tour three enticing and rarely visited spaces: the **National Museum of African Art** and the **Freer and Sackler Galleries of Asian Art.** The Freer is home to one of Washington's true treasures, James McNeill Whistler's outrageous *Peacock Room.*

People from around the world call Washington home; experience a twist on Turkish, Greek, and Lebanese cuisine at **Zaytinya** or check out **Mitsitam** in the **National Museum of the American Indian.** Celebrate the traditional and contemporary artistry of the Americas' indigenous population at the museum, which features sketches and drawings, paintings, basketry, and textiles from the hemisphere's original inhabitants.

Afterward, check out the history of cultural

identity as told by fabrics at the **Textile Museum,** containing clothing and carpets dating from 300 B.C. to the present.

Enjoy regional cuisine at **Georgia Brown's,** just a few blocks from the White House, with a menu of Southern favorites.

Finish out the evening with a drink and cool music at **Blues Alley,** a former 18th-century carriage house that hosts jazz musicians and some R&B and blues groups seven days a week.

Blues Alley, located in a former carriage house

through verdant Rock Creek Park or south for a daytime glimpse of the monuments. Paddlers and hikers can enjoy the views of wooded Roosevelt Island.

Check out historic Georgetown for lunch and shopping. Upscale fashion, stylish home furnishings, and fancy footwear can be found in Urban Chic, Cady's Alley, and Hu's Shoes. The Tombs is Georgetown University's quintessential college bar, perfect

for a pub lunch, or try a wood-grilled pizza and *insalata mista* at Pizzeria Paradiso.

Finish out the afternoon across the river from the Lincoln Memorial at Arlington National Cemetery. Its 624 acres features the Tomb of the Unknowns, countless graves of military and civilian heroes, and Arlington House, the home of Robert E. Lee.

Enjoy the finest of DC's dining with reservations at Citronelle or CityZen, or consume a less budget-busting bite to eat at Hank's Oyster Bar.

Catch a show at the Arena Stage or head to U Street for live music, jazz at Bohemian Caverns, or the flavor of the night—reggae, pop, country, hip-hop, or rock—at the 9:30 Club. Top off the evening satisfying your late-night munchies with a chili half-smoke, DC's uniquely local smoked sausage, at Ben's Chili Bowl.

TOP 10 FOR KIDS

- At the **National Zoo,** gorillas touch the hands – and hearts – of kids through their glass containment areas.

- Tarantulas are fed daily in the **Orkin Insect Zoo** at the **National Museum of Natural History.** Great fun for kids, but not for the crickets.

- Even small children are awestruck by the **Lincoln Memorial's** 19-foot-high seated statue of the 16th president.

- The **National Air and Space Museum** is a wonderland of technology and opportunity: Kids can walk through planes and a space station and participate in experiments.

- The smell of fried seafood wafts across the parking lots and along the busy waterfront at the **Maine Avenue Fish Market,** a carnival of food kiosks and vendors selling fried fish, fresh oysters, soft- and hard-shell crabs and nearly every type of fascinating, weird, edible creature of the deep.

- Kids are captivated at **Adventure Theatre,** a professional theater group that caters exclusively to children with shows like the beloved *Charlotte's Web* and the amusing adventures of *Frog and Toad.*

- Something's always growing, harvested, dyed, dried, or crafted at **Claude Moore Colonial Farm** in McLean, Virginia, a rendition of a modest circa-1771 frontier farm.

- The Washingtons were a tad wealthier than the residents of Claude Moore: From the Orangery to its vast veranda overlooking the Potomac River and the winding path that leads to Washington's grave, **Mount Vernon** offers children a world of excitement and room to roam.

- Tweens and teens like the **International Spy Museum,** which features one of James Bond's Aston Martins and tutorials on shadowing, trailing, and losing a tail.

- No need to drive all the way to Baltimore to check out an aquarium; the **National Aquarium** in the basement of the Commerce Building is a hidden delight, unknown to many locals.

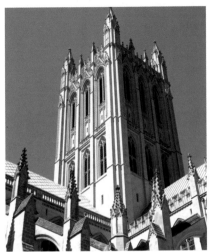

Washington National Cathedral

Day 3

Depending on your interests, mood, or the age of your fellow travelers, view pandas, big cats, and gorillas at the National Zoo or steel yourself for a heart-wrenching visit to the U.S. Holocaust Memorial Museum, with its permanent exhibit of more than 900 artifacts, films, and testimonies from the Nazi concentration and death camps.

If you've opted for walking among the animals at the zoo, consider eating lunch at Lebanese Taverna on Connecticut Avenue, dining on gyros, *shawarma,* and hummus, or if you've gone to the Holocaust Museum and still have the stomach to eat, check out the views and southern fare at Sou'wester in the Mandarin Oriental Hotel, sure to lift your spirits.

From the zoo, head up Connecticut Avenue to the Washington National Cathedral, the country's second largest, with groomed grounds and landscaping, breathtaking stained glass, interesting Gothic architecture, and great gargoyles and grotesques.

If you are on the National Mall, stroll over to the Newseum to peruse the day's front pages and admire Pulitzer Prize–winning photos. Another option? Check out the city's oldest art museum, the Corcoran, with its collection of American portraiture, landscapes, and photography.

Hop the Metro to hotfoot it downtown to the National Portrait Gallery and National Museum of American Art, which stay open until 7 P.M. daily.

Linger in the downtown area's stores, and dine nearby on Mediterranean mezes at Zaytinya or grab a burger, crab-cake sandwich, or a beer at Clyde's of Gallery Place.

See if you can score tickets to a sporting event or concert at Verizon Center, home to the Washington Capitals, Mystics, and Wizards pro sports teams and the Georgetown men's basketball team.

Sip a nightcap after the game or show at Proof, a wine bar with 40 wines by the glass.

Day 4

The morning begins with fortifying sustenance from Bagels & Baguettes on Capitol Hill on the Senate side; bring cash for the tasty eggwiches, bagels, and "schmear." Or sit down to enormous Belgian waffles at Jimmy T's.

Jump in line to watch the U.S. Supreme Court in action: stay for an entire procedure or opt for the three-minute quick-view line. If court is not in session, take in an informational video and wander the building's vast halls.

Take in the exhibits, including a flawless Gutenberg Bible and Thomas Jefferson's personal book collection, at the Library of Congress, the world's largest book repository.

For lunch, drop by the House of Representatives' Longworth House Office Building and head to its cafeteria, with the widest menu selection of any congressional dining room and great people watching—congressional staff, representatives, lobbyists, the media, and more.

Burn off lunch by strolling down Capitol Hill to the U.S. Botanic Gardens, a tropical paradise with thousands of flowering plants, blooms, towering trees, a waterfall, hanging plants, and a canopy walk.

Check out the indoor and outdoor modern collection at the Hirshhorn Museum and Sculpture Garden; its avant-garde works by artists like De Kooning, Ellsworth, Matisse, Calder, Warhol, and Rodin challenge conventional parameters. For more traditional portfolios, consider the quiet spaces of the Freer and Sackler galleries, featuring a vast selection of Asian art as well as the world's largest collection of James Whistler, and the National Museum of African Art, with an excellent collection of decorative arts from across the continent.

If art museums don't tickle your fancy, spend the afternoon getting lost in the "nation's attic," the National Museum of American History.

Union Station is worth a brief detour before dinner; the grand Main and East Halls of this massive beaux arts–style building, designed by Daniel Burnham, feature massive coffered ceilings, murals, columns, and statuary as well as shops and restaurants.

the winged figure of Democracy at Union Station

Enjoy the music and food of the Big Easy like char-grilled oysters, gumbo, and étouffée, as well as tastes from the Chesapeake Bay, including soft-shell crabs in season at Johnny's Half Shell, a lively place to linger over a Sazerac.

If you're in the mood to dance, hop a cab to Dupont Circle, where you can salsa the night away at Café Citron. Or chill out on a comfy couch at 18th Street Lounge.

Day 5

Take the car, hire a cab, or if you're fit, rent a bike for a morning trip to George Washington's Mount Vernon, the first president's impressive plantation home, eight miles south of Alexandria, Virginia. Don't miss the gift shop, one of the area's best.

Return to Alexandria, Virginia, to continue the colonial experience, dining at a favorite restaurant for the founding fathers, Gadsby's Tavern, famous for serving Washington, Adams, Jefferson, and Madison.

Roam the streets of Old Town Alexandria, with more than 4,000 historic buildings, including Christ Church and its graveyard and the Stabler-Leadbeater Apothecary Shop, where Martha Washington bought her medical supplies.

Window-shop along King Street before settling into a table at The Majestic, an art deco–style eatery serving locally-sourced down-home cooking, or dine in style at the nationally recognized Restaurant Eve. Or skip the fancy tabletops and head to The Birchmere for a bar meal on red-checked tablecloths and an acoustic, jazz, blues, or country show.

If you've elected to stay in Old Town, hit up Murphy's, an Alexandria Irish pub standard that has been around nearly 30 years, for a pint and the chance to pound on the tables while belting out a rambunctious rendition of "Red Rover."

SIGHTS

Ask a Washingtonian what they like to do in their city and you'll get a wide variety of answers. Ask what they like best about their town and you'll likely get one response: There's so much to do, and most of it is *free*. From watching orangutans and seeing your member of Congress grandstand during a hearing, to riding to the top of the world's tallest obelisk and taking in the works of great masters, it's all free. So much of the city's entertainment is gratis that it is not uncommon to hear locals grumbling over admission fees at commercial venues like the International Spy Museum or the Newseum. Washingtonians are definitely spoiled, but they appreciate their good fortune: "It's an incredible place. I wouldn't live anywhere else," says Javier Loureiro, a Madrid-born transplant and concierge at the posh Four Seasons Hotel.

DC's wallet-friendly climate, paired with its raison d'être as the U.S. capital, make it a top travel destination. Many come here to see the National Mall, loaded with iconic monuments and memorials. But the city is more than a collection of landmarks. Its neighborhoods host a wealth of museums, galleries, historic houses, and entertainment venues, many accessible by Metro or the low-cost Circulator bus.

Thanks to Washington's original urban designer, Pierre L'Enfant, and later planners, DC is extremely walkable: Distances between sights are minimal, although they might seem longer in the summer heat. In terms of safety, Washington is also relatively secure. It has shed its unsavory 1990s-era status as the nation's murder capital, but out-of-towners should remain alert, especially at night. Tourist areas stay busy

© STEPHEN FINN/123RF.COM

SIGHTS

HIGHLIGHTS

LOOK FOR  TO FIND RECOMMENDED SIGHTS.

◖ **Most Romantic Spot:** At night, the monument is bathed in light, casting a magical spell on the **Jefferson Memorial,** the perfect place to take a date (page 36).

◖ **Best Place to Feel National Pride:** You can't *not* feel proud standing on the **Lincoln Memorial** steps surrounded by visitors from around the world. The view is world-class too (page 37).

◖ **Best View:** The **Washington Monument**'s observation deck affords a bird's-eye view of the city and beyond. On a clear day, Virginia's Blue Ridge Mountains are visible nearly 60 miles to the west, and to the southeast, the Potomac River meanders through the Maryland and Virginia countryside (page 41).

◖ **Best Museum:** In a city of museums, it's nearly impossible to pick one, but the **National Museum of Natural History** comes close, with the Hope Diamond, dinosaur bones, a live coral reef, and bird-eating spiders (page 44).

◖ **Best Place for a Protest:** Someone's always mad in **Lafayette Square,** the park across from the White House. Nuclear disarmament protesters have been rallying here for more than 30 years, often joined by Lyndon LaRouche supporters, gay rights activists, Tea Party factions, and others (page 50).

◖ **Best Place for a Picnic:** The people-watching on the **U.S. Capitol Grounds** is among the best in the city. Grab lunch from nearby Union Station or a deli and treat yourself to the parade of senators, lobbyists, lawmakers, and celebrities (page 60).

◖ **The Sight Most Likely to Leave You Speechless:** Technically not in the city proper, the hallowed grounds of **Arlington National Cemetery,** across Memorial Bridge, are a solemn reminder of the price of freedom (page 67).

◖ **Best Hill:** The nearly mile-long walk from the **National Zoo**'s D Lot to Connecticut Avenue is steep, but along the way you'll see gorillas, prairie dogs, elephants, tigers, and orangutans. And when you're tired, it's a downhill trek to your car (page 74).

◖ **Best Gargoyles:** The **Washington National Cathedral,** the second largest in the United States, is loaded with classical Gothic detail — flying buttresses, rose windows, pointed arches, and hundreds of gargoyles and grotesques, including a likeness of Darth Vader (page 77).

© LISSANDRA RECICAR/123RF.COM

visitors at the Lincoln Memorial

and are well patrolled at nearly all hours, but the distances between often aren't well lit; traveling in groups is recommended. As for attractions in fringe neighborhoods, including parts of southeast and northeast DC, it's advisable to take a cab or drive directly to your destination if you believe it to be in a questionable area.

Three things are needed to enjoy Washington to its fullest: a good pair of walking shoes, some stamina, and a plan. Getting into some sights requires prior preparation, and in some cases, the legwork must be done months in advance. See each listing for details regarding ticketing and reservation requirements. When drafting your plan, choose an area of interest or your personal top 10. Are you here for the history? The art? The halls of state? A little of it all? Chances are that you won't see everything on your first or even second trip. It's tempting to rush from one place to another, but try to forego a frenetic pace. Savor the greatness of this capital city; the best memories often happen during the unplanned moments.

The National Mall West   Map 1

CONSTITUTION GARDENS
South of the intersection of Constitution Ave. and 19th St. NW, 202/426-6841, www.nps.gov/coga
HOURS: Daily 24 hours
COST: Free

This quiet spot near the Mall bordering on Constitution Avenue made national headlines in 2003 when a disgruntled tobacco farmer drove his fertilizer-laden tractor into the garden's pond and held police at bay for more than two days. But usually, this peaceful landscape belongs to mallards, fishermen, and runners. Adjacent to the Reflecting Pool, Constitution Gardens is home to an often overlooked monument honoring the signers of the Declaration of Independence. The Signers Memorial spotlights the 56 men who endorsed the document, from the calligraphically blessed John Hancock to those lost to history like New Hampshire's William Whipple. At the corner of Constitution Gardens is a circa-1835 lockkeeper's house, built when Constitution Avenue was a canal, part of the Chesapeake and Ohio waterways system.

FRANKLIN DELANO ROOSEVELT MEMORIAL
On the Tidal Basin at 900 Ohio Dr. SW, 202/426-6841, www.nps.gov/frde
HOURS: Daily 24 hours; rangers on duty daily 9:30 A.M.-11:30 P.M.
COST: Free

Since many tour it when walking from the Jefferson Memorial to the Lincoln Memorial, it's wise to take the extra steps and enter by the front, as it actually consists of four outdoor rooms and an antechamber that capture Roosevelt's presidency chronologically, one plaza representing each of his four presidential terms. Designed by Lawrence Halprin and dedicated in 1997, the seven-acre memorial is a captivating mix of statues, famous quotes, stonework, waterfalls, and greenery. Visitors begin their trip through time in an anteroom called Prologue that contains a sculpture by Robert Graham depicting Roosevelt in a wheelchair. The Great Depression area contains a sculpture, *Bread Line,* that's a popular spot for a photo op, as well as a bronze of a man listening to one of Roosevelt's fireside chats. The complexity of the New Deal and chaos of World War II is represented in the third chamber by a choppy waterfall but also includes a massive sculpture of a robust FDR seated with his beloved Scottish terrier, Fala. The memorial ends with quiet—a silent pool symbolizing the somberness of FDR's death in 1945, just 82 days after starting his fourth term. This was the first memorial in the city to feature a statue of a first lady; Eleanor Roosevelt is honored for her work as the nation's volunteer in chief and with the United Nations. Notably, this memorial was built without the Prologue sculpture. This artwork was installed near the front entrance in

THEY (WHO) SEEK TO ESTABLISH
SYSTEMS OF GOVERNMENT BASED ON
THE REGIMENTATION OF ALL HUMAN
BEINGS BY A HANDFUL OF INDIVIDUAL
RULERS... CALL THIS A NEW ORDER.
IT IS NOT NEW AND IT IS NOT ORDER

© PATRICIA KIME

FDR and his dog, Fala, as depicted in the Franklin Delano Roosevelt Memorial

2001 after advocates for the disabled lobbied and raised money for it. Halprin's original design respected Roosevelt's wishes that he never be seen in a wheelchair; the architect later guided installation of the new addition and said he welcomed it. At one time, park rangers allowed visitors to romp in the beautiful fountains and pools, but this is no longer allowed.

◀ JEFFERSON MEMORIAL

Ohio Dr. SW, 202/426-6841, www.nps.gov/thje
HOURS: Daily 24 hours; rangers on
duty daily 9:30 A.M.-11:30 P.M.
COST: Free

Off the Mall's beaten pathways across the Tidal Basin lies the Jefferson Memorial, which, like the Lincoln Memorial, boasts stately columns, a 19-foot-tall statue of the president, and engravings of his famous writings. But the interior of this monument lacks the emotional punch of its predecessor a mile away: The long passages from the Declaration of Independence, various bills, and Jefferson's letters don't adequately demonstrate the complexity of this founding father, who served as minister to France, secretary of state, and vice president, and negotiated the Louisiana Purchase. Still, the building itself is magnificent, a circular colonnade of Ionic columns topped by a shallow dome, a neoclassical design that pays homage to Jefferson's architectural inspirations, the Pantheon in Rome, and Palladio's Villa Capra, and calls to mind the third president's finest architectural legacy, the Rotunda at the University of Virginia. I enjoy gazing at this memorial from afar, recalling the three things the great redhead wanted to be remembered for: writing the Declaration of Independence and the Statute of Virginia for Religious Freedom, and founding the University of Virginia. The Jefferson Memorial is at its most stunning in spring, when the cherry trees that surround it are in full bloom.

KOREAN WAR VETERANS MEMORIAL

10 Daniel French Dr. SW, 202/426-6841,
www.nps.gov/kowa

HOURS: Daily 24 hours; rangers on
duty daily 9:30 A.M.-11:30 P.M.

COST: Free

Most of Washington's sights are at their finest from spring through fall; the Korean War
Veterans Memorial is the exception. Winter's
tough landscape sets the stage for this evoca-
tive memorial, which features the sculptures of
19 service members on patrol in the unforgiv-
ing landscape of Korea. The larger-than-life
statues are reflected in a backdrop of a black
granite wall, creating the illusion of 38 soldiers,
representing the 38th Parallel, the latitudinal
line along which the Koreas remain separated
today. Etched into the wall are the images
of more than 2,400 personnel and pieces of
equipment used in the war. When seen from
afar, these form a pattern of light on the dark
wall in the shape of Korea's mountains. One of
Washington's newest memorials, the Korean
War Veterans Memorial was designed by Frank
Gaylord and dedicated in 1995 by President
Bill Clinton and South Korean President Kim
Young Sam.

◖ LINCOLN MEMORIAL

Independence Ave. and 23rd St. SW, 202/426-6841,
www.nps.gov/linc

HOURS: Daily 24 hours; rangers on duty daily
9:30 A.M.-11:30 P.M.; tours daily on the hour 10 A.M.-11 P.M.

COST: Free

This colossal monument to the humble 16th
president is modeled after a Greek temple, a
limestone and marble tribute completed in
1922 to honor the man whose leadership abol-
ished slavery and kept the United States intact
despite a devastating civil war. Designed by architect Henry Bacon, the Lincoln Memorial
was built on land reclaimed from the Potomac
River and contains the iconic seated sculpture
of Lincoln by Daniel Chester French, which,
despite its massive size of 19 feet tall, humanizes
the mythical man, with its pensive stare and
lined, sorrowful face. The Great Emancipator's
eloquence is also celebrated here: The words of

the Gettysburg Address and Lincoln's Second
Inaugural speech are etched onto the memorial's walls. Views from the top of the memorial's 57 steps are among the city's finest, and the
landing just 18 steps below also marks one of
the city's most historic places—the spot where
Martin Luther King Jr. stood during the 1963
March on Washington. The Lincoln Memorial
features a tiny museum on the first floor, an
air-conditioned area that contains restrooms
and serves as a cool refuge for the overheated
during the sweaty summer months.

MARTIN LUTHER KING JR. NATIONAL MEMORIAL

Independence Ave. and Basin Dr. SW, 888/484-3373,
www.mlkmemorial.org

HOURS: Daily 24 hours; rangers on duty daily
9:30 A.M.-11:30 P.M.

COST: Free

Forty-eight years to the week Martin Luther
King, Jr., delivered his 17-minute "I Have a
Dream" speech on the steps of the Lincoln
Memorial, the nation's capital welcomed a
memorial to the great civil rights leader. The
memorial, which opened the week of Aug. 22,
2011, features a mountainous granite entryway, cleaved in two, symbolizing the despair
African-Americans felt under segregation and
the Jim Crow laws. At its center, a 28-foot-tall
sculpture of King, designed by Chinese artist
Lei Yixin, emerges from a rock known as the
Stone of Hope. Curved walls embrace the site,
etched with inspiring King quotes. Of note,
though, is the abbreviated quote to the right
of King on the Stone of Hope. Here are the
words from the original sermon: "Yes, if you
want to say that I was a drum major, say that I
was a drum major for justice. Say that I was a
drum major for peace. I was a drum major for
righteousness."

NATIONAL WORLD WAR II MEMORIAL

17th St. SW, 202/426-6841, www.nps.gov/nwwm

HOURS: Daily 24 hours; rangers on
duty daily 9:30 A.M.-11:30 P.M.

COST: Free

Sixteen million Americans helped lead the

Allies to victory in World War II, and despite earning the moniker "the Greatest Generation" in 1998 from NBC News anchor Tom Brokaw, they didn't have a single unifying memorial until 2004, more than 20 years after the Vietnam Veterans Memorial was dedicated. This impressive, if vaguely Teutonic, memorial, designed by Friedrich St. Florian, features a series of arches and pillars surrounding a pool and fountains. Each state and U.S. territory is represented, as is each combat theater; a curved wall of gold stars represents the more than 400,000 Americans killed. While its site between the Washington Monument and the Lincoln Memorial initially drew criticism for adding "clutter" to the Mall, many locals rejoiced, as the new monument revitalized a decrepit fountain and pool once filled with pond scum and trash. Kids will enjoy hunting for classic Yank "graffiti" declaring "Kilroy was here" on the memorial. (Hint: It's on the outside.)

TIDAL BASIN

1501 Maine Ave. SW

HOURS: Daily dawn-dusk

COST: Free

A 107-acre pond engineered to keep the Washington Channel clear of pollution and silt, the Tidal Basin is the main attraction during the city's Cherry Blossom Festival in late March and early April, when its more than 3,700 Yoshino and Akebino ornamental cherry trees are in bloom. The trees were a gift from the mayor of Tokyo in 1912, who sent more than 2,000 to the city to thank the United States for supporting Japan during the Russo-Japanese War. Today, roughly 4 percent of the trees are originals (the Yoshino cherry has a life span of roughly 40 years); several of these can be found near the 360-year-old Japanese Stone Lantern located in a grove just west of the Kutz Bridge. Some of the replacement trees, especially those planted in the past decade, bear the originals' genetic lineage, having been cultivated from their cuttings. While the Tidal Basin is most popular in the spring, it shouldn't be overlooked in the fall, when the trees' leaves

BLACK SQUIRRELS

With all the great sights in DC, it's funny that one small critter captivates nearly every visitor: the black squirrel. While Washington is a native habitat for the eastern gray squirrel, the city also is home to an eye-catching variety – the Canadian melanistic squirrel. The Smithsonian imported 18 of these special rodents in the early 1900s to the grounds of the National Zoo, ostensibly to bolster an area population decimated by hunting. Today, the all-black descendants of that small group range from just south of the city in Virginia to Rockville, Maryland, and they can be found in nearly every local neighborhood. In the last few years, a single albino squirrel has also been spotted on the Mall. If you see Albie, consider posting on Facebook's "Albino Squirrel Watch" page.

© MARCO METZLER (FOQUS)/FLICKR.COM

A black squirrel enjoys a snack in a Washington DC yard.

blaze vermilion. The Tidal Basin is a popular spot for light recreation: From mid-March to Columbus Day, the National Park Service operates a paddle boat kiosk with 2- and 4-person launches for rent, weather permitting (www.tidalbasinpeddleboats.com). For walkers, the basin's five-mile circumference offers a flat, scenic trail for taking in the sights.

U.S. BUREAU OF ENGRAVING AND PRINTING

14th St. and C St. SW, 202/874-2330 or 866/874-2330, www.moneyfactory.gov

HOURS: Mon.-Fri. 8:30 A.M.-3 P.M.; tours every 15 minutes Mon.-Fri. 9-10:45 A.M. and 12:30-2 P.M.; closed federal holidays

COST: Free

A tour of a working factory that is dated yet interesting, if just to see where the federal government makes money rather than spends it, the Bureau of Engraving and Printing is where the country prints paper bills and important documents like passports, White House invitations, and military identification cards. The tour begins with a short video and leads through a passageway over the assembly line where visitors watch thousands of dollars rolling off the presses. Tickets are required for entry and are available on a first-come, first-served basis for the day, starting at 8 A.M. at a ticket booth on Raoul Wallenberg Place near the Holocaust Museum. During peak season, March through August, a line forms and tickets go quickly, usually by 9 A.M.

U.S. HOLOCAUST MEMORIAL MUSEUM

100 Raoul Wallenberg Place SW, 202/488-0400, www.ushmm.org

HOURS: Daily 10 A.M.-5:20 P.M.; closed Yom Kippur and Christmas Day

COST: Free

Undoubtedly DC's most heart-wrenching museum, the U.S. Holocaust Memorial Museum is a chilling reminder of mankind's ability to commit atrocities and heinous acts, yet is also a tribute to humankind's courageousness, relaying stories of heroism, bravery, and faith. With a collection of nearly 13,000 artifacts, the museum tells of the ordeal that Jewish people in Europe faced from the early 1930s to the liberation of the concentration camps in 1945. In the permanent exhibit, *The Holocaust,* history is chronicled from the Nazis' rise to power and the corralling of Jewish people into ghettos to deportation and the Final Solution, the Nazi plan to eradicate all Jewish people. One section recounts the stories of gentiles who reached out to hide, protect, and save Jewish people, including the now-famous Oskar Schindler; Japanese diplomat Chiune Sugihara, who approved visas

© PATRICIA KIME

U.S. Holocaust Memorial Museum

for 6,000 Jewish people to leave Lithuania; and Raoul Wallenberg, the Swedish diplomat for whom the museum's street is named, whose work acquiring fake passports and papers is estimated to have saved 100,000 people. Other exhibits focus on the liberation of the concentration camps, the Nuremberg trials, and the stories of the survivors. There is also a Hall of Remembrance where visitors can light a candle in honor of the victims.

Visitors often ask why Washington DC was selected to host this museum. The facility and its education center were the result of a commission ordered by President Jimmy Carter and headed by author and Holocaust survivor Elie Wiesel, assigned to study the feasibility of creating a memorial to honor the 6 million Jewish and 5 million non-Jewish victims of the genocide. The museum was designed by architect James Freed, who fled his native Germany as a child in 1939 and was a partner in the well-known architectural firm Pei Cobb Freed.

Timed passes are required to visit the museum during its busiest season, March through early August. If you plan to visit during this

time, go online at least two months before your visit to secure a spot. A few same-day tickets are available at the front desk, but these go quickly in the morning at opening time. This museum is recommended for people age 12 and older; it's wise to gauge the emotional maturity of your child before planning a visit. The museum keeps its most graphic images behind privacy walls, allowing visitors to decide whether they want to view them, but the entire space is filled with disturbing images and heartbreaking stories.

VIETNAM VETERANS MEMORIAL

Henry Bacon Dr. and Constitution Ave., 202/426-6841, www.nps.gov/vive

HOURS: Daily 24 hours; rangers on duty daily 9:30 A.M.-11:30 P.M.

COST: Free

Hidden from Constitution Avenue below grade, the 493-foot-long black granite Vietnam Veterans Memorial, a.k.a. the Wall, contains the names of the 58,267 service members who died as a result of the Vietnam war. Its haunting design—an arrow containing the names

Vietnam Veterans Memorial

of the dead etched in chronological order that starts and ends in the center with the years of the conflict (1959 and 1974)—was conceived by architect Maya Lin when she was a 21-year-old undergraduate at Yale. Controversial from the start, the black gash struck a nerve in a country still raw from the war. But the Wall has become one of DC's most beloved memorials, its minimalist design elevating rather than overshadowing the sacrifices of the individuals whose names are on it. It was dedicated in 1982 and later amended with sculptures to broaden its appeal. An accompanying sculpture, *The Three Soldiers* by Frederick Hart, was added in 1984, while the Glenna Goodacre–designed *Vietnam Women's Memorial* sculpture of three nurses attending an injured service member was added in 1994.

◨ WASHINGTON MONUMENT

Constitution Ave. and 15th St. NW, 877/444-6777, www.nps.gov/wamo

HOURS: Memorial Day-Labor Day daily 9 A.M.-10 P.M.; Labor Day-Memorial Day daily 9 A.M.-5 P.M.; closed Independence Day and Christmas Day

COST: Free, but ticket required; $1.50 per ticket if ordered online

The 555-foot-tall Washington Monument honors the military service of America's first president and is the tallest stone structure and obelisk in the world. Built 1848–1854 and 1876–1874, the monument was first conceived by Robert Mills as a flat-topped obelisk rising from a circular colonnade containing statues of the founding fathers. But funding problems, political turmoil, and the Civil War halted production, and when construction resumed more than 20 years later, Army engineer Lt. Col. Thomas Casey opted for the simpler Egyptian obelisk. The marble monument, with walls 15 feet thick at its base, bears the distinctive mark of its construction woes; at roughly 150 feet up, its color turns to a creamier shade of white, the result of stone quarried from different locations in Maryland than the original. The monument is topped with a 5.5- by 9-inch solid aluminum pyramidal shaped capstone, intended to serve as a lightning rod to protect the structure.

© PATRICIA KIME

Washington Monument

At the top, visitors peer out eight small windows that afford 360-degree views of the city, the Potomac River, and the Maryland and Virginia countryside, including the Blue Ridge Mountains to the west. The elevator ride takes roughly 70 seconds, and while visitors are no longer allowed to ascend the monument's 897 steps, walk-down tours are sometimes offered at the discretion of the National Park Service. The slow-descent route allows a closer look at the monument's interior, lined with 192 carved stones honoring Washington, markers that hail from foreign countries, all 50 states, organizations, and private donors. All visitors get to glimpse some of these tributes, though; the descending glass-walled elevator slows as it passes several, including Michigan's, made of solid copper with a sterling silver coat of arms, and Alaska's, installed in 1982 and carved from solid jade.

Admission to the Washington Monument is free, but timed tickets must be obtained beforehand by phone or the Internet, or picked up at a nearby kiosk that opens at 8:30 A.M. daily.

During peak visiting times, tickets may be gone by 9 A.M., and during the summer, the line forms before 7 A.M. To order tickets, call the National Park Reservation Service at 877/444-6777 or go to www.recreation.gov. There is a $1.50 fee per ticket as well as a shipping and handling charge. You can order up to six tickets.

On August 23, 2011, a 5.8 magnitude earthquake struck 84 miles from DC. A number of the obelisk's stones were dislodged and the elevator was damaged. The monument remained closed through the end of 2011—check for updates before your visit.

The National Mall East   Map 2

NATIONAL AIR AND SPACE MUSEUM
Independence Ave. and 6th St. SW, 202/633-1000, www.nasm.si.edu
HOURS: Labor Day-Mar. 24 daily 10 A.M.-5:30 P.M.; Mar. 25-Labor Day daily 10 A.M.-7:30 P.M.; closed Christmas Day
COST: Free

Always crowded, never dull, the National Air and Space Museum is a testament to awesome feats of engineering, illustrating the history of flight from the Wright Brothers' 1903 Flyer through SpaceShip One, the first private craft to make repeat trips to space. The museum boasts 23 galleries of satellites, rockets, missiles, full-sized passenger aircraft, flight paraphernalia, and space ships—more than can be seen in an afternoon. There's a must-touch moon rock, brought to earth on Apollo 17 in 1972, as well as a number of for-fee activities, including Albert Einstein Planetarium shows and movies at the Lockheed Martin IMAX Theater, which still airs one of the earliest IMAX films, *To Fly,* as well as other titles. This museum is the most visited in Washington, with nearly 9 million coming through its doors each year. To avoid the crush, visit in January or February, or summer evenings. The Smithsonian also operates a companion museum, the Steven F. Udvar-Hazy Center in Chantilly, Virginia, a cavernous facility that contains large aircraft, including a Concorde, the Space Shuttle *Enterprise,* the *Enola Gay* B-29 bomber, and an SR-71 Blackbird. Chantilly lies 30 miles from the National Air and Space Museum and is accessible by car or via a privately run shuttle from Dulles International Airport. Entry is free, but be aware of the $15 parking fee (free after 4 P.M.).

NATIONAL ARCHIVES
700 Pennsylvania Ave. NW, 202/357-5000, www.archives.gov
HOURS: Mar. 15-Labor Day daily 10 A.M.-7 P.M.; Labor Day-Mar. 14 10 A.M.-5:30 P.M., closed Thanksgiving and Christmas Day
COST: Free

The three most important documents in the United States, known as the Charters of Freedom, are found in the great Rotunda of the National Archives in an engineered vault of glass, titanium, and argon gas that fascinates visitors almost as much as the documents themselves. The Declaration of Independence, the Bill of Rights, and the Constitution are the archives' most impressive artifacts, but the museum also contains other interesting items as well, including a 1297 copy of the Magna Carta. The *Public Vaults* exhibit holds the log of the USS *Nevada,* opened to December 7, 1941; telegrams sent by Lincoln to dignitaries; and a hilarious video of President George H. W. Bush declaring that he, as president, no longer needs to eat broccoli. The entryway to the Rotunda is on Constitution Avenue. Jammed in the spring with school groups, visitors should get to the archives first thing in the morning when there is no backup outside, or try to enter at lunchtime or right before closing to avoid lines. Also, Mondays tend to be the least crowded day of the week. Researchers interested in working in the Archives' vaults need to bring a government-issued identification card and enter the facility from Pennsylvania Avenue. The DC research center contains military records, census information, immigration records, and more.

NATIONAL GALLERY OF ART

4th St. and Constitution Ave. NE, 202/737-4215, www.nga.gov

HOURS: Mon.-Sat. 10 A.M.-5 P.M., Sun. 11 A.M.-6 P.M.; closed Christmas Day and New Year's Day

COST: Free

The collection of Western art in the National Gallery of Art is so large—more than 110,000 paintings, sculptures, and decorative arts objects—that it requires two buildings to house it. The West Building, which contains artwork spanning the Middle Ages to the late 1800s, is the original, a 1941 neoclassical marble structure designed by John Russell Pope, architect of the Jefferson Memorial and the National Archives, that features an immense dome with an oculus and towering interior garden courts. It contains nearly 100 galleries filled with the world's greatest works, including those by Dutch masters, American artists, French impressionists, and Renaissance geniuses. The only Da Vinci oil painting in the United States is here, *Ginevra di' Benci,* as are two Raphaels, a bevy of Renoirs, a few Vermeers, and numerous Monets, Gaugins, and Van Goghs. Across 4th Street NW is the East Building, a modern H-shaped wedge designed by I. M. Pei that showcases the museum's collection of contemporary works, including those by Picasso, Matisse, Pollock, Mondrian, Miró, O'Keeffe, LeWitt, and more. A huge Alexander Calder mobile greets entrants to the building; wings hold galleries organized by artist or genre. The two buildings are connected via an underground tunnel that is a favorite for youngsters, with a padded moving walkway that carries visitors through a groovy light show and feeds into a sunny cafeteria and gift shop. The coffee kiosk here is a personal favorite; nowhere else in DC can you enjoy top-shelf gelato and relax to the sounds of a rushing waterfall cascade surrounded by beautiful gifts and art.

THE NATIONAL MALL

Between Constitution Ave. NW and Independence Ave. SW from 3rd St. to 15th St., 202/426-6841, www.nps.gov/nama

HOURS: Daily 24 hours; rangers on duty daily 9:30 A.M.-11:30 P.M.

COST: Free

The Mall is the heart of Washington DC,

© PATRICIA KIME

National Gallery of Art

a vast expanse of lawn and trees first conceived by city designer Pierre L'Enfant as a grand boulevard connecting important buildings, halls, and museums. Today, the Mall is akin to the nation's front yard, a venue for festivals, concerts, marches, gatherings, picnics, and pickup games. Fringed by museums and trimmed with pea-gravel paths, the Mall is bookended by the U.S. Capitol and the Lincoln Memorial and contains the Washington Monument. Often appearing downtrodden, especially in the summer months, it suffers from heavy foot traffic, and the National Park Service is undertaking a years-long effort to restore its 650 acres. Projects include refreshing the Mall's turf, fixing sidewalks, curbs, and pathways, and repairing features like the Lincoln Memorial Reflecting Pool.

NATIONAL MUSEUM OF AMERICAN HISTORY

Constitution Ave. at 12th St. NW, 202/633-1000, www.americanhistory.si.edu
HOURS: Labor Day–Memorial Day daily 10 A.M.–5:30 P.M.; Memorial Day–Labor Day daily 10 A.M.–7:30 P.M.; closed Christmas Day; highlight tours daily 10:15 A.M. and 1 P.M.
COST: Free

The National Museum of American History has rightly earned the nickname "The Nation's Attic," owning more than 3 million artifacts with roughly 2 percent on display at any one time. A renovation in 2008 greatly improved the museum's space, infusing it with light and creating special galleries for precious objects like the Star-spangled Banner, the flag that flew over Fort McHenry in the War of 1812, inspiring poet Francis Scott Key to pen what's now the national anthem. Despite the museum's redesign, however, its collection remains somewhat of a hodgepodge, with some of its best relics getting lost in clutter. Case in point: George Washington's uniform, held in a darkened glass case to protect the fabric and often overlooked precisely because it is not well-lit or widely announced. "Is this it?" a recent visitor asked, somewhat confused

as she looked at her map and then the uniform. I've visited this exhibit space on military wars many times, and no matter how crowded it is, few passersby seem to take notice of this artifact, a splendid habit that shows how trim and tall the first president was. Another fantastic but often overlooked item is the original Woolworth's lunch counter where four brave African American college students staged a sit-in in Greensboro, North Carolina, in 1960. It sits in a hallway, decorating a space near escalators. The museum's pop culture and entertainment sections draw large crowds, as does the exhibit on the first ladies' ball dresses. Pop artifacts here include Dorothy's ruby slippers from *The Wizard of Oz* and Jim Henson's Kermit the Frog puppet. *The American Presidency: A Glorious Burden* is a can't-miss look at the country's 44 leaders.

NATIONAL MUSEUM OF NATURAL HISTORY

10th St. and Constitution Ave. NW, 202/357-2700, www.mnh.si.edu
HOURS: Labor Day–Mar. 24 daily 10 A.M.–5:30 P.M.; Mar. 25–Labor Day 10 A.M.–7:30 P.M.; closed Christmas Day; tours 10:30 A.M. and 1:30 P.M.
COST: Free

Renovations and new exhibits create a dynamic experience at the National Museum of Natural History, a trove of science beloved by children for its dinosaurs and outsize mammals, like a huge, hairy woolly mammoth and gigantic African bull elephant. This museum appeals to anyone interested in the earth and the universe's bounty, from the stunning sapphire-blue Hope Diamond to giant squid, from humankind's earliest tools to massive magnetic meteorites that arrived here from outer space. The newest galleries include the Hall of Human Origins, a 15,000-foot corridor that examines the genesis and evolution of our species, and the colorful Sant Ocean Hall, featuring a live coral reef aquarium, the fearsome jaws of a prehistoric shark, and a 48-foot right whale replica. The museum's older exhibits still capture the imagination:

SIGHTS

© PATRICIA KIME

Peruse the collection of presidential memorabilia at the National Museum of American History.

The Discovery Room allows children to touch and explore fossils and animal bones; the Hall of Mammals boasts more than 275 taxidermy specimens; and in the Dinosaur Hall, paleontologists are part of the attraction, often seen working behind glass as they mark and piece together fossils. Small children shouldn't miss the Orkin Insect Zoo, hidden at the end of a bones exhibit straight out of the Pleistocene era of museum design. The zoo features a live beehive that opens out onto the Mall along with daily tarantula and bug feedings. For a small fee, visitors also can tour the Butterfly Conservatory, spending time in an indoor garden with Blue Morpho butterflies, giant Atlas moths, and more. Outside, butterflies can be seen, for free during spring and summer, where they are drawn to the museum's local habitat garden planted along 9th Street NW.

NATIONAL MUSEUM OF THE AMERICAN INDIAN

Independence Ave. and 4th St. SW, 202/633-1000, www.nami.si.edu

HOURS: Daily 10 A.M.-5:30 P.M.; highlight tours Mon.-Fri. 1:30 P.M. and 3 P.M., Sat.-Sun. 11:30 A.M., 1:30 P.M., and 3 P.M.; closed Christmas Day

COST: Free

An architectural standout for its limestone layers seemingly eroded by wind and water, the National Museum of the American Indian is the first in the country devoted solely to the history of the Americas' indigenous peoples. This vast space is the antithesis of its busy neighbor next door, the National Air and Space Museum: Its spacious (and sometimes criticized as seemingly empty) hallways and floors showcase artifacts like ceremonial pieces, spiritual offerings, weapons, and clothing. This museum is best seen through the free one-hour tour that provides insight into the architect and designers' use of space and examines details that aren't readily apparent in the self-guided visit. The museum's gardens feature the habitats of Native Americans, with waterfalls and ponds, crops, and woodlands, a tranquil stop during a long visit to the Mall. The building's organic design was conceived by Canadian architect Douglas Cardinal, a member of the Blackfoot Nation, and it was implemented by the firm James Polshek & Partners, working closely with Native Americans to create the property's elemental feel.

THE SMITHSONIAN INSTITUTION

1000 Jefferson Dr. SW, 202/633-1000, www.si.edu

HOURS: Daily 8:30 A.M.–5:30 P.M.; closed Christmas Day

COST: Free

Can't decide which of the Smithsonian's 18 Washington museums you want to see? Start at the Smithsonian Institution Building, a fortress of sandstone nicknamed the Castle that serves as headquarters to the sprawling museum complex. The Castle contains a tasting menu of exhibits called *America's Treasure Chest* that highlights the collections found at the Smithsonian's other properties as well as an information booth that provides guides to the museum's other properties. It also houses the crypt of the man responsible for starting it all, James Smithson, a British geologist and chemist who oddly willed his fortune to the United States, even though he never visited the country. The Romanesque-style Castle was designed in 1846 by architect James Renwick, whose works include St. Patrick's Cathedral in New York City.

Downtown   Map 3

FORD'S THEATRE
NATIONAL HISTORIC SITE

511 10th St. NW, 202/347-4833, www.fordstheatre.org

HOURS: Daily 9 A.M.–4:30 P.M.; closed Thanksgiving and Christmas Day

COST: Free; advance individual tickets $2.50

Renovated in 2009, Ford's Theatre, where Abraham Lincoln was shot on April 14, 1865, contains a museum dedicated to the 16th president, with artifacts such as John Wilkes Booth's pistol and other memorabilia from that night as well as items that provide a comprehensive overview of Lincoln's life and development, from his birth in a Kentucky log cabin to his death at Petersen House across the street. Throughout the day, park rangers and actors at Ford's Theatre explore the questions that faced the country at the time of Lincoln's death—the Civil War, the assassination, slavery, the investigation into Lincoln's murder, and the conspiracy behind it. Ford's is also a working professional theater, staging shows of historic interest and significance as well as a Washington annual tradition, Dickens's *A Christmas Carol.* Timed tickets are required for the theater and museum as well as Petersen House; these are available online for a fee through the museum website. A limited number of free same-day tickets can also be obtained at the box office starting at 8:30 A.M.

INTERNATIONAL SPY MUSEUM

800 F St. NW, 202/393-7798, www.spymuseum.org

HOURS: Variable, so call ahead; closed Thanksgiving, Christmas Day, and New Year's Day

COST: $18 over age 11, $15 ages 5–11, $17 seniors, military, and intelligence community

Families with young children flock to this snazzy interactive museum, one of DC's first for-profit museums, which opened in 2002, but teens and adults are likely to get more out of the experience, which starts when visitors are given an intelligence "cover" to remember and carry with them throughout their self-guided tour. Highlights include exhibits on the art of espionage, the history of intelligence, and an overview of famous spies. Guests can pretend they are part of *Mission: Impossible,* crawling through a mock ventilation system, or try to escape their "tails" by working on their surveillance and reconnaissance skills. An Aston Martin DB5, the ultimate James Bond car, is here, as is a collection of historic spy gear. Near the end is a comprehensive look at the human toll and national security breaches resulting from the work of the nation's most notorious double agents. The Spy Museum gift shop is

© DESTINATION DC

The International Spy Museum will inspire your inner sleuth.

great fun, featuring high-tech and low-tech spy gadgets, CDs of spy-themed music, and all sorts of kitschy items for the kids like invisible ink pens and *Spy vs. Spy* paraphernalia.

MADAME TUSSAUDS WAX MUSEUM

1025 F St. NW, 202/942-7300, www.madametussauds.com/washington
HOURS: Mon.-Thurs. 10 A.M.-4 P.M., Fri.-Sun. 10 A.M.-6 P.M.
COST: $20 over age 11, $15 ages 3-12, $18 over age 59

For a steep $20, you can stand next to, ogle, and touch wax figures of celebrities at Madame Tussauds, the only place in DC where you can see the likenesses of all 44 presidents in one place along with numerous celebrities. The Washington locale of this museum brings a decided political bent, with figures of the Obamas and other world leaders as well as famous activists like Rosa Parks. But stargazers will find a hefty dose of Hollywood as well, with figurines of the Jonas Brothers, Johnny Depp, Angelina Jolie, Oprah Winfrey, Denzel Washington, and others. Unfortunately, this version—one of 12 worldwide—doesn't bear the original's signature chamber of horrors, the

only thing most kids seem to remember years after their visit.

MARIAN KOSHLAND SCIENCE MUSEUM

6th St. and E St. NW, 202/334-1201, www.koshland-science-museum.org
HOURS: Wed.-Mon. 10 A.M.-6 P.M.; closed Thanksgiving, Christmas Day, and New Year's Day
COST: $5 adults, $3 seniors, students, and active-duty military

The Marian Koshland Science Museum is less a museum than it is a thinking space, a place targeted at people over the age of 14 who have a passion for scientific method and examination. At the time of this publication, the museum's main exhibits were *Global Warming Facts and Our Future* and *Infectious Diseases*. Visitors watch an introductory film about the nature of science and then explore interactive computer models and lessons that shed light on matters such as the consequences of climate change and the problems facing public health, including eradication of infectious diseases, epidemics, and drug-resistant bacteria. If you are confused by the museum's complex nature, ask a docent for guidance; they are friendly and patient, and more than likely, a retired scientist or former health worker. Bring your thinking caps.

NATIONAL AQUARIUM

1401 Constitution Ave., Commerce Building basement, 202/482-2825, www.nationalaquarium.org
HOURS: Daily 9 A.M.-5 P.M.
COST: $9.95 ages 11-59, $8.95 seniors, $8.95 military personnel and family members, $4.95 ages 3-11, free under age 3

A stowaway in the basement of the Commerce Building and accessed through a door that faces 14th Street, the National Aquarium is a favorite for families with young children and anyone who enjoys getting close to small sharks, puffer fish, moray eels, and baby sea turtles. This is a small, manageable adventure into the underwater realm, a branch of the larger aquarium in Baltimore that is rarely crowded. Highlights include fish feedings and exhibits based on national marine sanctuary habitats. It's a great space for those with toddlers—no worries about losing them—and anyone who likes communing in the dark with the cast of *Finding Nemo*. Beyoncé, the aquarium's Giant Pacific Octopus, is a staff favorite, a huge cephalopod that needs numerous toys to keep her amused.

NATIONAL BUILDING MUSEUM

410 F St. NW, 202/272-2448, www.nbm.org
HOURS: Mon.-Sat. 10 A.M.-5 P.M., Sun. 11 A.M.-5 P.M.; closed Thanksgiving and Christmas Day
COST: Free; a small charge for certain special exhibits

The former Pension Bureau office for Civil War veterans, the National Building Museum is a stunning historic structure that holds an eclectic variety of permanent and temporary exhibits, appealing mainly to architecture fans and, oddly, preschool children, who find great joy in the museum's Building Zone, which contains giant blocks and foam architectural elements, dress-up clothes, and accessories for interactive play. For the grown-ups, permanent exhibits include a detailed look at the planning and development of Washington DC and an examination of the cityscapes, architecture, materials, and construction practices

used in America's cities. In the past year, the museum has hosted temporary exhibits on a variety of subjects: world's fairs held in the United States, Lego models of famous buildings, and the works of Andrea Palladio. The building's Great Hall measures 316 by 116 feet and is considered one of the most attractive entertainment spaces in the city, used for galas, balls, and fund-raising events. During normal daytime hours, it is a welcoming space containing plants and a central fountain, a popular spot for sharing a cup of coffee and reading.

NATIONAL LAW ENFORCEMENT OFFICERS MEMORIAL

605 E St. NW, 202/737-3400, www.nleomf.com
HOURS: Daily 24 hours; Visitors Center Mon.-Fri. 9 A.M.-5 P.M., Sat. 10 A.M.-5 P.M., Sun. noon-5 P.M.; closed Thanksgiving, Christmas Day, and New Year's Day
COST: Free

The National Law Enforcement Officers Memorial is a gathering place at Judiciary Square for police and peace officers as well as families who have lost loved ones to public service. Displaying 19,000 names of law-enforcement officers who have lost their lives since 1792, the gray marble memorial, installed in 1991, was designed by architect Davis Buckley. Numerous ceremonies are held each year here; in early spring, the memorial is awash in yellow thanks to thousands of daffodils planted along the perimeter. The memorial's visitors center contains information about the officers honored on the memorial's panels; a museum showcasing the history of law enforcement is slated to open nearby in 2013.

NATIONAL MUSEUM OF CRIME AND PUNISHMENT

575 F St. NW, 202/393-1099, www.crimemuseum.org
HOURS: Sept. 1-May 20 Sun.-Thurs. 10 A.M.-7 P.M., Fri.-Sat. 10 A.M.-8 P.M.; May 21-Aug. 30 Mon.-Sat. 9 A.M.-9 P.M., Sun. 10 A.M.-7 P.M.; closed Thanksgiving and Christmas Day
COST: $19.95 over age 11, $14.95 age 5-11, $16.95 seniors, military, and law enforcement community; $2 discount for all tickets except children if purchased online

As sensational as a reality television show, this

for-profit museum is designed to enthrall fans of *CSI* and pulp fiction with macabre exhibits on serial killers, gangsters, outlaws, and the men and women who toil to apprehend them. For a place that seems more theater and fluff than fact, this museum is surprisingly reader-intensive, with lengthy explanations and detailed information of nearly every artifact and reproduction. It also has a number of interactive activities, including the opportunity to test your knowledge of gruesome crimes; drive a police-car simulator; or decide, in an interactive shooting "game," whether to apply deadly use-of-force against offenders. The display commentary, rife with typos and grammatical errors, calls into question the veracity of the information presented, and many of the items on display are replicas or Hollywood film items, which may disappoint serious museum goers. Still, one of its starring artifacts is on view in the lobby to passersby and is 100 percent genuine: Ted Bundy's 1968 Volkswagen Beetle, a carriage of death into which he lured young women, assaulted them, and brutally murdered them.

NEWSEUM

555 Pennsylvania Ave. NW, 888/639-7386, www.newseum.org

HOURS: Daily 9 A.M.–5 P.M.; closed Thanksgiving, Christmas Day, and New Year's Day

COST: $21.95 adults, $17.95 over age 64, military, and students with ID, $12.95 ages 7-18, free under age 7; 10 percent discount if ordered online

A museum that sucks you in for hours and leaves you wanting more, the Newseum is the finest of DC's pay-to-play museums: seven floors of interactive exhibits, moving films, historic lessons, and activities on the past, present, and future of newsgathering. If the hundreds of front pages on display or the videos of journalistic ethics don't grab you, the 9/11 Gallery, containing a 360-foot piece of the World Trade Center's North Tower antenna, intense videos, and numerous artifacts will haunt you, as will the laptop computer belonging to *Wall Street Journal* reporter Daniel Pearl or Nick Ut's devastating photo of children running from a napalm attack in Trang Bang, Vietnam. Serious subjects are tempered with fun activities that appeal to all

© PATRICIA KIME

Newseum

ages: opportunities to pretend you're a weather reporter or a news anchor; tests to see how well you'd do as an editor, photojournalist, or reporter; and other interactive games. The

Newseum is funded by the Freedom Forum, a foundation dedicated to preserving the First Amendment established by *USA Today* founder Al Neuharth.

Foggy Bottom   Map 4

DAUGHTERS OF THE
AMERICAN REVOLUTION MUSEUM

1776 D St. NW, 202/628-1776, www.dar.org/museum
HOURS: Mon.-Fri. 9:30 A.M.-4 P.M., Sat. 9 A.M.-5 P.M.;
tours of period rooms Mon.-Fri. 10 A.M.-2:30 P.M.,
Sat. 9 A.M.-4:30 P.M.
HOURS: Daily 24 hours
COST: Free

Easier to access than the State Department's Diplomatic Rooms, the Daughters of the American Revolution (DAR) Museum holds numerous treasures from America's past and boasts 31 rooms that showcase different periods in American decorating and furnishings from 30 states and the District of Columbia. Precious artifacts in the museum include a 1775 printing of the map of Virginia drawn by Joshua Fry and Peter Jefferson (Thomas's father), a teapot made by Paul Revere, and a fanciful Chippendale sofa owned by Declaration of Independence signer Thomas McKean. Surprisingly, this museum of fussy furniture is also child-friendly, or at least American Girl fan friendly. Lovers of Felicity from the book series usually enjoy the museum's collection of clothing, toys, china, quilts, and furnishings. The DAR also displays a small collection of abolitionist items, including purses, cameos, and china featuring chained slaves begging for mercy—a depiction intended during its day to rouse sympathy and gain publicity for the abolitionist cause. It also has several artifacts belonging to suffragettes.

GEORGE WASHINGTON UNIVERSITY

2121 I St. NW, 202/994-6602, www.gwu.edu
HOURS: Daily 24 hours
COST: Free

Having a college named for you just isn't the same as starting one of your own. George

Washington had the former—Washington College in Chestertown, Maryland, established in 1782—but he aimed for the latter and left money in his will to do it. Washington's endowment led to the creation of Columbian College in 1821, the precursor to "GW," as George Washington University is known around the city. The school offers the gamut of undergraduate and graduate programs and can brag about having hundreds of famous alumni thanks to its expansive law school and executive business programs. Noted undergraduates include Jacqueline Kennedy Onassis, Virginia Sen. Mark Warner, and former Boston Celtics coach Red Auerbach. GW is a sprawling urban campus that consumes several city blocks and has a number of satellite campuses. If you are interested in touring the university, pick up a map at the Admissions Visitor Center near 22nd and H Streets.

◖ LAFAYETTE SQUARE

1601 Pennsylvania Ave. NW
HOURS: Daily 24 hours
COST: Free

The statue in the middle of Lafayette Square isn't of Revolutionary War general the Marquis de Lafayette; it's Andrew Jackson by Clark Mills, who later cast a similar sculpture for Jackson Square in New Orleans. Named in 1824, the park honors the soldier whose assistance during the Revolution contributed significantly to the colonies' victory over Britain. Statues of famous foreign military leaders who also aided the United States during the Revolution mark the square's corners: Maj. Gen. Jean de Rochambeau, Gen. Thaddeus Kosciuszko, Maj. Gen. Friedrich Wilhelm von Steuben, and Lafayette. One of the city's most

the North Portico of the White House, as seen from Lafayette Square

fashionable neighborhoods in the 1800s, the square is lined with Federal style buildings, including Blair House, the official guesthouse for visiting heads of state, and Decatur House, the 1818 home of U.S. naval hero Stephen Decatur, designed by America's first professional architect, Benjamin Latrobe. Lafayette Square, separated from the White House by the long-closed Pennsylvania Avenue, is a hot spot for protests. One group, opposing nuclear armament, has been there since 1981.

NATIONAL ACADEMY OF SCIENCES

2101 Constitution Ave. NW, 202/334-2346, www.nationalacademies.org
HOURS: Closed for restoration until 2012
COST: Free

The giant sculpture of Albert Einstein by Robert Berks in front of the National Academy of Sciences is one of DC's most popular sites for snapshots; groups love climbing into the lap of this oversized likeness of the famous physicist. The National Academy of Sciences is an organization that advises the government on scientific matters, and according to its charter, on the arts

as well. Its Constitution Avenue headquarters is currently undergoing renovations, but it usually hosts exhibits, symposia, and speaking events on various scientific and artistic subjects. Recent displays include highlights of the Academy's collection, including artwork that explores relationships between the arts and sciences, and *An Iconography of Contagion,* a collection of 20 health posters spanning the period between 1920 and 1990 that explore the public health industry's efforts to raise awareness of contagious diseases from syphilis and malaria to AIDS.

ST. JOHN'S CHURCH

1525 H St. NW, 202/347-8766, www.stjohns-dc.org
HOURS: Mon.-Sat. 9 A.M.-3 P.M.
COST: Free

Known as the "Church of the Presidents," St. John's, an Episcopal church located on Lafayette Square, has hosted every U.S. president since 1816 for at least one service; Barack Obama attended the morning of his inauguration, following in the footsteps of both presidents Bush and Ronald Reagan. Pew 54 is reserved for the commander-in-chief when he is in attendance.

St. John's was designed and built by Benjamin Latrobe, considered America's first professional architect, in the shape of a Greek cross; it was the second building constructed on Lafayette Square after the White House. It has been renovated over the years, most notably in the 1880s under the watch of architect James Renwick, who expanded the space and oversaw the installation of stained glass windows. The church's bell was cast by Joseph Revere, Paul Revere's son, in Boston in 1822. It weighs nearly 1,000 pounds and is the only Revere bell in continuous use in the District since that time.

U.S. STATE DEPARTMENT

22nd St. and C St. NW, 202/647-3241,
www.diplomaticrooms.state.gov
HOURS: Tours Mon.-Fri. 9:30 A.M., 10:30 A.M., and
2:45 P.M.; reservations required; closed federal holidays
COST: Free

Admirers of American period furniture and decorative arts should go the extra mile to obtain tickets for the U.S. State Department's Diplomatic Rooms, a 42-room suite located on the building's eighth floor used by the Secretary of State, Cabinet members, and the vice president for official business, including meetings, negotiations, and treaty signings. Decorated to showcase the finest of 18th and early 19th century American art, architecture, and casework, these rooms—salons, ballrooms and halls—hold magnificent early American furnishings, including the desk where the Treaty of Paris was signed as well as works by Paul Revere and Gilbert Stuart. Tours are by advanced reservation; the State Department recommends visitors contact them up to 90 days in advance. The visit is not recommended for children under 12.

THE WHITE HOUSE

1600 Pennsylvania Ave. NW, 202/456-7041,
www.whitehouse.gov
HOURS: Only by advance ticket, Tues.-Thurs.
7:30-11 A.M. Fri. 7:30 A.M.-noon, Sat. 7:30 A.M.-1 P.M.
COST: Free

Home to every U.S. president since John Adams, the White House is more than a residence: It contains the executive offices of the president and those of the first lady's staff as well. More difficult to see since security concerns arose after the September 11, 2001, terrorist attacks, the White House still is a "people's house," open for tours, a practice started by Thomas Jefferson when he threw open the home for a public reception following his second inauguration. Designed by Irish-born architect James Hoban and built between 1792 and 1800, the White House is considered to be neoclassical Federal style, constructed of sandstone quarried from Aquia, Virginia, and painted with more than 570 gallons of white paint. Once designed as a three-story structure, George Washington, who selected Hoban's drawings, tweaked them so the main building appears to have two stories on an English basement, although in actuality it is six stories high. In 1814 the White House was set on fire by the British and nearly burned to the ground; only a serendipitous rain shower saved it from complete ruin. Another fire torched the West Wing in 1929, and in the late 1940s, when the building was found to be unsound, the entire interior was gutted, reinforced, and renovated. The Trumans, occupants of the White House at the time, lived across the street in Blair House during the renovations. The White House has undergone extensive remodeling and renovations during its existence, and each president and first lady leave their mark on the home in some fashion. Teddy Roosevelt rid the house of the Victorian influences that had crept in since Abraham Lincoln's era; Jacqueline Kennedy was a major force in ridding it of replicas and inaccurate furniture, raising funds to bring in original antiques and period-appropriate fabrics and upholstery; the Obamas have added a vegetable garden.

The White House has 132 rooms and 35 bathrooms and sits on eight acres: The South Portico, a round two-story porch with Ionic columns, faces the Ellipse, the site used each December to host the National Christmas Tree and National Menorah; the North Portico, which is considered the home's front door, faces Lafayette Square.

Tickets for the self-guided White House tour are challenging to obtain. Requests must be submitted through the offices of members of Congress up to six months in advance and are available for groups of 10 or more. Often, congressional offices will keep a list of open spaces within a tour for smaller groups. It's recommended that once you make a request of your representative's or senator's office, follow up frequently so they don't forget you. The tour is brief, but visitors aren't rushed. Rooms one can expect to see include the Green Room, named by John Quincy Adams, likely in reference to the green canvas floor covering placed in it by Jefferson when he used it as a dining room, and not for the green moiré silk wallpaper that now adorns the walls; the Blue Room, the circular room above the Oval Office; the Red Room, with rich silk-upholstered walls and Empire furnishings; and the East Room, the largest room in the White House, used as a reception space and for state dinners. In the East Room hangs the mammoth Gilbert Stuart portrait of George Washington, one of a dozen painted by the artist and the copy famously saved from the British during the War of 1812 by First Lady Dolley Madison, who instructed slave Paul Jennings and others to rescue it in advance of the British invasion.

WHITE HOUSE VISITORS CENTER

1450 Pennsylvania Ave. NW, www.whitehouse.gov
HOURS: Daily 7:30 A.M.-4 P.M.; closed Thanksgiving, Christmas Day, and New Year's Day
COST: Free

Don't have tickets to the White House? Take pictures of the outside, and if you are interesting in learning more, head to the small visitors center on the first floor of the Commerce Building for a film and exhibits on its history. The displays highlight some of the home's furnishings and profile many of its occupants, including family members like Theodore Roosevelt's rambunctious children and Chelsea Clinton's cat, Sox. The National Park Service runs an information booth here that distributes pamphlets on area sights while the White House Historical Association operates a small gift shop, a place to buy a favorite Washington keepsake: the annual White House Christmas Ornament.

Capitol Hill   Map 5

FOLGER SHAKESPEARE LIBRARY

201 East Capitol St. SE, 202/544-4600, www.folger.edu
HOURS: Mon.-Sat. 10 A.M.-5 P.M.; tours Mon.-Fri. 11 A.M. and 3 P.M., Sat. 11 A.M. and 1 P.M.; garden tours Apr.-Oct. third Sat. of month 10 A.M. and 11 A.M.; closed federal holidays
COST: Free

Fans of the Bard will enjoy Folger Shakespeare Library, home to the largest collection of Shakespeare's works in the world as well as rare Renaissance books, manuscripts, and art. Although much of the Folger's collection is open to researchers only, the library owns 79 copies of the playwright's First Folio, and one is prominently displayed in library's oak-paneled exhibit hall. This dark barrel-ceilinged hall usually displays rotating exhibits on subjects pertaining to the Elizabethan era or Shakespeare. The Folger is one of Washington's performing arts gems, producing Shakespearean and other classical works at least three times a year in the library's theater, a painstakingly reproduced Elizabethan courtyard open to the public for viewing during the day. Outside, an Elizabethan garden showcases plants found in Shakespeare's works, as well as those common to his English gardens during his lifetime. The Folger's biggest yearly event occurs on the Saturday closest to Shakespeare's birthday, April 23, an Open House that draws large crowds with its performers, crafts, readings, and birthday cake.

LIBRARY OF CONGRESS

101 Independence Ave. SE, 202/707-8000, www.loc.gov

HOURS: Mon.-Sat. 8:30 A.M.-4:30 P.M.; tours Mon.-Fri. 10:30 A.M., 11:30 A.M., 2:30 P.M., and 3:30 P.M., Sat. 10:30 A.M., 11:30 A.M., and 2:30 P.M.; closed Thanksgiving, Christmas Day, and New Year's Day

COST: Free

Add one more thing the country owes to Thomas Jefferson, besides importing ice cream and waffles and drafting the Declaration of Independence: In financial straits near the end of his life, he sold his personal library of 6,487 books to Congress after its collection was burned by the British in 1814, supplying the basis for what has grown into the largest library in the world, with 147 million items, including 33 million books and other print materials on nearly 840 miles of shelves. The Library of Congress occupies three buildings on Capitol Hill and has numerous facilities elsewhere, including a high-density storage warehouse at Fort Meade, Maryland, and a film preservation center underground in Culpeper, Virginia. The primary structure of the Library of Congress is the Jefferson Building, a grand Italian Renaissance building that opened to the public in 1897 and contains several of the country's most valuable artifacts, including one of only three existing perfect copies of the Gutenberg Bible printed on vellum. Rotating exhibits off the Jefferson Building's Great Hall highlight the history of the nation's great documents—the Declaration of Independence, the Constitution, and the Bill of Rights—or focus on the importance of communication and the written word in societies throughout history. A spectator's gallery over the Main Reading Room can be accessed by a stairway in the Great Hall, giving visitors a glimpse of the library's majestic four-story research room. This vast domed space features stained glass replicas of the seals of 48 states, an elaborate gilt frieze, and 16 statues that depict famous representatives of subjects ranging from art and commerce to religion and history.

Visitors who see the reading room often wonder how they can get a library card. Passes are available to anyone conducting research

© PATRICIA KIME

Library of Congress

STAY TO THE RIGHT

Washington has a name for the habit tourists have of standing in large groups on Metro escalators: It is called escalefting – meaning people are hanging out across the entire step of an escalator, the right and the left sides. It is frequently used as a noun: "An escalefter blocked my way, and I missed the train."

DC is a working town, and many people rely on the Metro for commuting and getting to meetings. For these armchair warriors, riding the Metro is not unique, fun, or novel; it's functional. And protocol on the DC Metro system is for people on escalators to stand on the right to allow people to pass on the left.

We know you have lots to talk about – your experience at the Air and Space Museum, the bucket-drummers you listened to on K Street, the cute boy you saw on the last train – but please don't share while standing side-by-side with your BFF on a Metro escalator. Welcome to Washington, and thank you for staying to the right.

over the age of 18 who holds a valid ID card and proof of address. Requests can be made at the library's Madison Building. It can take librarians up to 45 minutes to retrieve a book or material if it is located on-site. If the item is elsewhere, it can take a few days. The Library of Congress is not a lending library; all research must be done on the premises.

LINCOLN PARK

East Capitol St. and 11th St. NE, 202/619-7225, www.nps.gov/cahi
HOURS: Daily 5 A.M.-midnight
COST: Free

This neighborhood park, overseen by the National Park Service, lies off the beaten path for visitors but is an important African American history site, containing a statue of Lincoln paid for by freed slaves and the city's first sculpture solely honoring an

African American. At the park's center sits the 1876 Emancipation Memorial, a monument funded by Civil War veterans and freed slaves that portrays a slave whose chains are snapped as Lincoln proffers the Emancipation Proclamation. From the start, the statue, designed by artist Thomas Ball, was controversial; Frederick Douglass, who delivered the keynote speech during its dedication, criticized its design for perpetuating negative stereotypes of blacks as subservient or dependent. Yet it became a popular tourist attraction, and in 1974 the National Council of Negro Women chose the same park to honor their founder, Mary McLeod Bethune, with a sculpture by Robert Berks. The daughter of former slaves, Bethune fought for equal education opportunities for African Americans. Her work led to the creation of Bethune Cookman College, and she later served as an advisor to President Franklin Roosevelt on race matters.

MARINE BARRACKS WASHINGTON

8th St. and I St. SE, 202/433-4073
HOURS: Tours Wed. 10 A.M.; evening parade Memorial Day-Labor Day Fri. 8:45 P.M.; reservations required
COST: Free

At the corner of 8th and I Streets stands the oldest post in the U.S. Marine Corps, a barracks sited in 1801 by President Thomas Jefferson and Lt. Col. William Ward Burrows, the Corps' second commandant. Chosen for its proximity to the Washington Navy Yard and the U.S. Capitol, the base contains the oldest continuously occupied public building in the District of Columbia, the commandant's home, which escaped being burned by the British in 1814. It is also home to music halls and facilities used by John Philip Sousa while he wrote several of his famous marches. Today, Marines assigned to the post largely perform ceremonial and security duties, although they must maintain combat readiness and can be deployed. The barracks is home to the Marine Corps Band, the ensemble once headed by Sousa that plays at White House and other official functions; the Marine Corps Drum and Bugle Corps; and the Corps' precision drill team, the Silent Drill

SIGHTS

Platoon. From Memorial Day through Labor Day, the barracks hosts a ceremonial parade on Friday nights, and its units participate in a Sunset Parade Tuesday evenings at the Marine Corps War Memorial.

NATIONAL JAPANESE AMERICAN MEMORIAL

Louisiana Ave. and New Jersey Ave. NW, 202/530-0015, www.njamf.com
HOURS: Daily 24 hours
COST: Free

A dark chapter in American history is remembered, as are the heroes who served the United States despite discrimination and the incarceration of their families, at the National Japanese American Memorial, a tribute to the 120,000 Americans interned at camps in the United States during World War II and the 33,000 soldiers of Japanese ancestry who fought for the United States. At the center of the memorial is a striking sculpture by artist Nina Akumu—two cranes fighting to free themselves of the barbed wire that binds them. The monument, installed in 2000, honors members of the 100th Battalion and 442nd Regimental Combat Teams and other World War II fighting units made up exclusively of *nissei* troops—U.S. citizens whose parents were Japanese.

NATIONAL POSTAL MUSEUM

2 Massachusetts Ave. NE, 202/633-5555, www.postalmuseum.si.edu
HOURS: Daily 10 A.M.-5:30 P.M.; tours 10 A.M. and 1 P.M., based on docent availability; closed Christmas Day
COST: Free

Mail is delivered to every household in the United States six days a week. The National Postal Museum, part of the Smithsonian complex, highlights this remarkable feat with exhibits that literally walk visitors from mail delivery in the colonial era to mailing methods of modern times. One doesn't have to be a philatelist to enjoy this airy, inviting museum, although it helps. While some might find the subject matter to be dry, toddlers love exploring the mail car and climbing into the cab of a mail truck, and teenagers like the exhibits on crime, mail fraud, and postal inspections, including an in-depth look at the search for Unabomber Ted Kaczynski and the perpetrator of the 2001 DC anthrax mailings. History buffs and artists appreciate the museum's vast stores of stamps, including those sold to support Amelia Earhart's daring journeys.

SEWALL-BELMONT HOUSE

144 Constitution Ave. NE, 202/544-4600, www.sewallbelmont.org
HOURS: Wed.-Sun. noon-5 P.M.
COST: $5 suggested donation

The names of suffragists don't exactly roll off most Americans' tongues, but the memories and artifacts of remarkable women like Elizabeth Cady Stanton and Susan B. Anthony are honored at the Sewall-Belmont House, headquarters to the National Woman's Party and a museum for those who campaigned for equal rights. Once home to suffragette and party founder Alice Paul, the 1800 building is the oldest house in DC that's not in Georgetown. It contains an extensive collection of suffrage and equal-rights documentation as well as the country's first feminist library. Newly reopened in 2011 following extensive renovations of its exhibit rooms, the Sewall-Belmont House is one of only a handful of museums in the country solely dedicated to the history of women in America.

THE SUPREME COURT OF THE UNITED STATES

1st St. NE, 202/479-3000, www.supremecourt.gov
HOURS: Mon.-Fri. 9 A.M.-4:30 P.M.; closed federal holidays
COST: Free

The Supreme Court doesn't exactly exude hospitality. With monumental steps, imposing Corinthian columns, and the stern phrase "Equal Justice Under the Law" etched on its neoclassical facade, it's formidable. And the justices seem to agree: "Why is it that we have an elegant, astonishingly beautiful, imposing, impressive structure? It's to remind us we have an important function and to remind the public, when it sees the building, of the importance and centrality of the law," Associate Justice Anthony Kennedy told C-SPAN. But past the checkpoints and lines, the ominous court is visitor-friendly, welcoming spectators and encouraging visitors to explore. Americans can spend a lifetime never seeing a president or a senator, but the opportunity to watch the most powerful members of the Judicial Branch is guaranteed two days a week for at least two weeks a month, from early October until late April. The Supreme Court is an appellate court, meaning it considers cases on appeal from federal circuit courts, and in some cases state supreme courts if the case involves constitutional or federal law. The Supreme Court receives more than 8,000 requests, known as petitions for writ of certiorari, each year. The nine justices—currently one chief justice and eight associate justices—decide which to accept (usually 75 to 80 cases a year), and then they hear them and rule. Only an act of Congress can overturn a Supreme Court decision.

Before its impressive building opened in 1935, the Supreme Court met in various settings, starting with the Merchants Exchange Building in New York City in 1790, moving to Philadelphia and eventually to the U.S. Capitol. The current building was proposed by chief justice and former president William Howard Taft, who felt the court should be contained in an edifice on par with the other two branches of government. Architect Cass Gilbert, who designed the neo-Gothic Woolworth Building in New York City, was selected to draft the design. Among the Supreme Court building's notable details are its massive bronze doors with bas reliefs depicting scenes from the development of Western law; the pediment sculpture on the little-visited East Front that includes lawgivers of three great civilizations—Moses, Confucius, and Solon; and two courtroom friezes that depict 18 historic lawmakers, including Hammurabi, Caesar Augustus, Charlemagne, and Muhammad. Surprisingly, the famous "Equal Justice" phrase found on the building's architrave,

which has become the Court's de facto motto, was created by architect Gilbert simply "because it fit," Supreme Court historians say.

Spectators hoping to watch the court in session can line up the day of a case in two lines: one that allows them to stay for three minutes, or another for the entire procedure. Lines begin forming around 8 A.M., earlier for high-profile cases, and hearings last roughly an hour. For information on cases, check out the Supreme Court website or the *Washington Post* for the daily docket.

The Supreme Court doesn't have official tours, but visitors can explore much of the building at their leisure. A 30-minute C-SPAN film about the court runs continuously in two theaters, and the exhibit hall contains several important court artifacts, including Chief Justice John Marshall's original chair and Justice Sandra Day O'Connor's robes. Visitors can also wander through the Great Hall and see the courtroom through a cordoned-off open doorway. Courtroom lectures are offered when court is not in session, usually every hour on the half hour starting at 9:30 A.M. Stop by the information desk to learn more about these opportunities.

UNION STATION

50 Massachusetts Ave. NE, 202/289-1908, www.unionstationdc.com

HOURS: Shops: Mon.-Sat. 10 A.M.-9 P.M., Sun. noon-6 P.M.; food court: Mon.-Sat. 7 A.M.-9 P.M. Sun. 7 A.M.-6 P.M.

COST: Free

It is hard to imagine, but in 1981, Union Station, the city's magnificent beaux arts train terminal designed by famed architect Daniel Burnham, was shuttered, its roof partially collapsed and its centurion statues in disrepair. Mushrooms grew along its 96-foot barrel-vaulted ceiling. Built in 1908 during the heyday of rail travel, the ornate station, modeled after the Diocletian and Caracalla baths in Rome, no longer seemed relevant in the world of affordable airline tickets and interstate highways. But a group of senators joined forces with Amtrak to save this architectural masterpiece. The $160 million renovation called for returning the terminal to a functional passenger station and adding shops, restaurants, movie theaters, and parking. The effort worked: Today, Union Station is on the National Register of Historic Places, a major commuter hub that is the busiest tourist sight in Washington DC drawing nearly 30 million to its impressive spaces each year.

Union Station consists of several impressive spaces: a central hall, two wings, and a main concourse. The Main Hall dazzles with its coffered barrel ceiling, gilded with more than 70 pounds of 22-karat gold leaf. Thirty-six Roman centurion statues by artist Louis St. Gaudens—younger brother of famed sculptor Augustus Saint-Gaudens—stand watch over travelers, their shields readied for battle (and covering their bare legs; Saint-Gaudens was asked by the commission overseeing construction to modify his statues for modesty's sake). The East Hall, a quiet shopping area of jewelry kiosks and boutique stores, features grand architectural tracery as well as a hand-painted ceiling and walls. Retail stores and eateries are found in the Main Concourse, which serves Amtrak and commuter rail passengers.

UNITED STATES CAPITOL

Between Constitution Ave. and Independence Ave. at 1st St., 202/226-8000, www.aoc.gov or www.visitthecapitol.gov

HOURS: Mon.-Sat. 8:30 A.M.-4:30 P.M.; tours Mon.-Sat. 8:50 A.M.-3:20 P.M.; closed Thanksgiving, Christmas Day, New Year's Day, and Inauguration Day

COST: Free

The majestic dome of the U.S. Capitol dominates the Washington skyline, an enduring symbol of the U.S. government and not unintentionally of democracy and freedom. Rising 288 feet above high ground once known as Jenkins Hill, the Capitol dome—at 4,455 tons, the largest cast-iron dome in the world—and its building are the centerpiece of the 450-acre Capitol Campus, which contains Congress, the Supreme Court, and the Library of Congress.

Often assumed by visitors to be the White House, the U.S. Capitol is home to the Senate and House of Representatives, which have met here since 1800, with one interruption between 1814 and 1819 (after the British burned the building in the War of 1812) and despite the noted absence of the Confederate States during the Civil War. Designed over the course of 200 years by at least five architects, the Capitol originally was conceived by physician and amateur architect Dr. William Thornton as a sandstone structure with two wings for the chambers of the bicameral legislature, connected by a round center hall topped with a neoclassical dome. President George Washington approved the design and laid the building's cornerstone in 1793. But less than 50 years later, as the country expanded, Congress needed more space. A new design called for doubling the Capitol's size and encapsulating the facade in marble. Since the redesign dwarfed the building's existing classical dome, Architect Thomas U. Walter drafted plans for a larger cast-iron dome. Construction began in 1856, and although funds became tight at the onset of the Civil War in 1861, President Abraham Lincoln insisted the work continue—a move that cemented the dome's role as a symbol of the republic. "If people see the Capitol going on, it is a sign we intend the Union shall go on," Lincoln told Army chaplain John Eaton. The exterior was completed in 1863, topped by a 19-foot bronze statue, *Freedom,* by sculptor Thomas Crawford.

The newest addition to the Capitol was finished in 2008, a 580,000-square-foot Capitol Visitor Center tucked under the historic Capitol's East Front that serves as a sheltered entrance and exhibit hall for the 3–5 million people who visit the building each year. The visitor center is the jumping-off point for most Capitol tours, which is the only way to view the historic Capitol's interior.

The highlight of any Capitol visit is the **Rotunda,** a 96-foot-wide circular hall at the heart of the building that is used largely for ceremonial events. In this grand space, under a ceiling that stretches 180 feet high, 10 U.S. presidents—the most recent being Gerald Ford

© PATRICIA KIME

The United States Capitol Rotunda is known for its impressive historical art collection.

in 2007—have lain in state, an honor given to senators, representatives, notable military leaders, and a few noteworthy civilians, including FBI Director J. Edgar Hoover and civil rights activist Rosa Parks. The Rotunda is known for its grand architecture and impressive art, including the fresco masterpiece *The Apotheosis of Washington* by Italian painter Constantino Brumidi, and eight 12- by 18-foot historical paintings of historic American events such as the much-replicated *Declaration of Independence* by Connecticut artist John Trumbull, seen on the $2 bill.

Adjacent to the Rotunda is the opulent **National Statuary Hall,** where nearly all the statues in the complex were crammed until 2008. Each state is allowed to display two statues within the U.S. Capitol. Statuary Hall served as the House of Representatives from 1819 to 1857, but it was never considered adequate for the purpose because its half-domed roof causes echoes throughout the chamber. The design also created what is called a "whispering gallery" in the space: be careful what you say here, because in some locations, a hushed exchange can be heard clearly and audibly at the opposite end of the hall.

During the capital's slow season (often November through February, excluding a brief period around Christmas and New Year's) or if a tour group is small, Capitol guides may show off the **Old Supreme Court Chamber** (which served justices from 1819 to 1860) and the **Old Senate Chamber,** both richly decorated halls that illustrate the Capitol architects' design genius and their Bicentennial-era redecorator's penchant for red drapes. Of note in the Old Senate Chamber is a porthole portrait of George Washington by Rembrandt Peale and the vice president's desk, a curved mahogany table topped with a canopy featuring a mahogany valance, gilt eagle, and shield.

Capitol tours take up to an hour. Those interested in the history of the building will want to leave time to explore the Capitol Visitor Center's exhibit hall, which features models of the capitol and architectural artifacts of the building. To obtain tickets, contact your senator or representative, or book them through www.visitthecapitol.gov.

U.S. BOTANIC GARDENS

100 Maryland Ave. SW, 202/225-8333, www.usbg.gov
HOURS: Mon.-Sun. 10 A.M.-5 P.M.
COST: Free

The toastiest place in DC on a chilly winter day is the conservatory of the U.S. Botanic Gardens, a subtropical paradise southeast of the Capitol containing more than 40,000 plants, including 5,000 orchids and thousands of roses. This greenhouse, built in 1932 and completely renovated in the late 1990s, charms the senses: The fragrance of lingering blooms wafts through the air; the sun's rays warm the hothouse; vibrant orchids and roses dance with the slightest movement; the sounds of a jungle waterfall tickle the ear. The concept for a national botanic garden dates to the founding fathers: Thomas Jefferson, George Washington, and James Madison worked to establish one on the Mall by 1820. Today, the space comprises the conservatory; the lovely National Garden, with a Butterfly Garden, Rose Garden, and the First Ladies' Water Garden; and Bartholdi Park, a formal, lavish landscape that contains an ornate Victorian-era fountain and examples of current American horticulture. Crowds flock to the conservatory after Thanksgiving and through the month of December for the garden's holiday display of model trains, festive poinsettias, Christmas trees, sparkling lights, and miniatures of buildings found in the nation's capital, all created from all-natural materials.

◖ THE U.S. CAPITOL GROUNDS

Between Constitution Ave. and Independence Ave. at 1st St.
HOURS: Daily 24 hours
COST: Free

The 59 acres surrounding the Capitol are tailor-made for picnicking and people-watching, especially in good weather when lawmakers stroll from their offices to the Capitol rather than use the building's underground tramway. Created by renowned landscape architect Frederick Law Olmsted, whose works include New York's Central Park and the National Zoo, the Capitol Grounds were intended to enhance the Capitol's beauty without detracting from the imposing structure. The grounds encompass eight miles of walkways, more than 4,000 trees (many of which are labeled with common and scientific names), and architectural flourishes such as massive stone pylons, terraces, and hidden treasures like the unusual brick and terra-cotta Summerhouse northwest of the Capitol building, designed by Olmsted as a water-stop for weary walkers. A popular spot for photographers is the West Front Reflecting Pool and its colossal Ulysses S. Grant Memorial, featuring lions, artillerymen, infantry troops, and the Civil War–winning general astride his steed, Cincinnatus. In the summer, the Capitol Grounds host free concerts by area military bands and orchestras, and at Christmas, the West Front showcases the Capitol Christmas Tree, a genteel cousin to the flashier National Christmas Tree that draws small crowds to see its radiant lights and handmade decorations.

Dupont Circle   Map 6

ANDERSON HOUSE

2118 Massachusetts Ave. NW, 202/785-2040, www.societyofthecincinatti.org
HOURS: Tues.-Sat. 1-4 P.M.; tours 1:15 P.M., 2:15 P.M., and 3:15 P.M.; closed Thanksgiving, Christmas Day, and New Year's Day
COST: Free

The magnificent Anderson House is head-quarters to the Society of the Cincinnati, an organization started in 1783 by officers of the Continental Army that exists today as an organization of descendents of these revolutionaries. The home was built by diplomat Larz Anderson III, whose posts included an ambassadorship to Japan, and his heiress wife, Isabel Perkins Anderson, a member of a prominent

Boston family. The elaborately decorated house has a decidedly European feel; the Andersons filled their entertainment spaces with English paintings, Flemish tapestries, French furniture, rugs, decorative arts, and more. When Larz died in 1937, Isabel gave it to the society (Anderson had been a member). Besides the couples' elaborate furnishings and decorative touches, which include wall murals depicting American history and maps of driving routes in Washington, the home contains society memorabilia and Revolutionary War exhibits, including a fantastic set of military miniatures from the United States and France.

CATHEDRAL OF ST. MATTHEW THE APOSTLE

1725 Rhode Island Ave., 202/347-3215, www.stmatthewscathedral.org

HOURS: Daily, daytime and early evening

COST: Free

St. Matthew the Apostle is an imposing red-brick Italian Renaissance building constructed in 1889 that serves as the seat of the Archdiocese of Washington DC. Its stately facade gives no hint to its kaleidoscopic interior, a Byzantine cacophony of gilded ceilings, mosaics, stained glass, and artwork centered around a massive central dome. Named for the patron saint of civil servants, the cathedral hosted John F. Kennedy's funeral in 1963 and Chief Justice William Rehnquist's in 2005. St. Matthews is open for exploration during the day and early evening; self guided tour pamphlets are available inside the entrance.

EMBASSY ROW

Massachusetts Ave. NW between Observatory Circle and Dupont Circle

More than 60 embassies line Massachusetts Avenue in mansions once owned by barons of the Gilded Age, men who made their money in mining, railroads, banking, and industry. Economic woes, including the Great Depression, led many to sell their homes, often for pennies on the dollar, to associations, nonprofits, and foreign countries. While many of these beaux arts–style buildings aren't open for tours, at least one is, by reservation—the opulent Embassy of Indonesia (2020 Massachusetts

© PATRICIA KIME

Embassy Row

Ave., 202/775-5306). The 15-minute tour of the former Walsh Mansion, built by mining industrialist Thomas Walsh, offers a glimpse into the lifestyle of a captain of industry. At its heyday, the Walsh Mansion hosted President Theodore Roosevelt as well as a debutante ball for Roosevelt's daughter Alice, and it served as the site of a state dinner for Queen Elizabeth. It was inherited by Walsh's daughter Evalyn Walsh McLean, the last private owner of the Hope Diamond, and eventually passed into private hands and the Republic of Indonesia. Reservations can be made by calling the embassy.

Another architectural gem on Embassy Row is the Haitian Embassy (2311 Massachusetts Ave.), with its Second Empire–influenced facade, and the elaborate embassies of Cameroon and Pakistan (2349 and 2315 Massachusetts Ave.), both designed by architect George Oakley Totten Jr., standouts for their Turkish-influenced architecture. In May, many embassies throw open their doors to the public as part of Passport DC, a month-long festival celebrating international cultures hosted by Cultural Tourism DC (www.culturaltourismdc.org).

MARY MCLEOD BETHUNE COUNCIL HOUSE NATIONAL HISTORIC SITE

1318 Vermont Ave. NW, 202/673-2402, www.nps.gov/mamc
HOURS: Mon.-Sat. 9 A.M.-5 P.M.; closed Sun., Thanksgiving, Christmas Day, and New Year's Day
COST: Free

The first headquarters of the National Council of Negro Women (NCNW) and the last home of civil rights activist and educator Mary McLeod Bethune, this redbrick townhome, on the National Register of Historic Places, is managed by the National Park Service and pays tribute to Bethune, known best for founding the NCNW but also for establishing a college in Florida for black women (now Bethune-Cookman University) and serving as one of Franklin Delano Roosevelt's advisors on race relations, a member of the president's then-called "Black Cabinet."

NATIONAL GEOGRAPHIC MUSEUM

1145 17th St. NW, 202/857-7588, www.nationalgeographic.com/museum
HOURS: Daily 9 A.M.-5 P.M.; closed Christmas Day
COST: Free; special exhibits admission varies

Some of the world's greatest photography—published and never seen before—can be viewed at the National Geographic Museum at Explorers Hall, which rotates exhibits exploring the earth, its inhabitants, and the environment. Past and future exhibitions include a traveling display of China's terra-cotta warriors and treasures of Etruscan civilization. Each month, this facility also hosts a speaker series; participants have included humanitarian Greg Mortenson, travel writer and former actor Andrew McCarthy, and adventurer Andrew Skurka.

TEXTILE MUSEUM

2320 S St. NW, 202/667-0441, www.textilemuseum.org
HOURS: Tues.-Sat. 10 A.M.-5 P.M., Sun. 1-5 P.M.; closed federal holidays and Christmas Eve
COST: $8 suggested donation

Weaving the history of cultures as told by their fabrics, the Textile Museum features clothing, rugs, tapestries, and artifacts, some of which date to 3000 B.C. At the museum, visitors can learn what it takes to make a Persian carpet and appreciate the artistry that goes into making some of the world's finest cloth. The exhibit halls are divided into two spaces: the Collection Gallery, a soothing art museum that showcases beautiful works, and the Activity Gallery, with instructional stations on weaving, dyeing, and finishing. The museum also features a lovely garden and a fine, pricey gift shop with unique handmade wares.

WOODROW WILSON HOUSE

2340 S St. NW, 202/387-4062, www.woodrowwilsonhouse.org
HOURS: Tues.-Sun. 10 A.M.-4 P.M.
COST: $10 adults, $8 seniors, $5 students

The only presidential home museum in Washington, the Woodrow Wilson House is preserved as it stood when Wilson lived there in the last three years of his life, containing furnishings, White House memorabilia, family items, and gifts presented to him and wife Edith while he served in the presidency. The couple moved to the 1915 Georgian Revival–style mansion after they left the White House in 1921. Wilson had suffered a stroke in 1919 and left the presidency at a time when his League of Nations proposal failed to pass Congress. Defeated, he retreated to this glamorous townhome. After Wilson died, Edith donated the house to the National Historic Trust and remained living in it until she died in 1961. The five-bedroom home contains a collection of Edith Wilson's dresses, autographed photos of world leaders, china, decorative arts, and more. Of particular interest is the leather chair Wilson favored during Cabinet meetings and the Bible he used during his swearing-in ceremonies as governor of New Jersey and as president.

Adams Morgan and U Street   Map 7

AFRICAN AMERICAN CIVIL WAR MUSEUM AND MEMORIAL

1925 Vermont Ave. NW, 202/667-2667, www.afroamcivilwar.org

HOURS: Mon.-Fri. 10 A.M.-5 P.M., Sat. 10 A.M.-2 P.M.

COST: Free

More than 209,000 "colored troops" served in the U.S. Army and Navy during the Civil War, and at the African American Civil War Memorial, they are honored for their heroism and sacrifice in preserving the Union and contributing to efforts to end slavery in the United States. The memorial, designed by Kentucky sculptor Ed Hamilton, depicts uniformed soldiers and a sailor heading off to service, leaving their loved ones. The powerful statue, unveiled in 1998, is accompanied by a listing of the 209,145 service members and officers assigned to the Bureau of United States Colored Troops. The museum, which took up residence in spring 2011 in its new home, a refurbished former school building across the street from the memorial, seeks to educate the public on the role of colored troops during the Civil War—their backgrounds, service, and heroism. Among its artifacts are an original copy of the Emancipation Proclamation, troop letters, and records. Curator Hari Jones is as much a treasure as the museum's artifacts, a master of creative nonfiction who often mesmerizes visitors with stories of the people honored at the museum.

HOWARD UNIVERSITY

1739 7th St. NW, 202/806-2755, www.howard.edu

One of the country's most prestigious historically black colleges and universities, Howard University was founded in 1867, named for Gen. Oliver Howard, then commissioner of the Freedman's Bureau who advocated for safe labor conditions and standards for former slaves. Notable alumni include Nobel Laureate Toni Morrison, former New York City mayor David Dinkins, and actress Phylicia Rashad as well as Howard Law School alumni Supreme Court Justice Thurgood Marshall, former congressman Harold Ford Sr., and former Washington mayor Adrian Fenty. The university's most notable building is its Founders Library, a 1937 Georgian-style structure that holds the largest collection of African American literature in the country.

Georgetown

Map 8

DUMBARTON HOUSE

2715 Q St. NW, 202/337-2288,
www.dumbartonhouse.org

HOURS: Mid-Mar.-mid-Dec. Tues.-Fri. 10 A.M.-4 P.M.,
Sat.-Sun. 11 A.M.-3 P.M.; mid-Dec.-mid-Mar. Tues.-Sun.
11 A.M.-3 P.M.; tours by appointment mid-Mar.-mid-Dec.
Tues.-Sun. 11 A.M., noon, and 1 P.M.

COST: $5 adults, free for children, youth, and students
with ID

One of the city's most complete homes from
the Federal period, the circa-1801 Dumbarton
House is a shrine to early American handi-
work, with more than 1,000 pieces of fine furniture, artwork, textiles, silver, and decorative
arts dating to 1790 through 1830. Initially
occupied by civil servant Joseph Nourse, the
home itself is of federal design or, more specifically, Adams design, characterized by curved
walls and elaborate plasterwork. The home is
managed by the Colonial Dames of America,
who take delight in offering tours of the home
as well as hosting special events, including a
spring Federal Ball, before which attendees
take classes to learn the etiquette of the day, attend in period dress, and dance the night away
in the candlelit ballroom. Often confused with
Dumbarton Oaks and Gardens, a circa-1800
mansion, art gallery, and gardens half a mile
away, Dumbarton House is reputedly where
Dolley Madison fled for a few hours after the
British invaded the capital in 1814.

GEORGETOWN UNIVERSITY

37th St. and O St. NW, 202/687-0100,
www.georgetown.edu

The oldest Roman Catholic university in the
United States, Georgetown was founded in 1789
by John Carroll, who became the country's first
Catholic bishop, and in 1805 came under management of the Jesuits, who continue to play a
role in the school's leadership today. The university has roughly 7,000 undergraduates and
just slightly more grad students, who come to
study at the school's renowned schools of foreign service and business as well as the colleges

of arts and sciences, law, and medicine. While
Georgetown has been revered for years in academic circles, it became known nationally in the
1980s and 1990s for its men's basketball team,
winning a national championship in 1984. The
Hoyas (their name is derived from Latin and
Greek and translates roughly as "What Rocks!")
have one of the prettiest campuses in the region,
open to exploring at all hours. Healy Hall, with
its tall clock tower and imposing gray stone architecture of Flemish and Romanesque design,
was built in 1879 and named for the first black
college president in the United States, Father
Patrick Healy, who led Georgetown from 1874
to 1882. Campus tours are available through the
admissions office in White-Gravenor Hall.

OAK HILL CEMETERY

3001 R St. NW, 202/337-2835,
www.oakhillcemeterydc.org

HOURS: Mon.-Fri. 9 A.M.-4 P.M., Sun. 1-4 P.M.;
closed Sat. and federal holidays

COST: Free

Washington is home to several great cemeteries, including Oak Hill, a contemplative
22-acre burial ground that contains architect
James Renwick's only Gothic-style chapel in
DC, lovely gardens, and the burial plots of famous Washingtonians like William Wilson
Corcoran, founder of Riggs Bank and the
Corcoran Art Museum; Civil War Secretary
of War Edwin Stanton; Secretary of State Dean
Acheson; and *Washington Post* publisher and
owner Katharine Graham.

OLD STONE HOUSE

3051 M St. NW, 202/426-6851,
www.nps.gov/rocr/oldstonehouse

HOURS: Wed.-Sun. noon-5 P.M.; closed New Year's Day,
Independence Day, Thanksgiving, and Christmas Day

COST: Free

The oldest standing building in Washington
DC, this simple home, built in 1765 of locally
quarried blue granite, is a sample of the region's
"vernacular" architecture, basically a home

MOVIE MAGIC IN GEORGETOWN

Hollywood loves DC – aerial shots of famous sites and close-ups with a monument in the background. The city has been film-friendly since 1915, when *Birth of a Nation* showed supremacist groups marching down Pennsylvania Avenue. More recently, robots battled it out on the Mall in *Transformers: Dark of the Moon*. While the National Mall tops the list of desirable movie locations, filmmakers are also drawn to one neighborhood like june bugs to a lightbulb – Georgetown. Here is a sampling of the flicks that made this 18th-century village a household word:

- **The Exorcist:** One of the most popular exercise spots in the city is tied to the groundbreaking 1973 horror movie – a flight of steep stairs that connects a gas station parking lot on M Street to Prospect Street. Known as the Exorcist Steps, the stairs are literally a butt-kicker that attract runners wanting to work on their glutes.

- **No Way Out:** The neighborhood features prominently in the movie that put Kevin Costner on the path to stardom. One of the film's exciting foot chases runs through the

neighborhood's nonexistent Metro station, actually filmed in Georgetown Park Mall and in Baltimore. Other DC locales in the movie include the Omni Shoreham and Hay-Adams Hotels and the Hotel Washington, now the W on Pennsylvania Avenue.

- **St. Elmo's Fire:** One of Georgetown's most beloved bars, The Tombs, inspired the watering hole in this movie. But the outdoor shots where stars Andrew McCarthy, Emilio Estevez, Demi Moore, and Rob Lowe were filmed are actually of another pub, Third Edition (1218 Wisconsin Ave.).

- **Wedding Crashers:** This movie is full of gratuitous shots of the monuments and the Capitol Building, but at least one scene, a fight between two divorce mediators, takes place in Georgetown not far from the university.

Too bad the producers of *Burn After Reading* couldn't maneuver the bureaucracy it takes to close streets in DC; they simply painted over a few row houses in Brooklyn to make it look like they filmed in Georgetown.

© PATRICIA KIME

Georgetown sites and streets are popular with movie-makers.

common to the area and built by an ordinary citizen, in this case, cabinetmaker Christopher Layman. Contrast this simple five-room house with George Washington's Mount Vernon, constructed 20 years earlier by Washington's brother Lawrence, a wealthy landowner and member of the Virginia House of Burgesses. A trip through this cottage is a quick trip through history; visitors often prefer lingering in the garden, with colonial-era shrubs and flowers. Both are worth a look if you need a break from a day of shopping in Georgetown.

Greater Washington DC   Map 9

AMERICAN UNIVERSITY
4400 Massachusetts Ave. NW, 202/885-3620,
www.american.edu

American University is a private school of nearly 10,000 undergrad and graduate students established in 1893 by the Methodist Church, originally as a graduate school. Located in an upscale neighborhood near Embassy Row, it is recognized nationally for its programs in political science, communications, international relations, and business; its undergraduates consistently land internships at many of the area's government agencies and contracting businesses. Despite its founding by the Methodist Church, the school is largely sectarian, attracting applicants from all 50 states and more than 150 countries worldwide.

ANACOSTIA COMMUNITY MUSEUM
1901 Fort Place SE, 202/633-1000,
www.anacostia.si.edu
HOURS: Daily 9 A.M.–5 P.M.; closed Christmas Day
COST: Free

The Anacostia Community Museum focuses on black history and culture in the city, with exhibits on the surrounding neighborhood as well as widespread issues that affect African Americans. Past topics have highlighted subjects like the region's African American baseball leagues and historic celebrations like the African American Family Day at the National Zoo on Easter Monday. The museum hosts numerous events, such as free concerts, films, and outreach programs for children.

ARLINGTON HOUSE
Arlington National Cemetery, 703/235-1530,
www.nps.gov/arho

Built by George Washington Parke Custis, grandson of Martha Washington and raised by her husband and his step-grandfather George Washington, Arlington House is more widely known as the pre–Civil War home of Robert E. Lee, who married Custis's daughter Mary Randolph Custis, who inherited the home in 1857. Lee lived in Arlington House between 1831 and 1861, with periods of absence due to military service. After Fort Sumter fell in April 1861, Lee, in Richmond at the time, resigned his commission in the Union Army; Mary left the home in May, and it soon became the domain of Northern troops and home to a Freedman's Village of former slaves. When U.S. Quartermaster Gen. Montgomery Meigs searched for a location to bury the growing number of war dead in the area, he zeroed in on Arlington House. As far as Meigs was concerned, the closer the Union dead were buried to the mansion, the better; Meigs wanted to punish Lee for siding with the Confederacy and to ensure Lee would never return to the home. Currently undergoing renovations, Arlington House is unfurnished and remains a construction site but is open for visits. Park officials estimate that the work will be concluded and the house refurnished by 2012. In front of this Georgian Revival mansion lies the grave of Washington city planner and Revolutionary War hero Pierre L'Enfant. Recognizing L'Enfant's importance to the nation and the city, government officials relocated his body from Prince George County, Maryland, to a prominent spot in the cemetery in 1909.

◀ ARLINGTON NATIONAL CEMETERY

Across Memorial Bridge from the Lincoln Memorial,
Arlington, Va., 703/607-8585,
www.arlingtoncemetery.org
HOURS: Apr.-Sept. daily 8 A.M.-7 P.M.;
Oct.-Mar. daily 8 A.M.-5 P.M.
COST: Free; parking $1.75 per hour for 3 hours,
$3.50 per hour after 3 hours

The country's second-oldest national cemetery, Arlington carries a powerful emotional punch, with its uniform rows of white marble markers, silent Changing of the Guard ceremony, and monuments that memorialize the country's greatest conflicts and tragedies, including every war since the Revolution. Heralded here are those who perished in many historic events: the loss of the Space Shuttles *Challenger* and *Columbia;* the sinking of the USS *Maine;* the bombing of Pan Am Flight 103 just before Christmas 1988; and others.

Roughly 300,000 sets of remains are buried on the 612-acre property, which is expected to grow by another 60 acres in the next decade. Those interred on this hallowed land, which once belonged to Martha Washington's granddaughter Mary Randolph Custis, include service members killed on active duty, retired military members, spouses, presidents, former slaves, and honored civilians.

When visiting Arlington, the Visitors Center is the recommended first stop. Here, guests can pick up a detailed map of the grounds, see exhibits on the cemetery's history, and inquire as to whether bus service has resumed for mobile tours throughout the cemetery. Until October 2011, that service was provided by Tourmobile, an open tram system that made stops at every major site within the cemetery. The physically fit can save some money and tour the burial grounds on foot, and until the National Park Service contracts with another company for bus tours, walking is the only way to get around Arlington National Cemetery, unless you have a relative buried there, in which case you may be eligible for a day pass for your car. Inquire at the Visitors Center. Be aware: Distances between the sites are vast. Arlington contains a few can't-miss places:

The Tomb of the Unknowns: Holding the remains of unidentified soldiers from World War I, World War II, and the Korean War, the tomb dates to 1926, built from more than 50 tons of white Yule marble quarried from Colorado—the same type of stone used to

© PATRICIA KIME

Arlington National Cemetery is an emotional must-see.

UNSUNG MEMORIALS, STATUES, AND MONUMENTS

DC is chockablock with statues, little known memorials, and monuments. Here's a sampling of those you might not go out of your way to see, but if you pass them, you'll now know what they are:

• Downtown, next to the Archives Metro stop, the **Navy Memorial** is a large pavilion that honors the men and women of the U.S. Navy. It contains a sculpture, *The Lone Sailor*, as well as fountains, nautical flagpoles, and a huge map of the world etched into the pavement. Next door, offering a great overhead view of the memorial, is the **Naval Heritage Center,** a compact yet extensive museum containing naval artifacts and a research library.

• The lovely bandstand near the Korean and World War II Memorials off Independence Avenue is actually a monument itself, the **DC World War I Memorial,** installed by the city in 1931 to honor city residents who served in the Great War. The Doric temple can accommodate a large orchestra and in fact was built to accommodate the Marine Corps Band led by John Philip Sousa. It is currently being restored to its former glory and hopefully will be used for performances.

• On the northern end of East Potomac Park near the Jefferson Memorial lies the **George Mason Memorial,** a tribute to the author of the Virginia Declaration of Rights, whose lobbying efforts regarding states and individual rights contributed to the creation of the Bill of Rights. This quiet respite contains a statue of Mason in repose, flanked by samples of his writings.

• President Harry Truman had a point when he called the building next to the White House the "greatest monstrosity in America." Ouch. The facility is the **Eisenhower Executive Office Building,** formerly the Old Executive Office Building, home to the offices of the vice president and numerous executive-branch suites. Other buildings in Washington that share its unique French Second Empire architecture include the Willard Hotel and the Renwick Art Gallery.

• The redbrick and multihued-tile building on the Mall that vaguely resembles the Smithsonian Castle but isn't, the **Arts and Industries Building** is part of the museum complex but is currently under extensive renovations, including replacement of its deteriorating roof and repairs to its structural problems. Built in 1881 to house artifacts from the 1876 Centennial Exposition, it contained much of the Smithsonian's collection for years, and during the Bicentennial housed a retrospective of the 1876 artifacts. A carousel, on the Mall directly in front of the building, operates year-round; the cost of a ride is $2.50.

• Near Embassy Row is the **Islamic Center** (2551 Massachusetts Ave.), the national mosque for American Muslims. Open to the public, visitors can wander around the grounds and tour the limestone structure, which contains intricate tile work, Persian carpets, and stunning ceilings detailed with gilded verses from the Koran.

• The weird fish sculpture at the corner of 7th Street and Pennsylvania Avenue is a **Temperance Fountain,** a long-dry memorial built by California dentist and abstainer Henry Cogswell to encourage people to drink water instead of booze.

• It's an iconic, often imitated scene in the movie *Titanic:* Star Kate Winslet leans from the bow of the ship, arms outstretched, after her love, played by Leonardo DiCaprio, declares he's king of the world. But this image isn't new: It was sculpted into stone in 1931 by Gertrude Vanderbilt Whitney for the **Women's Titanic Memorial,** at 4th and P Streets near the Washington Marina. No word as to whether Titanic director and writer James Cameron ever visited the monument, which was paid for by private donations from women to honor the men who gave their lives on the ill-fated ship.

build the Lincoln Memorial. It is guarded 24 hours a day by soldiers from the Army's 3rd Infantry, called the Old Guard, headquartered at nearby Fort Myer, Virginia. To become a tomb sentinel, soldiers must meet specific physical standards and pass a rigorous series of tests to ensure their ability to handle the task, which include marching 21 steps back and forth in front of the tomb in a wool uniform during the heat of the summer. From April to September, the unit changes the guard every half hour in a silent ceremony that draws large crowds. During winter months and at night, the guard is changed every hour in the same manner. Until 1998 the tomb held the remains of a Vietnam war veteran; DNA evidence revealed that the unknown buried there was 1st Lt. Michael Blassie, an Air Force pilot shot down near An Loc in 1972. Blassie was disinterred and reburied at a veteran's cemetery near his hometown of St. Louis, Missouri.

The Kennedy graves: The Eternal Flame shines perpetually above the grave of President John F. Kennedy, on a grassy knoll that affords a magnificent view of the National Mall and its memorials. The spot, actually visited by Kennedy before his death, was approved by his wife, Jacqueline Kennedy, who also requested the placement of the flame. Also buried at the John Carl Warnecke–designed site are wife Jacqueline Kennedy Onassis as well as two infant children who predeceased them. Their fourth child, John F. Kennedy Jr., was buried at sea in 1999. The grave of Sen. Robert Kennedy, Kennedy's brother, attorney general, and civil rights leader, is nearby, as is the grave of Sen. Ted Kennedy, the longest-serving Kennedy in public office; both are marked with simple white crosses and footstones.

Women in Military Service Memorial: Incorporating the original ceremonial entryway of Arlington Cemetery, this memorial, dedicated in 1997, pays tribute to women who have served in all five armed services and their affiliate women's auxiliaries, including the World War II–era WAVES and WACS. The often overlooked structure contains a small exhibit hall, a hall of honor, and a register containing the names, service records, and photos of nearly 250,000 servicewomen.

BASILICA OF THE NATIONAL SHRINE OF THE IMMACULATE CONCEPTION

400 Michigan Ave. NE, 202/526-8300, www.nationalshrine.com
HOURS: Apr. 1–Oct. 31 daily 7 A.M.–7 P.M.; Nov. 1–Mar. 31 daily 7 A.M.–6 P.M.
COST: Free

In a city not known for its churches, a few stand out, one being the Basilica of the National Shrine of the Immaculate Conception. The largest Catholic church in North America, the basilica is defined by its blend of Byzantine and Romanesque architecture, which features a central dome just eight feet smaller in circumference than the one at the U.S. Capitol, a towering campanile similar to those in Italy, and a vast interior festooned with gilded mosaics, artwork, sculptures, and decorative arts. Built between 1921 and 1959, work continues today on this vast structure. The Great Upper Church is home to a number of significant

Basilica of the National Shrine of the Immaculate Conception

© OLIVIER LE QUEINEC/123RF.COM

pieces of artwork, including the mosaic *Christ in Majesty,* one of the world's largest mosaic images of Jesus, featuring roughly 4,000 colors, and a mosaic copy of the Vatican's *Immaculate Conception* by Murillo. The ceiling of the upper church contains six domes in addition to the main one; each is lined with colorful Byzantine-style mosaics. The lower level contains a memorial hall, numerous chapels, and exhibits that include the stunning—and probably very heavy—coronation tiara of Pope Paul IV. The Crypt Church shouldn't be missed; it was modeled after the early Christian catacombs and features a low ceiling of archways held up by 10-ton columns. Despite its size, the church is not the home of the Archdiocese of Washington; St. Matthew the Apostle Cathedral on Rhode Island Avenue houses the diocese headquarters and is the archbishop's chair. The National Shrine was honored as a minor basilica in 1990 by Pope John Paul II and is a national pilgrimage site for Roman Catholics.

CATHOLIC UNIVERSITY OF AMERICA
620 Michigan Ave. NE, 202/319-5305, www.cua.edu

Established in 1887 as a graduate university and expanded in 1904 to teach undergraduates, Catholic University of America is a 193-acre campus northeast of the U.S. Capitol that aims for students to learn from more than 80 major areas within the context of religious freedom and spiritual pluralism. The school attracts students of all faiths from around the world, and while it is known for its philosophy and religion programs, it also boasts a highly acclaimed architecture program, music program, and renowned drama program—notable alumni include actors Susan Sarandon, Chris Sarandon, and Jon Voight.

CONGRESSIONAL CEMETERY
1801 E St. SW, 202/543-0539, www.congressionalcemetery.org

HOURS: Daily dawn-dusk; tours Sat. 11 A.M.; Civil War tour Apr.-Oct. third Sat. of the month 1 P.M.

COST: Free

A still-active cemetery dating to 1807, the Congressional Cemetery is the final resting place for vice presidents, members of Congress, military heroes, and Washington VIPs as well as ordinary citizens, such as 21 women workers who died when the Washington Arsenal

John Philip Sousa's grave, Congressional Cemetery

© PATRICIA KIME

exploded in 1864. The 35-acre burial ground contains more than 55,000 sets of remains, including those of John Philip Sousa, Mathew Brady, and J. Edgar Hoover. Two prominent Native Americans are here as well: Pushmataha, a Choctaw chief who served with Andrew Jackson at the Battle of New Orleans, and Taza, son of Apache chief Cochise. Unusual monuments and memorials dot the natural landscape, including 165 oddly shaped sandstone markers that indicate the burial plots of representatives and senators who died in office, and several table stones, popular in the Victorian era, when families like to enjoy picnics with their departed. Pamphlets for a variety of self-guided tours are available in the cemetery office, including an introductory tour and a suffrage tour, noting the graves of famous women's rights activists. The Congressional Cemetery is run by a nonprofit group that has managed to raise money and the cemetery's visibility by allowing its space to be used for dog walking. Especially busy on weekends, the cemetery turns into one big dog party when members of its K9 Corps come out in droves. While this seems like an odd arrangement, the presence of dogs at nearly all hours has minimized vandalism and at the same time raised revenue for the cemetery (dog owners pay a hefty $250 for the privilege of bringing a dog here). There is a waiting list; if you are not a member, you cannot bring your dog.

DEA MUSEUM

700 Army Navy Dr., 202/307-3463,
www.deamuseum.org
HOURS: Tues.-Fri. 10 A.M.-4 P.M.
COST: Free

Surprisingly, the Drug Enforcement Administration Museum doesn't hit visitors on the head about the dangers of drug use; instead, it allows the warning to announce itself, relayed through numerous historic artifacts, wall panels and documents, a 150-year history of drug use in America, and the efforts undertaken by law-enforcement agents to quash it. The museum is full of fascinating tidbits and factoids (by the 1900s, the typical drug addict was a middle-class female hooked on prescription drugs like laudanum; it seems there has always been a "mother's little helper" of some sort), and there are even drugs on display—seized samples of pot, pills, and vessels with narcotics residue. The reproduction 1970s-era "head shop" showcases bongs and water pipes; a display on the modern use of drugs calls musicians like Charlie Parker, Jimi Hendrix, and Kurt Cobain on the carpet for glamorizing drug use. The museum also maintains a wall of honor for those who have died in the effort to eradicate the illegal drug trade.

FRANCISCAN MONASTERY OF THE HOLY LAND

1400 Quincy St. NE, 202/526-6800,
www.myfranciscan.com
HOURS: Daily 9 A.M.-4:45 P.M.; tours of monastery and shrines Mon.-Sat. 10 A.M., 11 A.M., 1 P.M., and 3 P.M.; Sun. 1 P.M., 2 P.M., and 3 P.M.
COST: Donation

Unknown to many Washingtonians, the Franciscan Monastery of the Holy Land replicates some of Christianity's most holy sites and was built for pilgrims who may otherwise never get to Israel to see the originals. The Franciscans are actually caretakers of the real sites; it makes sense they'd want to extend their ministry to the United States, and they have, in a remote corner of Washington DC, maintaining a stunning set of gardens, buildings, and shrines. The Church of the Holy Sepulcher, built in 1889, is in Byzantine style and contains replicas of famous spaces like the Cloister of St. John Lateran and St. Paul Outside the Walls in Rome. It also features 15 chapels with the *Hail Mary* written in 200 ancient and modern languages. Under the monastery next door lies a reproduction of early Christian catacombs; in the gardens, visitors will find replicas of Jesus' tomb, the Gardens of Gethsemane, the Grotto of Lourdes, and a pathway that traces the Stations of the Cross. The church and grounds are enormously popular on Good Friday; on that day the friars also spearhead a national collection effort to preserve the actual sites in Israel.

FREDERICK DOUGLASS NATIONAL HISTORIC SITE

1411 W St. SE, 202/426-5961, www.nps.gov/frdo

HOURS: Apr. 16–Oct. 15 daily 9 A.M.–5 P.M.; Oct. 16–Apr. 15 daily 9 A.M.–4:30 P.M.; closed Thanksgiving, Christmas Day, and New Year's Day

COST: Free

The last home of abolitionist Frederick Douglass, who lived here from 1877 until his death in 1895, Cedar Hill gives insight into the abolitionist's private and professional life and serves as a time capsule of day-to-day life in the last quarter of the 19th century. This well-furnished home contains gifts to Douglass from luminaries like Abraham Lincoln and Harriet Beecher Stowe. It also holds a collection of Douglass's books, several diaries, and copies of his writings as well as furniture, artwork, decorative items, and home goods typical of a house of the period. In the kitchen stands a wood-burning cookstove, an upgrade from the open-fire cooking common during an earlier period, and a Sears icebox. Douglass bought the home shortly after homes in the once all-white neighborhood became available for black ownership. The house underwent a three-year $2 million restoration to return it to the state it was in when Douglass and his family members lived in it.

GALLAUDET UNIVERSITY

800 Florida Ave., 202/651-5505, www.gallaudet.edu

The foundation for Gallaudet University, the country's only liberal arts college for the hearing impaired, was laid in 1856 when a Dartmouth educated journalist named Amos Kendall established a school for the deaf in the city. As the facility grew, it hired Dr. Edward Miner Gallaudet, whose father, Thomas, had established the first school for the deaf in the United States, to oversee it. Today, Gallaudet has roughly 1,000 undergraduates and 800 grad students who can study in more than 30 majors and participate in athletic activities, clubs, sororities, and fraternities. The school claims the football huddle was invented here in the 1890s as a way to keep the opposing team from trying to interpret the sign language used for plays. The campus has a number of fine Victorian

buildings and lovely grounds laid out by landscape architect Frederick Law Olmsted.

KENILWORTH AQUATIC GARDENS

1550 Anacostia Ave. NE, 202/426-6905, www.nps.gov/kepa

HOURS: Daily 7 A.M.–4 P.M.; closed Thanksgiving, Christmas Day, and New Year's Day

COST: Free

The only national park devoted to water lilies and other aquatic plants, these gardens, in Anacostia Park, started as a hobby by Civil War veteran W. B. Shaw, who shipped 12 plants from his native Maine in the early 1880s to remind him of home. He began cultivating them and crossbreeding varieties; eventually the venture went commercial, and Shaw and his daughter sold plants to collectors and landscapers across the country. The land became public in 1926. The gardens are at their peak during the summer months, but the lilies prefer temperatures under 90°F, so the optimal time for visiting is in the morning. In late July, the park hosts a lotus festival to celebrate this exotic Asian flower's blooms. The park also contains several trails to the Anacostia River that offer opportunities for wildlife viewing.

NATIONAL ARBORETUM

3501 New York Ave. NE, 202/245-2726, www.usna.usda.gov

HOURS: Daily 8 A.M.–5 P.M.; closed Christmas Day

COST: Free

This "Trees R Us" covers 412 acres and contains thousands of plants and shrubs in a setting that preserves the native landscape of the region. The Arboretum was founded in 1927 and is federally supported; many of its plantings are the result of research conducted at the facility. One of the most photographed sites here is actually artificial—a copse of sandstone Corinthian columns from the U.S. Capitol that were removed when the building was expanded in the 1950s. The Arboretum is home to the National Bonsai and Penjing Museum, with a 400-year-old Japanese white pine bonsai tree that survived the bombing of Hiroshima. The average age of the collection is 100 years; just the thought that someone

© PATRICIA KIME

National Capitol Columns, the National Arboretum

could maintain a houseplant for more than a century is mind-boggling. The Arboretum contains nine miles of roads and numerous hiking trails. The busiest time to visit is in spring, when the rhododendrons and azaleas are in bloom, but the Arboretum is worth a look at other times of the year—attractions include a Koi pond, the Friendship Garden, and the National Herb Garden.

NATIONAL MUSEUM OF HEALTH AND MEDICINE

Brookville Rd., Silver Spring, Md., 202/782-2200, www.nmhm.washingtondc.museum
HOURS: Daily 10 A.M.–5:30 P.M.; tours first and third Sat. 1 P.M.; closed Christmas Day;
COST: Free

The grisly and macabre collection at the National Museum of Health and Medicine showcases the evolution of military medicine from the Civil War to the present day and examines the art of treating the thousands of maladies that can afflict the human body. Not for the weak of stomach, the displays include fetal and baby skeletons, some with birth defects like cyclopia (having one eye) and hydrocephalus, the leg of a Civil War soldier who lost it at the Battle of Gettysburg, and a giant hairball removed from the stomach of a girl who suffered from trichotillomania (pulling out one's hair). For presidential scholars, the bullet that killed Abraham Lincoln is here, as are fragments of Lincoln's skull. The vertebrae of assassin John Wilkes Booth are in a separate case nearby. The museum moved to Silver Spring, Maryland, from its original home on the grounds of Walter Reed Army Medical Center. It is expected to be fully operational in 2012.

NATIONAL MUSEUM OF THE U.S. NAVY

805 Kidder Breese St. SW, 202/433-6826 or 202/433-3377 for the USS *Barry* display ship, www.history.navy.mil/branches/org8-1.htm
HOURS: Mon.-Fri. 9 A.M.–5 P.M., Sat.-Sun. 10 A.M.–5 P.M.; closed Thanksgiving, Christmas Eve, Christmas Day, and New Year's Day. USS *Barry* Mon.-Sat. 9 A.M.–5 P.M.
COST: Free

Housed in a former breech mechanism shop of the naval gun factory that once occupied this site, the National Museum of the U.S. Navy, at the Washington Naval Yard, contains artwork, artifacts, and ship models that span the Navy's history, beginning before the Revolution and moving into the evolution of today's modern service. The place is big fun for kids, with "toys" they won't find anywhere else, like two periscopes that allow visitors to peer outside the building and submarine models that float up and down. In the warmer months, the display ship USS *Barry* is open for tours; this 1950s-era Sherman Class destroyer earned two battle flags in Vietnam and participated in the blockade of Cuba during the Cuban Missile Crisis.

◀ NATIONAL ZOO

3001 Connecticut Ave. NW, 202/673-4800,
www.nationalzoo.si.edu
HOURS: Nov.-Mar. daily 10 A.M.-6 P.M.;
Apr.-Oct. daily 10 A.M.-4:30 P.M.
COST: Free; parking $15 for the first 3 hours, $20 over 3 hours

The National Zoological Park is one of the greatest perks of Washington DC: a park you can jog through, play in, and picnic in that is free and home to more than 2,400 animals. The stars of the National Zoo continue to be its two giant pandas, Mei Xiang and Tian Tian, who have lived here since 2000. On loan from China, the bears are set to remain at the zoo until 2015. Their baby, Tai Shan, born in 2005, was sent to China in 2010 under a prior agreement between the United States and China regarding the couple's offspring. The National Zoo is full of other wonders to be discovered: two major pathways lead through the zoo, with offshoots to various exhibits and halls. Along the Olmsted Walk, visitors might see orangutans swinging overhead on their daily commute between the Ape House and the Think Tank, loads of lions (seven were born in 2010), tigers, gorillas, zebras, camels, kangaroos, and alligators. Along the walk also are the Reptile House, the Small Mammal House, and the Great Ape House. An offshoot leads to a personal favorite, the Invertebrate House, home to cute cuttlefish, huge Madagascar hissing cockroaches, and a giant Pacific octopus. Along the Valley Trail are exhibits showcasing bald eagles, beavers, and bears. The Asia Trail

© NATALIA BRATSLAVSKY/123RF.COM

Giant pandas are the main attraction at the National Zoo.

is home to clouded leopards, fishing casts, red pandas, and sloth bears. In 2011, the elephants got a new home; the spacious facility, off the Elephant Trail, features new yards and play spaces for the institution's pachyderms. In the far reaches of the park is a huge Bird House with dozens of colorful species like toucans, parrots, and hornbills.

The nearest Metro stop to the zoo is Woodley Park; when you leave the station, head left up the hill on Connecticut Avenue until you reach the zoo's gates. The zoo's education building, with park information, is just inside the entrance. If you drive to the zoo, use Parking Lot D. It's at the bottom of the hill, which means when you and your guests are tired toward the end of your visit, you'll be walking downhill back to your car.

THE PENTAGON AND PENTAGON MEMORIAL

Boundary Channel Dr., Arlington, Va., 703/697-1776, www.pentagon.afis.osd.mil and www.whs.mil/memorial
HOURS: Mon.-Fri. 9 A.M.-3 P.M.; Memorial: daily 24 hours
COST: Free

Want to get a look at the inside of the world's largest office building? You can, and hopefully you won't be disappointed; it's a building the size of a medium city, and hence, it basically includes doorways, offices, a barber shop, a hair salon, banks, fast-food joints, and little cars—OK, they're more like golf carts— darting through the corridors. It's nice to see that this building, struck by an airliner on September 11, 2001, is so normal, given the enormous tragedy that occurred here. During the roughly one-hour tour of the facility, visitors are ushered around a maze of corridors by an active-duty service member, stopping to look at artwork, portraiture, and artifacts on display. It's hard to grasp the enormity of this place, which houses 30,000 employees and 3,705,793 square feet of office space. The U.S. Capitol Building could fit in one of the five wedges. The interior courtyard alone covers five acres.

Open to the public, no reservations needed, the Pentagon Memorial honors the 184 people murdered on September 11, 2001, when terrorists steered American Airlines Flight 77 into the building. The memorial features 184 cantilevered benches aligned along the aircraft's path, each etched with a victim's name, from the youngest, 3-year-old Dana Falkenberg, on her way to Australia on a family trip, to the oldest, 71-year-old defense contractor John Yamnicky, flying to California on a business trip. The memorial differentiates between those who died on the aircraft and those who were in the building by the direction of the benches: 59 face one way, symbolizing the passengers; 125 face the other direction. The grounds also feature memorial trees and an age wall that rises in height according to the ages of the victims, from three inches for Falkenberg to 71 inches for Yamnicky. The memorial was designed by Keith Kaseman and Julie Beckman, friends and architects who worked at separate firms in New York City at the time of the attacks and who witnessed the collapse of the World Trade Center that day.

PRESIDENT LINCOLN'S COTTAGE

Rock Creek Church Rd. and Upshur Rd. NW, 202/829-0436, www.lincolncottage.org
HOURS: Mon.-Sat. 9:30 A.M.-4:30 P.M., first tour 10 A.M., last tour 3 P.M.; Sun. 11:30 A.M.-5:30 P.M., first tour noon, last tour 3 P.M.; closed Thanksgiving, Christmas Day, and New Year's Day
COST: $12 adults, $5 ages 6-12, $6 National Trust members, $10 active-duty military, $8 Girl Scouts

Abraham Lincoln spent one-quarter of his presidency at this Gothic Revival home on the grounds of the Soldier's Home, now called the Armed Forces Retirement Home, in northeast DC. For Lincoln and his family, the house, on a verdant hillside three miles from the White House, served as a hideaway from office seekers and the troops that crowded into the city once the war began. It also provided a retreat for a grieving family who lost son Will, 11, to typhoid fever in 1862. Lincoln often commuted to work from this 34-room house; he is said to have written the first draft of the Emancipation Proclamation here during the summer of 1862. The home was also used as a summer getaway for Presidents Rutherford Hayes and Chester

Arthur. Restored by the National Trust for Historic Preservation, it contains few furnishings and is preserved mostly as it was when the National Trust acquired it, with one notable exception: They removed bookshelves and 23 layers of paint and varnish from the walls of the library to reveal the beauty of its longleaf pine paneling, which likely was admired by Lincoln, who spent many hours in the room and often had to be reminded to take breaks from it.

U.S. AIR FORCE MEMORIAL

Columbia Pike and Air Force Memorial Dr.,
703/979-0674, www.airforcememorial.org
HOURS: Apr. 1-Sept. 30 daily 8 A.M.-11 P.M.;
Oct. 1-Mar. 31 daily 8 A.M.-9 P.M.
COST: Free

A monumental piece of abstract art just a short walk uphill from the Pentagon Memorial, the Air Force Memorial, with a spire that rises 270 feet over surrounding buildings, is visible from all neighboring highways and parts of DC. The work, which symbolizes the contrails of the Air Force's precision flight team the Thunderbirds

as they perform a "bomb burst" maneuver, was designed by James Freed, architect of the U.S. Holocaust Memorial Museum. People either love it or hate it; critics questioned whether a monument inspired by a demonstration team adequately reflects the sacrifices made by members of the U.S. Air Force in the past 60 years. The memorial is one to look at throughout the day; its brushed stainless steel points change appearance based on the position of the sun, the weather, and the hour. At the base is a collection of engraved inscriptions that highlight Air Force history, including a list of the service's Medal of Honor recipients and historic quotes.

U.S. MARINE CORPS WAR MEMORIAL

N. Marshall Dr., Arlington, Va., 703/289-2500,
www.nps.gov/gwmp/marinecorpswarmemorial.htm
HOURS: Daily 24 hours
COST: Free

A mile from the Arlington Cemetery Visitors Center, the U.S. Marine Corps War Memorial, colloquially referred to as the Iwo Jima

© PATRICIA KIME

U.S. Marine Corps War Memorial in winter

Memorial, is one of the world's largest bronze sculptures, crafted by artist and former Navy sailor Felix de Weldon and based on Associated Press photographer Joe Rosenthal's Pulitzer Prize–winning photo of U.S. Marines raising the American flag on Mount Suribachi, Iwo Jima, on February 23, 1945. The statue depicts the five Marines and one Navy corpsman who actually took part in the event: Mike Strank, Ira Hayes, Harlon Block, Franklin Sousley, Rene Gagnon, and John Bradley; three, Hayes, Bradley, and Gagnon, survived the battle and were able to serve as models for de Weldon. Block, Strank, and Sousley died on the island in other phases of the battle, and their photos were used for the design. The statue's figures stand 32 feet tall and are raising a 60-foot flagpole. At 100 tons, it is considered one of the world's largest free-standing bronzes.

On Tuesday evenings from Memorial Day through the final week of August, the Marine Corps holds a Sunset Parade in front of the memorial. The event features performances by the Corps' Drum and Bugle Corps and Silent Drill Platoon and begins at 7 P.M. Admission to the event is free; bring lawn chairs or a picnic blanket.

U.S. NAVAL OBSERVATORY

3450 Massachusetts Ave. NW, 202/762-1438, www.usno.navy.mil

HOURS: Tours on alternate Mon. 8:30-10 P.M., reservations required

COST: Free

When the U.S. Naval Observatory was built in the 1840s, Washington DC didn't suffer the light pollution it has today. The telescope's importance as a star-finder has waned, but the facility is still used by the Navy and the Defense Department for positioning and timing. The observatory is home to the U.S. Navy's master clock, actually a set of atomic clocks that keep the official time for the military services. Tours of the historic facility are given every other Monday evening and include a film on the observatory's history, a look at the master clock system, and weather permitting, a peek

through one of its telescopes. The observatory grounds also are home to the vice president, who lives at 1 Observatory Circle, an 1893 Queen Anne Victorian built originally to house the facility's superintendent.

◀ WASHINGTON NATIONAL CATHEDRAL

3101 Wisconsin Ave. NW, 202/537-6200, www.nationalcathedral.org

HOURS: Mon.-Fri. 10 A.M.-5:30 P.M.; tours 10-11:30 A.M. and 12:45-3:30 P.M.; nave level June 1-Aug. 31 Tues. and Thurs. 10 A.M.-8 P.M., Sat. 10 A.M.-4:30 P.M.; tours 10 A.M., 11:30 A.M., 12:45 P.M., and 3 P.M.

COST: $5 suggested contribution

Perched on high ground not far from the city's highest point, Washington National Cathedral dominates the DC skyline, a Gothic masterpiece that took 83 years to build. It is the second-largest cathedral in the United States after St. John the Divine in New York City, and the sixth-largest in the world. Technically named the Cathedral of Saints Peter and Paul, the church is home to the bishop of the Episcopal Diocese of Washington as well as the bishop of the Episcopal Church USA. It holds more than 1,200 services each year and has a growing neighborhood congregation of its own.

The plan for a national house of worship was actually pitched by Pierre L'Enfant, whose design for Washington included such a worship space of national significance. It wasn't until the early 1900s that work began on one, however. In 1907, President Roosevelt laid the foundation stone, using the same mallet that George Washington used to install the Capitol cornerstone. Construction ebbed and flowed between wars and economic crises, and the last stone was installed in 1990. The church was built entirely with private funds; although its organizational body was chartered by Congress to establish a "cathedral for the promotion of religion," it has no official governmental role. But that's not to say it hasn't hosted its share of historic events. It held the funerals of Presidents Gerald Ford, Ronald Reagan, and Dwight D. Eisenhower, was President George W. Bush's place of worship for the National Prayer and

Washington National Cathedral is also known as the Cathedral of Saints Peter and Paul.

Remembrance Service on September 14, 2001, and has served as the gathering place for inaugural prayer services. It is the site of President Woodrow Wilson's grave as well as Helen Keller's and Anne Sullivan's.

The cathedral's principal designers, British architect George Frederick Bodley, and later, Philip Hubert Frohman, set out to build a church to rival Europe's finest: The Gothic National Cathedral features flying buttresses; spires; 231 stained glass windows, including one that contains a moon rock obtained during the Apollo 11 mission; 112 creepy gargoyles; and 288 angels and grotesques, including the likeness of Darth Vader.

On Aug. 23, 2011, a 5.8 magnitude earthquake struck the DC area, shaking many of the city's historic buildings. Two—the Cathedral and the Washington Monument—remained closed for months afterward. The cathedral lost two stone finials from its tallest tower and suffered structural damage. While the church remained closed at the time this book went to press, the grounds remain open.

RESTAURANTS

Washington's dining scene has mushroomed in the past 20 years, thanks partly to an influx of celebrity chefs attracted to the city's vibrancy and economic stability, and primarily to a new crop of ambitious restaurateurs eager to make a name for themselves among the city's neighborhoods. DC boasts a plethora of upscale eateries led by chefs with last names like Ducasse, Puck, Richard, and Andrés that afford diners the chance to vie competitively for reservations and shell out significant coin for a memorable meal. Expensive steak houses also dominate DC dining; business deals continue to be made over a dinner of aged beef, creamed spinach, and sautéed mushrooms. Fortunately, the restaurant boom has also given rise to a number of low- to mid-priced restaurants, mainly neighborhood bistros that cook contemporary American or ethnic cuisine that reflects the city's diversity. From Spanish tapas to Ethiopian, Middle Eastern and Vietnamese to New American, there's something for every taste and budget throughout the city.

Washington is a crossroads of visitors, business travelers, conventioneers, marchers, politicians, and residents, and as such it boasts a lively dining scene nearly every night of the week. Until I moved to DC, I never knew anyone who said "I don't cook" and meant it. There are people in this city who eat out every single night. And given their number of dining options, they can do this for a year without repeating a restaurant; they'd never have to step into a fast food joint either. But they do have to plan ahead: They usually must dine between 6 P.M. and 10 P.M. or find a late-night

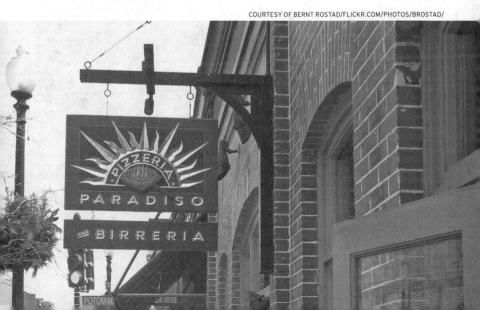

HIGHLIGHTS

LOOK FOR  TO FIND RECOMMENDED RESTAURANTS.

Best Seafood: It's hard to choose between a city original, **Kinkead's** (page 94), with its primo crab cakes and comfy piano bar, and the stunning art deco dining room and raw bar at **Oceanaire** (page 89).

Best Restaurant to Spot Celebs: A quintessential new American bistro that serves french fries cooked in duck fat and a perfect apple pie, the **Blue Duck Tavern** attracts an A-list crowd, including Faith Hill and Tim McGraw, Bono, Tom Hanks, and the Obamas (page 90).

Best Burgers: It's a matter of taste, but in a city full of new burger joints, a homegrown original stands tall: **Five Guys** began in a humble strip mall in Arlington, Virginia, serving consistently excellent and inexpensive burgers and fries (page 93).

Best Place to Spot Politicians: When Congress is in session, it's nearly impossible not to see someone important at **The Monocle** on the Senate side of Capitol Hill. Recent sightings include Sen. Joe Lieberman, Speaker of the House John Boehner, and Rep. Peter King (page 97).

Best Place to Seal the Deal: According to the Federal Election Commission, congressional candidates spend more money at **Charlie Palmer Steak** than at any other restaurant in DC. This probably has nothing to do with its Capitol Hill location or sky-high prices (page 102).

Best Sausages: The lunch line is half the fun at **Ben's Chili Bowl,** enjoying the hip-hop music, the lunch crew's antics, and the rapid-fire preparation of the city's signature dish, the half-smoke (page 107).

Most Kid-Friendly Restaurant: Old **Glory Bar-B-Que** is a place kids and parents can both love: the pulled pork, brisket, mac and cheese, and corn on the cob menu pleases youngsters, while the bar, with 80 different bourbons, appeals to the older folks (page 112).

Best Views: At **Sequoia,** food and service can be spotty, but who cares? It's all about hanging out with good friends while gazing out at the Potomac (page 112).

Most Romantic Restaurant: Your date will love the fireplaces, exposed beams, antiques, and a table for two set with Limoges china and crystal at **1789** (page 112).

Best Pizza: A crispy but chewy crust, unusual toppings, and microbrews – there should be a **Pizzeria Paradiso** in my neighborhood. Thankfully, it's close enough (page 114).

© DESTINATION DC

Head to Ben's Chili Bowl for the best chili-cheese fries and half-smokes.

PRICE KEY

$ Entrées less than $10
$$ Entrées $10-20
$$$ Entrées more than $20

gastropub or bar for a meal. For all its cosmopolitan airs, DC still closes up shop in many neighborhoods by 10 P.M.

George Washington hoped his city would someday become an economic powerhouse, but it was founded on transiency, and the very design of the federal government ensures that the population turns over with every election cycle. The ebb and flow is also influenced by foreign elections and the influx of emissaries and their entourages, creating a city that is one giant melting pot. Since fewer than 40 percent of its residents were actually born here, the city has no real regional cuisine to call its own. Many menus around the city draw heavily on Southern ingredients—items like blue crab, Virginia ham, grits, or polenta and greens—but little can be considered uniquely Washingtonian (with the exception, perhaps, of the half-smoke—a spicy sausage served on a bun like a hot dog). The silver lining in this transiency is the variety of cuisine that's available within five miles of the U.S. Capitol; Ethiopian, Thai, Chinese, Salvadoran, Lebanese, Spanish, Tex-Mex, Mediterranean, Italian, Korean, Malaysian, French, American, Irish, Moroccan, and more, it's all here.

Adventurous eaters can find food to suit their tastes throughout the city, but they shouldn't restrict themselves to sit-down restaurants. A great meal can be had in a museum or theater café, at walk-up counters and food trucks, in bars and at diners across the map. It can even be found in the suburbs—especially the suburbs—where prices are slightly lower but the quality is anything but.

RESTAURANTS

The National Mall East

Map 2

CONTEMPORARY AMERICAN
CITYZEN $$$
Mandarin Oriental, 1330 Maryland Ave. SW,
202/787-6006,
www.mandarinoriental.com/washington/dining
HOURS: Tues.-Thurs. 6–9:30 P.M., Fri.-Sat. 5:30–9:30 P.M.

A temple to the creativity of chef Eric Zeibold, formerly of Napa, California's Mobil five-star French Laundry, CityZen is a destination for gourmands, with a three- and six-course chef's tasting menu that varies depending on the availability of ingredients, the season, and the whims of the chef, whose American menu blends classic French and Asian ingredients with California contemporary. The restaurant's mood itself is Zen-like, with stone pillars, soaring ceilings, and soft lighting emanating from single-tiered chandeliers and table votives. Some tables overlook the Tidal Basin and the Jefferson Memorial; nearly all have a view of the exhibition kitchen, where Ziebold often is seen preparing a flawless duck Bolognese or sautéed Mulard duck foie gras with béarnaise. Make sure you allot hours to savor CityZen, starting with the box of handcrafted Parker rolls and ending with a ginger beignet with vanilla-ginger cream or other sweet treasure. You can enjoy a similarly well-prepared meal with a more casual menu for less money in Zen Bar, which features an amazing 30-foot wall of fire as a decorative touch.

SOU'WESTER $$
Mandarin Oriental, 1330 Maryland Ave. SW,
202/787-6006,
www.mandarinoriental.com/washington/dining
HOURS: Daily 6:30–10:30 A.M., 11:30 A.M.–4 P.M.,
5:30–10 P.M.; brunch Sat.-Sun. 11:30 A.M.–4 P.M.

This part of the city isn't replete with dining options, but the Mandarin Oriental Hotel boasts two: Sou'Wester is the laid back Georgia cousin to CityZen's exotic New Yorker, with a

The decor at Mandarin Oriental's CityZen truly fits the name.

© DESTINATION DC

menu of Southern favorites, including crispy fried chicken, hush-puppies with honey butter, coleslaw, fried oysters, and snapper with Old Bay. Desserts also hail from the Deep South: banana cream and mud pies, red velvet cake, and homemade ice cream. The vibe is comfortable, and some tables offer great waterfront views. During cherry blossom season, Sou'Wester is ideal for sipping a cocktail and enjoying views of the blooms and the crowds.

EUROPEAN
GARDEN CAFÉ $$

National Gallery of Art West Building, 4th St. and Constitution Ave. NE, 202/842-6353, www.nga.gov/dining

HOURS: Mon.-Sat. 11:30 A.M.-3 P.M., Sun. noon-4 P.M.

For years, this dining hall featured a French menu reflecting the culinary preferences of the impressionist masters. Currently, to celebrate a Canaletto exhibit as well as the National Gallery's collection by Italian artists, the Garden Café showcases northern Italian fare, a menu created by Fabio Trabocchi, head chef

of Fiola Restaurant downtown. The buffet is the most popular choice, featuring a selection of salads, soups, and pasta with pancetta and eggplant parmigiana, but the menu also has à la carte items such as the popular basil tortellini with buffalo mozzarella.

NATIVE AMERICAN
MITSITAM NATIVE FOODS $$

National Museum of the American Indian, 4th St. and Independence Ave. SW, 202/633-1000, www.mitsitamcafe.com

HOURS: Daily 10 A.M.-5 P.M.

Word is out about this culinary oasis in the desert of National Mall dining options. A cafeteria that steps outside the bounds of salads, wraps, and pizza, Mitsitam taps its museum's themes for culinary inspiration: Menu choices include Native American staples such as grilled venison, cedar-planked roasted salmon and bison, and Mesoamerican foods that include chorizos and green-pepper peach salsa. The setting is institutional, with the exception of the wood-paneled dining room that echoes the building's curves, but the aroma rising from its open fires lends it an ambience not normally found in a museum canteen. Avoid the crowds by planning a late meal, around 1:30 P.M.

QUICK BITES
CASTLE CAFÉ $

Smithsonian Castle, 1000 Jefferson Dr. SW, 202/633-1000, www.si.edu/dining
HOURS: Daily 8:30 A.M.-5:30 P.M.

As with any dining option in a museum, the Castle Café is not inexpensive—nearly $3 for a cup of coffee? Sheesh. But it is located in a world-class museum—one that doesn't charge an entry fee—and offers free Wi-Fi. Plus it is convenient and a lovely place to plan a day, with high stools and large stained glass windows. It's quiet too—no one seems to know about it and its menu of sandwiches, wraps, salads, and panini.

ESPRESSO AND GELATO BAR $

National Gallery of Art East Building, 4th St. and Constitution Ave. NE, 202/712-7458, www.nga.gov/dining
HOURS: Mon.-Sat. 10 A.M.-4:30 P.M., Sun. 11 A.M.-5:30 P.M.

There's no finer place in Washington to "take a coffee" and enjoy afternoon gelato than the espresso bar in the National Gallery. Located beneath street level in a corridor connecting the gallery's east and west buildings, the walk-up counter features an array of coffee drinks and

19 flavors of house-made gelato—chocolate, blueberry-cranberry, *frutti de bosco,* and more. Its small tables face a cascading waterfall, creating a sense of the outdoors underground. For substantial fare and bigger tables that accommodate large groups, the Gallery's Cascades Café lies behind the bar's table and a hedge of houseplants. The cafeteria's menu features salads, sandwiches, panini, and soups.

PAVILION CAFÉ $

National Gallery of Art Sculpture Garden, Constitution Ave. and 7th St. NW, 202/289-3360, www.nga.gov/dining
HOURS: Mid-Mar.-Labor Day Mon.-Sat. 10 A.M.-4 P.M., Sun. 11 A.M.-5 P.M.

This seasonal café epitomizes the best of urban living—the chance to dine in a beautiful garden setting surrounded by works of the world's greatest artists. The Pavilion's retro space is set among flowers and trees; contemporary sculptures by Claes Oldenburg, Roy Lichtenstein, and others; and is in itself a work of art: The Mall-side terrace incorporates a genuine art nouveau entrance from the Paris Metro. The Pavilion's menu selection includes typical lunch fare—wraps, salads and sandwiches—as well as beer and wine. On summer Friday evenings, the Sculpture Garden turns into a concert venue; the café swaps out its menu for light dinner fare to accommodate those attending the free live jazz events. Concerts start at 5:30 P.M.

Downtown   Map 3

AMERICAN
CEDAR $$$

822 E St. NW, 202/637-0012, www.cedardc.com
HOURS: Lunch Mon.-Fri. 11:30 A.M.-2:30 P.M., dinner Mon.-Sat. 5:30-10:00 P.M., brunch Sat. 11 A.M.-3 P.M., Sun. 10 A.M.-3 P.M.

Cedar is a solid choice for American fare in an area of often overcrowded restaurants. Designed to resemble a forest, this cozy dining room is a basement decorated in cedar paneling, twig wallpaper, and stone, a 70-seat

establishment that aims to please, from bartenders who whip up a smooth Sazerac to the friendly hostess, attentive waitstaff, and a chef that doesn't hold back on ingredients like cream, butter, and bacon. Virginia pan-roasted oysters and duck-fat fries are among the most popular dishes. Cedars offers a three-course fixed-price menu for theatergoers; nearby venues include the Shakespeare Theatre Company and the Woolly Mammoth Theatre Company.

RESTAURANTS

RESTAURANTS

CENTRAL MICHEL RICHARD 💲💲💲
1001 Pennsylvania Ave. NW, 202/626-0015,
www.centralmichelrichard.com
HOURS: Lunch Mon.-Fri. 11:30 A.M.-2:30 P.M.,
dinner Mon.-Thurs. 5-10:30 P.M., Fri.-Sat. 5-11 P.M.

A bucket of fried chicken to go, mashed potatoes, cheeseburgers, and Apple Brown Betty from a renowned French chef? Central is Michel Richard's ultimate irony: The French enjoy sniffing at the plebian offerings of the average American diner, but Richard, originally from Brittany, has abandoned his native country's collective snobbery and embraced such lowbrow fare, preparing it with French techniques and adding a dash of tasty French staples to round out the menu. The setting is no diner—blond wood tables, neutral walls, drum chandeliers—and the extensive wine and drink list wouldn't be found in the average American restaurant either, but the menu is complete Americana: meatloaf, liver and onions, rib-eye steak, and bacon cheeseburgers. For those who can't see visiting a Michel Richard restaurant and not sampling the chef's native cooking, there are mussels, steak tartare, *pommes frites*, and a frisée salad. Save room for the whimsically served banana split.

CLYDE'S OF GALLERY PLACE 💲💲
707 7th St. NW, 202/349-3700, www.clydes.com
HOURS: Lunch Mon.-Fri. 11 A.M.-5 P.M.,
dinner Mon.-Fri. 5 P.M.-midnight,
Sat.-Sun. 4 P.M.-midnight, brunch Sat.-Sun. 10 A.M.-4 P.M.

Is this restaurant a standout in the Clyde's family, a local restaurant group that runs the Old Ebbitt Grill and 1789? No. But the Gallery Place venue, decorated as a Victorian-era saloon from the days when the Brits ruled Hong Kong (a theme that recalls its location, Chinatown), is conveniently located near the

DC FOOD TRUCKS

If it's edible, it's probably available from a DC food truck. Gourmet food trucks that sell more than the usual hot dog, slice of pizza, or pupusa began setting up shop in the city in 2009, and now they appear to be here to stay. Among the trucks, a number of these mobile kitchens stand out. They change location daily and post the addresses on Twitter, which tends to work fine, except on those days when it's 12:30 p.m., you're hungry, and you log in to be told, "Twitter is at capacity. Please try again later." Cue the growling stomach.

- **Red Hook Lobster Truck** (@Lobster truckDC): A mobile offshoot of the Red Hook Lobster Pound in Brooklyn, New York, Red Hook dishes out a bit of the Pine Tree State — rolls stuffed with chunks of fresh-steamed lobster or shrimp, homemade whoopie pies, Maine Root soda, and tangy real lemonade.

- **District of Pi** (@PiTruckDC): Sister truck to the original in St. Louis, Pi rolls out Chicago-style pizza in four varieties, usually two meat and two veggie options. The Beltway features a cornmeal crust topped with kalamata olives, zucchini, feta cheese, and basil; the Central West End is piled with mozzarella, prosciutto, goat cheese, tomatoes, onions, and arugula.

- **Takorean** (@takorean): A wedding of Korean barbeque with Mexican toppings satisfies the lunch crowd at bargain prices (three tacos for $8). Meat and vegetable choices are Korean through and through – *bulgogi*, tangy chicken, tofu in hoisin, cabbage, and kimchi – but the toppings hail from south of the border, lime *crema* and cilantro.

- **Sauca** (@wheresauca): A truck whose offerings span the globe, Sauca sells diversity in a wrap, beef *shawarma*, fish tacos, Indian butter chicken, and pork *banh mi*. These sandwiches don't need embellishment, but if you feel inspired, the truck offers a large variety of sauces.

Verizon Center and several museums, making it appealing for families seeking a decent meal after a long day of touring or work. Clyde's offers typical American comfort food: burgers, crab cakes, nachos, and appetizers like crab with artichoke dip and hummus in a typical American comfort space: cavernous and dark with banquettes, booths, and big tables. It's the place to go when you don't want to think about where to go, the restaurant where you know the food will be decent, the waitstaff will be friendly, and you don't have to worry about paying for bottled water.

ASIAN
FULL KEE $\textbf{\$\$}$

509 H St. NW, 202/371-2233, www.fullkeedc.com
HOURS: Mon.-Sun. 11 A.M.-2 A.M.

Chinese restaurants are becoming a rarity in the neighborhood that still bears the name "Chinatown" on its Metro stop. The Full Kee is a throwback to this area's origins. It is a large two-story place that serves Cantonese and American favorites. Area residents recommend that to make the most of a visit here, order dumplings or noodle dishes from the card inserted into the menu, or stick to the chef's specials. Among the most popular meals is beef chow fun, rice noodles piled with beef, mushrooms, and Chinese broccoli and wok-fried to lend the noodles a smoky flavor. Don't expect lavish decor or cloying service, just inexpensive food in a simple space.

OYA $\textbf{\$\$}$

777 9th St. NW, 202/393-1400, www.oyadc.com
HOURS: Lunch Mon.-Fri. 11:30 A.M.-2 P.M.,
dinner Mon.-Thurs. 5:30-10 P.M., Fri.-Sat. 5:30-11:30 P.M.,
Sun. 5:30-9 P.M.

A stunning interior greets guests at Oya, a fire-and-ice design of blinding white banquettes, leather chairs, and stone, with fireplaces built into the walls and a two-ton chain curtain separating the bar from the dining room. Oya is as close to LA sexy-chic as DC gets in terms of atmosphere, and people definitely go to this upscale eatery for the vibe. The menu

leans heavily toward fish and seafood, with a spicy bluefin tuna tartare appetizer that tantalizes and entrées of fresh turbot with delicately poached oysters or lobster macaroni and cheese. Stick with the ocean offerings, sushi, and the martini menu.

THE SOURCE $\textbf{\$\$\$}$

575 Pennsylvania Ave. NW, 202/637-6100,
www.wolfgangpuck.com/restaurants/fine-dining/3941
HOURS: Lunch Mon.-Fri. 11:30 A.M.-2 P.M.,
dinner Mon.-Thurs. 5:30-10 P.M., Fri.-Sat. 5:30-11 P.M.,
brunch Sat. 11:30 A.M.-3 P.M.

One of only two Wolfgang Puck fine restaurants on the East Coast, The Source is a sparkling two-story eatery, a modern space of glass and steel with a comfortable lounge and a long bar downstairs and a minimalist dining room upstairs. In this stark setting, the food provides the color: deep-pink tuna tartare in miso-sesame cones, pork-belly dumplings in ink-black sauce speckled with leafy green cilantro, red Thai-curry shrimp and rockfish tempered with yellow pineapple. The lounge menu ranges from small bites like Kobe beef sliders and sushi to more filling fare, including black cod with noodle salad and Chinese barbecue spareribs. At lunchtime, The Source offers a three-course fixed-price menu featuring soup or pot stickers, cheeseburgers, salmon, and a surprise: select the prix fixe, and you can attend the neighboring Newseum for $7.

BREAKFAST
LINCOLN'S WAFFLE SHOP $\textbf{\$}$

504 10th St. NW, 202/638-4008
HOURS: Mon.-Fri. 5:30 A.M.-6:30 P.M.,
Sat.-Sun. 5:30 A.M.-3 P.M.

It is dingy and located by a few tacky tourist shops (Lincoln and Kennedy conspiracy pennies! The U.S. Capitol in a plastic snow globe!), but if your hotel doesn't offer breakfast, or you have business near Ford's Theatre and enjoy dining on a hearty breakfast at a greasy spoon, Lincoln's Waffle Shop is a cheap, dependable hole-in-the-wall that serves pancakes, waffles, eggs, and regional specialties that include salmon cakes and grits from the South and scrapple, a fried Pennsylvania Dutch specialty of leftover butcher scraps, corn meal, and flour, from north of the Mason-Dixon Line.

DESSERTS
RED VELVET CUPCAKERY ⑤
501 7th St. NW, 202/347-7895,
www.redvelvetcupcakery.com
HOURS: Mon.-Fri. 8 A.M.-11 P.M., Sat.-Sun. 10 A.M.-11 P.M.

Area office workers enjoy an afternoon stop at Red Velvet Cupcakery, known for its eponymous cupcake, a red treat topped with fluffy cream-cheese icing, and other frosted delights. Flavors vary by season, with the bakers trying new recipes that include Guinness cupcakes at Saint Patrick's Day and carrot cake near Easter. They've also perfected the chocolate gluten-free cupcake, no small feat.

FRENCH
BISTRO D'OC ⑤⑤
518 10th St. NW, 202/393-5444, www.bistrodoc.com
HOURS: Lunch Mon.-Sat. 11:30 A.M.-2:30 P.M.,
dinner Mon.-Thurs. 5:30-9:45 P.M.,
Fri.-Sat. 5:30-10:45 P.M., Sun. 11:30 A.M.-8:30 P.M.

A pleasant French bistro sandwiched between the home where Abraham Lincoln took his last breath and a souvenir stand, Bistro D'Oc is a quaint place to kick back and savor traditional French fare like cassoulet and steak frites. Never quite as crowded as nearby eateries, even on a Friday or Saturday night, the relaxed café invites diners to linger over their meals. The bar boasts a rotating selection of wine by the glass, which draws heavily from the Languedoc region, as well as three makes of absinthe, adding to the place's Gallic experience. Hearty entrées include roasted rack of lamb with béarnaise and roasted eggplant, braised veal with wine, tomatoes, and olives, and braised short ribs with mushrooms. A few of the dishes are tinged with Thai accents, including chicken sautéed with Thai green curry and sea scallops with Thai fried rice—a nod to chef Bernard Grenier's wife, who hails from southeast Asia.

HAUTE CUISINE
MINIBAR AT CAFÉ ATLANTICO ⑤⑤⑤
405 8th St. NW, 202/393-0812,
www.cafeatlantico.com/miniBar
HOURS: Tues.-Sat. seatings at 6 P.M. and 8:30 P.M.

To make a reservation at MiniBar, diners must pick up the phone at precisely 10 A.M. a month before they want to go and be prepared to hit the redial until they get through. If they're lucky, they will secure one or two of the six seats at the two sittings per night for the chance to sample 27 to 30 courses from chef José Andrés's imagination. What they get for their fixed price of $120 is the culinary equivalent of Mr. Wonka's chocolate factory—a romp with a group of golden ticket holders through the thermosphere of culinary space: prawns that swim on a wave of brioche-flavored foam, a Philadelphia cheesesteak (wafer-thin slices of beef hugging a cheddar-filled pita), a dessert that is made of sweet ingredients—coconut milk ice cream and frozen peanut powder—but tastes like pad thai. MiniBar is an event; guests interact with the chefs and are encouraged to ask questions. Despite the number of portions, big eaters should understand that they might not leave full. Like many tasting menus, this one consists basically of 27 bites—all flavorful, all delicious, but individualized and small.

INDIAN
RASIKA ⑤⑤
633 D St. NW, 202/637-1222,
www.rasikarestaurant.com
HOURS: Lunch Mon.-Fri. 11:30 A.M.-2:30 P.M.,
dinner Mon.-Thurs. 5:30-10:30 P.M., Fri. 5:30-11 P.M.,
Sat. 5-11 P.M.

The spices of India contrast with the coolness of the trendy Penn Quarter restaurant Rasika, where young staffers and newly landed professionals sip drinks and dive into naan among the beaded and silk decor. One of the many überchic restaurants to pop up in DC in the past decade, Rasika delivers with its menu, drawing rave reviews for its inventive takes on traditional Indian. The best Indian food I've ever had was in London—not having been to India—and luckily, chef Vikram Sunderam hopped across the pond from England in 2005 to bring the flavors of his native Mumbai to this country. If you are unfamiliar with Indian food, the waitstaff is very helpful; Rasika also offers a chef's tasting menu to sample the best of Sunderam's talents. Popular appetizers include the *palak chaat,* a crispy spinach dish served with tamarind sauce, and the naan with goat cheese. For a main meal, the *dal makhani,* a stew of spicy red lentils, satisfies, as does the lamb *roganjosh* with garam masala and caramelized onions. Dessert eaters will enjoy the apple *jalebi,* a crispy fried apple topped with orange cardamom ice cream.

ITALIAN
TOSCA $$$

1112 F St. NW, 202/367-1990, www.toscadc.com
HOURS: Lunch Mon.-Fri. 11:30 A.M.-2:30 P.M., dinner Mon.-Thurs. 5:30-10:30 P.M., Fri.-Sat. 5:30-11 P.M.

Impeccably prepared northern Italian fare, including handcrafted pastas with rich fillings and sauces as well as artfully plated meats, rarely fail to please at Tosca, an upscale restaurant amid the bustle of downtown. The atmosphere is nondescript, reminiscent to some extent of an office that should hold cubicles instead of dark wood tables, and the service is stiff and a bit stuffy, but the food is sublime, drawing crowds of business executives at lunch and a well-heeled throng most evenings for dinner. Popular dishes include tortelli stuffed with robiola cheese and rich black truffle accompanied by a porcini and leek sauce, and the roasted veal ravioli, filled with delicate white meat, prosciutto, and pistachio mortadella. The wine list is long on Italian reds and offers five by the glass as well as an American chianti. To enjoy Tosca for less, patrons can sit at the bar and order half portions of a number of pastas.

MEDITERRANEAN AND MIDDLE EASTERN
ZAYTINYA $$

701 9th St. NW, 202/638-0800, www.zaytinya.com
HOURS: Sun.-Mon. 11:30 A.M.-10 P.M., Tues.-Thurs. 11:30 A.M.-11:30 P.M., Fri.-Sat. 11:30 A.M.-midnight

Another lively eatery from Jaleo chef José Andrés, Zaytinya's menu consists of mezes

Zaytinya

with Turkish and Greek delights, delicious little plates of meats, vegetables, and sauces that leave you wanting to sample everything listed. On being seated in comfortable leather banquettes or at a table overlooking passersby on 9th Street, servers bring the restaurant's namesake (*zaytinya* is Turkish for "olive oil") and warm pillowy wedges of pita to snack on as you peruse the menu. Helpful staff will answer your questions and make recommendations: Familiar Middle Eastern snacks (hummus, baba ghanoush, *labneh*) are available, along with surprises that will change your preconceived notions about some foods—crispy brussels sprouts with coriander and garlic yogurt, crispy veal sweetbreads with baby fennel, and braised goat. The wine menu consists exclusively of Middle Eastern vintages. Again, the waitstaff can help you make decisions. The only drawback to Zaytinya is the overeager busing: On more than one occasion, they've whisked away a dish containing the remnants of a delectable sauce meant to be swabbed with bread. If you are dining at Zaytinya or walking past it, take note of the dark gray building across the street: The city's Martin Luther King Jr. Memorial Library is DC's only Mies van der Rohe–designed building.

MEXICAN
OYAMEL $$
401 7th St. NW, 202/628-1005, www.oyamel.com
HOURS: Sun.-Mon. 11:30 A.M.-10 P.M., Tues.-Thurs. 11:30 A.M.-11:30 P.M., Fri.-Sat. 11:30 A.M.-midnight

Yes, this restaurant offers grasshopper tacos, one of the many small plates of Mexican and, in the case of the locusts, pre-Colombian fare offered by chef José Andrés, who crafts meals with authentic ingredients like ground corn, hominy, *guajillo* chilies, pork belly, tongue, and for the less adventurous, chicken, barbecued pork, and braised lamb. For starters, the house-made guacamole, prepared and served in a *molcajete,* pairs wonderfully with freshly made masa chips and a pitcher of the classic margaritas. Like many Andrés restaurants, the *antojitos,* or little plates, are intended to be savored and shared. Prime picks includes the pork tacos with pickled red onions and grilled skirt steaks. Chocolate cake, served with a Mexican hot-chocolate froth and tinged with cinnamon and other uncommon spices, melts in your mouth. The grasshoppers are more a gimmick than anything; besides the crunchy little legs that get stuck in your teeth, the taste differs little from the salsa and guacamole.

NEW AMERICAN
PROOF $$$
775 G St. NW, 202/737-7663, www.proofdc.com
HOURS: Lunch Tues.-Fri. 11:30 A.M.-2 P.M., dinner Mon.-Thurs. 5:30-10:30 P.M., Fri.-Sat. 5:30-11 P.M., Sun. 5:30-9:30 P.M.

Proof is a wine bar that delivers on its food and whose cuisine is not limited to the cheese plates that guests can build from a selection of 20 dairy, goat, and blue varieties or the charcuterie. In this restaurant, on the first floor of a nondescript office building, chef and co-owner Haider Karoum has created a menu that draws heavily on Mediterranean flavors with a bit of Asian thrown in—Karoum helmed Asia Nora, a now-closed DC restaurant. A Peking duck breast is served with a pomegranate emulsion and sweet potato puree; tuna tartare and *hamachi crudo* are as popular as the gnocchi and pork ragout. Proof

Customers enjoy the extensive wine collection at Proof.

© DESTINATION DC

has more than 40 wines by the glass that can be ordered in 2-, 6-, and 8-ounce pours. This restaurant is trendy and usually low-key, but with the Verizon Center just down the street, it's wise to check out the venue's schedule, as the place fills up with boisterous fans after a game or concert.

QUICK BITES
CAPITAL Q $
707 H St. NW, 202/347-8396, www.capitalqbbq.com
HOURS: Mon.-Wed. 11 A.M.-9 P.M.,
Thurs.-Sat. 11 A.M.-midnight

Barbecue is such a controversial topic. What defines barbecue—the sauce, the cooking method, the spices? Is Capital Q authentic Texas barbecue, with menu choices like beef brisket and jalapeño corn bread? I don't know, but a friend and transplant from Amarillo has her parties in DC catered by Capital Q. In addition to its brisket, the Q offers smoky and delicious chicken and pulled pork and a variety of sauces, served in a place with entertaining decor—corrugated walls plastered with steer heads, signed pictures of congressional patrons, and $1 bills. The Q is also one of the few places in DC that serves sweet tea.

FOOD COURT,
RONALD REAGAN BUILDING $
1300 Pennsylvania Ave. NW, 202/312-1300,
www.itcdc.com
HOURS: Mon.-Fri. 7 A.M.-7 P.M., Sat. 11 A.M.-6 P.M.,
Sun. noon-5 P.M.

Normally I wouldn't mention a food court, but there are so few dining options near the eastern National Mall that it's a requirement here. The Ronald Reagan's food court is less than two blocks from the National Mall—perfect for the masses exhausted by sightseeing and those who'd rather not spend money in a museum cafeteria or at a hot dog vendor. The dining hall has deli sandwiches, hamburgers, sushi, Cajun food, nachos, wraps, Chinese food, pitas, Italian, and the ubiquitous Subway. Be prepared to go through security to enter the building, a working office for government officials and contractors.

TEAISM PENN QUARTER $
400 8th St. NW, 202/638-6010, www.teaism.com
HOURS: Mon.-Fri. 7:30 A.M.-10 P.M., Sat.-Sun.
9:30 A.M.-9 P.M., brunch Sat.-Sun. 9:30 A.M.-2:30 P.M.

Tea plays a prominent role in this Asian-themed deli, which draws lines at lunch for its edibles, including sandwiches, bento boxes, salads, and entrées like chicken curry. At breakfast time it is a place to enjoy an inexpensive meal of chai with waffles or cut Irish oatmeal topped with raisins and mango. Teaism invites patrons to linger; the Penn Quarter location contains a Koi pond.

SEAFOOD
OCEANAIRE $$$
1201 F St. NW, 202/347-2277, www.oceanaire.com
HOURS: Lunch Mon.-Fri. 11:30 A.M.-5 P.M., dinner
Mon.-Thurs. 5-10 P.M., Fri.-Sat. 5-11 P.M., Sun. 5-9 P.M.

Oceanaire's ambience is art deco chic, with neon lighting, mahogany banquettes, and etched glass accented with stainless steel. Supposedly modeled after a dining room on a 1930s-era cruise ship, it's more 1920s supper club; if it had a stage, you'd expect Fred Astaire and Ginger Rogers to waltz out on it. This is a place where guests can easily rack up a tab dining on fresh oysters, dirty martinis, and more. The seafood sampler is always a table pleaser, with large crab and lobster claws, oysters, clams, and shrimp heaped on mounds of ice. The wine list tends to the pricey side—Oceanaire is basically like a high-end steak house that serves fish instead of dry-aged beef or Kobe; it's a great place for a special dinner with friends or those dining on an expense account. Service, while attentive, can be slow; expect to make an evening of it.

SPANISH AND LATIN
CAFÉ ATLÁNTICO $$$
405 8th St. NW, 202/393-0812, www.cafeatlantico.com
HOURS: Lunch Tues.-Fri. 11:30 A.M.-2:30 P.M.,
dinner Tues.-Thurs. 5-10 P.M., Fri.-Sat. 5-11 P.M.,
Sun. 5-10 P.M., brunch Sat. 11:30 A.M.-2:30 P.M.,
Sun. 11:30 A.M.-2:30 P.M., last dim sum seating 1:30 P.M.

Another of chef José Andrés's colorful, boisterous restaurants, Café Atlántico serves what it calls Nuevo Latino, dishes of Central and South American fare with a dash of the islands

RESTAURANTS

thrown in, containing touches of coconut milk, pineapple, and banana foam. Guacamole made table-side is a must for starters, accompanied by a creative handcrafted—read expensive— cocktail such as the Dark and Stormy, made with house-made ginger beer, or the manly "Daisy If You Do:" leather-infused tequila, rye-infused St. Germain, and a dash of peaty Lagavulin single malt. As with many Andrés restaurants, the menu features a three-course fixed-price theater menu as well as a tasting menu. Bring your sense of adventure; very little on this menu is "the usual."

JALEO $$
480 7th St. NW, 202/628-7949, www.jaleo.com
HOURS: Daily from 11:30 A.M., evening closing time varies

The history of DC's restaurant revolution and chef José Andrés are inextricably entwined; Andrés, one of *GQ* magazine's Men of the Year in 2009 and overseer of five top restaurants in DC, began with Jaleo in 1993, the first restaurant outside of Chinatown to serve small plates. Nearly 20 years later, Jaleo remains as popular as ever, buzzing with noise and the clinking of plates and glasses, with guests happily diving into the menu of more than 70 tapas offerings. With so many choices, decisions are difficult: The menu includes six varieties of paella that serve up to four people, interesting meats like quail and Canary Island rabbit, trout wrapped in serrano ham, and *gambas al ajillo*—shrimp sautéed in garlic. Jaleo, which means "merry-making" in Spanish, truly was a pioneering restaurant in this neighborhood: Andrés opened this colorful spot two years before the Verizon Center broke ground.

STEAK
CAPITAL GRILLE $$$
601 Pennsylvania Ave. NW, 202/737-6200, www.capitalgrille.com
HOURS: Lunch Mon.-Sat. 11:30 A.M.-3 P.M., dinner Sun.-Thurs. 5-10 P.M., Fri.-Sat. 5-11 P.M.

Just inside the doorway of the Capital Grille is a glass refrigerator showcasing heaping slabs of dry-aged beef. Near the host stand, cherry wine lockers contain secret stashes of cigars and fine wines belonging to some of Washington's famous and infamous residents—people like hockey great Alex Ovechkin and disgraced defense contractor Brent Wilkes—along with a slew of aliases. The bar is usually filled with attractive young women and older men, and in the dining room, some of the city's heaviest hitters feast on thick steaks and wedge salads. For a place seemingly straight out of Hollywood as a "power dining" site, the food is excellent. Steaks are cooked to perfection (although the au poivre has quite a kick), and the creamed spinach is the best in town. This is a top place for dinner, but if you happen to be in DC for lunch, are wearing a suit, and have a few hours to spare, consider reliving the days of the three-martini lunch here.

Foggy Bottom   Map 4

AMERICAN
C BLUE DUCK TAVERN $$$
1201 24th St. NW, 202/419-6755, www.blueducktavern.com
HOURS: Breakfast Mon.-Fri. 6:30 A.M.-10:30 A.M., Sat.-Sun. 11 A.M.-2:30 P.M., lunch Mon.-Fri. 11:30 A.M.-2:30 P.M., Sat.-Sun. noon-2:30 P.M., dinner daily 5:30-10:30 P.M.

Windsor rockers, birdhouses, and jarred fruit greet guests at Blue Duck Tavern, heralding the restaurant's American focus, but the design is anything but "country" in this chic eatery. In view of the dining room of dark oak, blue burlap, and handcrafted furniture, chef Brian McBride prepares contemporary American cuisine with mainly local ingredients: wild striped bass, thick hanger steak, and duck breast with huckleberries. The Blue Duck, in the Park Hyatt, is a favorite for visiting celebrities as well as those who live here. President and Mrs. Obama celebrated their 17th wedding anniversary in this contemporary space; Bono is known to stay at the Park Hyatt and dine at the Blue Duck, and country stars Faith Hill and Tim McGraw have eaten more than one meal here. Save room for the delicious apple pie.

EQUINOX ❺❺❺

818 Connecticut Ave. NW, 202/331-8118, www.equinoxrestaurant.com

HOURS: Lunch Mon.-Fri. 11:30 A.M.-2:30 P.M., dinner Mon.-Thurs. 5:30-10 P.M., Fri.-Sun. 5:30-10:30 P.M.

A pioneer of the DC locavore dining movement, chef Todd Gray's Equinox landed in DC in 1998, mining the region's organic farms to create elegant mouthwatering dishes influenced by Italian cuisine. Equinox suffered a kitchen fire in 2010 and within six months was reopened for business. Gone is the neutral-toned starchy interior in favor of frosted glass panels, limestone and granite walls, an open fireplace, and a glass divider between the bar and dining room, which opens up the space. The food remains the star, highlighting the best of the mid-Atlantic region: meats from Shenandoah-area farms, fish from Chesapeake Bay, softshell crab, and shad roe. Little touches, like cookies with the check, make diners feel pampered.

FOUNDING FARMERS ❺❺

1924 Pennsylvania Ave. NW, 202/822-8783, www.wearefoundingfarmers.com

HOURS: Breakfast Mon.-Fri. 8-11 A.M., Sat.-Sun. 9 A.M.-2 P.M., lunch and dinner Mon. 11 A.M.-10 P.M., Tues.-Thurs. 11 A.M.-11 P.M., Fri. 11 A.M.-midnight, Sat. 2 P.M.-midnight, Sun. 2-10 P.M.

Shortly after it opened, *Travel + Leisure* magazine named Founding Farmers one of the country's best new restaurants. Its concept appeals to the green at heart—a dining room in an environmentally certified building that serves sustainable and local cuisine, the restaurant itself being owned by the North Dakota Farmers Union. Its execution is less than perfect, but on several levels, Founding Farmers delivers. First, it's among the few places in town that strives to serve regional ingredients and actually be affordable, and second,

its effort to be "green" extends to the menus printed in soy ink on recycled paper, organic cleaning products, and biodegradable paper products and trash bags. At night, the bar and large communal tables on the first floor pack in crowds that include students from nearby George Washington University and policy workers from the International Monetary Fund, which shares its building. The upstairs dining room is quieter, a place to savor the vast eclectic menu. The Southern dishes seem to work here—fried green tomatoes, deviled eggs, shrimp, and grits. The desserts are pleasing gargantuan servings of cheesecake and carrot cake. Warning: The portions are huge at Founding Farmers; *Washington Post* food critic Tom Sietsema has called it an eco-friendly version of the Cheesecake Factory.

OLD EBBITT GRILL ❺❺

675 15th St. NW, 202/347-4800, www.ebbitt.com

HOURS: Mon.-Fri. 7:30 A.M.-1 A.M., Sat.-Sun. 8:30 A.M.-1 P.M.

The Old Ebbitt Grill is a sentimental DC favorite. The food isn't cutting-edge, and the line is often long, but for location, clubby ambience, price, and friendly service, the Grill is a dependable eatery in a neighborhood lacking budget-friendly and family-friendly options. Old Ebbitt hails itself as "Washington's oldest saloon," established by an innkeeper at the edge of Chinatown in 1856 and relocated several times before landing at its present location in 1983, with portions of its old interior either intact or embellished to resemble its Theodore Roosevelt–era heyday. Gas lamps, dark wood, and forest-green booths combine with antique touches like the clock in the entryway from the restaurant's F Street location and a marble-and-iron staircase from the former National Metropolitan Bank building next door. Featuring a menu heavy on pub fare and steak, a few choices stand out—oysters, crab cakes, and eggs Chesapeake, and for dessert, peanut butter pie—and the bar shines because of the friendly, funny bartenders. Reservations are recommended but not required.

FRENCH

CAFÉ DU PARC ⑤⑤⑤

1401 Pennsylvania Ave. NW, 202/942-7000,
www.cafeduparc.com

HOURS: Breakfast Mon.-Fri. 6:30-10:30 A.M.,
Sat.-Sun. 7-11 A.M., lunch Mon.-Fri. 11:30 A.M.-2 P.M.,
Sat.-Sun. noon-2:30 P.M.,
dinner Mon.-Fri. 5:30-10:30 P.M., Sat.-Sun. 6-10 P.M.

The charm of blue umbrellas on the sidewalk
in front of one of the city's most architectur-
ally beautiful hotels draws diners to Café du
Parc, a French bistro at the Willard Hotel that
boasts views of Pershing Park, the Ellipse, and
the White House's gatehouses. The feel of Paris
extends indoors to a bright café with wooden
tables, creamy walls, and blue banquettes, and
upstairs to the main restaurant with an open
kitchen. An unsung eatery among DC bistros, this café begins its day with breakfast—
croque-monsieur and crepes, fresh brioche, and
croissants—and skips through the day with a
menu of traditional French cuisine—steaming
pots of simmering mussels, onion soup drip-
ping with cheese, a slow-cooked lamb stew,
and satisfying cassoulet. Pastry chef Morgan
Bomboy has created a litany of tarts, cakes,
chocolate croissants, madeleines, and mille-
feuille that can be taken to go. For dining in,
the chocolate mousse is as good as you'd find
in the City of Lights.

MARCEL'S ⑤⑤⑤

2401 Pennsylvania Ave. NW, 202/296-1166,
www.marcelsdc.com

HOURS: Mon.-Thurs. 5:30-10 P.M., Fri.-Sat. 5:30-11 P.M.,
Sun. 5:30-9:30 P.M.

The French-country ocher walls, red banquettes, and Pierre Deux upholstery create a
cozy feel in this formal restaurant, a throwback to the days when waiters wore suits, chefs
donned toques, and male patrons wore coats
and ties. Jackets are still required at Marcel's,
but this is a restaurant to dress up for, an intimate space that sets the mood for a great menu
that, surprisingly, is not dated. The boudin
blanc is this restaurant's ace in the hole, a sausage crafted from mousse of chicken and foie
gras. A snail fricassee with garlic flan mixes

textures and flavors, as does lamb tenderloins in
phyllo with a spicy Madeira sauce. The ordering format is flexible: Guests can choose three-,
four-, and seven-course meals. A pretheater option is available throughout the evening.

ITALIAN

NOTTI BIANCHE ⑤⑤

824 New Hampshire Ave. NW, 202/298-8085,
www.nottibianche.com

HOURS: Breakfast Mon.-Fri. 7-10 A.M.,
Sat.-Sun. 8-11 A.M., lunch Tues.-Fri. 11:30 A.M.-2:30 P.M.,
Sat.-Sun. noon-2:30 P.M., dinner Tues.-Thurs. and
Sun. 5-10 P.M., Fri.-Sat. 5-11 P.M.

A quiet place near the Kennedy Center that
draws diners in for a pretheater meal, Notti
Bianche is a neighborhood favorite, with exacting service and an authentic Northern Italian
menu that includes pasta dishes, risotto, grilled
meats with fresh vegetables, and more. Patrons
feel at home in this 42-seat dining room at
the ground level of the George Washington
University Inn. The decor is comfortable but
forgettable, but the service is warm and welcoming, and the food is a surprise, thanks to
a chef who once served as *chef de la cuisine* at
Equinox. Ingredients are fresh and well-prepared, and dishes are plated as beautifully as
in restaurants that charge twice the price. At
the height of tomato season, the caprese salad
is sublime, with pillows of fresh mozzarella, vibrant fruit, and pungent basil. The bruschetta
is tossed up with thin rings of squid and capers.
Grilled hanger steak and chicken breasts come
from the kitchen redolent and juicy, with su-
perbly prepared side dishes like fingerling potatoes, balsamic onions, or asparagus. Save room
for dessert: The pistachio gelato topped with
crunchy cocoa-nib brittle goes well with a fresh
cup of Illy.

MALAYSIAN

MALAYSIA KOPITIAM ⑤⑤

1827 M St. NW, 202/833-6232,
www.malaysiakopitiam.com

HOURS: Mon.-Thurs. 11:30 A.M.-10 P.M.,
Fri.-Sat. 11:30 A.M.-11 P.M., Sun. noon-10 P.M.

This sketchy place, in the basement of a row

house next to a strip club, doesn't look like much outside or inside, but it's the only place in DC to enjoy Malaysian cuisine, a blend of Chinese, Indian, Indonesian, and native flavors. *Satay* is a popular dish, as is *roti canai,* a skillet-fried flatbread accompanying curried meats and sauces. Malaysia Kopitiam feels like the neighborhood counters my friends and I went to for snacks in the suburbs of Kuala Lumpur, down to the menus with pictures and the slightly surly Chinese owners. The food—curries, *mee* soup, sticky rice with mango—tastes fairly authentic as well. Dishes guaranteed to give diners a taste of Malaysia include the *roti canai,* the curry puffs, *mee siam,* raja chicken, and of course, the *satay.* The curry *laksas* are available with a choice of noodles and various meats and vegetables.

QUICK BITES

BREADLINE ⑤

1751 Pennsylvania Ave., 202/822-8900, www.breadline.com

HOURS: Mon.-Fri. 7:30 A.M.-3:30 P.M.

Its reputation as Washington's version of the *Seinfeld* soup-Nazi counter is overrated, but it does help the line go more quickly if you know what you want before you get to the front. Always chaotic during lunchtime, this soup, salad, and sandwich place hits the spot with meats piled high on chewy baguettes, creamy egg salad served on crispy-soft olive bread, daily sandwich specials, and salads that come plain or dressed with roast beef, Greek vegetables, Persian chicken, or lentils, depending on the day. The setup is slightly confusing, with lines not well defined and the drink and snack refrigerator off in the corner away from the checkout; it's also sometimes hard to get a table. But in good weather, you can pick up your lunch to go and head to nearby Lafayette Square for an impromptu picnic.

DICKEY'S FROZEN CUSTARD ⑤

1710 I St. NW, 202/293-7100

HOURS: Mon.-Fri. 9 A.M.-4 P.M.

On a wilting summer day, a chocolate-vanilla swirl from Dickey's is coolness in a cup, a brief breeze on a simmering city sidewalk. But Dickey's is more than just a dessert and snack shop; it's a great place to go for sandwiches, cookies, coffee, or a cold drink. The Panini Amor comes stuffed with turkey, provolone, artichoke, avocado, and pesto mayonnaise on warm bread. The grilled cheese is crispy on the outside and oozing with melted cheese. Still, any meal at Dickey's begs to be finished with a cone of creamy frozen custard. The question of what makes Dickey's product different than soft-serve ice cream or frozen yogurt is more technical than one would think: Frozen custard is at least 10 percent butterfat, defined by the Food and Drug Administration as ice cream, but it also contains at least 1.4 percent egg yolk, another FDA requirement. It is prepared in a special machine that mixes it and freezes it so that it has a denser texture and feel than regular ice cream.

◖ FIVE GUYS ⑤

1400 I St. NW, 202/450-3412, www.fiveguys.com

HOURS: Daily 11 A.M.-10 P.M.

Five Guys is ubiquitous now, in 40 states and in Canada, but it started as a burger shack in a strip mall in Arlington, Virginia, a family business that built its success on a mix of fresh ground sirloin and chuck, locally made buns, Idaho potatoes, and free peanuts. The menu is simple—burgers, hot dogs, and fries cooked in peanut oil—but exacting, with 13 topping choices, cooking methods that dictate a burger can only be pressed once per side on the grill, and a requirement to use only Mount Holly brand pickles. The atmosphere is pretty much the same in every Five Guys, with a walk-up counter, oak tables, trademark white tile with red trim on the walls, and vintage '70s and '80s music playing on the sound system. The original locations, though, have something most of the newer places don't—a grubby charm that makes it OK to drop your peanut shells on the floor. Washingtonians are amused by the natural rivalry that has popped up between

RESTAURANTS

Five Guys is an area original.

East Coast and West Coast fans of In-N-Out Burger and Five Guys, chains that both favor hand-pressed, never frozen patties; the burger winner is a matter of preference, but In-N-Out french fries are no match for the fried-in-peanut-oil fries at Five Guys.

LINDY'S BON APPETIT $

2040 I St. NW, 202/452-0055

HOURS: Mon.-Thurs. 8 A.M.-9 P.M., Fri. 8 A.M.-midnight, Sat. 10 A.M.-midnight, Sun. 10 A.M.-9 P.M.

A George Washington University favorite, Lindy's is a place where students, residents, and area visitors chow down on burgers, available in 23 varieties, along with beer. Downstairs has a college hangout–takeout feel (which it is), while upstairs, called Lindy's Red Lion, is a bar and restaurant where guests find a calmer atmosphere with the same menu. Lindy's has more than meat burgers on the menu, but not much—vegetarian and turkey are alternate choices, as are gyros and other sandwiches. The fries are salty and piping hot, always served straight from their cooking oil.

SEAFOOD
◖ KINKEAD'S $$

2000 Pennsylvania Ave. NW, 202/296-7700, www.kinkead.com

HOURS: Mon.-Thurs. 11:30 A.M.-10 P.M., Fri. 11:30 A.M.-11 P.M., Sat. 5-11 P.M., Sun. 5-9 P.M.

Kinkead's has endured since 1993 as the local favorite for premier seafood and regional cooking—massive crab cakes, pan-seared softshells and Smithfield ham, oyster and crab chowder, mounds of fresh seafood on ice served to guests in a huge two-story restaurant that takes up a number of storefronts. The piano bar on the first floor, with live jazz nightly, hums with energy and banter, a lively spot for quick meal and a couple of drinks. The upstairs dining room feels like a different restaurant, more serious and subdued with neutral decor, better suited for a business meeting or quiet night out. The menu spans the gamut of seafood preparation. Chef Bob Kinkead hails from New England, and patrons will find classic dishes from the region on the menu, like fried Ipswich clams, lobster rolls, and hearty fish chowder. But the menu also includes delicate tuna tartare, mussels in a mustard and cream sauce, and sweet grilled prawns over polenta.

SOUTHERN

GEORGIA BROWN'S $$

950 15th St. NW, 202/393-4499, www.gbrowns.com
HOURS: Mon.-Thurs. 11:30 A.M.-10 P.M., Fri. 11 A.M.-11 P.M., Sat. noon-11 P.M., Sun. 10 A.M.-2:30 P.M. and 5:30-10 P.M.

Georgia Brown's opening its doors within months of Vidalia made 1993 a big year for Southern cooking in the city. A block from the White House, GB's concentrates heavily on cuisine from South Carolina's Low Country, a broad stretch of salt marshes, islands, and beaches that contains Charleston at its heart. Executive chef Jim Foss puts his stamp on this cuisine, sprinkling in touches of creole and Cajun spice and cooking methods. The menu focuses on Southern staples like seafood and chicken, spices, and fresh produce—okra, corn, and sweet potatoes. The fried green tomato appetizer with a dollop of goat cheese and served with green-tomato relish is a mouthwatering updated version of an old favorite; black-eyed pea cakes are dressed with smoky grilled vegetables and a piquant lemon-cayenne mayonnaise. Comfort food seekers enjoy the bacon-wrapped meatloaf and crispy, moist fried chicken. Live jazz music is served up every Wednesday during dinner as well.

VIDALIA $$$

1990 M St. NW, 202/659-1990, www.vidaliadc.com
HOURS: Lunch Mon.-Fri. 11:30 A.M.-2:30 P.M., dinner Mon.-Thurs. 5:30-9:30 P.M., Fri.-Sat. 5:30-10 P.M., Sun. 5-9 P.M., closed Sun. July-Aug., except Restaurant Week.

The point of Southern cooking is comfort—satisfying dishes of rich, creamy, buttery, or crackling ingredients prepared as lovingly as a Sunday dinner, served in heaping mounds of gastronomic goodness. Food is the soul of a region, so when Vidalia first opened its doors in 1993, Washingtonians wondered if the city was ready for an expensive, fussy version of a favorite genre. Chef Jeffrey Bubin and wife Sally proved it was. In a sophisticated dining-room setting, Vidalia serves Southern dishes prepared from locally sourced meats, fish, and produce, artfully served and distinctive—old favorites, only better. Satisfying shrimp and grits include ingredients like delicate tasso ham instead of overpowering bacon, a sprinkling of greens, and a shellfish emulsion. Frogmore stew, prepared throughout the South dumped onto papered tables, is more refined—served on a plate—and includes Chesapeake Bay's finest rockfish in addition to smoky sausage and confit potatoes. Not surprisingly, the mint julep and chess pie are among the best in town.

STEAK

BLT STEAK $$$

1625 I St. NW, 202/689-8999, www.bltsteak.com
HOURS: Lunch Mon.-Fri. 11:30 A.M.-2:30 P.M., dinner Mon.-Thurs. 5:30-11 P.M., Fri.-Sat. 5:30-11:30 P.M., closed Sun.

It's tough to beat a meal that starts with complimentary gruyère popovers and pâté upon sitting down. BLT Steak, in which the *BLT* stands for Bistro Laurent Tourondel, is a special-occasion place, the hip 20-something urbanite to your father's classic steak house. The menu teems with traditional steak house choices—shrimp cocktail, heirloom tomato salads, and New York strip—but the setting is anything but stodgy, with throbbing techno music and suede-covered banquettes littered with pillows. The Kobe beef selections are among the most expensive entrée choices in the city: at more than $25 per ounce, those in the know recommend buying one for the table as an accompaniment to sample its deep, rich, marbled-pink, melt-in-your-mouth texture. Entrées, whether fish, fowl, lamb, or cow, are treated with utmost care at BLT Steak, unusual for this genre of restaurant, where nonbeef options sometimes take a backseat to the bovines. Like many high-end seafood and steak rooms, side dishes are served family style to share with the table. BLT's best bets are the creamed spinach and the onion rings.

Many DC restaurants, such as Thai Coast, have sidewalk dining.

© PATRICIA KIME

THAI
THAI COAST $$
2514 L St. NW, 202/333-2460

HOURS: Mon.-Thurs. 11:30 A.M.-3 P.M. and 4:30-10:30 P.M., Fri.-Sat. 11:30 A.M.-11 P.M., Sun. 11:30 A.M.-10:30 P.M.

For a late meal or an easygoing, inexpensive place to grab a bite, Thai Coast is a neighborhood choice for standards such as drunken noodles, penang curry with chicken, red curry with duck, and pad thai. Its location near several hotels makes it a convenient and less expensive alternative to the neighborhood's high-end restaurants. The place has a full bar with a number of fun umbrella drinks on the cocktail menu, and outdoor seating is available in good weather, a draw for locals at happy hour. Will your meal at Thai Coast be one of the best you've ever had? No, but in a city crammed with trendy eateries, destination restaurants, and expense-account cafés, it's nice to enjoy a decent meal in a laid-back place.

Capitol Hill   Map 5

AMERICAN AND NEW AMERICAN
JIMMY T'S $
501 East Capitol St. SE, 202/546-3646

HOURS: Wed.-Fri. 6:30 A.M.-3 P.M., Sat.-Sun. 8 A.M.-3 P.M.

Hip and retro Jimmy T's is not. This diner is the real deal, a neighborhood greasy spoon where eggs, bacon, and hot coffee are its raison d'être. Located in a Victorian row house, Jimmy T's is a no-frills grill, with a long Formica counter, cramped booths, and mismatched mugs. The menu is largely breakfast fare, with eggs and Belgian waffles favored over pancakes or healthy offerings like fruit. Jimmy T's is an everyman's diner in a neighborhood made over through gentrification, a place where locals can find creamy grits done right and eggs done to order. Jimmy T's is not large; on weekends, the booths and seats fill up fast, and patrons linger over coffee and the *Post*. If you don't want to wait for a table on weekends, arrive before 10 A.M.

MATCHBOX 🌑🌑

521 8th St. SE, 202/548-0369, www.matchbox369.com
HOURS: Mon.-Fri. 11 A.M.-close, Sat.-Sun. 10 A.M.-close

The wait for a table can be interminable, and whether it's worth it is debatable, but if you're craving a wood-fired pizza with a thin chewy crust loaded with cheese and unusual toppings like chipotle peppers and smoked gouda or sliders topped with crispy fried onions, Matchbox is the place. The warm dining room, with its exposed brick and French doors that open onto a sidewalk patio, and a large bar entices diners to linger over meals, which contributes to the wait. Don't have the time? The place does a brisk business in takeout orders.

🅒 THE MONOCLE 🌑🌑🌑

107 D St. NE, 202/546-4488, www.themonocle.com
HOURS: Mon.-Fri. 11:30 A.M.-midnight, Sat. 5-10 P.M.

It's hard not to stare when you're dining at the Monocle; usually half the people in the dining room appear regularly on CNN and C-SPAN. For more than 50 years, this old-school Washington power restaurant has managed to stay fresh and relevant, maybe because of its location—within spitting distance of the Hart and Dirksen Senate office buildings—or its attentive waitstaff that treats all patrons like they're VIPs, including the lunching visitors in blue jeans. The menu—simple, fresh fare such as steaks and chops, and heaping main salads at lunch, draws in those who have little time to cook or enjoy a meal at home. The interior is pure Washington politics: Walls are plastered with photos of famous diners; beams and moldings are hand-stenciled with sage aphorisms ("If you want a friend in Washington—get a dog," "An empty stomach is not a good political advisor"). Upstairs rooms are heavily favored for political strategy sessions and private celebrations. The Monocle is not a place to eat if politics makes you ill. Its allure is the atmosphere; if you want to see how lawmakers spend their off-duty time, the opportunity is practically guaranteed.

RESTAURANTS

© PATRICIA KIME

The Monocle

DINING ALFRESCO IN DC

In fine weather the city's sidewalks sprout outdoor tables and umbrellas, and restaurants turn their patios into small oases of greenery and candlelight. Dining outdoors is a summertime treat, and even in Washington, where the humidity sends visitors into air-conditioned spaces during the day, they clamor at night for an outside table. The best outdoor dining spaces in DC:

The people-watching is tops at **Johnny's Half Shell** on Capitol Hill, and the menu isn't too shabby either. Johnny's is where Hill staffers and capitol VIPs go to blow off steam after work, enjoying camaraderie Capitol Hill-style on the patio. Dining on **Citronelle**'s haute cuisine under the stars on its patio adds another dimension to a memorable evening.

You know you are in Washington when you sit under one of **Café du Parc**'s bright blue umbrellas, with the historic Willard Hotel at your back and the White House grounds across the street. Crowds of visitors, businessmen, and locals stroll past, heading to the White House, the Mall, or a nearby museum.

At **Sequoia,** it's really all about the view and not the food or even the drink. With a three-tiered patio on the Potomac River, guests overlook the stunning river, the Kennedy Center, and in warm weather, the fleet of yachts and powerboats that tie up in the river, their owners enjoying old fashioned summertime fun like swimming, sunbathing, and knocking back a few beers.

You don't have to have deep pockets to enjoy outdoor dining in DC. The delightful outdoor patio at **Hank's Oyster Bar** in Georgetown is scheduled to double in capacity in 2011, a welcome change for those dreaming of an evening with friends, drinking beer and eating oysters outside. The patio at **Cashion's Eat Place** has more seating than many Adams Morgan restaurants. It still manages to fill quickly, but it is worth the wait for the inventive cuisine and friendly patrons.

FRENCH

BISTRO BIS $$$

15 E St. NW, 202/661-2700, www.bistrobis.com
HOURS: Mon.-Fri. 7-10 A.M. and 11:30 A.M.-2:30 P.M., dinner daily 5:30-10:30 P.M.,
brunch Sat.-Sun. 11:30 A.M.-2:30 P.M.

The mouthwatering menu at Bistro Bis is not for waist-watchers. Considered one of Washington's top destinations for French fare, the selections at Bistro Bis, inside the haute Hotel George, favor the flavorful, fatty, and forbidden: sweetbreads with chanterelle mushrooms and tomato Madeira *ravigote,* steak frites, pan roasted quail with foie gras, slow-cooked lamb with creamy polenta and flageolet. Heavily favored by lobbyists and politicians for breakfast meetings, Bistro Bis's morning and brunch menus feature selections such as Eggs Chesapeake (eggs Benedict with a heaping portion of lump crabmeat) and a country ham-and-cheese omelet oozing with gruyère. Bistro Bis has a modern yet warm dining room with sleek cherry chairs, comfortable and private booths, mirrored walls, a zinc bar, and an inviting fireplace. The bar menu, which features tempting snacks such as steak tartare, crispy garlic potato chips, and sliders topped with duck bacon, is as skillfully prepared as the offerings in the main restaurant, but lighter on the wallet.

MONTMARTRE $$

327 7th St. SE, 202/544-1244, www.montmartredc.com
HOURS: Tues.-Thurs. 11:30 A.M.-2:30 P.M. and 5-10 P.M.,
Fri.-Sat. 11:30 A.M.-2:30 P.M. and 5-10:30 P.M.

A neighborhood charmer that offers some of the city's finest French bistro fare, Montmartre is a crowd pleaser, packing in patrons most evenings and on weekends for brunch. Set in a former row house near Eastern Market, the space is cramped and noisy but comfortable, with seating outside during good weather as well as at the bar and amid tightly packed tables in the dining room. Top-sellers include appetizer mussels in a broth of pastis, shallots, and basil; escargots drenched in garlic butter; and house-made country pâté. A favorite entrée, braised rabbit over linguine, never fails to please, its succulent meat served with olives and drizzled with truffle oil. Reservations are recommended for dinner but aren't taken for lunch.

GERMAN
CAFÉ BERLIN $$

322 Massachusetts Ave. NE, 202/543-7656, www.cafeberlindc.com
HOURS: Mon.-Thurs. 11:30 A.M.-10 P.M., Fri.-Sat. 11:30 A.M.-11 P.M., Sun. 10 A.M.-10 P.M.

On a warm summer evening, the sidewalk patio at Café Berlin beckons, drawing patrons with the promise of a half-liter-size boot of beer and German fare. Much of the menu isn't authentic, with choices like a baked brie appetizer and turkey roulade, and the goulash is Hungarian, but there are enough traditional offerings to satisfy a Teutonic craving, including wurst, wiener schnitzel, and *kartoffel pfannkuches* (latkes). The interior decor is circa 1980s, but the setting doesn't stop diners from enjoying their meals, finished with a scrumptious piece of Black Forest cake.

ITALIAN
AQUA AL 2 $$

212 7th St. SE, 202/525-4375, www.acquaal2dc.com
HOURS: Tues.-Sun. 11:30 A.M.-2:30 P.M. and 5:30-11 P.M., Fri.-Sat. 5:30-11:30 P.M., bar Mon.-Fri. 11:30 A.M.-1 A.M.

Known for delicious steaks, Aqua Al 2 (the number is pronounced DOO-eh, as in *due,* "two" in Italian) is a branch of an original in Florence that is popular with Americans. In DC you'll find a restaurant in a former row house that oozes Old World charm, a place that feels nearly more Italian than its Florence counterpart, with mottled yellow walls, exposed brick, and back windows that "overlook" the Arno and the Ponte Vecchio (done in murals). This Aqua Al 2 (there's also one in San Diego's Gaslamp district) also duplicates the original's authentic menu down to the carpaccio di bresaola. Highlights include the signature filet mignon with blueberry glaze, creamy gorgonzola gnocchi, and tender veal with a mushroom wine and garlic sauce.

TRATTORIA ALBERTO $$

506 8th St. SE, 202/544-2007, www.trattoriaalbertodc.com
HOURS: Lunch Mon.-Fri. 11:30 A.M.-2:30 P.M., dinner Mon.-Sun. 5:30-10:30 P.M.

A solid choice for southern Italian cuisine on Barracks Row, this neighborhood restaurant is a comfortable neighborhood hangout, with red-checked tablecloths, a dependable house red, and hearty fare—overstuffed ravioli, creamy fettuccine with pesto, and tasty veal scaloppini. Dining takes place on one of three floors in this converted row house or outdoors when the weather is nice. It's not hip or cool, just comfortable.

MEXICAN AND LATIN
LA PLAZA $

629 Pennsylvania Ave. SE, 202/546-9512
HOURS: Mon.-Fri. 11:30 A.M.-3 P.M. and 5-10:30 P.M., Sat. noon-11 P.M., Sun. noon-10 P.M.

The kitschy decor at neighborhood cantina La Plaza—piñatas dangling from the ceiling, sombreros on the walls—creates a festive mood where the margaritas flow freely and the friendly staff makes everyone feel like a regular. Typical of many Washington "Mexican" restaurants, La Plaza serves a variety of Latin American dishes, including Salvadoran and Tex-Mex as well as Mexican. House specialties include seafood enchiladas, paella, and tamales. Friendly owner-chef Henry Mendoza often travels from table to table, greeting customers and inquiring about the food and the service. Don't be surprised if a free plate of yucca or a round of tequila shots arrives on your table gratis. Such little touches make La Plaza a favorite with Capitol Hill families as well as Hill staffers looking for a place for a relaxing lunch.

TORTILLA COAST $$

400 1st St. SE, 202/546-6768, www.tortillacoast.com
HOURS: Mon.-Wed. 11:30 A.M.-10 P.M., Thurs.-Fri. 11:30 A.M.-11 P.M., Sat. 11:30 A.M.-10 P.M., Sun. 11 A.M.-9 P.M.

Tortilla Coast has been in business nearly 25 years, a somewhat surprising fact given that the food is acceptable but not spectacular. But TC

RESTAURANTS

has two reasons it continues packing 'em in: location, catty-corner from the Capitol South Metro Station, the closest restaurant to the three House office buildings; and booze—its frozen margaritas and sangria swirls are catnip to young Hill staffers. The spacious dining room makes it easy to get a table at lunch or early in the evening. The menu is mainly Tex-Mex, with ground beef and chicken featured prominently as entrée fillings. Nachos and pitchers of frozen margaritas appear to be among the hottest sellers any time of day. Tortilla Coast is a convenient spot for a quick lunch and a great hangout on Thursday and Friday nights for the Hill set.

PUB FARE
DUBLINER PUB $$
520 North Capitol St. NW, 202/737-3773, www.dublinerdc.com

HOURS: Sun.-Thurs. 11 A.M.-1:30 A.M., Fri.-Sat. 11 A.M.-2:30 A.M.

Dependable for a hearty lunch or an after-work pub dinner within crawling distance of Union Station, patrons appreciate Dubliner's

decent tap selection that includes Guinness, Harp, Smithwick's, Kilkenny, and two delicious house brews produced by Old Dominion Brewery. The menu features typical Irish fare, such as a body-warming shepherd's pie and pollack fried to perfection (the fries are less than stellar, though, and are usually mealy). Most of the Dubliner bartenders and waitstaff have melodic Irish accents, and Irish music plays on the sound system all day long, from pennywhistle tunes to ballads by Sinéad O'Connor and the Corrs. Musicians take over a corner of the bar every evening at 9 P.M., playing traditional pub songs. Next door, Kelly's Irish Times, a separate pub unaffiliated with the Dubliner, attracts a rowdier young crowd with its fraternity-party style and American-Irish bar vibe, complete with repeat sing-alongs of "The Unicorn" song.

TUNNICLIFF'S TAVERN $$
222 7th St. SE, 202/544-5680

HOURS: Mon.-Thurs. 11 A.M.-2 A.M., Fri. 11 A.M.-3 A.M., Sat. 10 A.M.-3 A.M., Sun. 10 A.M.-2 A.M.

A popular spot for brunch with weekend

Dubliner Pub, near Union Station, is a convenient after-work dinner spot for locals.

© PATRICIA KIME

Eastern Market shoppers, Tunnicliff's has the feel of an established neighborhood locale even though it opened less than a decade ago. Known for comfort food like mountainous Reuben sandwiches, burgers, gooey grilled cheese stuffed with bacon, pigs in a blanket, and draft beer on tap, Tunnicliff's is a busy, friendly place to kick back and spend an afternoon. On weekends, when Eastern Market comes alive with a farmers market and street vendors, shoppers pack the pub for brunch, featuring crab omelets and farm eggs stuffed with mashed potatoes, cheese, and bacon. It's best to arrive right when it opens; by 11 A.M. the line for the table is out the door.

QUICK BITES
BAGELS & BAGUETTES $
236 Massachusetts Ave. NE, 202/544-1141, www.bnbcafe.net
HOURS: Mon.-Fri. 7 A.M.-4 P.M., Sat.-Sun. 8 A.M.-3 P.M.

If you're searching to fuel up before work or sightseeing, Bagels & Baguettes is a cash-only favorite for breakfast bagels and tasty lunch sandwiches, a small counter that draws neighbors and nearby office workers for its protein-rich egg and cheese bagel sandwiches, lox and cream cheese, or satisfying salads. Seating is limited, but in nice weather the storefront has outdoor seating facing Massachusetts Avenue. Better yet, grab your meal and head to a bench in Stanton Park or the Capital Grounds.

GOOD STUFF EATERY $
303 Pennsylvania Ave. SE, 202/543-8222, www.goodstuffeatery.com
HOURS: Daily 11:30 A.M.-11 P.M.

For the past few years, Washington has been embroiled in a burger war, and Good Stuff Eatery is one of the many combatants. But can there be a clear-cut winner? Preference is a matter of taste, and each contender offers something the others don't. In Good Stuff Eatery's case, it is the mayonnaise bar, with Chesapeake Bay, mango, and Sriracha varieties to slather on fries as well as handspun milk shakes in rich flavors such as Toasted Marshmallow, Milky Way, and Black and White. Patrons often try

Good Stuff to see what former *Top Chef* contestant Spike Mendelsohn offers but they return mainly for the shakes and the variety: In addition to thin burgers piled with toppings, GSE has turkey and vegetarian burgers and traditional as well as inventive wedge salads. It's also one of the few places to find a Southern favorite, the one-eyed bacon cheeseburger ("Sunnyside" on chef Spike's menu), comprising a burger, a fried egg, bacon, cheese, and barbecue sauce—greasy goodness that settles a stomach roiling from a night of partying.

MARKET LUNCH $$
225 7th St. SE, 202/547-8444
HOURS: Wed.-Fri. 7:30 A.M.-2:30 P.M., Sat. 8 A.M.-3 P.M., Sun. 9 A.M.-3 P.M.

There's a reason this cash-only stand in Eastern Market makes it into all the guidebooks. Locals really, really like it. We wait in line on Saturday mornings for a heaping plate of blueberry buckwheat pancakes or sneak in before closing for a gargantuan, nearly breadless crab cake or zingy fried green tomatoes served with a side of tart rémoulade. Market Lunch serves plate-licking Southern food quickly, if not cheaply, alongside a cup of sweet tea or lemonade, to be eaten at the 30-seat-long market table. Prices might seem steep for a counter joint, but the food speaks for itself. Not a fan of fried oysters or crab soup? The North Carolina barbecue sandwich is eastern Carolina perfection; a bite of the zesty vinegar pork is guaranteed to induce homesickness in a Tar Heel.

TAQUERIA NACIONAL $
400 North Capitol St. NW, 202/737-7070, www.taquerianacional.com
HOURS: Mon.-Fri. 7:30 A.M.-3 P.M.

This takeout joint near Union Station has simple meat, onions, and cilantro tacos. Try the chorizo and cheese or the shredded carnitas with a side of fried yucca and an *agua fresca*. On a sunny day, sidling up to the counter and taking your lunch to a nearby park—the Japanese American Memorial is just across the way—beats heading inside to the mammoth food court inside Union Station.

UNION STATION FOOD COURT $

50 Massachusetts Ave. NE, 202/289-1908,
www.unionstationdc.com

HOURS: Mon.-Sat. 7 A.M.-9 P.M., Sun. 7 A.M.-6 P.M.

This food court rates mentioning for its convenience, selection, and sheer size, a white-tiled cavern beneath the station's Main Concourse that spans the length of nearly two football fields placed end-to-end. Seating is plentiful in this vast basement, and dining choices are ample, from a self-contained sushi bar to Cajun, barbecue, Jamaican, Italian, and more. Vittorio's Gelato Bar offers sweet treats, and the usual suspects are here as well, including Subway and Taco Bell.

SEAFOOD

JOHNNY'S HALF SHELL $$$

400 North Capitol St. NW, 202/737-0400,
www.johnnyshalfshell.net

HOURS: Mon.-Fri. 7-9:30 A.M., 11:30 A.M.-2:30 P.M., and 4:30-10 P.M., Sat. 5-10 P.M.

Cocktails flow freely from morning until closing time at Johnny's Half Shell, a seafood house on the Capitol's Senate side that brings the atmosphere and menu of the Big Easy to Washington. Politicos and media execs love Johnny's, which features retro octagonal tile floors, a lively bar, friendly waitstaff, and at peak hours, a clamorous crowd. Piano music floats through the dining room at lunch, and live jazz energizes the joint on weekends. The menu leans heavily toward southern Louisiana's creole and Cajun styles, with a dash of Chesapeake Bay thrown in. Popular eats include creamy étouffée, crab cakes (heavy on the crab, light on any filling), and barbecue crabs in season. This is the go-to place for anyone in DC craving an authentic po'boy; chef-owner Ann Cashion flies in the real deal's key ingredient, the crusty, airy, never-duplicated French bread, from Leidenheimer Baking Company in New Orleans and serves them with fried shrimp, oysters, or brisket with debris.

STEAK

◖ CHARLIE PALMER STEAK $$$

101 Constitution Ave. NW, 202/547-8100

HOURS: Mon.-Fri. 11:30 A.M.-2:30 P.M. and 5:30-10 P.M., Sat. 5-10:30 P.M.

Offering power dining at extravagant prices in the shadow of the Capitol Dome, Charlie

Johnny's Half Shell is a favorite for lunch and dinner.

© PATRICIA KIME

Palmer is a haven for Washington VIPs and diners living on an expense account. Do senators, representatives, or celebrities eat like this every day? Dry-aged thick-cut steaks, cooked to perfection, are the draw, and the iced shellfish platter of lobster, shrimp, king crab, and oysters never fails to impress. The wine list, exclusively American with at least one selection from each state, is handed to customers on an electronic wine book; sommeliers can help diners choose from one of the dozen offered by the glass, from the 3,500 bottles in the restaurant's snazzy wine cube (a cooler that appears to float above a fountain), or one of the 7,500 additional bottles stored elsewhere on the premises. If you're saving a special bottle for an occasion, the restaurant waives the corkage fee as long as the bottle you've brought is American. Washington has no shortage in the steak house genre; Charlie Palmer, with its high ceilings, aqua and steel interior, and modern design bears a chophouse menu without the clubhouse feel.

Dupont Circle

Map 6

AMERICAN
LUNA GRILL 🟢🟢
1301 Connecticut Ave., 202/835-2280,
www.lunagrillanddiner.com
HOURS: Sun.-Thurs. 8 A.M.-11 P.M.,
Fri.-Sun. 8 A.M.-midnight

Because every meal doesn't have to break the bank or be an over-the-top experience, Luna Grill wins accolades for its simple diner fare in a neighborhood not known for understatement. With Reuben sandwiches, all-day breakfast, nachos, sweet potato fries, hamburgers, and root beer floats on the menu, there's something for everyone to like—except the lines, which are especially long on weekend mornings.

ASIAN
RAKU 🟢
1900 Q St. NW, 202/265-7258,
www.rakuasiandining.com
HOURS: Sun.-Thurs. 5-9:30 P.M., Fri.-Sat. 5-10:30 P.M.

An affordable place to grab a bite to eat before heading to a movie or hitting up the Dupont Circle First Fridays at area galleries, Raku serves sushi and a number of Asian dishes, including pad thai and *kway teow,* Singaporean curry noodles, dumplings, and tuna tartare. If it seems that the menu is diverse, Raku calls itself an Asian diner, with something on the menu to suit any Asian yen. Decorated in touches of rich oranges and reds, Raku is usually noisy and bustling, perfect for its location within view of happening Dupont Circle.

CONTEMPORARY AMERICAN
KRAMERBOOKS & AFTERWORDS CAFÉ 🟢🟢
1517 Connecticut Ave., 202/387-3825,
www.kramers.com
HOURS: Sun-Thurs. 7:30 A.M.-1 A.M., Fri.-Sat. 24 hours

There's a novelty to eating in a bookstore, especially one that's open 24 hours on weekends. Kramerbooks & Afterwords Café is a Dupont Circle staple, established the year of the Bicentennial. The "café" is actually a full-service restaurant, dishing out omelets, French toast, and steak and eggs in the morning; salads, filet mignon, and duck tacos for lunch; and grilled leg of lamb, pan-seared scallops, or lobster ravioli in the evening. The live music Wednesday through Saturday completes the experience. The place claims to be disabled accessible, but be aware that people in wheelchairs or those who have difficulty using stairs have trouble navigating this space.

RESTAURANT NORA 🟢🟢🟢
2312 Florida Ave. NW, 202/462-5143, www.noras.com
HOURS: Mon.-Thurs. 5-10 P.M., Fri.-Sat. 5:30-10 P.M.

A pioneer in the DC organic and locally-sourced-ingredient restaurant scene, Restaurant

RESTAURANTS

© PATRICIA KIME

Restaurant Nora, Washington's first certified organic restaurant

Nora claims to be the first certified organic restaurant in the United States, which leads one to wonder exactly what that means. It turns out that in 1999, the Oregon Tilth, one of six private organic certifiers in the country, bequeathed the title on Restaurant Nora after it developed a set of strict criteria. For diners at Nora, this means that 95 percent or more of everything consumed in the restaurant has been produced by organic farmers and devotees of sustainable agriculture. Naturally, healthy eater First Lady Michelle Obama chose it as the venue to celebrate her 46th birthday. Restaurant Nora is housed in a beautiful 19th-century corner shop that was once a grocery store. Its menu varies with the seasons but offers a variety of dishes—wild salmon with asparagus, garlic kale and a light chive hollandaise, herbed goat cheese, and leek-stuffed chicken breast with crispy artichokes. Some things may not appeal to everyone—stewed dandelion is one that comes to mind, but maybe that's just because of a memory of my mom cooking those embarrassingly pungent greens for me to take to

a fourth-grade ethnic-fare potluck. Who knew Mom was so cutting-edge?

TABARD INN 🪙🪙🪙

1739 N St. NW, 202/331-8528, www.tabardinn.com
HOURS: Breakfast Mon.-Fri. 7-10 A.M., Sat. 8-9:45 A.M., Sun. 8-9:15 A.M., brunch Sat. 11 A.M.-2:30 P.M., Sun. 10:30 A.M.-2:30 P.M., lunch Mon.-Fri. 11:30 A.M.-2:30 P.M., dinner Sun.-Thurs. 6-9:30 P.M., Fri.-Sat. 6-10 P.M.

The Tabard Inn is best known in DC for its weekend brunch, where area residents flock for fresh homemade doughnuts and the poached eggs. But it's also a nice dinner find, a cozy restaurant in one of DC's oldest hotels that features quality contemporary American cuisine and a nice lounge area, often hosting live music alongside its crackling fireplace. Outstanding menu choices include the charcuterie, gnocchi with wild mushrooms and pine nuts, and broiled sea bass with cauliflower flan and bok choy. Try one of bartender Chantal Tseng's delicious concoctions, which include a Mark Twain (scotch, lemon, simple syrup, and bitters) or, after dinner, an Aperitivo Italo-Franco (Prosecco, elderflower liqueur, grapefruit peel, and Cocchi Americano).

FRENCH
BISTROT DU COIN 🪙🪙

1738 Connecticut Ave. NW, 202/234-6969, www.bistrotducoin.com
HOURS: Mon.-Wed. 11:30 A.M.-11 P.M., Thurs.-Fri. 11:30 A.M.-1 A.M., Sat. 11 A.M.-1 A.M., Sun. 11 A.M.-11 P.M.

Bistrot Du Coin is that neighborhood place to go for house wine, dependable French fare, and a lively atmosphere. It is a charming establishment for a bistro that has only been around since 2000, with warm yellow walls, a huge mirrored bar back, a zinc-topped bar, and friendly patrons enjoying the hubbub. The best dishes are those you'd find in a Paris neighborhood café: a salad of grilled scallions and duck-gizzard confit, escargots, onion soup, and daily specials that range from classic ratatouille to a juicy T-bone steak with fries. A glass of Veuve Clicquot (yellow label) is still just $10 per glass; the remainder of the wine list is, naturally, completely French.

GOING GREEN IN DC

So many of the city's restaurants use locally sourced ingredients that there are too many to list. A few, however, take their eco-consciousness to another level, pledging to use either 100 percent organic ingredients, biodegradable cleaning products and supplies, or give portions of their proceeds to environmental causes. These eating spots take their commitment to Mother Earth seriously:

The queen of the DC organic dining scene, **Restaurant Nora** has served eco-friendly meals since it first opened in 1979. Certified as an organic restaurant 20 years later, Nora's menu consists of nearly 100 percent certified organic ingredients. Owner Nora Pouillon sits on a number of environmental boards, including the Amazon Conservation Team, Fresh Farm Markets, and the Environmental Film Festival.

The Four Seasons grows its own herbs, vegetables, and leafy greens in a pocket garden on its property along the C&O Canal for its popular steakhouse, **Bourbon Steak.** In 1999, chef Michael Mina oversaw the effort to bring in 400 plants from an Amish farm to start the beds that are cultivated using organic methods. What Mina can't grow himself he brings in from organic and Amish farms, including meats, fruits, and other ingredients.

In the super-trendy, super-crowded environment of **Founding Farmers,** it's easy to question just how "green" this restaurant is. But it is owned by a farmers' collective, is housed in a LEED Gold-Certified building, and is Green Restaurant certified, committed to using sustainably farmed and organically grown ingredients.

High-end seafood house **Hook** and its less-expensive sibling **Tackle Box** both promote restaurateur Jonathan Umbel's commitment to sustainable seafood. They strive to use locally grown ingredients and humanely raised meat and dairy products. Best of all, dining at one of these two establishments helps the environment, if just a little bit: Hook and Tackle Box donate generously to several ocean and water conservation organizations.

RESTAURANTS

ITALIAN
OBELISK $$$

2029 P St. NW, 202/872-1180

HOURS: Tues.-Sat. 6-10 P.M.

There's no sign in front of the unassuming row house that contains Obelisk, a 30-seat restaurant that serves creative Italian fare by chef Peter Pastan. Apparently, it fell down, and Pastan decided not to replace it. You know you are in the right place because there's a small obelisk cutout on the side of the building as well as a menu on display. And once you step inside, you're likely to feel like you're in someone's living room. If you're not quite convinced that this is where you want to spend your money, concerns should be assuaged by the first plate, a creamy cheese served with olive oil, salt, and pepper. Continue with the four-course prix fixe dinner and several antipasti offerings before moving on to several simply prepared, delicious courses. Dishes might include pickled anchovy and pork belly, duck ragout and pasta, boar chop, duck breast with rapini, or black bass with olive relish.

MEDITERRANEAN
KOMI $$$

1509 17th St. NW, 202/332-9200, www.komirestaurant.com

HOURS: Tues.-Sat. 5:30-9:30 P.M.

Komi has stayed at the top of favorite local magazine *Washingtonian*'s "100 Very Best Restaurants" lists since 2009—no small feat for a restaurant that opened less than a decade ago. Why has it earned such high praise? Consistency, a memorable dining experience, passion, and "energy," writes magazine food critic Todd Kliman. "Does the place deliver what it promises, and does it attain all it reaches for?" asks Kliman. Reviews say it does. At Komi, there are only 12 tables. There aren't any menus; the only decision a patron has to make is whether to get the wine pairing. Chef Johnny Monis sets a nightly menu based on Greek and Mediterranean dishes. Dinner is an event, with plates of mezes, delivered in intervals, starting out the experience and moving through to succulent meats and fish, perhaps a roasted baby pig or goat for two, and scallops dabbed with black truffle and dill.

ZORBA'S CAFÉ ⑤⑤
1612 20th St. NW, 202/387-8555, www.zorbascafe.com
HOURS: Mon.-Sat. 11 A.M.-11:30 P.M., Sun. 11 A.M.-10:30 P.M.
Zorba's has no waitstaff. Patrons order at the kitchen and then stand and wait for their food while another member of their party goes and finds a table on one of two levels or, in the summer, outside. It has no frills but is not short on flavor. The menu is standard Greek fare: souvlaki, gyros, roast leg of lamb, and kebabs, but with a variety of vegetarian options. The Greek-fire feta spread is among the popular appetizers, and the *taramosalata,* a dip made of roe, lemon juice, and olive oil, is delicious with piping hot pita.

QUICK BITES
BGR THE BURGER JOINT ⑤
1514 Connecticut Ave. NW, 202/299-1071,
www.bgrtheburgerjoint.com
HOURS: Sun.-Thurs. 11 A.M.-10 P.M., Fri.-Sat. 11 A.M.-11 P.M.
The decor in BGR The Burger Joint is pure nostalgia for those of us who are products of the 1980s and retro-cool for the current generation of adolescents who have come to appreciate that era and its music. Album covers on the walls reflect what may or may not be playing loudly over the stereo—Prince, U2, Journey, AC/DC, the Cars—and neat mosaic tables evoke memories of simple elementary school days, Nestlé Quik, and the MTV logo. The Lee Highway, Virginia, location even has a *Partridge Family* lunchbox. But enough about the atmosphere. BGR is about burgers: huge six-ouncers cooked to order on buttery brioche buns brought in from Philadelphia. The meat is hormone-free aged prime beef, big thick patties like you'd make at home if you were grilling. Toppings include thick

slabs of onion and tomato, lettuce, pickles, optional cheese or apple-wood smoked bacon, and something called "mojo sauce," BGR's twist on Thousand Island dressing. Not in the mood for ground beef? BGR also has vegetarian and turkey burgers on the menu as well as Cuban sandwiches.

MR. YOGATO ⑤
1515 17th St. NW, 202/629-3531, www.mryogato.com
HOURS: Sun.-Thurs. noon-11 P.M., Fri.-Sat. noon-1 A.M.
Making customers happy like kids in a candy store, Mr. Yogato is a top choice for frozen yogurt in DC because of its selection, quality, and the absurd little games you can play to earn a discount. You can get 10 percent off for stamping your forehead with their information, 5 percent for ordering in a funny voice, or 5 percent for answering a trivia question incorrectly. There's a spot to read books and play Nintendo and board games. But what about the yogurt? It comes in two styles: original soft, the sweeter of the two, and original tangy, in numerous flavors with a selection of 45 toppings to choose from.

SEAFOOD
HANK'S OYSTER BAR ⑤⑤
1624 Q St. NW, 202/462-4265, www.hanksdc.com
HOURS: Sun.-Tues. 5:30-10 P.M.,
Wed.-Thurs. 5:30-11 P.M., Fri.-Sat. 5:30 P.M.-midnight,
brunch Sat.-Sun. 11 A.M.-3 P.M.
Hank's Oyster Bar is the place Washingtonians go to get their fill of briny bivalves without breaking the bank. The joint's blackboards always have at least five kinds of oysters advertised, and the menu also contains a number of Northern coast dishes—lobster rolls and fried clams—in addition to some Southern recipes such as collards and fried chicken on some days. Among the choice items here are sake oyster shooters, fried shrimp and calamari, and an oyster po'boy. Hank's sponsors a particularly budget-friendly happy hour Sunday through Friday with raw oysters on the half shell for $1 each. Reservations are more like a waiting list; you can call ahead to let them know you are coming, but you'll still have to wait.

Adams Morgan and U Street Map 7

AMERICAN
BEN'S CHILI BOWL $

1213 U St. NW, 202/667-0909, www.benschilibowl.com
HOURS: Mon.-Thurs. 6 A.M.-10:45 P.M., Fri. 6 A.M.-4 A.M.,
Sat. 7 A.M.-4 A.M., Sun. 11 A.M.-11 P.M.

The sign on the fridge behind the register reads: "The only people who eat free at Ben's are the Obamas and Bill Cosby. Everyone else pays." At Ben's Chili Bowl, this is just plain good business sense. With the endless stream of city politicians, government VIPs, and celebrities that line up for a half-smoke at this DC institution, Ben's has to protect its bottom line. Ben's was founded by DC residents Ben and Virginia Ali in 1958 at its present location in the then-hopping neighborhood known as "Black Broadway," a corridor of jazz clubs, restaurants, and nightspots where luminaries like Ella Fitzgerald, Cab Calloway, and Duke Ellington hung out. This all changed in 1968, when Martin Luther King Jr. was killed and the businesses along U Street and much of the city were torched during days-long riots. Ben's

managed to stay open, serving the firefighters, activists, and police officers working to save the city. For the next 20 years, Ben's saw the neighborhood struggle with poverty, drugs, and a paralyzed city structure. It became a place where few would venture. Enter Bill Cosby in 1985. Ben's had been a personal favorite since he had courted his wife here, and he held a press conference at Ben's to announce that his show was the top TV sitcom in the country. Things began looking up, even as construction of the Metro line ripped up the streets and changed the surrounding neighborhood. Today, Ben's is not just a great place to grab lunch or a late-night snack, it is a symbol of the spirit of African American entrepreneurship and of the human character in general. Sure, this is a lofty assignation for a mere restaurant, but Ben's deserves this high praise as well as the countless awards it has received over the years. Regarding the food, Ben's seriously does have the best chili-cheese fries and half-smokes—chunky, spicy sausages—in town. Ben's has

RESTAURANTS

© PATRICIA KIME

Ben's Chili Bowl is warm and friendly.

long lines and is cash-only, so come prepared. But with the friendly service, hip-hop beat, messy meals, social line-standers, and vintage 1950s decor, you'll find it worth the wait.

BUSBOYS AND POETS $

2021 14th St. NW, 202/387-7638,
www.busboysandpoets.com
HOURS: Mon.-Thurs. 8 A.M.-midnight, Fri. 8 A.M.-2 A.M.,
Sat. 9 A.M.-2 A.M., Sun. 9 A.M.-midnight

Bookstore, coffeehouse, and poetry-reading venue, Busboys and Poets is a DC original, a place where locals can go for progressive (read "Blue State") literature and books; listen to readings, music, or whatever happens to be going on during open-mike night; and grab a bite to eat. The cuisine is simple and considered affordable in this pricey restaurant city: pizzas for less than $12; a huge made-to-order hamburger of locally farmed beef for $12; and a heaping plate of fried catfish with collards and lemon caper sauce for $16. Some events like staged readings and slam poetry have a cover charge, and others are free. Check out the website for details. Browsing the books, however, is always free. Proceeds benefit the nonprofit Teaching for Change.

THE DINER $

2453 18th St. NW, 202/232-8800, www.dinerdc.com
HOURS: Daily 24 hours

The Diner is one of those places where you go for a simple meal and end up leaving full, happy, and surprised by the check, which will be pretty low compared to many in this city given the quality of food you just consumed. The only bad thing about the Diner is that it is not a secret; hence the wait for a table can be fairly long on a weekend morning. Fans love the Croque and Dagger, a breakfast twist on a *croque-madame* made with two eggs, bacon, and béchamel on French bread and topped with gooey

Busboys and Poets

gruyère; the Irish Benedict, which swaps out corned beef hash as the main meat; and the fresh homemade pies and the inventive milk shakes, including frozen adult libations like mint liqueur and chocolate. Morning people can avoid lines by getting there by 8 A.M. on weekends.

CONTEMPORARY AMERICAN
CASHION'S EAT PLACE ⑤⑤
1819 Columbia Rd. NW, 202/797-1819, www.cashionseatplace.com
HOURS: Tues. 5:30-10 P.M., Wed.-Sat. 5:30-11 P.M., Sun. 11:30 A.M.-2:30 P.M. and 5:30-10 P.M.

Original owner Ann Cashion, co-owner of Johnny's Half Shell on Capitol Hill, opened Cashion's in 1995 with the goal of creating a friendly neighborhood eatery that serves anything-but-ordinary cuisine. Today, chef John Manolatos has kept that goal, adding a few dishes that hint at his own Greek ancestry but preserving an overall menu of contemporary American with subtle Southern touches and keeping the funky decor, which features family photos of the restaurant's employees as well as reclaimed windows and drapes. Recent popular menu choices include a goose egg with ramp appetizer, bison hanger steak served with spicy kale, and spit-roasted goat. Cashion's is a popular local brunch spot as well, featuring a filling array of breakfast and lunch choices.

PERRY'S ⑤⑤
1811 Columbia Rd. NW, 202/234-6218, www.perrysadamsmorgan.com
HOURS: Sun.-Thurs. 5:30-10:30 P.M., Fri.-Sat. 5:30-11:30 P.M., Sat. 11 A.M.-3 P.M., brunch Sun. 10 A.M.-2:30 P.M.

Drag queen brunch: Yes, Perry's is open for dinner and lunch on other days, but most locals know it for its Sunday experience, a full spread of brunch items and a sassy drag show, held twice during the day at 10:30 A.M. and 12:30 P.M. Reservations are not taken, so patrons begin lining up around 9 A.M. to get a table for one of the shows, which is a blend of comedy, lip-synching, and sexual harassment

at its playful best. The buffet is largely typical buffet fare—eggs and breakfast meats, waffles, salads, seafood, and chicken, with some Asian dishes thrown in (Perry's primarily is a seafood and sushi place the rest of the week) along with desserts and pastries. Bring some $1 bills if you'd like to be a part of the comedic action; most people tip the queens regardless. Every other day of the week, Perry's boasts the largest open-air dining room in the neighborhood.

ETHIOPIAN
ETETE ⑤⑤
1942 9th St. NW, 202/232-7600, www.eteterestaurant.com
HOURS: Daily 11 A.M.-1 A.M.

Washington DC is home to one of the country's largest Ethiopian populations, and the city benefits in many ways, not least of which is having several fine Ethiopian restaurants, including Etete, a family-run operation that serves traditional fare at relatively inexpensive prices. The dining room is cozy if crowded in the evenings, and the chairs are very (almost too) close together, but this adds a dash of authenticity to the experience. Lamb, beef, chicken, and vegetarian dishes are served in groups on a platter lined with *injera,* the tangy flatbread that doubles as a utensil (don't expect forks and knives). *Doro wat,* chicken in red-pepper paste, is the country's national dish and tops the menu at Etete, but if you aren't afraid to eat raw meat, the *kitfo,* a spicy steak tartare, outshines it on the menu.

MEXICAN
LAURIOL PLAZA ⑤⑤
1835 18th St. NW, 202/387-0035, www.lauriolplaza.com
HOURS: Mon.-Thurs. 11:30 A.M.-11 P.M., Fri.-Sat. 11:30 A.M.-midnight, Sun. 11 A.M.-11 P.M.

Locals pack Lauriol Plaza for tasty pitchers of strong margaritas and the cuisine, which, like nearly every "Mexican" restaurant in DC, includes Peruvian and El Salvadoran dishes. The interior is light and airy, a two-story restaurant

DANIEL LOBO – DAQUELLAMANERA.ORG

Lauriol Plaza is popular with locals craving Mexican favorites.

with large windows and an outdoor patio. Enchiladas, fajitas, and chiles rellenos are on the "Mexican favorites" menu; more adventurous choices can be found under "oven and sautéed dishes": Cuban pork marinated and roasted with oranges or lamb with peppers, tomatoes, and potatoes.

QUICK BITES
FAST GOURMET $
1400 W St. NW, 202/448–9217
HOURS: Mon.-Thurs. 11 A.M.-11 P.M., Fri.-Sat. 11 A.M.-3 A.M., Sun. 11 A.M.-10 P.M.

Just south of DC along small country roads, travelers will find an unusual genre of eatery—the gas station restaurant. They usually have great names like "Gas-n-Stuff," "Gas-n-Grits," "Pump-n-Munch," or "Mr. Gas Food Mart." Fast Gourmet doesn't have a similarly memorable moniker, but it does bring this unique type of takeout counter to DC in a place called a "Lowest Price" gas station. Past the cashier is a takeout spot that serves up some of DC's tastiest sandwiches, wraps, and salads.

And this being the Adams Morgan–U Street area, the menu is ripe with international flavors. There's a Cuban sandwich stuffed with shredded pork butt, a pita that overflows with falafel, hummus, and cucumbers, a yellowfin tuna sandwich with caper mayonnaise, lamb wraps, and more. Side dishes reflect the owners' Uruguayan heritage: fried plantains and fried yucca.

JULIA'S EMPANADAS $
2452 18th St. NW, 202/789-1641,
www.juliasempanadas.com
HOURS: Mon.-Thurs. 10 A.M.-2 A.M., Fri.-Sat. 10 A.M.-4 A.M.

Hot pocket sandwiches stuffed with hearty fillings like beef, chorizo, chicken, turkey, black beans, and potatoes hit the spot after a long night in the bars in Adams Morgan. The owner hails from Chile, but the empanadas are based on recipes from across the Americas, including a Jamaican one with a hint of curry. The dessert empanadas, little pies stuffed with apples, pears, or blueberries, satisfy a sweet tooth as well.

JUMBO SLICE $

2341 18th St. NW, 202/234-2200

HOURS: Daily 11 A.M.-4 A.M.

The Jumbo Slice is more than 1,000 calories of bread, cheese, oil, and tomato sauce that soaks up all the alcohol imbibed over the course of the night in Adams Morgan. This piece of pizza is basically a pizza in itself, only conquered by folding it over and eating it while leaning over so as not to spill gooey cheese or grease all over your clothes. While $5 for a slice of pizza might seem pricey, when you consider that it takes two paper plates to hold this wedge that's larger than your head, it makes sense. Should the line be too long, simply go next door to Pizza Mart (2445 18th St.), owned by the brother of Jumbo Slice's proprietor and serving the same mammoth pieces.

TRYST $

2459 18th St. NW, 202/232-5500, www.trystdc.com

HOURS: Mon.-Wed. 6:30 A.M.-midnight, Thurs. 6:30 A.M.-2 A.M., Fri.-Sat. 6:30 A.M.-3 A.M., Sun. 7 A.M.-midnight

Tryst is like something from the set of *Friends*, with comfy couches, tables for lingering over espresso, and plush velvet armchairs. But in addition to the usual coffee drinks, you can also get food—muffins, sandwiches, salads, croissants, or a baguette topped with *lebneh* yogurt spread, olive oil, mint, cucumber, and tomato—and even a cocktail. Tryst wants its customers to stay for a while, sip their coffee or cocktail, and relax. It's meant to be like home, only with pretty designs crafted into the cappuccino foam.

Georgetown   Map 8

BREAKFAST

CAFÉ TU-O-TU $

2816 Pennsylvania Ave. NW, 202/298-7777, www.cafetuotu.com

HOURS: Mon.-Fri. 9 A.M.-7 P.M., Sat. 10 A.M.-7 P.M., Sun. 10 A.M.-6 P.M.

Café Tu-O-Tu (the name is a play on the city's area code) serves Mediterranean-inspired sandwiches, salads, and paninis in a row house that looks tiny but actually manages to seat 40 people. Breakfast items hit the spot if you're looking to charge yourself for a busy day. A smoked turkey, provolone, and egg sandwich on a croissant packs a protein punch, and the Mediterranean breakfast, with feta, olives, smoked turkey, cucumbers, and baguette, is a plate right out of owner Miro Sarano's native Turkey. For lunch, salads and paninis shine.

SEASONS $$$

2800 Pennsylvania Ave. NW, 202/342-0444, www.fourseasons.com

HOURS: Mon.-Fri. 6:30-10:30 A.M., Sat.-Sun. 7 A.M.-10:30 P.M., brunch Sun. 10:30 A.M.-2:30 P.M.

Breakfast at Seasons can only be described as luxurious: attentive but unobtrusive service, fine linens, silver and china, perfectly brewed coffee, fresh-squeezed juices, impeccably prepared eggs, frittatas, waffles, and truffle skillets. Favored by the diplomatic crowd and Washington power brokers as well as a stream of regulars, the tables at Seasons are set far apart in the airy, light-filled dining room, allowing for discreet conversations or a quiet, contemplative meal. In terms of choices, the lemon ricotta pancakes have been a bestseller since the restaurant opened; the smoked salmon Benedict and Mediterranean egg-white omelet also rank among the top-sellers. Daily diners can spend their morning reading one of 80 newspapers on a complimentary loaner Kindle. Sunday brunch is an event, a feast of divine offerings: a seafood bar overflowing with crab claws, oysters, shrimp, seviche, and three kinds of salmon along with carving stations and rack of lamb, cheese and fruit sections, vegetables, and meat dishes. An entire room holds desserts.

RESTAURANTS

CONTEMPORARY AMERICAN

◖ OLD GLORY BAR-B-QUE $$

3939 M St. NW, 202/337-3406, www.oldglorybbq.com

HOURS: Mon.-Thurs. 11:30 A.M.-2 A.M.,
Fri.-Sat. 11:30 A.M.-3 A.M., Sun. 11 A.M.-2 A.M.,
brunch Sun. 11 A.M.-3 P.M.

The decor is theme-park barbecue restaurant—red-checked tablecloths, a 1959 Chevy bumper hanging over the door, country-primitive versions of the Stars and Stripes everywhere, and cocktails served in mason jars—but this makes Old Glory a great place to take the kids or go with a group that likes to roll up their sleeves and tackle a rack of ribs or a giant pulled pork sandwich. A basket of biscuits and cornbread arrives with the drinks, served with honey-peach butter that will entice you into swabbing out the butter dishes' remnants with a piece of bread or your finger. The menu features a combination of regional barbecues, Texas brisket, North Carolina pulled pork, chicken, and St. Louis ribs, served with a choice of sauces and sides. Don't expect to have the world's best 'cue (after all, Old Glory lacks the requisite outrageous neon sign, nor it is it a shack off in the woods near Tuscaloosa, Alabama), but go hungry because the portions are large, and be willing to try all the sauces and maybe one of the 82 bourbons on offer.

◖ SEQUOIA $$$

3000 K St. NW, 202/944-4200,
www.arkrestaurants.com/sequoia_dc.html

HOURS: Mon.-Thurs. 11:30 A.M.-11 P.M.,
Fri.-Sat. 11:30 A.M.-midnight, Sun. 4-11 P.M.,
brunch Sun. 10:30 A.M.-3 P.M.

People don't actually go to Sequoia for the food; they go for the views and the atmosphere, the stunning floor-to-ceiling windows that look out over the Potomac River, and in the summer months, the three-level outdoor patio where young Washingtonians party late into the evening. Named for the former presidential yacht parked just down the river, Sequoia is a gathering place for fun. Get there early for a table, and dress well if you plan to stay late; otherwise, go for a cocktail and appetizer to enjoy the experience, which in the

summertime includes watching boaters spark up their own happy hours berthed alongside one another in the river, and then head elsewhere in Georgetown for a decent meal.

◖ 1789 $$$

1226 36th St. NW, 202/965-1789,
www.1789restaurant.com

HOURS: Mon.-Thurs. 6-10 P.M., Fri. 6-11 P.M.,
Sat. 5:30-11 P.M., Sun. 5:30-10 P.M.

If a restaurant has survived in Washington since the 1960s, it has earned the title "institution," and 1789 is one of the few venerable dining spots able to claim that honor. Its name refers to the date the city of Washington incorporated Georgetown and the year the archbishop purchased the land for the university. Occupying a Federal-style row built in the mid 1800s, for years 1789 has drawn couples young and old, celebrants, parents taking their Georgetown students out for a special meal, and wedding parties. The restaurant is separated into rooms that each have a distinct decor, but all are cozy spaces, with fireplaces, gas lamps, candlelight, exposed beams, and fine linens. Managed by Clyde's Restaurant Group, the menu has managed to stay relevant in a city replete with new dining options. Young chef Daniel Giusti has added his stamp to the traditional menu, including sourcing the ingredients and adding selections like venison loin with sweet potatoes and crispy skate to a menu known mainly for its tenderloin and leg of lamb. The formal service is friendly and not overbearing. Jackets are required for men, a fact that is usually discretely mentioned while making the reservations.

FRENCH

BISTRO FRANÇAIS $$

3124 M St. NW, 202/338-3830,
www.bistrofrancaisdc.com

HOURS: Mon.-Thurs. and Sun. 11 A.M.-3 A.M.,
Fri.-Sat. 11 A.M.-4 A.M.

One of M Street's most enduring eateries, Bistro Français offers daily specials, an early bird price break, and the latest hours of any full-service restaurant in Georgetown, helping bring in patrons to sit elbow-to-elbow at the tables crowded into this brass and glass bistro to dine on French fare, trying not to overhear their neighbors' conversations (nearly impossible). For $24.95 the early bird special, available 5–7 P.M. and 10:30 P.M.–1 A.M., is a deal in the city—a glass of wine; soup du jour or appetizer, such as mussels or liver mousse; choice on entrée; and a pastry to top it off. The menu features minimally prepared dishes, including steak frites, steak au poivre, coq au vin, and Dover sole. Late in the evening, Bistro Français becomes a destination for hungry barflies and chefs who have closed their own places elsewhere.

CITRONELLE ⓈⓈⓈ

3000 M St. NW, 202/625-2150, www.citronelledc.com
HOURS: Mon.-Thurs. 6-10 P.M., Fri.-Sat. 6-10:30 P.M.

Chef Michel Richard's flagship restaurant, Citronelle, is one of the city's world-renowned restaurants and winner of numerous awards, including twice being named to *Gourmet* magazine's Top 20 Restaurants in the Country and also earning the Best Fine Dining Restaurant of the Year in DC in 2002. Several chefs in the city have been named to the James Beard Foundation's Who's Who in American Food and Wine; Richard received his honors way back in 1988, landing in DC in 1994 with Citronelle after opening a version at the Santa Barbara Inn in California. But enough of the backstory: What is it about Citronelle that makes it so special? It's a triple threat: an atmosphere that sets the stage for an event meal, flawless service, and creative presentation of artfully prepared ingredients. As with Richard's other restaurants, the menu is imbued with the chef's sense of humor: an "egg" symphony that doesn't contain any eggs, and the tartare is served resembling stained glass. The preparations are surprising yet classically prepared. If you are lucky enough to be here on a night when Richard is here, consider ordering off-menu, asking for the chef to decide. True foodies should also consider reserving a place at the chef's table. Starting at $350 per person, guests enjoy a food-and-wine pairing at a table inside Richard's exhibition kitchen, the chance to interact with Richard in planning, preparing, and enjoying a menu. Call for details. For a less expensive way to enjoy Richard's creations, head to the lounge. Jackets are required for men.

© PATRICIA KIME

Michel Richard's Citronelle

MIDDLE EASTERN
CAFÉ DIVAN ❸❸

1834 Wisconsin Ave., 202/338-1747,
www.cafedivan.com

HOURS: Mon.-Thurs. 11 A.M.-10:30 P.M.,
Fri.-Sat. 11 A.M.-11 P.M., Sun. 11 A.M.-10 P.M.

Directly across from Georgetown's "Social
Safeway" (so nicknamed because young singles have been finding dates over the produce
since at least the early 1980s), Café Divan is a
Turkish delight with a menu full of tasty kebabs and, on Thursday nights only, spicy rotisserie lamb cooked over an open wood fire
and served on a bed of rice, spring onions, and
scrumptious yogurt sauce. The space is notably
unusual, a trapezoidal dining room with modern minimalist decoration. Start with the meze
platter and a glass of house wine; if you are
not lucky enough to be there on a Thursday,
the Iskendar kebab, marinated lamb and veal
shaved over toasted pita and served with roasted
tomatoes, makes a satisfying meal.

PIZZA
❿ PIZZERIA PARADISO ❸❸

3282 M St. NW, 202/337-1245, www.eatyourpizza.com

HOURS: Mon.-Thurs. 11:30 A.M.-11 P.M.,
Fri.-Sat. 11:30 A.M.-midnight, Sun. noon-10 P.M.

Wood-fired Neapolitan pies make up the bulk of
the menu at Pizzeria Paradiso, which fills daily
with hungry diners seeking some of the city's finest pizza. The crust is crispy yet chewy, and the
topping selection is vast, with a variety of vegetable toppings not found at other pizza places,
including eggplant, roasted garlic, zucchini, potatoes, pine nuts, and capers. The bottled beer selection is primarily microbrews; the draft choice
is a Baltimore-brewed Extra Special Bitter.

PUB FARE
THE TOMBS ❸❸

1226 36th St. NW, 202/337-6668, www.tombs.com

HOURS: Mon.-Thurs. 11:30 A.M.-1:15 A.M.,
Fri. 11:30 A.M.-2:15 A.M., Sat. 11 A.M.-2:15 A.M.,
Sun. 9:30 A.M.-1:15 A.M.

Hands down, The Tombs is the best college
bar in DC and has been since 1962. Boisterous,
loud, and lively at nearly any hour, this walk-

down establishment underneath 1789 is the
go-to place for Georgetown University students
and alumni, but it also draws clientele of all
ages, including GU administrators and pro-
fessors for weekday lunch and the after-church
crowd from nearby Holy Trinity Church on
Saturday evenings and for Sunday brunch.
There's just something about being crammed
into this brick-lined basement with hundreds
of other happy people that makes The Tombs
special. The food is typical bar fare, with burgers and Reuben sandwiches among the best
menu picks, and the tap offers six beers, from
low-brow Busch for the empty-pocketed college kids to Old Dominion. In the evenings,
entertainment varies: Wednesday nights often
are reserved for '80s music with a DJ spinning
the tunes, and occasionally a GU a cappella
group will pop in. The decor is now basically a
paean to the Georgetown crew team and other
university sports, thanks to a 1985 makeover
by the Clyde's Restaurant Group, but the basic
vibe hasn't changed since the 1960s. If you related to the movie *Animal House* or once owned
a copy of *The Preppy Handbook,* you'll love The
Tombs.

QUICK BITES
BAKED AND WIRED ❸

1052 Thomas Jefferson St., 202/333-2500,
www.bakedandwired.com

HOURS: Mon.-Thurs. 7 A.M.-8 P.M., Fri. 7 A.M.-9 P.M.,
Sat. 8 A.M.-9 P.M., Sun. 9 A.M.-8 P.M.

One of DC's homegrown cupcake bakeries,
the bipolar Baked and Wired, a bakery (baked)
and coffee shop (wired—get it?), draws lines
for its large cupcakes and artfully poured cap-
puccinos. The line is substantially shorter at
Baked and Wired than it is at its competitor,
Georgetown Cupcake, a few blocks away, and
the cupcakes are much larger than the competition's, which means that some cupcake lovers prefer it over its famous counterpart. The
Elvis cupcake is a true fan favorite—banana
with peanut-butter frosting drizzled with chocolate—while the Ménage à Trois draws fans for
its luxurious raspberry filling inside a chocolate
cupcake topped with vanilla icing. The biggest

© PATRICIA KIME

Enjoy the cupcakes and coffee at Baked and Wired.

complaint about Baked and Wired is its blessing and its curse: The size of the cupcakes dictates that you can only eat one in a sitting. At other places you can sample a couple and not leave feeling like you can't get out the door.

DEAN AND DELUCA $

3276 M St. NW, 202/342-2500, www.deandeluca.com
HOURS: Daily 7 A.M.-8 P.M.

An offshoot of the New York market chain, Dean and Deluca offers an à la carte menu of sandwiches, soups, salads, and gourmet coffee to be enjoyed in an open-air patio or nearly anywhere in Georgetown that you can find a bench. The market is a great place to pick up gourmet cheese, wine, baked goods, or nearly anything else you might want to take back to your hotel room to enjoy after a long day of business meetings or sightseeing.

GEORGETOWN CUPCAKE $

3301 M St. NW, 202/333-8448,
www.georgetowncupcake.com
HOURS: Mon.-Sat. 10 A.M.-9 P.M., Sun. 10 A.M.-7 P.M.

Their story is as adorable as the cute little cakes that sell out nearly every day: Two sisters grew up baking and decorating cupcakes in their mom's kitchen and decided they wanted to leave their corporate jobs—one a Princeton grad in the finance world, the other a Gucci special-events coordinator—to open Washington's first cupcakery, which they did on Valentine's Day 2008. Thousands of cupcakes, a move to a bigger space, and a reality series later, the women of Georgetown Cupcake have become minor celebrities, and their bakery continues to draw long lines, in part because of their successful show but repeatedly for the taste and beauty of their diminutive confections. The menu changes daily and seasonally: Cherry Blossom is a visually beautiful dessert that comes on the scene in late March and April, a Madagascar bourbon vanilla cupcake with cherries inside, topped with cream cheese frosting and a fondant cherry blossom; in November, Caramel Apple, an apple cake with a *dulce de leche* core, vanilla cream cheese frosting, and *dulce de leche* drizzle, makes an appearance. To avoid the line, go during the day on weekdays or head over to the Bethesda, Maryland, location (4834 Bethesda Ave.).

MOBY DICK'S HOUSE OF KABOB $

1070 31st St. NW, 202/333-4400,
www.mobysonline.com
HOURS: Mon.-Thurs. 11 A.M.-10 P.M., Fri. 11 A.M.-11 P.M., Sat. noon-11 P.M., Sun. noon-9 P.M.

Apparently, Iranians are as amused by the name Moby Dick as people in Washington DC are. It's definitely a funny name for a takeout joint that serves great Persian food until the wee hours. Moby Dick was the moniker of a sandwich shop near the American Embassy in Tehran back in the days when the country was ruled by the shah; the owner of that establishment liked the book, and the owner of the Washington string of Moby Dick's, now numbering 15 area restaurants, knew the name would tickle Iranian expats as well as former embassy employees. Popular with hungry late-night diners, the food is kabobs of ground sirloin or tenderloin, lamb kabobs (*barreh*), and chicken. The restaurants

CUPCAKE WARS

The days of thinking the cupcake phenomenon would pass are over. With several new cupcakeries opening up in DC in the past year and even an offshoot of LA's Sprinkles arriving in Georgetown in 2011, cupcake bakeries have joined dog biscuit shops in the catalog of excessive indulgence, places where, for a few dollars, you can purchase a confection that looks like it was personally crafted for you. I don't get the cupcake phenomenon because I don't possess a sweet tooth, but I polled cake-loving friends regarding their favorites, and setting aside the great unknown that is Sprinkles (it set up shop just blocks from Georgetown Cupcake while this book was being written), the votes came in heavily for two: Georgetown Cupcake and Baked and Wired. And not surprisingly, women favored Georgetown Cupcake while the guys gushed about Baked and Wired.

TLC cable TV fans are familiar with **Georgetown Cupcake,** the girl-powered shop that turns out beautifully crafted little cakes decorated with fondant hearts and flowers, gummy fruit, or an exacting touch of shaved coconut.

Truthfully, each cake is a work of art: Each variety is frosted with a flavored icing that complements the cupcake's recipe (no across-the-board use of butter cream) and is embellished as carefully as any full-sized sweet. Even though Georgetown Cupcake moved to larger digs in 2009, the line often wraps around the corner and down a city block. But fans don't mind. "It's no big deal. This is a treat that I love doing with my kids," says Virginia resident Deb Graves, who ventures into Georgetown a few times a year specifically for the experience.

Five blocks from Georgetown Cupcake sits **Baked and Wired,** the urban-chic antidote to Georgetown Cupcake's sugary perfections, serving up huge cupcakes in a shop with a retro candy store vibe. The cupcakes have less frosting than their competition, but this works, its sweetness providing counterbalance to the large airy cakes. Baked and Wired also draws crowds, the line forming down the block, but it's not as long as the one along M Street. The cupcakes are complimented perfectly by a coffee drink from the "wired" area, which has comfortable chairs.

Long lines form outside Georgetown Cupcake.

© PATRICIA KIME

also serve some Greek fare, including gyros and souvlaki, but the best bet for a late-night snack is a beef kabob with a side of *seer torshi*, garlic marinated in vinegar.

SEAFOOD
HOOK ❸❸❸

3241 M St. NW, 202/625-4488, www.hookdc.com
HOURS: Mon.-Wed. 5-10 P.M., Thurs. 11:30 A.M.-2:30 P.M. and 5-11 P.M., Fri. 11:30 A.M.-2:30 P.M. and 5 P.M.-midnight, Sat.-Sun. 5 P.M.-midnight, brunch Sat.-Sun. 10 A.M.-3:30 P.M.

For fresh fish and seafood without a hefty dose of eco-guilt, Hook offers a menu entirely based on sustainable ingredients—items that have not been overfished or are in danger of disappearing from the planet—which means the chef cooks up some things the average seafood lover may not have tried before, including wahoo, weakfish, bluefish, and rockfish (which has rebounded thanks to aggressive protection measures in Chesapeake Bay in the past 20 years). But old standards also make their way onto the menu, including lobster, oysters, and clams, served up in a modern white dining room with barrel-vaulted ceiling. A guide is delivered with the check to help patrons continue making sustainable dining choices when eating seafood.

TACKLE BOX ❸

3245 M St. NW, 202/337-8269,
www.tackleboxrestaurant.com
HOURS: Sun.-Thurs. 11 A.M.-11 P.M., Fri.-Sat. 11 A.M.-1 A.M.

A lobster shack plunked in the middle of Georgetown, Tackle Box is neighboring Hook's little sibling, down to its kid-friendly menu of fried shrimp, fish-and-chips, and lobster rolls. This is the spot to satisfy a West Coast craving for fish tacos, well-prepared with the requisite amount of cabbage, as well as New England cravings: The lobster rolls are stuffed to the brim with sweet, tender chunks of seafood. The decor of plastic chairs and picnic tables is what you'd find in any Northern coastal takeout joint. In 2011, Tackle Box opened an upstairs bar that features the same menu, now available with a cold beer.

STEAK
BOURBON STEAK ❸❸❸

Four Seasons Hotel, 2800 Pennsylvania Ave. NW, 202/944-2026, www.bourbonsteakdc.com
HOURS: Mon.-Fri. 11:30 A.M.-2:30 P.M., Sun.-Thurs. 6-10 P.M., Fri.-Sat. 5:30-10:30 P.M.

In the back of the Four Seasons Hotel, overlooking the C&O Canal, is one of the city's newest steak houses, favored by the celebrities who stay at the Four Seasons—people like the Jonas Brothers, Paul McCartney, area local Dave Grohl, Brad Pitt, and Angelina Jolie—as well as Washington power players that include Capitals and Wizards owner Ted Leonsis. Bourbon Steak is certainly the place for beautiful people with thick wallets, but for a night out, its dark dining room, reached through the lobby of the Four Seasons, a veritable art museum in itself with works by Andy Warhol and Robert Mangold on the walls, is a special place. From the welcoming staff that makes everyone feel like a VIP to the dishes prepared to perfection, including dry-aged porterhouse and New York strip, duck with foie gras, and Virginia swordfish with baby leeks, black garlic, and bacon *lardon*. Dress up, take a few hours, and enjoy being pampered; it's what the Four Seasons is all about.

THAI
BANGKOK BISTRO ❸❸

3251 Prospect St. NW, 202/337-2424,
www.bangkokbistrodc.com
HOURS: Mon.-Thurs. 11:30 A.M.-10:30 P.M., Fri.-Sat. 11:30 A.M.-11:30 P.M.

A no-fuss meal in a friendly place on a quiet street off the beaten path in Georgetown, Bangkok Bistro serves popular American versions of Thai fare, including Penang curry and drunken noodles as well as authentic dishes like *hamachi kama* and spicy soups. Vegetarians will appreciate the number of choices designed for them, and most everyone loves the wallet-friendly generous portions, served as spicy as you want. Bangkok Bistro is within walking distance of many hotels and has outdoor seating in good weather. Another bonus: the birthday special, $13 off an entrée on your special day.

Greater Washington DC

Map 9

CONTEMPORARY AMERICAN AND EUROPEAN

TALLULA RESTAURANT AND EAT BAR ❸❸

2761 Washington Blvd., Arlington, Va., 703/778-5051, www.tallularestaurant.com

HOURS: Sun.-Thurs. 5:30-10 P.M., Fri.-Sat. 5:30-11 P.M., brunch Sat. 11 A.M.-2:30 P.M., Sun. 10 A.M.-2:30 P.M.; Eat Bar daily from 4 P.M.

Locals are still scratching their heads over the fact that a swanky contemporary restaurant is operating in a place where many of them had their first beer, but Tallula, which opened in the mid-2000s, and its companion gastropub, Eat Bar, named for the neon "Eats" sign that once adorned Whitey's, the dive bar that once stood here, have wormed their way into area hearts with creative food, an extensive wine list, and a convivial atmosphere. For prices slightly less than you would pay downtown, diners enjoy a menu initially created by chefs whose past employers include Notti Bianche and Citronelle. Highlights include Maryland rockfish served with a side of *fregula,* fennel, and eggplant and dressed with *chermoula* sauce, as well as salmon poached in olive oil and served with a potato latke, sweet and sour red onions, and a horseradish crème fraîche. The food at Eat Bar is less fussy: burgers, sliders, mussels, and penne pasta. For nostalgia's sake, they should swap out the Asian fusion chicken wings for "broasted" chicken served with a side of jezebel sauce.

MIDDLE EASTERN

LEBANESE TAVERNA ❸❸

2641 Connecticut Ave. NW, 202/265-8681, www.lebanesetaverna.com

HOURS: Lunch Mon.-Fri. 11:30 A.M.-2:30 P.M., dinner Mon. 5-9 P.M., Tues.-Thurs. 5-10 P.M., Fri. 5-11 P.M., Sat. noon-11 P.M., Sun. noon-9 P.M.

Of the restaurants near the zoo and in Woodley Park, Lebanese Taverna consistently delivers great food, with filling plates that will leave you wanting to return. Lebanese Taverna is a local chain that began nearly 30 years ago in a corner café in Arlington, Virginia, and has locations throughout the region. The Woodley Park location has a crisp, clean interior that includes a lovely barrel-vaulted ceiling and stained glass windows as well as outdoor tables in nice weather. The hummus and baba ghanoush are great for starters, as are most of the mezes; for the main courses, the carved rotisserie meats are rich and flavorful, and the lamb *fatteh,* accented with pomegranate seeds, is fan favorite.

QUICK BITES

HEIDELBERG PASTRY SHOP ❸

2150 N. Culpeper St., Arlington, Va., 703/527-8394, www.heidelbergbakery.com

HOURS: Tues.-Fri. 6:30 A.M.-6:30 P.M., Sat. 8 A.M.-5 P.M., Sun. 8 A.M.-1 P.M.

The aroma of grilled bratwurst wafts across the parking lot summer Saturdays, and the scent of freshly baked bread and confectioner's sugar greets customers inside the area's only German bakery, Heidelberg, a destination for those seeking dense, chewy German breads, perfect pies, crunchy cookies, and European specialties like Sacher and *obst* tortes, strudel, and stollen at Christmas. Customers at the family-run store can pick up lunch or dinner to go: on Saturdays in the summer, employees grill German sausages and serve them with potato salad, or they can choose from a selection of made-on-the-spot deli sandwiches, from a classic Reuben to coarse and fine liverwurst. Heidelberg family members disagree on the store's tastiest item, but one cake wins high marks among the majority—the black and white mousse cake, a rich creamy confection of cake, airy mousse, and chocolate shavings that melts in your mouth.

ITALIAN STORE ❸

3123 Lee Hwy., Arlington, Va., 703/528-6266, www.italianstore.com

HOURS: Mon.-Fri. 10 A.M.-9 P.M., Sat. 10 A.M.-8 P.M., Sun. 11 A.M.-6 P.M.

Transplants from the New York City area and

Philadelphia have a home at the Italian Store, a deli known regionally for its submarine sandwiches and pizzas that possess that certain je ne sais quoi of authenticity not found elsewhere. The Capri is the top-seller, with prosciutto, Genoa salami, provolone, spiced *capocollo*, lettuce, onions, and oil and vinegar, served on a hard or soft roll, but the menu also offers eight other hot-sandwich options and 18 gourmet sandwiches, including one with pâté and brie. The pizzas are simple and large, and they come in seven varieties that use a house-made sauce recipe clearly created by someone who has lived well north of Arlington. Order ahead by phone to avoid the store's ordering line; you'll likely still have a wait to pay.

RAY'S HELL BURGER ●

1713 Wilson Blvd., Arlington, Va., 703/841-0001
HOURS: Mon.-Thurs. and Sun. 11 A.M.-10 P.M.,
Fri.-Sat. 11 A.M.-11 P.M.

It's easy for President Obama and Russian President Dmitry Medvedev to dine at Ray's Hell Burger, because one, they don't have to worry about parking, a chronic problem at this location, and two, even though it's cash-only, Obama probably didn't have to fish around in his pocket to make sure he had enough money. Oh, and three, they probably had no problem getting a seat (especially with the signs that effectively tell patrons they can be booted from their chairs if someone important comes in). The signs are, frankly, a turnoff. Still, Ray's packs patrons in from opening to closing, with massive burgers made to order and a selection of unusual toppings, including foie gras, cognac sautéed mushrooms, and jalapeños as well as the usual lettuce, tomato, and onion. Expect that you'll need a fork by the end of your burger; the buns don't hold up to the juicy meat or the condiments.

SEAFOOD
MAINE AVENUE FISH MARKET ●●

1100 Maine Ave. SW, 202/484-2722
HOURS: Mon.-Sun. 8 A.M.-9 P.M.

There's something decidedly un-Washington about the Maine Avenue Fish Market. Take a look around DC: It's practically spotless, with little grime and litter. Even its market—Eastern Market—is spotless, lacking the feel or grittiness of Philadelphia's Reading Terminal Market or 9th Street Italian Market. Enter the fish market, the closest thing the city has to a midway, with its pungent odors, carnivalesque awnings, hawkers promoting their wares, and live critters waiting to be cooked and eaten. At the fish market, customers can grab crab-cake sandwiches, raw and fried oysters, fried fish, and even dessert at Jimmy's, which serves pies and cakes. There are no seats, although there is a new covered area; most patrons grab their meals and stand at wooden tables that look out over the river. Even if you don't like seafood, the fish market is an experience, a chance to hang out by the river with locals in a relatively safe neighborhood and enjoy a vibe that seems to be disappearing with the slow gentrification of each section of the city.

STEAKS
RAY'S THE STEAKS ●●

2300 Wilson Blvd, Arlington, Va., 703/841-7297
HOURS: Sun.-Thurs. 5-10:30 P.M., Fri.-Sat. 5-11 P.M.

When Ray's the Steaks opened in an aging strip mall in Arlington, Virginia, fans of Ruth's Chris and Morton's rejoiced: Here was a place they could go for quality steaks and not break the bank. The setting wasn't fancy, but owner Michael Landrum delivered what he intended: quality steaks for about half the price of the competition and side dishes that came with a meal. Ray's has moved to a larger, more upscale location a few blocks away, but it hasn't strayed from its roots, still serving fine cuts of beef with buttery red-bliss mashed potatoes and creamed spinach. On a recent visit, a steak arrived at the table overcooked; when the meal was whisked away to be replaced, a cup of crab bisque arrived, a flavorful surprise that turned out to be the meal's most memorable part. Ray's has a loyal following that includes regulars who dine here weekly.

RESTAURANTS

NIGHTLIFE

The night is young and so are the residents of DC: With the median age a youthful 35, the city is alive with college-age students, hipsters, party girls, the newly employed, and up-and-comers, all looking to let off some steam after hours. It also has its share of longtime locals, a sophisticated, learned bunch who've grown up on the city's after-work party scene and continue to expect much from it. And as a government town somewhat insulated from economic turmoil, Washington's population seems to have the cash to spare for a night out. What's on your agenda—cool jazz served with smooth martinis? A punk show punctuated by smoke and strobes? A gin and house-made tonic sipped in an übersleek space listening to Esperanza Spalding? Maybe it's a late-night burger and jukebox tunes at the city's finest hole-in-the-wall. Fortunately, all of it can be found in Washington DC. Just two decades ago, much of the city's late-night entertainment was restricted to two main neighborhoods: Georgetown and the then-edgy Adams Morgan. Today, revitalization has attracted a bevy of entrepreneurs seeking to create the best thing across the city, and traditional nightlife borders have disappeared. Excitement and entertainment can be found citywide: on U Street, in Dupont Circle, in the Atlas District, and in Arlington. There's also no shortage of revelers; lines are often out the door, and tickets for shows stay in hot demand, regardless of the night of the week.

Georgetown and Adams Morgan continue to reign as legendary nightlife destinations, especially for the young and boisterous. Bars and pubs line the main streets, a mix of casual nightspots and tightly packed dance

© PATRICIA KIME

HIGHLIGHTS

LOOK FOR  TO FIND RECOMMENDED NIGHTLIFE.

Best Beer Selection: ChurchKey is to beer lovers what Proof and Vinoteca are for oenophiles, with more than 500 beer offerings listed on the menu by flavor or taste rather than place of origin or style – a boon for those who don't know the difference between a *weissbier* and a *hefeweisen* (page 123).

Best Live Music Venue: Adams Morgan's most popular bar, **Madam's Organ** packs patrons in nightly with live music on the first floor, a DJ on the second floor, a rooftop patio, and five bars (page 124).

Best Drink With a View: The name of the rooftop terrace at the W Hotel Washington DC says it all: **POV** (Point of View). Indoor and outdoor spaces overlook the White House, the Washington Monument, and the National Mall, with views clear to the river, the Jefferson Memorial, the Pentagon, and the Air Force Memorial (page 127).

Best Neighborhood Bar: I'm not sure why everyone – *Esquire* magazine and the Food Network included – classifies the **Tune Inn** as a dive. Sure, it has taxidermy and vinyl seats sagging from the weight of thousands of derrieres, and the service is sometimes brusque, but the floor and the bathrooms are clean, the beer is cold, and the chili cheese fries are gooey sticks of deliciousness. It's an awesome place (page 128).

Best Place to Get Your Groove On: Maybe it's not as upscale as other clubs in DC, lacking the strict "no sneakers, no Timberlands, no ball caps" dress code found elsewhere, but **U-Street Music Hall** pulses, with a huge dance floor, a body-thumping Martin sound system, and DJs who get the crowd moving (page 130).

Best Alternative Music Venue: From artists on the cusp of playing Coachella to big alternative names to groups you've never heard of, the **Black Cat** has it all (page 132).

Best Jazz Club: The competition is stiffer than ever, but **Blues Alley,** the District's longest-running jazz hall, wins with aficionados for its supper-club ambience and top-notch musicians (page 132).

Only in DC: An unmarked door leads upstairs to **18th Street Lounge,** a nightclub set in a townhome once rented by Teddy Roosevelt. Kudos to the decorators who made Queen Anne Victorian style cool (page 133).

Best Spot to Take a Date: Dimly lit, cozy yet chic, and with a wine menu that offers full or half pours, the wine bar at **Bistrot Lepic** is like a mini break to contemporary Paris without the airfare (page 135).

just a few of ChurchKey's 500 beer offerings

floors, urban lounges, and eclectic small music venues. Georgetown tends to attract more out-of-towners and college kids (it is, after all, sandwiched between Georgetown and George Washington Universities), while Adams Morgan is more diverse, drawing visitors and locals alike, a post-21 set seeking a night of letting loose. U Street has emerged as the destination for live music and sophisticated revelry, with venues ranging from the rambunctious to the high-end, including rocking live music halls, jazz halls, clubs, and packed dance floors. Dupont Circle is very much a local scene, with chic clubs, lounges, and sports bars, while Capitol Hill's few watering holes fill up, especially at happy hour during the week, with congressional staffers and interns seeking cheap eats and drinks.

DC's drinking age is 21, as it is elsewhere in the United States. But some of the city's music venues allow patrons 18 and over to get in the door for a show and to dance. Having an identification card is a must. Without one, you stand very little chance of getting in the door. Over 18 gets you inside; over 21 and you'll get a hand stamp that allows you to buy alcohol. Details regarding bars' policies are included in the listings.

For a good sense of what's happening in DC at any giving time, check out the *Washington Post*'s Going Out Gurus, who seem to be among the most savvy folks on the planet when it comes to fun in Washington. They have a blog (www.washingtonpost.com/blogs/going-out-gurus) and are contributors to the *Post*'s Going Out Guide, also found on the web. Also, at www.dcist.com, editor in chief Aaron Morrissey has assembled a litany of DC-nophiles who keep current concert listings and other items of local interest.

Bars

BILLY MARTIN'S TAVERN
1264 Wisconsin Ave. NW, 202/333-7370,
www.martins-tavern.com
HOURS: Mon.-Thurs. 11 A.M.-1:30 A.M., Fri.
11 A.M.-2:30 A.M., Sat. 9 A.M.-2:30 A.M., Sun.
9 A.M.-1:30 A.M.
Map 8

Brunch is the most popular meal at Billy Martin's Tavern, but having been founded by an Irishman, it's a popular watering hole as well, filled with regulars who like bar food and Guinness in a traditional pub atmosphere. Its rich history—every president from Harry Truman to George W. Bush has stopped by, and John F. Kennedy was a regular when he was a neighbor and a senator—draws the curious, but it's also a neighborhood hangout for residents, Georgetown alumni, students with their parents, and older Washington business types. The atmosphere is clubby but genuine: The bar is nearly 80 years old, with dark oak booths, Tiffany lamps, and hunter-green accents. Beer is the most popular beverage ordered here, with

Guinness, Smithwick's, and Yuengling on tap, but traditional drinks like Dark and Stormy are also in demand. If Aniko is behind the bar, request one of her Bloody Marys, which comes in an Old Bay rimmed glass.

CHI-CHA LOUNGE
1624 U St. NW, 202/234-8400,
www.latinconcepts.com
HOURS: Sun.-Thur. 5 P.M.-2 A.M., Fri.-Sat. 5 P.M.-3 A.M.
Map 7

Named for a fermented drink brewed in South America from corn, Chi-Cha calls itself "modern Andean," with a menu that focuses on Central and South American tapas and a chill candlelit lounge where guests relax on couches around tables, sipping cocktails and, if they feel the need, smoking a hookah. With a popular house sangria and smoking pipes on the menu, Chi-Cha draws a very diverse crowd, groups of all nationalities from various walks of life. The lounge, with warm orange walls and red accents, is set up so you can't help overhearing others' conversations, an intentional move by owner Maurico Fraga-Rosenfeld, who oversees a number of area nightspots and aims to encourage mingling among patrons.

☾ CHURCHKEY

1337 14th St. NW, 202/567-2576,
www.churchkeydc.com
HOURS: Mon.-Thurs. 4 P.M.–1 A.M., Fri. 4 P.M.–2 A.M., Sat. noon–2 A.M., Sun. noon–1 A.M.

Map 6

DC's largest selection of beer on tap can be found at ChurchKey, a beer bar located upstairs from sibling restaurant Birch & Barley, with 50 varieties of draft. But the selection doesn't stop there: ChurchKey also offers 500 bottled varieties and five English-style cask ales—less carbonated and smoother than most brews. The beer menu is organized by characteristics ("malt" and "tart"), and every beer is available in four-ounce pours, encouraging sampling. With such a selection and a small

ChurchKey is located above Birch & Barley.

DANIEL LOBO – DAQUELLAMANERA.ORG

space—ChurchKey has seating for 150—the place tends to fill up within an hour or so of its 4 P.M. opening. To avoid waiting in line, head over right at 4 P.M.

FADO

808 7th St. NW, 202/789-0066,
www.fadoirishpub.com
HOURS: Mon.-Thurs. 11 A.M.–2 A.M., Fri. 11 A.M.–3 A.M., Sat. opening depends on sports schedules, close 3 A.M., Sun. opening depends on sports schedules, close 2 A.M.

Map 3

With decor imported lock, stock, and barrel from an Irish company that makes Irish pubs, Fado's decor features a bit of everything from the Irish Pub Company catalog, including Celtic areas, country design, even a "bookstore" alcove. The interior, in the ever-more-Disney (or is it Las Vegas?) contrived Verizon Center area, is lovely, if a bit artificial, but the food and beverages are genuine. The tap selection is a mix of Irish and English, including Strongbow cider and Kilkenny cream ale along with the usual Harp, Guinness, and Bass, and the menu features boxties and Irish breakfast. Music on weekends is where Fado breaks the pub mold: DJs spin Top 40 and dance tunes, and everyone in the place enjoys the beat.

GATE 54 AT CAFÉ SAINT-EX

1847 14th St. NW, 202/265-7839, www.saint-ex.com
HOURS: Mon. 5 P.M.–1:30 A.M., Tues.-Thurs. 11 A.M.–1:30 A.M., Fri.-Sat. 11 A.M.–2:30 A.M., Sun. 11 A.M.–1:30 A.M.

Map 7

In the basement of restaurant Café Saint-Ex, Gate 54 hosts DJs five nights a week, never with a cover charge and always with variety. The music selection can range from rock, soul, and country to punk and alternative, depending on who is in the booth that night. The place is small and fills up quickly on weekends; bar patrons spill into the bistro and clog the hallways. On the flip side, sometimes the café is packed and the bar is empty. The specialty cocktails, with several riffs on bourbon drinks, can be purchased and enjoyed on either floor.

BULLFEATHERS

410 1st St. SE, 202/484-0228,
www.bullfeathersdc.com

HOURS: Sun.-Thurs. 11 A.M.-11 P.M., Fri.-Sat. 11 A.M.-2 A.M.

Map 5

Named for an exclamation Teddy Roosevelt
used to utter in lieu of cursing, Bullfeathers
is a Capitol Hill hangout, an institution of in-
temperance for the staff, congressional representatives, and politicos. Pub fare is the name
of the game in terms of food, with the burgers
among the top choices. For drinks, draft beers
are the popular choice, with more than 30
microbrews, imports, and a handful of domes-
tics on tap. Bullfeathers sucks patrons in for
happy hour, and keeps them there for the socializing long into the night; be aware, though,
if you are unhappy with Congress, this might
not be the place to go because you are guaranteed a spectator seat for the parade of lawmakers, lobbyists, and those who work for them.

KELLY'S IRISH TIMES

14 F St. NW, 202/543-5433, www.kellysirishtimes.com

HOURS: Sun.-Thurs. 11 A.M.-1:30 A.M., Fri.-Sat.
11 A.M.-2:30 A.M.

Map 5

For those in need of a low-brow Irish bar on
the Senate side, Kelly's Irish Times fills the
bill, a dark spot that draws area workers for an
after-hours pint but on Friday and Saturday
fills with throngs of raucous college kids and
postcollegiates singing along with the Irish entertainment or enjoying the pickup scene. The
downstairs thrums to a dance beat on weekends; the place also has a pool table. For a more
authentic Irish experience with a quieter crowd,
check out the Dubliner next door.

LUCKY BAR

1221 Connecticut Ave. NW, 202/331-3733,
www.luckybardc.com

HOURS: Mon.-Thurs. 3 P.M.-2 A.M., Fri. 3 P.M.-3 A.M.,
Sat. noon-3 A.M., Sun. 9 P.M.-2 A.M.

Map 6

Lucky Bar is a casual, if slightly grungy, place
that draws an after-work crowd that likes to
leave their business at the door—a rarity in a

town of self-important postcollege types. The
somewhat divey atmosphere is enhanced by
the cheap beer at happy hour; Thursday evening 3–8 P.M. draws college kids, interns, and
the just-over-21 crowd for the $3 Buds, Bud
Lights, and house cocktails. A DJ spins tunes
Thursday through Saturday. During the day on
weekends, Lucky Bar draws in soccer fans who
are likely to find their favorite team playing on
one of 25 TV sets. The place has a reputation
for being a meat market, but with a name like
"Lucky Bar," that shouldn't be a surprise.

MADAM'S ORGAN

2461 18th St. NW, 202/667-5370,
www.madamsorgan.com

HOURS: Mon.-Thurs. 5 P.M.-2 A.M., Fri. 5 P.M.-3 A.M.,
Sun. 5 P.M.-2 A.M.

COST: $5 Cover after 9 P.M.

Map 7

Madam's Organ has staying power, a bar whose
mural of a well-endowed redhead always turns
heads and announces in no uncertain terms
that you've arrived in Adams Morgan. The
painting and the bar, a multilevel ramshackle
row house that cemented its place in city
nightlife history by drawing crowds for 20
years to this lively neighborhood with nightly
live music, have become DC landmarks. The
party continues today: Bands playing blue-
grass, blues, or jazz set a lively, rowdy tone
and the dimly lit interior, and strong drinks
are a recipe for misbehavior. Madam's Organ's
catchphrase is "Where the beautiful people go
to get ugly," and in 2000, *Playboy* magazine
agreed: Madam's Organ was voted one of the
top bars in the United States. The rooftop deck
draws patrons year-round, and the place also
has a small balcony that overlooks 18th Street.
Redheads, take advantage: you pay just half
price for bottles of Rolling Rock.

MARVIN

2007 14th St. NW, 202/797-7171, www.marvindc.com

HOURS: Mon.-Thurs. 5:30 P.M.-2 A.M., Fri.-Sat.
5:30 P.M.-3 A.M., Sun. 11 P.M.-2 A.M.

Map 7

A restaurant, lounge, and Belgian *biergarten* that

pays homage to DC native son Marvin Gaye, Marvin draws an international crowd to its dimly lit spaces, who flock to its split personality decor—classic bistro restaurant downstairs, comfortable homespun lounge upstairs, with framed pictures of Motown stars, upholstered furniture, and floral banquettes. The back deck, with a covered bar, serves a variety of Belgian brews on tap and 30 in bottles that complement the Belgian menu. DJs spin soulful, fun, funky, or R&B tunes seven nights a week. Why a Belgian theme in a place dedicated to one of the kings of Motown? In 1981, Gaye faced a nadir in his personal life and professional career and fled to the seaside town of Ostend, Belgium, where he found inner peace, freedom from drugs, and inspiration for his hit "Sexual Healing."

PATTY BOOM BOOM

1359 U St. NW, 202/629-1712,
www.pattyboomboomdc.com
HOURS: Tues.-Thurs. and Sun. 8 P.M.-2 A.M.,
Fri.-Sat. 8 P.M.-3 A.M.
Map 7

Patty Boom Boom epitomizes U Street—a bar that celebrates a distinctive culture and pulls in a diverse crowd from all over DC, mainly because anyone who has ever visited the Caribbean wants to drink a Red Stripe and listen to reggae music every once in a while. Patty Boom Boom is an island getaway in the heart of DC, where Rastafarians stand side-by-side with policy wonks swaying to "No Woman, No Cry" or singing along to "Buffalo Soldier." The first floor sells takeout fare, mostly Jamaican patties—the country's version of an empanada—while DJs spin music upstairs, usually by 8 or 9 P.M., and bands sometimes strike up live reggae at 7 P.M. on weekends. Be warned: Just as it does in the islands, the rum punch will sneak up on you.

THE POUR HOUSE

319 Pennsylvania Ave. SE, 202/546-1001,
www.pourhousedc.com
HOURS: Mon.-Thurs. 4 P.M.-2 A.M., Fri. noon-3 A.M.,
Sat.-Sun. 10 A.M.-3 P.M.
Map 5

A hangout in the pub-crawl triumvirate that spans the 300 block of East Pennsylvania Avenue, the Pour House is three bars in itself: a sports bar on the main level that attracts

NIGHTLIFE

© C. DEAN KIME

Jamaican club Patty Boom Boom

OUTDOOR DRINKING SCENE

© PATRICIA KIME

Sequoia, on Georgetown's Waterfront

The downside to central air-conditioning in DC is that no one takes a break during the heat of the day in the summertime to sit under a canopy, sip a cool drink, and try to catch a slight breeze. But Washingtonians have taken that onetime summer ritual and pushed it back a few hours: Come quitting time, they're looking for a place to enjoy a cold beer or cocktail outside, either on a rooftop deck, patio, or porch under a sunshade or umbrella. Washington's bar owners have obliged, putting tables out on sidewalks and remodeling rooftops to accommodate customers. Some of the capital's best outdoor drinking scenes:

POV (Point of View): The place with the best views has indoor and outdoor seating. The covered terrace catches the breezes above Pennsylvania Avenue; in bad or cold weather, the staff drops plastic curtains and fires up the propane heaters as needed.

The waterside **Sequoia** bar draws the beautiful crowd, but a more relaxed waterfront drinking experience can be found at **Cantina Marina** (600 Water St. SW). Views of the Washington Channel and marinas combined with pitchers of margaritas make for a nice end to the business day. Their policy of making customers pay for chips and salsa is odd, though. **Perry's** in Adams Morgan and **Marvin** on 14th Street both offer great views of their neighborhoods.

Johnny's Half Shell offers the best of urban sidewalk happy hour: large umbrellas, drink specials, stunning views of the Capitol and tree-lined parks, and terrific people watching. **Lauriol Plaza** has a huge rooftop deck and free-flowing margaritas to make Lauriol Plaza especially appealing on a steamy summer night.

Pittsburgh fans as well as Florida Gators (a throwback to the days when the bar was decorated entirely with Steelers and Penguins memorabilia); a game room in the basement featuring skee ball, shuffleboard, darts, and electronic games; and the upstairs Top of the Hill martini lounge, offering leather chairs, red felt pool tables, and stiff drinks. While the food is uninspired, the pub games, the allure of hanging out with fellow sports fans, decent happy hour specials, and friendly bartenders draw in crowds.

◖ POV ROOF TERRACE AND LOUNGE
515 15th St. NW, 202/661-2400,
www.whotels.com/WashingtonDC
HOURS: Sun.-Thurs. 5 P.M.-2 A.M., Fri.-Sat. 5 P.M.-3 A.M.
Map 4

A great place for a celebratory drink, a special occasion, or to bring out-of-towners, POV (Point of View) at the W Hotel Washington DC has a view to rival the one enjoyed by the president from the White House's South Portico. Washington's skyline is laid out in bas-relief—the Washington Monument, the Lincoln Memorial, and the White House's East Wing. Lounge chairs, sofas, and cocktail tables in a black and metallic color scheme with pops of red establishes the place as a cool lounge. The cocktail menu is heavy on throwbacks, including Dark and Stormies, Pimms Cups, mint juleps, and old-fashioneds. As with any W, the service is impeccable and painstakingly hip; sometimes the W shtick feels more like a satire of hipster chic, especially when a line forms for POV down in the lobby and the place seems nearly empty when you arrive upstairs. Make a reservation if you plan to dine, or get there early—by 8 P.M. on Friday or Saturday for quick entry to the bar.

THE REEF
2446 18th St. NW, 202/518-3800, www.thereefdc.com
HOURS: Mon.-Thurs. 11 A.M.-1:30 A.M.,
Fri. 11 A.M.-2:30 A.M., Sat. 9 A.M.-2:30 A.M.,
Sun. 9 A.M.-1:30 A.M.
Map 7

A casual setting with three levels for relaxation, noshing, and drinking, the Reef is Adams Morgan's largest bar. The narrow first floor "lush" room has jungle decor with rock walls, vines, and greenery; the large second-floor space has floor-to-ceiling windows overlooking 18th Street and huge aquariums filled with tropical fish and colorful coral; and the third level, a covered and heated rooftop deck, is open year-round. The Reef is popular for its beer (the menu rotates nearly weekly, and a special selection is served every Thursday) and its kiddie happy hour, Friday nights 5–8 P.M., where parents can enjoy drink specials while their youngsters get discounts on food.

RHINO BAR AND PUMPHOUSE
3295 M St. NW, 202/333-3150, www.rhinobardc.com
HOURS: Mon.-Thurs. 6 P.M.-2 A.M., Fri. 5 P.M.-3 A.M.,
Sat. noon-3 A.M., Sun. noon-2 A.M.
Map 8

This bar is like three spots in one: On Saturday game days in the fall, Rhino Bar and Pumphouse is an Ohio State watering hole, with the Buckeyes playing on the TV and the area's OSU expats cheering their team on. On Sunday it becomes a Philadelphia Eagles hangout, full of screaming Eagles fans devouring $0.25 wings, and during baseball season, it's the same thing, only the Boston Red Sox are the team of choice. At night, though, it's the fraternity house that never got remodeled—the one where you took swan dives off the mantle or dropped a whole beer on the stained hardwood floor and no one noticed. It makes sense—Georgetown University doesn't officially have a fraternity scene, so where else would the students of the school, still the epitome of preppy, go? If you seek camaraderie with lax-bro guys and cute girls in sundresses, this is the place on weekends after 10 P.M. If that's not your scene, it's best to steer clear.

ROUND ROBIN BAR
Willard InterContinental Hotel,
1401 Pennsylvania Ave. NW, 202/637-7348,
www.washington.intercontinental.com
HOURS: Mon.-Thurs. noon-1 A.M., Fri. 3 P.M.-1 A.M.,
Sat. noon-1 A.M.
Map 4

Historians have spent some time debunking

NIGHTLIFE

the popular DC myth that the term *lobbying* was invented at the Willard Hotel in the vast room off what's now the Round Robin Bar, but the story is still quaint—President Ulysses S. Grant frequented the hotel, and favor-seekers often stopped him in the lobby for conversation. While the term originated earlier and elsewhere, the patrons of the Willard and the Round Robin don't seem to care. Many of them are lobbyists come home to roost, enjoying a single malt or mint julep in a space their predecessors enjoyed more than 100 years ago. Decor is traditional, with green upholstered walls, dark wood, and glittering barware, and the place is known for its traditional drink menu heavy on the scotch (100 choices, plus bourbon and cognac). One bit of Willard bar history is true: Famous orator Senator Henry Clay introduced the world to the classic Kentucky beverage the mint julep here when he shared his recipe with the bartender in 1850. Mint juleps continue to be among the most requested drinks at the Round Robin, made from Clay's original recipe using Maker's Mark.

SEQUOIA

3000 K St. NW, 202/944-4200,
www.arkrestaurants.com/sequoia_dc.html
HOURS: Mon.-Thurs. 11:30 A.M.-11 P.M., Fri.-Sat.
11:30 A.M.-midnight, Sun. 10:30 A.M.-3 P.M. and 4-11 P.M.
Map 8

The young and the beautiful park themselves on Sequoia's three-tiered patio on summer weekends, enjoying the social scene and the bar's incomparable views of the Potomac River. Most patrons are well-dressed, and flirting is de rigueur. The waterfront shows are entertaining as well: In spring around lunchtime, high school and college crew teams compete along the river, and on summer afternoons motorboats and yachts tie up along the Georgetown waterfront and start their own parties. The cocktails and drinks are known to be especially pricey—you are paying for the ambience— and the food is marginal and overpriced, so skip it. But on a sultry summer evening in Washington, a Corona and a cool river breeze at Sequoia are especially sweet.

(TUNE INN

331½ Pennsylvania Ave. SE, 202/543-2725
HOURS: Daily 8 A.M.-1 A.M.
Map 5

The Food Network hailed the Tune Inn as one of DC's greatest "dives," understandable for the duct-taped vinyl booths, walls adorned with taxidermy, and NASCAR on the TVs. But it's a clean place with rib-sticking food—cheeseburgers, fried okra, chicken fingers—that's artery-clogging and delicious along with beer that's cold and arrives quickly, served in plastic pitchers. A hideaway from DC's pretentiousness, the Tune attracts politicians and Hill heavies seeking a simple meal and a beer in a down-home space. A bipartisan crowd revels here: Political strategist and Tulane University professor James Carville and wife Mary Matalin were allegedly heading here for their first date when they found no room at the Inn; instead they went next door to the now-closed Hawk 'n' Dove. The 2010 election saw the Tune Inn robbed of its unofficial "mayor," perennial customer Gene Taylor, the perfectly coiffed, perpetually tan representative from Mississippi who got washed away with the incoming Republican tide. Newcomers need to check any airs they may have at the door.

© C. DEAN KIME

The Tune Inn is much more than your typical dive bar.

Dance Clubs

CAFÉ CITRON
1343 Connecticut Ave. NW, 202/530-8844,
www.cafecitrondc.com
HOURS: Mon.-Thur. 4 P.M.-2 A.M., Fri.-Sat. 4 P.M.-3 A.M.
Map 6

Deceptively small from the outside, this row-house club is known for its mango mojitos and free salsa lessons. The tunes get cranked up after 10 P.M., and those with inhibitions run out the door. Everyone else dances with abandon—many of them are very good at various Latin style dances and others who aren't, but

who cares? Weekdays are less crowded, with more time to work on your form; on Monday nights, enjoy a flamenco show.

ULTRABAR
911 F St. NW, 202/638-4663, www.ultrabardc.com
HOURS: Thur. 9:30 P.M.-2 A.M., Fri.-Sat. 9:30 P.M.-3 A.M.
COST: $20 (free passes available on website).
Map 3

Ultrabar is the total club experience, with four floors of music, laser lights, a VIP section, pricey bottle service, platforms for dancing,

GO-GO: THE MUSIC

In Washington, "go-go" doesn't imply women in high heel boots swinging around a pole or dancing in a cage, although that type of entertainment can be found here. Go-go refers to a homegrown genre of music that never quite entered the mainstream but has been a force in northeast DC clubs with young black residents who enjoy dancing to its complex rhythms and Afrocentric percussion and styling.

The essence of go-go is complex – the music is a mix of funk, R&B, and old school – delivered in a syncopated rhythm of quarter and eighth notes with a brief hold thrown in. The music is heavily underscored with drums, high hat, congas, and timbales with a hefty dose of cowbell (Bruce Dickinson would be proud). The music hit its peak in the 1980s, with local groups such as the Young Senators, the Soul Searchers, and Trouble Funk gaining a following, but the genre's flirtation with fame was somewhat limited: Beyoncé Knowles's hit "Crazy In Love" sampled heavily from a previous local go-go hit by the Chi-Lites, and some of her albums also have heavy go-go back-beats. Experience Unlimited, a go-go group, had some success after Spike Lee featured their song "Da Butt" in the movie *School Daze*.

But while clubs in DC continue to sponsor go-go nights, you won't find it played at the bars or dance clubs listed above. Go-go gatherings mainly occur in small clubs in northeast

DC and are not recommended for visitors, out-of-towners, or anyone not familiar with the hood. Sometimes Chuck Brown, considered the godfather of go-go, performs in a mainstream club like Blues Alley. A Chuck Brown concert is a venture into DC's roots as a majority African American city, well worth a look.

Follow the signs to find the go-go.

and a dress code that asks women to keep it "classy and sexy" and lists a litany of things guys can't wear (basically everything except button-down shirts and dark trousers with dress shoes). Music on the main floor is mainly Top 40; upper levels include Latin, electronica, and hip-hop. To avoid the long line, check out the club's website first and download a pass for free admission before 11 P.M. As with many clubs, if you are a woman who is dressed to kill and savvy enough to have downloaded a pass, you have a good shot at skipping the line altogether. Ultrabar is an 18-and-over club, and the overall crowd tends toward the youngish side.

U-STREET MUSIC HALL

1115 U St. NW, 202/588-1880,
www.ustreetmusichall.com
HOURS: Check calendar for live shows; usually 7-10 P.M.; DJ nights 10 P.M.-2 A.M.
Map 7

U-Street Music Hall is the place to go clubbing if pretention, pricey bottle service, and half-naked girls dancing in cages isn't your idea of fun. It has the best sound system in Washington, and it sells National Bohemian beer in cans—Baltimore's former home brew, now made by Pabst, which has a fan following in DC. Fortunately, U-Hall doesn't just appeal to hipsters drinking "Natty Bo": It's a club that attracts a diverse crowd, including young women dressed to the nines, boys in tight Ts and cowboy boots, and college prepsters. There's no dress code, so you won't get booted if you don't have the right look. Music varies, mainly spun by DJs and focusing on anything with a great bass beat—you can feel it rumbling through your chest from the 20,000-watt sound system—including techno, electronica, dance, and house. Concerts are sometimes held here as well, including hip-hop, punk, hard-core, and soul.

Gay and Lesbian

COBALT

1639 R St. NW, 202/232-4416, www.cobaltdc.com
HOURS: Mon.-Thurs. 4 P.M.-2 A.M., Fri.-Sat. 4 P.M.-3 A.M.
COST: $7-10 Cover charge.
Map 6

A three-tiered nightclub that claims to have DC's sexiest bartenders (well, they're shirtless and sculpted like Michelangelo's *David,* so that's a start), Cobalt has a restaurant on its first floor, a lounge on its second floor, and a dance floor on the third level with DJs spinning tunes. Happy hour activities occur nightly, including karaoke and flip-cup on Sunday, retro music on Tuesday, and, uh, a "best package" contest on Thursday.

JR'S BAR AND GRILL

1519 17th St. NW, 202/328-0090, www.myjrsdc.com
HOURS: Mon.-Thurs. 2 P.M.-2 A.M., Fri.-Sat. 2 P.M.-3 A.M.
Map 6

The future leaders of the Log Cabin Republicans enjoy JR's, a club that attracts gay wonks and staffers, noticeable for their Abercrombie & Fitch and Banana Republic conservative attire and work-hard, play-hard attitude. The decor is stained glass and brass railings, with a separate bar that has a big screen for music videos. There's also an upper level with a pool table and a more laid-back atmosphere than the crowded downstairs scene. JR's has showtunes night on Monday—videos, songs, and sing-alongs to Broadway hits, strengthened by the bravado of a few stiff drinks.

NELLIE'S SPORTS BAR

900 U St. NW, 202/332-6355,
www.nelliessportsbar.com
HOURS: Mon.-Thurs. 5 P.M.-1 A.M., Fri. 3 P.M.-2 A.M., Sat. 11 A.M.-2 A.M., Sun. 11 A.M.-1 A.M.
Map 7

Maybe it's the location, convenient for a preconcert drink for a show at the 9:30 Club, or that U Street draws such an eclectic crowd, but

© PATRICIA KIME

Nellie's Sports Bar

this bar doesn't exactly exude LGBT. It could be the fact that owner Douglas Schantz is on record as saying he opened the place as a neighborhood hangout for everyone, regardless of their sexual orientation, and the neighborhood has responded. The front room of Nellie's is beautiful for a sports bar—exposed brick, dark wood, and a fireplace that is more like a lounge. Through a set of doors, though, lies the sports memorabilia and several televisions, with a few more upstairs tuned to whatever team is playing, drawing a mixed crowd of regulars and sports fans. At night, the place transforms, with crowds of men flocking to the rooftop deck and Top 40 and dance music playing through the sound system. There's drag bingo on Tuesday night, outings to Nats games, and hideaways with checkers and chess boards.

PHASE 1

525 8th St. SE, 202/544-6831, www.phase1dc.com
HOURS: Mon.-Thurs. 4 P.M.-2 A.M., Fri. 4 P.M.-3 A.M., Sat. 7 P.M.-3 A.M., Sun. 7 P.M.-2 A.M.
COST: $8 Cover charge
Map 5

Phase 1 claims to be "the oldest lesbian bar in the country," opening in 1970, and who's to say when the Hideaway in St. Petersburg, Florida, which claims to have opened in 1969, applied for its liquor license? Regardless, Phase 1 is the oldest in DC, and still one of the few bars exclusively for women. Monthly activities include Jell-O wrestling, drag king shows, and burlesque events. It also has a pool table, a dance floor, and a well-stocked bar. Men are welcome, but they'll get the evil eye unless accompanied by a female friend.

TOWN DANCEBOUTIQUE

2009 8th St. NW, 202/234-8696, www.towndc.com
HOURS: Daily 9 P.M.-4 A.M., last entry 2:30 A.M.
COST: $10
Map 7

Town is where gay Washington goes simply to have a good time, to hang out on the dance floor and let loose. This huge club features two dance floors and a stage for drag shows. Music switches nightly; Friday is for 18 and older, with '80s music downstairs and electronica and Top 40 upstairs; Saturday is for 21 and older, with house and pop tunes. Drag shows occur both evenings at 9:30 and 11 P.M. Bring cash if you don't want to use the bar's ATM; the place doesn't take credit.

Live Music

◖ BLACK CAT

1811 14th St. NW, 202/667-7960, www.blackcatdc.com
HOURS: Sun.-Thurs. 8 P.M.-2 A.M., Fri.-Sat. 7 P.M.-3 A.M.
Map 7

Established in 1993 by a group of investors—mainly musicians, including local boy Dave Grohl who's hit it big playing for Nirvana and fronting the Foo Fighters—the Black Cat favors local groups, up-and-comers, and cutting-edge bands as well as world-touring DJs. The stage at the Black Cat rocks nightly, attracting a mixed 18-and-over crowd, depending on who is on stage. This dark, low-ceilinged space holds 550 people standing. The downstairs contains a small stage room and a lounge. Bring cash. There's an ATM next to the bar if you forget, but you won't want to pay the user fees.

◖ BLUES ALLEY

1073 Wisconsin Ave. NW, 202/337-4141,
www.bluesalley.com
HOURS: Daily 6 P.M.-12:30 A.M.
Map 8

Blues Alley is like a Hollywood set of a jazz club, with exposed brick walls, small round cocktail tables with tea lights, and art nouveau chairs tucked in a low-slung 19th-century carriage house not far from the C&O Canal. Its stage has hosted Dizzy Gillespie, Sarah Vaughan, and Nancy Wilson, and more recently, Melba Moore and Terence Blanchard. Although its main acts tend to favor jazz, promoters sometimes throw in something unique, like a three-night appearance by Chuck Brown, considered the godfather of DC's homegrown music genre, go-go. Blues Alley is a great place for a date, but only after you have established rapport with your partner: Patrons listen intently to the music, eschew small talk, and glare at anyone who chats through the music. Blues Alley usually offers two shows a night. Dinner is available, although the cuisine is secondary to the music. Consider booking a seat at a late performance and heading elsewhere for dinner beforehand.

© PATRICIA KIME

BOHEMIAN CAVERNS

2001 11th St. NW, 202/299-0801,
www.bohemiancaverns.com
HOURS: Mon.-Thurs. 7 P.M.-12 A.M.,
Fri.-Sat. 9:30 P.M.-2 A.M., Sun. 6 P.M.-12 A.M.
Map 7

The focal point of the four-level Bohemian Caverns is its historic basement, a unique setting of faux stalactites from yesteryear that once hosted jazz greats such as Duke Ellington and Cab Calloway. Established in 1926 underneath a drug store, Club Caverns, later called Crystal Caverns, was Washington's top club for jazz, a required stop on the circuit for Miles Davis, Billie Holiday, Shirley Horn, and Charlie Parker. The club's fortunes went south in 1968 when the neighborhood collapsed amid civil rights turmoil, but after it was purchased and renovated in the late 1990s, it has again claimed a spot as a top DC jazz and blues venue. The 17-piece house band takes the stage nearly every Monday; solo acts and small groups, such as Jimmie and Tootie Heath or Sachal Vasandani, perform on weekends.

9:30 CLUB

815 V St. NW, 202/265-0930, www.930.com
Map 7

DC's most popular small venue for rock and well-known for staging a broad spectrum of other genres, the 9:30 Club holds 1,200 patrons in a warehouse space with a vast first floor facing an elevated stage and an upstairs balcony overlooking the entire scene. Four bars keep the drinks flowing, and there's not a bad sightline in the house. Still, shorter people—me included—do better by queuing up well before the doors open to snag a spot near the stage. The 9:30 Club is an all-ages club; it's not uncommon to see a parent with a teen or two in tow, or a group of high-schoolers checking out a favorite obscure group. IDs are required for those wanting to drink alcohol, no exceptions. Recent appearances include Loretta Lynn, Death Cab for Cutie, The Cars, and Regina Spektor.

U-TOPIA

1418 U St. NW, 202/483-7669, www.utopiaindc.com
HOURS: Tues. 9:30 P.M.-1 A.M., Wed. 9 P.M.-1 A.M.,
Thurs. 9:30 P.M.-1:30 A.M., Fri. 11 P.M.-2:30 A.M., Sat.
11 P.M.-2:30 A.M.
Map 7

U-Topia, one of the first businesses to bring jazz back to historic U Street, is a celebration of the arts, a place to try a menu featuring international cuisine, admire art (the owner's paintings hang on the walls), and feel the music—usually American jazz, but Brazilian up-tempo on Thursday nights. U-Topia has a set calendar of bands, but musicians often drop by with their own instruments for impromptu jam sessions. The decor is sophisticated, featuring exposed brick, red accent walls, and drapes reminiscent of owner Jamal Sahri's native Morocco. An eclectic crowd packs in after about 10 P.M. on weekends; for the best views of the musicians, grab a seat at the mahogany bar.

Lounges

◖ 18TH STREET LOUNGE

1212 18th St. NW, 202/466-3922,
www.eighteenthstreetlounge.com
HOURS: Tues.-Thurs. 5:30 P.M.-2 A.M.,
Fri. 5:30 P.M.-3 A.M., Sat. 9:30 P.M.-3 A.M., Sun. 9 P.M.-2 A.M.
COST: $10-20
Map 6

The 18th Street Lounge, or ESL, gets points for creativity. Despite a setting in a Victorian mansion marred with rusting fire escapes set above a mattress store, ESL oozes exclusivity, with no sign outside, a strict dress code, and lines down the block of youngsters willing to pay a cover charge for a place to sit. Inside, the decor is Victorian, with rich fabrics, fussy couches, chandeliers, and fireplaces, setting a tone like partying in the home of a rich old friend or your great-grandma's house, depending on your perspective. DJs spin an eclectic mix of house, reggae, soul, or blues in this

NIGHTLIFE

two-story space, and live jazz often plays on the upper level on weekends. An outdoor patio has more modern furnishings and sometimes hosts guest DJs. Guys: The usual offenders like ball caps, sneakers, and light jeans will get you turned away at the door, but quite often khakis will too.

THE GIBSON

2009 14th St. NW, 202/232-2156,
www.thegibsondc.com
HOURS: Mon.-Thurs. and Sun. 6 P.M.-1 A.M., Fri.-Sat. 6 P.M.-2 A.M.
Map 7

A friend's family owned a pharmacy in DC during Prohibition and somehow made a killing; I like to imagine that the back door of their establishment was similar to the Gibson—no sign, a buzzer to enter, and inside, a candlelit space where patrons could break the law in near darkness, sipping forbidden cocktails. Today, there are no rules against imbibing fancy cocktails, with the exception being the drinking age, but the fantasy appeals: The Gibson prides itself on classic cocktails such as a flawless martini or Gibson (a martini garnished with a pickled onion), New Orleans Sazerac, and old-fashioneds. The bartenders have a thing against vodka drinks, as they explain that vodka wasn't popular during the Prohibition. But surprisingly, *pisco*, an import from Peru, was. Reservations are required; patrons are allowed to take a seat for two hours.

LOUNGE 201

201 Massachusetts Ave. NE, 202/544-5201,
www.lounge201.com
HOURS: Tues.-Fri. 4 P.M.-2 A.M.
Map 5

As smooth as Disaronno in a snifter, Lounge 201 has a cool upscale vibe that attracts a more refined, better-paid, older clientele than the many beer bar–happy hour joints on Pennsylvania Avenue that serve the Capitol Hill crowd. Drinks aren't cheap (a bottle of Veuve Clicquot is priced at $140), but the specialty cocktails are diverse and inventive; the Sinatra, with blueberry vodka, white cranberry juice, fresh lime, and tonic, is a splash of summer in a glass. And at 10 ounces, all the martinis pack a punch. Leather banquettes, a curved sweeping bar, and pool tables combine to create a chill atmosphere for policy wonks and politicos. A DJ spins great cuts from the '80s and '90s on Thursday nights.

RUSSIA HOUSE

1800 Connecticut Ave. NW, 202/234-9433,
www.russiahouselounge.com
HOURS: Mon.-Thurs. 5 P.M.-midnight, Fri. 5 P.M.-2 A.M., Sat. 6 P.M.-2 A.M., Sun. 6 P.M.-midnight
Map 6

The rich decor at the Russia House—red damask wallpaper or red leather-textured walls, long draperies, deep green marble, and twinkling chandeliers—coupled with the Eastern European accents of the patrons make a visit to Russia House a getaway to the motherland, a place to enjoy Russian food and vodka, the latter never enjoyed on its own without the former in Russia. Russia House has nearly 100 flavors and types of vodka on the menu despite the fact that plain vodka, namely Stoli, still rules in Moscow. With so many choices, the sampler of six vodkas is one of the most popular orders, with guests choosing among the selections that include Polish vodka tinged with herbs and milk-filtered vodka, which is thicker and smoother than a shot of Ketel One. Russia House is also one of the few places in DC to find Baltika beer. Of course, there's a selection of caviar to round out the experience.

Wine Bars

(BISTROT LEPIC

1736 Wisconsin Ave. NW, 202/333-0111,
www.bistrotlepic.com
HOURS: Daily 5:30 P.M.-midnight
Map 8

On its first floor, Bistrot Lepic is a quintessential French neighborhood dining spot, one that has been recognized for excellence by the critics of *Bon Appétit* and *Town & Country* magazines. Upstairs is the restaurant wine bar, opened in 2002 and greeted with great fanfare, the first of its kind in the city. The small space seats 50, an Asian-inspired room of rattan furniture and coconut-inlay tables touched with French accents such as bright floral oil paintings, gilt mirrors, and stained glass lamps. The wine bar features roughly 20 wines—all French—by the glass as well as a full menu, from "appeteasers" like escargot and onion tart to French bistro fare, including cassoulet and *coquilles Saint-Jacques*. On Tuesday 6–8 P.M., the wine bar hosts complimentary tastings; Wednesday 7–10 P.M. is live music night, and happy hour is every day (except Tuesday) 5:30–7 P.M., with half-price wines.

CORK

1720 14th St. NW, 202/265-2675, www.corkdc.com
HOURS: Tues.-Wed. and Sun. 5 P.M.-midnight,
Thurs.-Sat. 5 P.M.-1 A.M.
Map 7

The wine is the star at Cork, a bar that offers 50 wines by the glass and roughly 160

VINO IN DC

In the past decade, wine bars have become a staple of the DC dining and drinking scene, with some more focused on the food and others fixated on the wine, serving small plates of cheese or cured meats to complement the vintages. Among the pioneers is the wine bar at **Bistrot Lepic,** a second-floor hideaway above the Georgetown bistro that pours French varietals. Still going strong after a decade, Bistrot Lepic has inspired a generation of entrepreneurs and restaurateurs who've set up shop with just the dream of sharing their favorite beverage with Washington.

If a glass of wine and a bit of cheese is all you seek, check out the selections at Veritas and Cork. **Veritas,** near Dupont Circle, offers 70 wines by the glass, an international selection that draws from five continents. At **Cork** you'll find nearly 50 wines by the glass, mainly from France, Spain, Italy, and Germany – no New World offerings here.

For more substantial fare along with your pour, check out **Proof,** known for its numerous small plates and 50 wines by the glass, kept fresh in an Enomatic system that keeps the wines fresh by replacing oxygen in the open bottle with argon, eliminating oxidation. Proof's selection is from all over the world. **Vinoteca** features 100 wines, many of them available in half-glass tasting pours, along with a full menu of New American fare with locally sourced and organic ingredients. And although its name implies all things Californian, the wine list at **Sonoma** heavily favors the wines of Italy, although the menu is Californian.

The city also has a number of fine restaurants with outstanding wine lists, and the booming popularity of wine in the United States has prompted these eateries to move their collections out of their cellars and place them front and center in the dining room. In many of DC's top eateries, wine chillers are a central part of the decor. For a night out of big food and substantial wines, there's **Charlie Palmer Steak,** which only offers 10 wines by the glass, but rarely does a customer order a single serving. The restaurant's 3,500-bottle selection is exclusively American, and Charlie Palmer will waive the corkage fee for anyone who brings in a special bottle to drink with their meal, as long as it's American. The **Blue Duck Tavern** also has an encyclopedic wine list, with more than 30 by the glass, mainly American and including top Virginia wines.

bottles from small vineyards around the world, but the small plates are noteworthy as well: goat cheesecake, crispy duck confit, fried shrimp, and calamari tarted up with lemon and pepper. Wine neophytes appreciate the descriptions of the wines as well as the flights, which allow a taster to experience the different vintages without breaking the bank. Often crowded and noisy, Cork is less of a romantic date place and more a fun setting to kick back with friends and enjoy the fruit of the soil.

SONOMA
223 Pennsylvania Ave., 202/544-8088,
www.sonomadc.com
HOURS: Mon.-Thurs. 5-10 P.M., Fri.-Sat. 5-11 P.M., Sun. 5-9 P.M.
Map 5

Sonoma is a full-service restaurant and nightspot with a downstairs that serves a menu of small plates, charcuterie, and cheese platters designed to satisfy the hungry diner, and a wine bar upstairs with a more limited menu and, surprisingly, a smaller wine-by-the-glass list than downstairs, but with more selective choices. With low upholstered benches, leather cubes, and modern sofas, Sonoma's wine bar attracts a trendy upscale crowd. Oddly, given its name, the wine list leans heavily toward Italian offerings. The menu, though, stands firmly in the realm of Napa Valley. Specials include half-price bottles from the reserve list on Sunday.

VERITAS
2031 Florida Ave. NW, 202/265-6270,
www.veritasdc.com
HOURS: Daily 5 P.M.-close
Map 6

Cozy Veritas seats just 50 people in its exposed brick and burgundy interior, attracting customers with a wine list of 70 by the glass, nearly 200 bottles, and flights: half-glass tastings that center on a theme such as "backpacking in Italy" or "Lewis and Clark," with wines of Washington State. A few flights include the same varietal from different places—an adventure for the palate that demonstrates how differences in climate and soil affect a grape. Food offerings are mainly limited to appetizers that complement the vino, including cheese boards, charcuterie, dips, and chocolates.

VINOTECA
1940 11th St. NW, 202/332-9463, www.vinotecadc.com
HOURS: Mon.-Sat. 5 P.M.-close, Sun. 11 A.M.-close
Map 7

Vinoteca distinguishes itself from DC's other wine bars by offering a variety of entertainment and a bar that sells draft craft beer and Peroni to sip while playing boccie in the back court. Of course, its selling point is the wine, roughly 60 labels, many of them available in half-glass pours. The happy hour special, Tuesday–Friday 5–7 P.M. and all day Sunday, features 20 wines for $5 per glass. Sometimes this row-house space has live music, and it also features sidewalk seating, a bonus on a nice evening.

ARTS AND LEISURE

For roughly its entire first century, Washington grew as a political power but languished as a cultural backwater where arts played second fiddle to the day's decision-making. But by the beginning of the 20th century, the scales became more balanced, partly due to the city's natural maturation but also because philanthropy, especially that benefitting the arts, became fashionable in the Gilded Age. Coupled with the city's growing intellectual capital (Washington today has the largest percentage of residents with bachelor's degrees of any U.S. city, according to the Brookings Institution), the climate existed for a world-class arts and entertainment community. While the city has long been known as a destination for history, monuments, and the world's biggest library, it is slowly becoming a center for the arts as

well, with a vibrant theater scene nearly rivaling Chicago's second place to New York, an arts establishment that conserves some of the world's greatest works and nurtures new and emerging artists, and a stopover for musicians at all stages of their careers.

It's hard to walk down a street in DC and not bump into a museum or gallery, and it's impossible to find a night on the calendar when there's nothing to do. Washington's performers and artists are hard at work daily, vying for exhibit and stage space throughout the city at small appointment-only galleries and large exhibition halls, at the well-known performing arts venues like Kennedy Center for the Performing Arts, or an intimate off-the-beaten-path black box like the District of Columbia Arts Center. Washington DC is

DANIEL LOBO · DAQUELLAMANERA.ORG

HIGHLIGHTS

LOOK FOR (TO FIND RECOMMENDED ARTS AND ACTIVITIES.

(**Most Powerful Portraits:** The Hall of Presidents at the **National Portrait Gallery and National Museum of American Art** features the likenesses of 42 commanders in chief, including a surprisingly endearing portrait of Richard Nixon by Norman Rockwell (page 144).

(**Best Museum Space:** The **Phillips Collection,** housed in a gallery space that blends contemporary architecture with rooms in the former Phillips family home, displays the works of Degas, Cézanne, Van Gogh, and Matisse alongside art by Americans Whistler, Homer, Hopper, and O'Keeffe (page 144).

(**Best Theater Venue:** The city's first Regional Theatre Tony Award winner received a makeover in 2010; **Arena Stage** now has three theater venues, including its original theater-in-the-round, now under a glass-enclosed cantilevered big top (page 147).

(**Best Free Show:** Millennium Stage, in the Grand Foyer of the **John F. Kennedy Center for the Performing Arts,** showcases America's talent *for free,* no ticket required, daily at 6 P.M. On any given evening, audiences might see a children's storyteller, a Grammy nominee, a university dance troupe, or a one-act play (page 149).

(**Best Under-the-Radar Tony Award Winner:** The theater cognoscenti know **Signature Theatre,** but many of its own neighbors aren't familiar with this gem, founded to showcase the works of Stephen Sondheim. Signature has gone beyond playing a little night music to staging new works and reworking often ignored books, including a critically acclaimed revival of *Chess* in 2010 (page 151).

(**Best Place for a Movie Opening:** The decor — what looks to be circa-1970 with smooshed red seats and the funk of 40 years — is nothing to gush about, but the **AMC Loews Uptown**'s curved 32- by 70-foot single screen and 850 seats with a balcony still remains the best place to catch a midnight opening in DC (page 154).

(**Most Impressive Parade:** The Army calls their evening performances "tattoos," while the Marines call them "parades." Regardless, the Corps's Friday **Military Parades** at Marine Barracks 8th and I are unforgettable (page 163).

(**Best Short Hike:** Deciduous forests, marshland, the river, and a hidden memorial make **Theodore Roosevelt Island** a favorite for strolling and dog walking (page 170).

(**Best Museum Gardens:** Ten acres of French-, Italian-, and English-inspired gardens surround **Dumbarton Oaks,** a landscape straight out of Francis Hodgson Burnett's *The Secret Garden* (page 170).

(**Best Biking Trail:** The gentle uphill climb of the **Capital Crescent Trail** from Georgetown to Bethesda, Maryland, is a workout, but a treat waits at the end: Dolcezzo Gelato is just a few blocks down on the left on Bethesda Avenue (page 172).

© PFC RAIMONDO LESCAUD

Marine Corps's Friday Military Parade

home to one of the country's first art museums, the Corcoran, and numerous museum galleries, such as the Renwick, a Smithsonian outlet showcasing crafts and decorative arts, and the National Museum of African Art, a unique underground space that remains one of the city's best-kept secrets. There are also a number of small nonprofit and commercial galleries that support young and emerging artists and cater to new and experienced collectors. And, of course, the city contains the taxpayers' own National Gallery of Art, the country's premier free art museum, funded initially in 1937 as a gift by financier Andrew Mellon. Across the city, art devotees will find something to their liking in Foggy Bottom, Dupont Circle, Adams Morgan, U Street, or the National Mall.

For classical entertainment, Kennedy Center is the city's crown jewel, home to the National Symphony Orchestra, the Washington National Opera, and the Washington Ballet. Kennedy Center also stages Broadway touring shows and revamped works of classics such as *Ragtime*. Across the city, smaller entertainment venues, including George Washington University's Lisner Auditorium, hosts a variety of concerts and recitals. To enjoy dance music, jazz, rock, and punk, the city boasts a number of clubs and after-dark venues that celebrate these genres, long a part of the city's cultural fabric. Among the success stories is the revival of jazz, blues, and rock along U Street, a historic center for music where Duke Ellington, Shirley Horn, and Tony Taylor cut their teeth from the 1920s through the 1950s. The city is also known for its unique form of music, go-go, a blend of funk, swing, blues, and early hip-hop with a distinctive rhythmic style all its own, frequently heard in clubs on the fringes of town.

In terms of theater, Washington's community is blossoming into one of the nation's best, home to two Regional Theatre Tony Award–winning theaters and numerous stages that showcase new works and reworked versions of classics. In the past three years, the city has served as a launching pad for three shows to Broadway, including the blockbuster *Next to Normal,* winner of three Tony Awards and a Pulitzer Prize. From traditional musical theater to experimental shows to opera or straight plays, if it's on stage, you'll find it in DC.

Spring and summer are the biggest seasons for outdoor events and festivals in DC, although Washingtonians also like to brave December's chill to watch the lighting of the National Christmas Tree or crowd the banks of the Potomac River to be entertained by the city's waterskiing Santa. Annual events range from the renowned National Cherry Blossom Festival and American Folk Life Festival in the spring and summer to neighborhood favorites like the Halloween High Heel Drag Queen Race.

Sports fans also will find plenty in Washington. Its moderate four-season climate and waterside location provide numerous outlets for nearly any type of recreation, including rowing, running, cycling, hiking, skating, and surfing. Well, maybe not surfing, but stand-up paddleboarding—it's not just for Samoans anymore. There's also horseback riding, sailing, running, and tennis. Unsurprisingly, Washington is one of the fittest cities in the country, according to *Men's Health* magazine, evident in the number of runners, cyclists, and walkers out daily enjoying the city's trails and scenery. And if your love of sports leans more toward sitting on the edge of a foldout seat, beer in hand, the city has that too: Washington hosts five major-league sports teams and numerous collegiate teams whose schools participate in nearly every Division I sport available, including local favorites lacrosse and crew. Sparkling venues like the new Nationals stadium and the Verizon Center, with their great concession selections and safe, friendly atmosphere, enhance the experience.

The Arts

Washington's art scene is a kaleidoscope of mediums, styles, genres, and subjects, as diverse as the city that claims residents from nearly every other country. For the past century the arts have thrived in Washington, first supported by its socialites and captains of industry, who used their great wealth to widen the city's cultural appeal, and now sustained by an environment that enjoys relative economic stability and a population on the youngish side—35 being the median age—with disposable income to spend on experiences, whether a gallery opening, a new stage play, or the latest from an up-and-coming band. Today, the city's population has no shortage of choices for cultural edification.

In terms of visual arts, galleries and museums can be found in nearly every neighborhood, with the grand dame of art museums, the National Gallery of Art, located on the National Mall, its collection of 110,000 pieces—only a small percentage on display at any given time—so large that it spans two buildings. It is described in the *Sights* section of this book. But the National Gallery is not alone in boasting a premier art collection. Washington's historic museums, the Corcoran Gallery and the Phillips Collection, house well-known works, and each showcases an aspect of American art: the Corcoran has 19th century portraits, landscapes, and photography, and the Phillips has American realists

DC CELEBRITIES: NOT JUST HOME TO POWERBROKERS

Loads of famous people live in Washington DC for its ties to politics, the government, and the world stage. But the city has nurtured its share of residents in the arts: A surprising number of artists, writers, performers, scientists, and, quite naturally, satirists were born in DC or the immediate suburbs, or spent time here during their childhoods. Without them the American entertainment industry wouldn't be what it is today.

The city's U Street clubs were a nursery for jazz musicians, including **Duke Ellington,** pianist **Billy Taylor,** saxophonist **Frank Wess,** and jazz vocalist **Shirley Horn.** Years later, another Washingtonian lent his unique voice to African American music, influencing an entire generation of singers across genres: DC native **Marvin Gaye** played a pivotal role in the success of Motown and the label's unique sound. Other world-famous musicians from the area include **John Philip Sousa, Roberta Flack,** and the current darling of grunge and rock, **Dave Grohl.**

Two nearby Virginia high schools are known for their award-winning performers. The now-closed George Washington High School

in Alexandria counts singers **Jim Morrison, Mama Cass,** and **John Phillips** as alumni, and Arlington's Washington-Lee High School boasts three Oscar winners: **Warren Beatty, Shirley MacLaine,** and **Sandra Bullock.**

Actors abound, although many of them were born in the city and moved elsewhere, including **William Hurt, Samuel L. Jackson,** and **Katherine Heigl.** Those who rank among the stars raised here include **Helen Hayes, Yeardley Smith** (the voice of Lisa Simpson), and **John Heard.** Comedians **Ana Gasteyer** and **Stephen Colbert** have roots in DC as well.

DC hits the mother lode when it comes to famous journalists – **Carl Bernstein, Pat Buchanan, Maureen Dowd,** and others – but it was also home to literary figures, most notably **Sinclair Lewis** and **Walt Whitman.** Whitman's mark is nearly everywhere on the city: He was known for frequenting the Round Robin Bar at the historic Willard Hotel, serving as a nurse at the makeshift hospital in the Patent Office Building, now home to the National Portrait Gallery, and working as a copy boy for the U.S. Army at what is now the W Hotel Washington DC.

and abstract artists side-by-side with European impressionists. The city also has a number of nonprofit exhibit spaces showcasing local and emerging artists and commercial galleries that sell the works of newcomers as well as the established. Many of these are open during the week, but the fun happens on the first Friday of the month, especially near Dupont Circle, where many of the neighborhoods galleries stay open until 8 or 9 P.M. The city has a burgeoning number of multifunctional art spaces too, where patrons can examine a local artist's exhibit and catch a performance-art piece or a new play. The District of Columbia Arts Center in Adams Morgan satisfies fans of the avant-garde with its 750-square-foot gallery and 50-seat black box, a popular venue for staging experimental theater.

DC's theater scene is also hopping. The list of award-winning and renowned theaters is long for a city of its size. In no uncertain terms, Washington is finally on the radar of producers, Broadway performers, and playwrights as a city that takes risks and embraces bold productions in the name of theater. People want to work here, and audiences clamor for more. What's unfortunate is that most DC residents, when asked about the city's stages, can usually only name three: Kennedy Center, the National Theater, and the Warner; maybe they'll mention Arena Stage. But with the exception of theater addicts and aficionados, few can tell you that the Folger Theatre at the Folger Shakespeare Library differs from the Shakespeare Theater Company, or that the Woolly Mammoth Theater Company puts on original works like nothing seen elsewhere. In 2008, Washington's Arena Stage wrested *Next to Normal* from Chicago's Goodman Theatre; the musical went on to Broadway. Kennedy Center is still tops when it comes to national tours of Broadway megahits and potential Broadway launches, like the 2009 revival of *Ragtime* and the 2011 production of *Follies*. But theater patrons who can't afford the steep ticket prices at this premier venue can find incredible talent, thoughtful and entertaining shows, and visually stunning productions at

nearly every price point throughout the city in musical theater, contemporary and classical plays, movement pieces, and concerts.

Consider allotting time to explore the city's cultural landscape, to enjoy a place that offers everything from the classical and traditional to the contemporary and experimental. You might end up pondering something you never expected to see in the nation's capital or taking a bit of artistry home as a souvenir. Regardless, if you take the time to catch a show or visit a small gallery, you'll see a part of Washington few visitors take the time to get to know.

MUSEUMS

CORCORAN GALLERY OF ART

500 17th St. NW, 202/639-1700, www.corcoran.org
HOURS: Wed. and Fri.-Sun. 10 A.M.-5 P.M.,
Thurs. 10 A.M.-9 P.M.
COST: $10 adults, $8 over age 61 and students, free under age 12
Map 4

Washington's first art museum, the Corcoran Gallery features an extensive collection of American art, with an emphasis on 18th- and 19th-century portraiture and landscapes and including an extensive library of 20th-century works. Among its collection is the striking *Mount Corcoran* by Albert Bierstadt, an idealized vision of a Sierra Nevada peak named to please patron and museum founder William Corcoran. Other notable works include a Gilbert Stuart portrait of George Washington, *Madame Edouard Pailleron* by John Singer Sargent, and *Ground Swell* by Edward Hopper. The Corcoran also holds a vast collection of historic and modern photography. Past exhibits include Edward Burtynsky's *Oil* and *Native Land: Photographs from the Robert G. Lewis Collection*. The striking 1897 beaux arts building is also home to the Corcoran College of Art and Design, an undergraduate school that confers bachelor of fine arts degrees in the visual arts and master's degrees in design and art education. Once a year, usually in April, the school sponsors an sale of students' artworks, a great place to pick up jewelry and decorative arts at reasonable prices.

ARTS AND LEISURE

the Freer Gallery of Art

THE FREER GALLERY OF ART AND ARTHUR M. SACKLER GALLERY

1050 Independence Ave. SW, 202/633-4880, www.asia.si.edu
HOURS: Daily 10 A.M.–5:30 P.M.; closed Christmas Day
COST: Free
Map 2

Technically two separate museums but lumped together because they share a similar focus— Asian art—and twin buildings surrounding a center court, the Freer and Sackler Galleries are true oases on the Mall, often overlooked spaces that hold an exquisite collection of Asian art and decorative artifacts, including centuries-old ceramics, jades, and bronzes, Japanese porcelains, Chinese scrolls, screens, and Islamic art and books. The Freer Gallery, whose collection is largely derived from a gift by turn-of-the-20th-century industrialist Charles Lang Freer, also contains the world's largest collection of works by James McNeill Whistler, Freer's favorite artist. Not to be missed is Whistler's *Peacock Room,* designed for the home of British shipbuilder Frederick Leyland, a spectacularly embellished room the artist decorated without consulting the owner and then proceeded to hold parties in when Leyland wasn't home.

When the pair had a falling out over payment and the parties, Whistler reworked the room, painting it blue and adding a garish pair of gilt fighting peacocks. Freer had the *Peacock Room* disassembled and rebuilt at his home in Detroit before it eventually ended up in this Washington gallery.

HILLWOOD ESTATE

4155 Linnean Ave. NW, 202/686-5807 or 877/445-5966, www.hillwoodmuseum.org
HOURS: Tues.-Sat. 10 A.M.–5 P.M., select Sun.; closed Mon. and federal holidays
COST: Suggested donation $15 adults, $12 over age 64, $10 college students, $5 ages 6-18, free under age 6
Map 9

Containing one of the largest collections of Russian imperial art outside Russia, Hillwood is the former home of Marjorie Merriweather Post, heiress to the Post cereal fortune and onetime wife of Joseph E. Davies, ambassador to the Soviet Union from 1936 to 1938, when the couple purchased many works of art, often sold by the government at rock-bottom prices to raise hard currency in the challenging economic and political climate of the time. The home displays Russian icons, Fabergé eggs, porcelain, textiles, silver, and framed artwork in addition to Post's extensive collection of French furniture, art, and jewelry. The estate is most popular during spring, when its extensive gardens are in bloom. A café on the grounds serves a light lunch and afternoon tea. Reservations are recommended for the dining room. Visitors can also opt to purchase from the express menu and borrow a picnic blanket free of charge to enjoy dining among the spectacular landscaping.

THE HIRSHHORN MUSEUM AND SCULPTURE GARDEN

7th St. and Independence Ave. SW, 202/633-4674, www.hirshhorn.si.edu
HOURS: Museum daily 10 A.M.–5:30 P.M., plaza daily 7:30 A.M.–5:30 P.M., sculpture garden daily 7:30 A.M.–dusk; closed Christmas Day
COST: Free
Map 2

Kudos to architect Gordon Bunshaft for the

distinctive look of this midcentury modern doughnut-shaped museum, an unidentified picture of which hangs in nearly every full-service Marriott bathroom—at least the ones in Williamsburg, Virginia, St. Thomas in the U.S. Virgin Islands, Chicago, and Sydney. In addition to its distinctive shape and interior courtyard, the Hirshhorn has an equally impressive interior, a natural light-filled space containing a mind-bending collection of contemporary works that include mobiles from Alexander Calder, sculptures by Matisse, and paintings and silk screens by De Kooning, Warhol, and Miró. If you don't have time to tour the inside, at least walk through the museum's sunken **Sculpture Garden** as you make your way down the Mall. This space features the works of more than 70 artists; pieces include Rodin's *Burghers of Calais* and *Horse and Rider* by Marino Marini. The Hirshhorn also hosts art classes for children and youths; these artist-led mini courses on Saturday are among the most popular children's activities in the city.

KREEGER MUSEUM

2401 Foxhall Rd. NW, 202/338-3552 or 877/377-3050, www.kreegermuseum.org
HOURS: Sat. 10 A.M.-4 P.M., optional tours 10:30 A.M., noon, and 2 P.M.; by appointment Tues.-Fri.
COST: $10 adults, $7 over age 64 and students
Map 9

The Kreeger is one exclusive place, a midcentury modern home in the residential northwest section of the city, filled, appropriately, with contemporary artworks, including paintings by Mondrian, Munch, Monet, Miró, and Picasso and sculptures by Calder, Rodin, and Brancusi. The collection (displayed on rotation, so you never know what you'll see) can be viewed on weekdays during a 90-minute by-appointment-only tour or on Saturday, when the museum holds an open house. Saturday is really the best time to visit, taking one of the optional tours and having the time to explore the home and grounds, one of the few residences in DC designed by Philip Johnson, famous for his Glass House in New Canaan, Connecticut.

THE NATIONAL MUSEUM OF AFRICAN ART

950 Independence Ave. SW, 202/633-1000, www.nmafa.si.edu
HOURS: Daily 10 A.M.-5:30 P.M.; closed Christmas Day
COST: Free
Map 2

The aboveground and underground galleries of the National Museum of African Art hold treasures from across the vast continent—ancient and modern art from every region, including masks, textiles, baskets, pottery, ritual artifacts, and carved tusks and figurines, some of which date to the 15th century. If you don't know anything about African art, stop off at the information desk and ask if they have a copy of the informational tour, which highlights 15 artifacts and helps explain the creativity and methodology behind them. The museum is linked to the Freer and Sackler Galleries by an underground tunnel; the space is cool and restful, a perfect place to loiter for a few minutes during an otherwise hectic visit to the National Mall.

NATIONAL MUSEUM OF WOMEN IN THE ARTS

1250 New York Ave. NW, 202/783-5000, www.nmwa.org
HOURS: Mon.-Sat. 10 A.M.-5 P.M., Sun. noon-5 P.M.
COST: $10 adults, $8 over age 64 and students, free under age 18
Map 3

If you took art history in college more than 20 years ago, chances are your textbook was a version of H. W. Janson's *History of Art*. And if you purchased the book before 1986, you might not have noticed, but it featured no female artists—no Georgia O'Keeffe, no Mary Cassatt, no Frida Kahlo. The founders of the National Museum of Women in the Arts took notice of this oversight, inspiring them to create a museum devoted exclusively to artists of the feminine gender. The museum, located in a former Masonic Temple, now contains the works of more than 800 artists. Notable works on display include Adélaïde Labille-Guiard's *Presumed Portrait of the Marquise de Lafayette* and Mary

Cassatt's *The Bath*. The museum's Mezzanine Café is a popular spot with area office workers and ladies who lunch, and the gift shop is worth a look for its wide selection of books, posters, jewelry, and decorative arts made by women.

🌙 NATIONAL PORTRAIT GALLERY AND NATIONAL MUSEUM OF AMERICAN ART

8th St. and F St. NW, 202/633-8300 or 202/633-7970, www.npg.si.edu and www.americanart.si.edu
HOURS: Daily 11:30 A.M.-7 P.M.
COST: Free
Map 3

Housed in a stunning space that once served as the U.S. Patent Office, a Civil War hospital, and the site of Lincoln's second inaugural ball, these two museums share a square city block surrounding a central courtyard that, during a multimillion-dollar makeover in the 2000s, was enclosed with a striking fishnet glass canopy. The National Portrait Gallery is known for its exhibit featuring the likenesses of the U.S. presidents, including a copy of Gilbert Stuart's famous portrait of George Washington (which also hangs in the White House and was spirited out of the building before the British set it on fire in 1814) and a standing portrait of Ronald Reagan that, when it was unveiled, elicited the remark from Reagan, "Yep, that's the old buckaroo." Other exhibits include *American Origins,* featuring the likenesses of hundreds of famous Americans from the colonial era to the Gilded Age, with striking portraits of Benjamin Franklin, a photograph of Sojourner Truth, and a vast collection of daguerreotypes.

The National Portrait Gallery blends into the National Museum of American Art somewhere in the hallways of this vast building; no line defines the change, and only the artwork indicates that you have moved from one to the other. The American Art museum holds the world's largest collection of American art, including oil and watercolors, sculpture, photography, folk art, crafts, and prints. The museum also includes furniture and decorative arts. Not to be missed is the bizarre and complex *The Throne of the Third Heaven of the*

The White Girl, by James Abbott McNeill Whistler, can be seen at the National Portrait Gallery.

Nation's Millennium General Assembly, by James Hampton, a work of assemblage art located in the museum's folk art gallery. The piece was found in the artist's garage after he died. For more traditional items, check out the collection of Western art, including landscapes from members of the Hudson River School and portraits of Native Americans by George Catlin.

🌙 PHILLIPS COLLECTION

1600 21st St. NW, 202/387-2151,
www.phillipscollection.org
HOURS: Tues.-Wed. and Fri.-Sat. 10 A.M.-5 P.M., Thurs. 10 A.M.-8:30 P.M., Sun. 11 A.M.-6 P.M.
COST: Tues.-Fri. donation, Sat.-Sun. $10 adults, $8 over age 62 and students, free under age 18
Map 6

At its entryway, the Phillips's space resembles

nearly any other art museum, with stark walls and pinpoint lighting illuminating the masterpieces. Through this pristine hardwood and plaster facade, however, are tight hallways and opulent chambers, the 1897 Greek Revival townhome of collectors Duncan and Marjorie Phillips, which contains many of the museum's treasures. The manor home, with rooms of half-timbered walls and wood paneling, original furnishings, and unique fireplaces, is nearly as notable as the artwork that adorns its walls—paintings by Whistler, Chase, Homer, Hopper, Weber, and Eakins. The Phillips Collection is considered the nation's first museum devoted to modern art; its newer space holds the museum's most famous piece, Renoir's *Luncheon of the Boating Party,* as well as the renowned Rothko Room, a linear space showcasing three of Mark Rothko's saturated works of color. The artist is said to have loved the room's chapel-like design. The Phillips After 5 event, held the first Thursday of each month, features after-hours browsing, food, drink, and live jazz.

Phillips Collection

© PATRICIA KIME

RENWICK GALLERY

17th St. and Pennsylvania Ave. NW, 202/633-2850, www.americanart.si.edu/renwick/
HOURS: Daily 10 A.M.–5:30 P.M.; closed Christmas Day
COST: Free
Map 4

This lavish 1859 townhome was designed by architect James Renwick for art collector and banker William Corcoran to house the latter's growing collection of American and European Art. The red stone Second Empire building served as a museum for more than 20 years, before Corcoran opened a larger facility just down the street. Today, the Renwick is the Smithsonian's repository for contemporary craft and decorative arts, displaying sculpture, woodwork, furniture, and design pieces that scream to be touched, although that is verboten, especially Wendell Castle's *Ghost Clock,* an eye-popping work of illusion, and Larry Fuente's *Game Fish,* a whimsical trophy crafted from used toys, baubles, and beads. The Renwick's Grand Salon is a magnificent sample of 19th-century opulence: The recently restored two-story space features a vast skylight, lavish fabrics, and numerous artworks hung "salon style," nearly up to the ceiling.

GALLERIES
ADDISON/RIPLEY FINE ART

1670 Wisconsin Ave. NW, 202/338-5180, www.addisonripleyfineart.com
HOURS: Tues.-Sat. 11 A.M.–6 P.M.
Map 8

This contemporary gallery hosts exhibits of internationally recognized artists, specializing in landscapes, paintings, sculpture, and photography. A recent show by Julia von Eichel showcased the artist's flat and multidimensional pieces, her etched works on oil adorning the walls while her 3-D creations of molded Mylar and latex paint were strung throughout the room, creating planes and lines through which visitors maneuvered. The work was beautiful to gaze on in the simple confines of a gallery but wasn't exactly practical for home decor. Exhibits change often, making Addison/Ripley Fine Art a nice spot to visit every couple of months for new and contemporary works.

ARTS AND LEISURE

ALEX GALLERY AND GALLERY A

2106 R St. NW, 202/667-2599, www.alexgalleries.com
HOURS: Tues.-Sat. 11 A.M.-5 P.M.

Map 6

Sitting among a bevy of galleries, Alex Gallery is an independent shop that carries adventurous art and bold abstract works—paintings, sketches, and paper media—by well-known European and American artists. The gallery is housed on two floors of a row house, a cozy environment with fireplaces and period architecture that contrasts nicely with the contemporary works on display. Sibling Gallery A is a membership gallery that focuses on emerging professional artists.

BURTON MARINKOVICH FINE ART

1505 21st St. NW, 202/296-6563,
www.burtonmarinkovich.com
HOURS: Tues.-Sat. 11 A.M.-6 P.M.

Map 6

If you've been visiting Washington-area art museums and want to buy a work by a contemporary or modern master, this gallery is the place to go, selling the works of Matisse, Calder, Christo and Jeanne-Claude, Sol LeWitt, Miró, and more. The gallery showcases paintings, drawings, prints, and studies, on display in a Victorian row house.

GOVINDA GALLERY

1227 34th St. NW, 202/333-1180,
www.govindagallery.com
HOURS: Tues.-Sat. 11 A.M.-6 P.M.

Map 8

Music and art blend in beautiful harmony at Govinda, a gallery dedicated to figurative works, painting, photos, and drawings, with the subject or artist usually connected to music in some way. Works don't have to be as obvious as a photo taken by Linda McCartney or Annie Leibovitz (who held her first DC show here in 1984), or a black and white photo of Elvis. A recent exhibit showcased drawings by artist Carlotta Hester, who made pencil sketches of musicians performing at one of the biggest festivals in Ireland. The gallery is in Georgetown, not far from the university campus, and is often frequented by students who enjoy lusting after its vast collection or rock photography and posters.

HILLYER ART SPACE

9 Hillyer Court NW, 202/338-0680,
www.artsandartists.org
HOURS: Mon. 10 A.M.-5 P.M., Tues.-Fri. 10 A.M.-7 P.M.,
Sat. 11 A.M.-4 P.M.

Map 6

Hillyer Art Space is a meeting place for artists, buyers, and young patrons who enjoy socializing and taking part in exhibitions, poetry readings, and screenings as well as seeing something new. Also on display in the gallery and at the offices of parent company International Art & Artists are the unusual pieces of the Hechinger collection, donated in 2003 by home improvement warehouse pioneer John Hechinger Sr.: artworks, sculpture, pictures, prints, and paintings that incorporate tools. Hillyer, tucked behind the Phillips Collection adjacent to the venerable Cosmos Club, is a top spot for First Friday socializing, often the first gallery to fill up on these popular art evenings,

Hillyer Art Space

an unpretentious space for newcomers to dip their toes in the sea of art appreciation.

IRVINE CONTEMPORARY

1412 14th St. NW, 202/332-8767,
www.irvinecontemporary.com
HOURS: Tues.-Sat. 11 A.M.-6 P.M.
Map 6

Mixed-media experimental works coexist with lively drawings and paintings at Irvine Contemporary. The space wins rave reviews from fans for its ever-changing collection and pieces that challenge and teach. Owner Martin Irvine is an associate professor for Georgetown University's Communication, Culture, and Technology program; he's welcoming, approachable, and informative, willing to discuss and debate the merits of the pieces on display.

STUDIO GALLERY

2108 R St. NW, 202/232-8734,
www.studiogallerydc.com
HOURS: Wed.-Thurs. 1-7 P.M., Fri. 1-8 P.M., Sat. 1-6 P.M.
Map 6

A cooperative of more than 40 DC-based artists that has been around for more than 45 years, Studio Gallery highlights contemporary works in oil and watercolor, sculpture, multimedia, and canvas. The gallery hosts solo and group exhibits simultaneously in two main spaces, and in December holds a free-for-all with members showing their best and most spirited works. The co-op takes part in Dupont Circle's First Fridays, a chance to view the arts and speak with the artists and owners.

THEATER
◖ ARENA STAGE

1101 6th St. SW, 202/488-3300, www.arenastage.org
Map 9

After spending a few years holding performances in alternate venues while its own theater received an extreme makeover, Arena took the stage in the 2010–2011 season at the new Mead Center for American Theater with abandon, winning rave reviews for its unconventional casting and energetic presentation of old favorite *Oklahoma!* and launching a new production of Edward Albee's *Who's Afraid of Virginia Woolf?* to Broadway. Arena

Arena Stage shines in its new home at the Mead Center for American Theater.

© PATRICIA KIME

focuses on "the canvas of American theater," including classics and new works. It was the first theater to receive the Regional Theatre Tony Award when the award was introduced in 1976, and it has earned numerous Helen Hayes Awards (Washington's premier theater prize). The new Arena Stage preserves the old stage's 1970s-era theater in the round, technically a theater in the square, and includes two additional performance spaces, including an architectural twist on a black box that is ovoid and paneled in brown wood. It also features a vast lobby and self-service café by Washington top chef José Andrés.

DISTRICT OF COLUMBIA ARTS CENTER

2438 18th St. NW, 202/462-7833, www.dcartscenter.org

Map 7

The unexpected and experimental are found at the District of Columbia Arts Center, a small 50-seat black box and gallery space in Adams Morgan. Tucked on the second floor of a row house that doesn't look like it could contain a theater, patrons mingle before shows in the gallery space, and when the door opens, they're led through a mysterious passageway, down a few steps, outside, and through another doorway to the theater. DC Arts Center specializes in edgy fare staged previously at nationwide fringe festivals, immersion theater performances, or new works developed by established artists, such as the Virginia-based Performers Exchange Project's *Dido Versus the Squid Monster*. DC Arts Center is conveniently located for a complete night on the town. After catching a show, theater patrons can head across the street to one of Adams Morgan's lively nightspots for music, drinks, and dancing.

FOLGER THEATRE

1 East Capitol St. SE, 202/544-7077, www.folger.edu
HOURS: Box office phone Mon.-Sat. 10 A.M.-5 P.M., Sun. noon-5 P.M.

Map 5

The black-and-white half-timbered interior of the Folger Theatre provides an intimate setting for enjoying some of the English language's finest works. Many of the plays staged by the Folger are Shakespearean, but every season or so, the troupe throws in a few classical and contemporary works inspired by the Bard. In the last 20 years, the theater has been nominated for 76 Helen Hayes Awards and won 14. While the Folger's Elizabethan-style theater is a traditional setting, this isn't an indication that all its productions are conventional. Some stagings are classical while others are avant-garde; recent productions include *A Comedy of Errors* and *Orestes: A Tragic Romp*. The small space seats 200 in the orchestra and an additional 50 in the balconies. Those with balcony seating should be aware that some seats have obstructed views, while those seated along the rail may have to lean over for a clear view.

FORD'S THEATRE

511 10th St. NW, 202/638-2941 or 202/347-4833, www.fordstheatre.org

Map 3

There's something undeniably impressive about seeing a show in Ford's Theatre, sitting within feet of the box where President Lincoln

Ford's Theatre

was shot, imagining John Wilkes Booth jumping from the balcony and dashing across the stage, dragging his broken leg. The unshakeable sense that history was made in this theater clings to audience members regardless of how often they've watched something on its stage. Not surprisingly, Ford's Theatre's offerings usually have some kind of historical bent, and much of what is put on is lighthearted fare, appropriate for families, like the annual staging of *A Christmas Carol* or the 2011 production of *Liberty Smith,* a musical about a Forrest Gump of the American Revolution who stumbles into big events and meets nearly every Founding Father during the war. Some fare is more pointed and adult; in one recent production, the theater brought three of Washington's regional powerhouse actresses together for Horton Foote's *The Carpetbagger's Children,* a captivating tale of life in the postreconstruction South.

THE FRIDGE DC

Rear Alley, 516 8th St. SE, 202/644-4151,
www.thefridgedc.com
HOURS: Gallery Wed.-Sat. 1-7 P.M. and 1 hour before special events
`Map 5`

A funky space tucked in an alleyway near Barracks Row, The Fridge is a venue for performers as well as an exhibition space for artists, both established and up-and-coming. Once a month, the Fridge hosts a Sunday Circus featuring performances by artists ranging from magicians and musicians to poets and solo artists.

◖ THE JOHN F. KENNEDY CENTER FOR THE PERFORMING ARTS

2700 F St. NW, 202/467-4600 or 202/416-8000,
www.kennedy-center.org
`Map 4`

The Kennedy Center is the crown jewel of Washington's performing arts scene, home to the National Symphony Orchestra, the Washington Chamber Symphony, the Washington Opera, and the Washington Ballet, and it is the venue of choice for Broadway

---

CAPITOL STEPS

In a league of their own, the satirical singing troupe the Capitol Steps is a Washington favorite, performing irreverent comedy sketches that skewer politicians and administrators regardless of which side of the aisle they reside. Founded in 1981 by a group of congressional staffers who enjoyed poking fun at their bosses during office Christmas parties, the Steps now primarily consist of professionally trained performers, with a requisite handful of former political staffers and administrators thrown in to keep it all "fair and balanced." The shows are a 90-minute musical satire of current news items and headline-making personalities; songs include titles like "Berlusconi Amore," "Obama Mia," and the "Ballad of the Queen Berets," and stand-up comedy sketches include "Lirty Dies," a routine delivered in a pig latin-like language that makes no sense – yet it does.

The Capitol Steps perform on weekends at the Ronald Reagan Building (1300 Pennsylvania Ave. NW) and at fund-raising venues throughout the DC area as part of its community outreach campaign. For information, call 202/312-1427 or check out www.capsteps.com.

---

touring groups, orchestras, operas, and internationally known solo performers as well as large musicals hoping to make it to the Great White Way. The Kennedy Center opened in 1971, its gleaming white marble structure designed by Edward Durrell Stone and later named a living memorial to John F. Kennedy, who supported funding for a national cultural center and whose wife, Jackie, served as honorary chairwoman for the project while she was first lady. The Kennedy Center has three main performance spaces: the Concert Hall, the largest of the three, has seating for 2,400. The Opera House is slightly smaller, able to accommodate 2,300. The newly renovated Eisenhower Theater holds just over 1,100. The center also houses a theater lab, a family theater, and a terrace theater.

Among the most popular free events in DC are the Kennedy Center's shows on the **Millennium Stage,** performances that occur nightly at 6 P.M. in the Grand Foyer, a stunning space that overlooks the river and is one of the largest rooms in the world (at 630 feet long, it is 75 feet longer than the Washington Monument is tall). When the Kennedy Center launched the Millennium Stage concept in 1997, most Washingtonians thought the practice would end by New Year's Eve 2001, but the city has been blessed by its continuance, part of an initiative by the center to ensure that the performing arts are within reach of everyone regardless of budget. Millennium Stage performances include concerts, children's shows, dance troupes, and works celebrating musical theater.

Tickets for events at the Kennedy Center often sell out; call the box office directly to inquire about the chances of obtaining tickets or release of tickets on the day of the performance. Also, the venue has a special program that sells discount tickets to seniors, disabled people, full-time students, low-income people, and junior enlisted personnel, based on availability. Call the box office for additional information.

LINCOLN THEATER
1215 U St. NW, 202/328-6000,
www.thelincolntheatre.org
Map 7

This historic theater once hosted music greats Duke Ellington, Ella Fitzgerald, Billie Holiday, and Nat King Cole. Today, the refurbished 1922 stage aims to continue celebrating its African American roots, staging shows and concerts that highlight multicultural experiences and expression. Recent events have included a night with Spike Lee, plays focusing on African American issues, and film premieres. The theater is on the National Register of Historic Places, not only for its historic significance but for its architecture; the plain facade belies the space's lavish interior's chandeliers, elegant boxes, rich upholstery, and fine wallpapers.

NATIONAL THEATRE
1321 Pennsylvania Ave. NW, 202/783-3372,
www.nationaltheatre.org
Map 3

The ornate National Theatre is the country's third-oldest theater and the longest in continuous operation in Washington. It held the first performance of *Hamlet* in Washington just two days after opening on December 7, 1835. Numerous acting greats have crossed the National's stage, including John Barrymore, Helen Hayes, Vivian Leigh, Jack Lemmon, John Gielgud, and John Travolta. The place even has its own ghost: According to lore, actor John McCullough was killed during an argument with another actor at the theater and was allegedly buried beneath the stage. The National Theatre seats 1,676 on three levels, with an especially steep balcony that allows for decent views but is not for acrophobics. It also has very tight rows, which can be uncomfortable for tall patrons. But it is still a top spot to see a touring Broadway show like *Avenue Q* or *Spamalot,* and on some Monday nights, it sponsors free events such as concerts, dance performances, and one-act plays. It also hosts free children's performances on Saturday. The National Theatre was last renovated in 1984 in a style designed to recall the era of its founding. Prepare yourself for its garish paint scheme, popular in the early 1800s.

THE SHAKESPEARE THEATRE COMPANY
450 7th St. NW, 202/547-1122, www.shakespearedc.org
Map 3

The Shakespeare Theatre Company has become so popular and so critically acclaimed that one theater wasn't enough to house it. In 2008 the 775-seat Sidney Harman Hall joined its neighbor, the Lansburgh Theatre, as dual venues for the company, which aims to stage classic theater—both written by Shakespeare or thought-provoking works along some classical vein—through a uniquely American lens. The Shakespeare Theatre Company was named by the *Wall Street Journal* as "the nation's foremost Shakespeare theater." It has won 59 Helen Hayes Awards in the past 20 years. Recent performances include *As You Like It* and *Richard II* as well as Oscar Wilde's *An Ideal Husband.* The theater often sets aside nights for young theatergoers, offering discounts to those under age 35, and it is a popular venue for a night out; many neighboring restaurants offer fixed-price pretheater dinner discounts, and area bars stay open late for patrons to enjoy an after-show cocktail.

SIGNATURE THEATRE

4200 Campbell Ave., Arlington, Va., 703/820-9771, www.signature-theatre.org

Map 9

Signature has come a long way from its roots as a suburban theater housed in a converted garage set in an industrial park. In 2007 it moved to a modern space—just across the creek and worlds away from the old venue—featuring two black-box theaters, ample rehearsal space, a vast lobby, and a bar. And two years after that, it won a Tony Award for regional theater, the same award earned by Arena Stage in 1976 and Chicago's Goodman Theatre in 1992. But it wasn't the space that earned the kudos; when Signature opened in 1990, it aimed to fill a void of medium-sized theaters in DC and a nationwide gap of those producing new works, especially musicals. "Signature has broadened and brightened the region's cultural landscape with its bold productions of challenging new and established works," the Broadway League and the American Theatre Wing wrote when they announced the award. At Signature, standard classics are never done traditionally: A recent production of *Sweeney Todd* was more bloodthirsty than most, and *Les Misérables,* presented without a rotating stage or marching hordes, was as dark and complex as Victor Hugo's book. Broadway flops also come to life, like a 2010 staging of *Chess.* Signature gives voice to new playwrights as well, often staging straight plays in the smaller Ark Theatre.

© PATRICIA KIME

Signature Theatre, Arlington

STUDIO THEATER

1501 14th St. NW, 202/332-3300,
www.studiotheatre.org
Map 6

Studio is another Washington gift to audiences and actors, a place that started in 1978 as an acting conservatory and stages contemporary works and Pulitzer Prize- and Obie Award–winning plays. Studio has four performance spaces designed to forge a connection between the attendees and the stage, and there's not a bad seat in any of the houses, although audiences often report being uncomfortably close to the actors, which is the point. Themes are often thought-provoking, dark, or raunchy, and past performances have included *Fat Pig, Guantanamo,* and *Jerry Springer, The Musical.* The Studio space is sleek and modern, with great views overlooking 14th Street along with a great lobby to linger in and enjoy drinks and snacks. Studio's consistent community involvement served as the cornerstone for the neighborhood's revitalization; without the theater, it is safe to say that the area, long-scarred after the 1960s riots, would be behind in its redevelopment. Today, the neighborhood is as hip as the theater that proudly calls 14th Street its home.

THEATER J

1529 16th St. NW, 202/777-3229,
www.washingtondcjcc.org/center-for-arts/theater-j/
Map 6

Award-winning Theater J, located in DC's Jewish Community Center, produces roughly six shows a year, including new works and revivals designed to showcase the Jewish cultural legacy or explore issues of humanity, including political, moral, and social dialogue. Theater J is on the cutting edge of the performing arts, encouraging new playwrights and commissioning works. The 2011 season includes productions of Arthur Miller's *After the Fall* and a nod to the sesquicentennial of the Civil War, *The Whipping Man,* about two newly freed slaves and the son of their former master, a Jewish Confederate soldier. All is not dark, however: The season also includes

a romantic comedy and performances by the Kinsey Sicks, a "dragapella quartet" that performs outrageous, salacious, and hysterical musical comedy.

WARNER THEATRE

513 13th St. NW, 202/783-4000,
www.warnertheatre.com
Map 3

The Warner Theatre, less than a block from the National Theatre, is a gilded art deco masterpiece constructed in 1924 as a movie house and vaudeville stage. It now hosts a variety of performances, including national tours of Broadway shows (*Stomp* and *Rent*), concerts ranging from Tony Bennett to Bobby McFerrin, comedy acts and television personalities, including an evening with Anthony Bourdain, and speakers like Maya Angelou. The Warner is the city's traditional venue for the Washington Ballet's annual staging of *The Nutcracker;* the opulent setting and beautifully crafted show is a family favorite for many Washingtonians.

WOOLLY MAMMOTH THEATRE COMPANY

614 D St. NW, 202/289-2443,
www.woollymammoth.net
Map 3

For a show you won't find in New York or Chicago, check out Woolly Mammoth Theatre Company, Washington's avant-garde troupe that specializes in new works, quirky plays, and devilishly fun performances. Stagings have included *A Girl's Guide to Washington Politics* from Second City and Charlie Ross's hilarious *One Man Lord of the Rings* and *One Man Star Wars.* On a more serious note, plays like *The Agony and Ecstasy of Steve Jobs,* a one-man show by political activist Mike Daisey about the Apple CEO and the company's impact on Chinese laborers, grip audiences as well, serving more as food for thought than entertainment. Woolly Mammoth's new digs, which the company moved into in 2005, are sophisticated: Concrete, polycarbonate, and metal surfaces define a bright cavernous space improbably located in an office building basement.

CHILDREN'S THEATER
DISCOVERY THEATRE
Smithsonian Institution's Ripley Center,
1100 Jefferson Dr. SW, 202/633-8700,
www.discoverytheatre.org
Map 2

For shows of perfect length and subjects beloved by kids, consider heading to the National
Mall for a show at Discovery Theatre, in the
Smithsonian's Ripley Center, accessible through
a copper-domed kiosk next to the Castle.
Discovery Theatre stages children's shows,
including puppet and magic shows, one-act
plays, concerts, and musical events that cap-
tivate young imaginations. Afterward, children can take in a nearby museum or ride the
Smithsonian Carousel, a 1947 merry-go-round
with 60 fleet-footed steeds.

CONCERT VENUES
Live music can be found nearly nightly across
the Washington region, with headliners not
always choosing to appear at the large venues
listed. Often the familiar or most recent iTunes
favorite can be found playing at a smaller club
or pubs in offbeat neighborhoods. Check out
the *Nightlife* listings for the inside track to
small music venues in DC.

DAR CONSTITUTION HALL
311 18th St. NW, 202/628-4780, www.dar.org/conthall
Map 4

DAR Constitution Hall is the city's largest
auditorium, a beautiful 1929 limestone neoclassical structure originally built to host the
Daughters of the American Revolution's annual convention. Today, this 3,700 seat venue
is a popular meeting space, holding area high
school graduations, World Bank assemblages,
and speaker series, and it is a great small concert venue, with decent sight lines from all
seats and small enough that it has no "nose-
bleed" section. Recent performers include Janet
Jackson, John Mellencamp, Paul Simon, Cake,
and the Isley Brothers. DAR Constitution Hall
is widely known as having denied Marian
Anderson the chance to perform there in
1939, prompting Eleanor Roosevelt to resign

her membership in the organization. But the
DAR overturned its discriminatory policies toward African Americans immediately following the uproar over the segregationist policy,
and Anderson performed at Constitution Hall
for a Red Cross benefit in 1943. She later chose
the auditorium as the first stop on her farewell
concert tour in 1964.

VERIZON CENTER
601 F St. NW, 202/661-5000, www.verizoncenter.com
Map 3

The stars sell out the more than 20,000-seat
Verizon Center, a venue for concerts by U2,
Beyoncé, Lady Gaga, and Bon Jovi, and other
headliners. It has also served as a stage for the
Dalai Lama and family-friendly entertainment
such as the Washington International Horse
Show and Disney on Ice. This spotless, modern
arena opened in 1997, commissioned by visionary developer Abe Pollin, who wanted DC's
professional sports teams to play in the city (the
Washington Wizards, formerly the Bullets,
and the Capitals used to play in Landover,
Maryland). Today, the Verizon Center is a centerpiece of the downtown area, bringing music
and sports fans nightly to this lively neighborhood. The Verizon Center is managed by a
company owned by Ted Leonsis, owner of the
teams that Pollin formerly owned, the Wizards
and the Capitals, as well as the Washington
Mystics WNBA franchise.

WOLF TRAP FOUNDATION
FOR THE PERFORMING ARTS
1645 Trap Rd., Vienna, Va., 703/255-1900,
www.wolftrap.org
Map 9

Wolf Trap is a Washington summertime tradition, a chance to hear a remarkable lineup
of singing groups and shows under the stars
in suburban Virginia. Nearly every night of
the summer, area residents and visitors traipse
out to Vienna, Virginia, with cooler and picnic blanket in hand, to line up at the gate for
the mad dash to the prime lawn seats at this
outdoor amphitheater. Considered the nation's
only national park devoted to the performing

arts, Wolf Trap hosts a variety of musicians and performers, including Lyle Lovett, the Goo Goo Dolls, Tony Bennett, Aretha Franklin, Maxi Priest, Huey Lewis and the News, and others. The venue also serves as the stage for summertime performances by Atlanta's Theater of the Stars, national opera groups, and movies with scores played live by the National Symphony Orchestra. Wolf Trap's vast lawn is first-come, first-served seating; lawn chairs are only allowed in designated areas in the back, and most people bring blankets or cushions. Coolers and outside food and drink are allowed, even encouraged, as part of the experience. The amphitheater also has covered seats under the loggia and in the orchestra; most people who purchase seats tailgate in the venue's parking lot before the show. Ticketed seats are closer to the stage than the lawn, and they offer another bonus: a roof when it rains. Concerts and shows go on regardless of weather; in 2008, Wolf Trap's matinee performance of *Les Misérables* took place in the middle of a raging Hurricane Hanna. The Filene Center, as the amphitheater is known, is open from early June through Labor Day. Wolf Trap hosts smaller events such as concerts and stand-up comedy acts in the Barns of Wolf Trap, a smaller indoor stage, during the winter.

CINEMA
AFI SILVER THEATER AND CULTURAL CENTER
8633 Colesville Rd., Silver Spring, Md., 301/495-6720, www.afi.com/silver
HOURS: Daily noon-midnight, check website for listings
Map 9

The American Film Institute, an organization dedicated to the preservation and celebration of the motion picture industry, screens new productions, classics, the quirky and forgotten in Silver Spring's Silver Theater, a restored 1938 movie house and expanded cultural center that contains three screens, conference and meeting spaces and concession stands. The institute often shows films in themes—every Hitchcock movie over the course of a couple of months, or "Movies from the '80's," or "Great Westerns."

It's one of the few places in America outside a university setting where you can see *Lawrence of Arabia, A Clockwork Orange,* or *The Muppet Movie* on the big screen.

LANDMARK'S E STREET CINEMA
555 11th St. NW, 202/452-7672, www.landmarktheatres.com
Map 3

E Street Cinema is exactly what many urbanites want in a movie house: Eight screens that show films beyond the Hollywood blockbusters, such as foreign and domestic films, independent works, and shorts. It also has a gourmet concession stand whose menu includes vegetarian pizza, espresso drinks, beer, and wine. Each theater's screen is diminutive, and while the sound quality is average, this isn't a place you'd necessarily need the latest in audio technology.

LOEWS GEORGETOWN 14
K St. and Wisconsin Ave. NW, 202/342-6441, www.enjoytheshow.com
Map 8

This is your basic multiplex in a convenient location, boasting great stadium seating, a top-notch sound system, numerous bathrooms, and first-run movies. The downside of the Georgetown locale is parking: Moviegoers must either walk, locate hard-to-find street parking, or use the expensive garage. The concession stands are also frequently understaffed. But there's a silver lining to the parking challenges and the expense; the obstacles help bring down the number of people who insist on bringing their babies and toddlers to inappropriate R-rated movies, a breach in common sense that seems to be growing in prevalence. While this theater seems out of the way and inconvenient for many, if you live or are staying within a mile or two and want to catch the latest in Hollywood blockbusters, it's a winner.

AMC LOEWS UPTOWN
3426 Connecticut Ave. NW, 202/966-8805
Map 9

The interior of the Uptown in Cleveland Park

© PATRICIA KIME

AMC Loews Uptown

doesn't exactly match this magnificent building's art deco exterior, but no one seems to care; the Uptown is the most popular place in DC to catch a movie, mainly because it boasts the very definition of "big screen"—a 40- by 70-foot curved screen designed to show Cinerama and widescreen Panavision films. It hosted the world premiere of *2001: A Space Odyssey* in 1968. The Uptown also offers that rarest of movie-house seating options nowadays: a balcony. The Uptown is the one place in DC where theatergoers are likely to encounter attendees in costume; for days following the first screening of *Harry Potter and the Deathly Hallows,* audience members showed up in wizard finery or sporting Gryffindor scarves. The Uptown is far from a movie palace, however. The lobby and the concession stands are tiny, although a moveable cart that sells sodas and candy helps sate the hungry, and the bathrooms, on the second floor, while clean, are the only ones in the theater and nearly always have a line. During the world premiere of *The Guardian,* actress Sela Ward joined the mass exodus from the theater to the restrooms, but she looked less than happy. No one was willing to ask whether this was because she very publicly had to stand in line or because much of her performance wound up on the cutting-room floor.

SMITHSONIAN IMAX THEATERS

National Air and Space Museum, 6th St. and Independence Ave. SE; National Museum of Natural History, 10th St. and Constitution Ave. NW, 202/633-1000, www.si.edu/imax

`Map 2`

Hundreds of thousands of people in the United States saw their first IMAX movie at the National Air and Space Museum, which had one of the country's first IMAX theaters and began showing To Fly, about the magic of flight, in 1976. While the movie wasn't the world's first IMAX offering, it is among the most widely viewed and is still shown today in the Lockheed Martin IMAX Theater. Nearly all the movies shown on the Smithsonian's three IMAX screens, including the one at the National Museum of Natural History and the Udvar-Hazy Center in Chantilly, Virginia, have a science bent, exploring subjects like dinosaurs, the Hubble Space Telescope, and the International

ARTS AND LEISURE

Space Station. Sometimes, however, the theaters host special screenings of Hollywood IMAX productions, including *Harry Potter and the Deathly Hallows* and *U2 3D*. The Hollywood films often screen at night and sell out quickly; consult the Smithsonian's website for schedules.

WEST END CINEMA

2301 M St. NW, 202/419-3456,
www.westendcinema.com
Map 4

A new addition to DC's small group of art-house theaters, West End Cinema opened in 2010 and quickly gained a following among those whose tastes run to the obscure and practically unknown. Its theaters are miniscule, more like a friend's media room than a movie theater, but the movie offerings and the concessions stand—with a full bar—more than make up for the space's cushioned folding chairs and small screens. Not surprisingly, the staff is friendly and chatty, very up on movies, and always willing to strike up a conversation about the latest.

Festivals and Events

The streets, sidewalks, and venues of Washington—even the National Zoo—host yearly events in the city, from celebrations of food during two Restaurant Weeks to cavalcades heralding the arrival of cherry blossoms in the spring. With its festivals and events, DC seems more a Southern city than a Northern one, focusing on a defining theme such as the cherry blossoms, Memorial Day, or July 4 rather than a neighborhood ethnicity or heritage. The reason is simple: The city's growth as a federal town rather than an industrial center drew transplants from across the country for white-collar positions instead of attracting large immigrant populations needed for an industrial workforce. Thus, neighborhoods didn't develop around a single ethnicity. Even the city's Chinatown wasn't settled until the 1930s, and today, the area barely resembles the Asian neighborhoods found in New York, San Francisco, or Philadelphia. What Washington does offer are several distinct traditions honoring its legacy as the U.S. capital and its heritage as a majority African American city. Major events occur on nearly every federal holiday, including President's Day, Independence Day, Christmas Day, and presidential inaugurations, and local events celebrate the city's strong African American heritage.

Washington is home to a number of commercial events that draw spectators from across the city, including the Washington Auto Show; Restaurant Week, in which diners can enjoy selected meals at the city's top restaurants for a fraction of regular prices; and the International Wine and Food Festival. Some festivals aren't single events at a central venue; the DC Jazz Festival takes place during two weeks with performances at venues across the city, and the Capital Fringe Festival, a celebration of new plays and experimental theater, is a 17-day carnival of performance that occurs on stages across the city.

Washington also has its share of quirky events that locals hate to miss—short occasions that spin wildly into all-night parties on the streets and neighborhood bars, like the Halloween High Heel Drag Queen Race, Halloween in Georgetown, and annual events at the French Embassy and area French restaurants on Bastille Day.

WINTER

BOTANIC GARDENS HOLIDAY DISPLAY

100 Maryland Ave. SW, www.usbg.gov

One of the area's most popular holiday events is indoors, in the warm, moist environs of the Botanic Gardens. Each year, starting the day after Thanksgiving and running until New Year's Day, the gardens decorates for the holidays, with lights, model trains, and replicas of DC's buildings made entirely from organic materials—seeds, flowers, straw, hay, and more. Families enjoy seeing the displays and then meandering through the warm tropical conservatory or orchid room afterward.

THE CAMPAGNA CENTER'S SCOTTISH CHRISTMAS WALK

George Washington Masonic National Memorial, Alexandria, Va., www.scottishchristmaswalk.com

For the past 40 years, the city of Alexandria, seven miles from downtown DC, kicks off the holiday season with a Scottish Christmas Walk Weekend and Parade, an extravaganza of bagpipes, kilts, dogs, and pipe and drum bands that is unique to the area. The festival includes a Scottish marketplace, a heather and greens sale, scotch tastings, a tea party for children, and the parade in Old Town, which draws more than 100 clans and bands. The event raises money for a local nonprofit that serves needy children. The same weekend, the city of Alexandria usually holds its Holiday Boat Parade of Lights, welcoming Santa by water and featuring local boats decked out in holiday regalia.

CHRISTMAS AT NATIONAL HARBOR

National Harbor, Oxon Hill, Md., www.gaylordhotels.com/gaylord-national

For the past couple of years, the National Harbor complex has become a local destination to experience holiday fun, with the Gaylord National Harbor creating an enormous palace of ice decorations, slides, and wintertime activities for children. The festive spirit permeates the area, with the development's streets and trees lit like a veritable Whoville. This is Christmas at its most commercial, a staged winter wonderland that some people like, but if you prefer the style and substance of Charlie Brown's Christmas tree, you should look elsewhere. For the last two years, National Harbor has been the only location to see DC's water-skiing Santa. For the past 25 years, Santa has arrived in Washington by boat, accompanied by knee-boarding reindeer, elves, and the

OUTDOOR CONCERTS AND EVENTS

During the summer, the National Mall hums at night with the sounds of free concerts and events. Locals bring lawn chairs, coolers, and such, but all you really need is a hotel blanket and a picnic from a local deli to make a memory.

The U.S. Capitol's West Front hosts free military-band concerts during the summer at 8 P.M.: the Navy Band plays Mondays, the Air Force Band on Tuesdays, the Marine Corps Band on Wednesdays, and the Army Band on Fridays. If you're at the Mall on Thursday, head to the grounds of the Washington Monument, where you'll find the Marine Band performing at 8 P.M.

The National Art Gallery also hosts a summer music series, jazz in its sculpture garden every Friday 5–8:30 P.M. Bring your own picnic or pick one up at the Pavilion Café in the garden, but get there early for good seats; this event is a Washington after-work favorite.

The outdoor film series Screen on the Green takes place on the National Mall between 4th Street and 7th Street NW on Mondays during the summer and features classic movies under the stars. Past screenings have included *Twelve Angry Men* and *Goldfinger*. Bring a picnic, bug spray, and a blanket or one of those short beach chairs, and plan to arrive by 7 P.M. for a decent seat. (The movie starts when it's nearly dark, around 9 P.M.)

The biggest event on the Mall during the summer is the July 4 concert and fireworks, but locals head to the U.S. Capitol's West Front on July 3 for the dress rehearsal, which usually starts around 7:30 P.M. The event is not exactly a secret, and the closest lawn spaces fill quickly, but the crowds are nowhere near the size they'll be the following day. Also, don't expect to see everyone who's scheduled; some performers, like the Beach Boys a few years back, skip the rehearsal.

Grinch riding a Jet Ski; it's definitely something worth seeing if you're in the nation's capital on December 24.

GEORGE WASHINGTON BIRTHDAY CELEBRATION
Various locations, Alexandria, Va.,
www.washingtonbirthdayparade.net

A number of events are held in Washington honoring the city's namesake, like a ceremony held February 22 at the Washington Monument, but the best Washington's Birthday events occur in downtown Alexandria, Virginia, and at Mount Vernon, Washington's home, 13 miles from the city. Alexandria hosts a mile-long parade with bands, color guards, reenactors, antique vehicles, and marchers as well as a road race, open houses of historical buildings, and a birthday ball. At Mount Vernon, the highlight is a wreath-laying at the first president's tomb, sometimes by the current president or his representative, usually the commanding general of the Military District of Washington, followed by a military pass in review on the manor's bowling green by costumed soldiers, usually from the U.S. Army's Old Guard and Fife and Drum Corps.

MARTIN LUTHER KING JR.'S BIRTHDAY
Various locations, www.kennedy-center.org,
www.nationalcathedral.org, www.nps.gov/frdo

Many in Washington mark King's birthday, a federal holiday, performing community service. But a number of events are also held around the city focusing on civil rights and its leader. The recent completion of King's memorial on the Tidal Basin in August 2011 is expected to expand the number of commemorations held here each year. Traditional events honoring King include a free concert at the Kennedy Center, *Let Freedom Ring*, heralding King's memory with music; a civil rights film festival at Frederick Douglass National Historic Site in southeast Washington; and a service at the National Cathedral honoring King, who spoke from its pulpit the Sunday before his assassination in 1968.

NATIONAL CHRISTMAS TREE LIGHTING AND PAGEANT OF PEACE
The Ellipse in front of the White House,
www.thenationaltree.org

Around the beginning of the second week of December, the president lights the National Christmas Tree on the Ellipse in front of the White House, an event usually accompanied by music and choral concerts; in 2010 the great B. B. King played, along with Maroon 5 and Sara Bareilles. The lighting ceremony kicks off a nearly four-week celebration of the holidays downtown called the Pageant of Peace, which features trees decorated by every state and territory, nightly Yule logs, and choral and band performances. While many Washingtonians steer clear of the crowds that show up for the Christmas tree lighting, a trip to the Mall to see the tree on another night and enjoy the Pageant of Peace, followed by hot chocolate or a toddy at a nearby restaurant, is a holiday tradition for many DC families. The first year the current Colorado blue spruce was decorated as the national Christmas tree was 2011; its 42-feet-tall predecessor, which stood on the Ellipse for more than 30 years, fell over in a strong windstorm in February 2011. The Ellipse also hosts a National Menorah. If the crowds at the garishly decorated national tree aren't your thing, consider heading over to Capitol Hill to check out the legislative branch's subtler one, decorated with ornaments handmade by children and artists from various states.

WASHINGTON AUTO SHOW
Washington Convention Center,
www.washingtonautoshow.com

America's love affair with cars is manifested at the mammoth Washington Auto Show, held in the vast cavern of the Washington Convention Center, with nine acres of exhibits spread across two floors. In 2011 the event featured more than 700 cars, trucks, and other vehicles, ranging from the latest versions of luxury sports cars to energy-efficient vehicles, electric cars, family sedans, and more. New in 2011 was an exhibit that displayed cars that run on myriad alternative fuels as well as those that have star power, including vehicles from movies such as *American Graffiti* and *Transformers* and television shows like *Magnum, P.I.* and *Starsky and Hutch.*

WASHINGTON DC INTERNATIONAL WINE AND FOOD FESTIVAL

Various locations, www.wineandfooddc.com

The emphasis at the International Wine and Food Festival is more on wine than on food, although a number of city restaurants participate in this annual event at the Ronald Reagan Building, and some fine dishes are available for purchase. With the admission fee, attendees can enjoy cooking demonstrations, a variety of snacks and cheeses, and, of course, wine. In 2011 roughly 100 wineries poured more than 500 different wines.

WINTER RESTAURANT WEEK

Various locations,
http://washington.org/restaurantwk

More than 100 restaurants participate in Restaurant Week for two weeks in January, much to the delight of budget-conscious foodies throughout the city. Participating restaurants offer either their full menu or something from a Restaurant Week menu at a set price for lunch, dinner, or both. For Washingtonians who've wanted to try one of the city's fine restaurants, including Jaleo, Charlie Palmer Steak, Café Atlántico, or even Tallula in Arlington, and not break the bank, Restaurant Week is the time to do it.

SPRING

AFRICAN AMERICAN FAMILY DAY AT THE NATIONAL ZOO

The National Zoo, 3001 Connecticut Ave.,
www.nationalzoo.si.edu

On Easter Monday, African American families in Washington often head to the National Zoo to celebrate a tradition that began in 1889, the year the zoo opened. Back then and for many years, the servants who worked in Washington's finest homes had to work on Easter Sunday serving holiday dinners. They celebrated their Easters on Monday, often going with their families to the zoo to enjoy a spring day of picnicking and the sights. Today, Family Day continues, sanctioned by the zoo, and features music, Easter egg rolls and hunts, and festival activities like face painting and dancing.

BLOSSOM KITE FESTIVAL

The National Mall, www.kitefestival.org

At the start of the Cherry Blossom Festival, the Blossom Kite Festival, formerly the Smithsonian Kite Festival, held annually since 1967, is a cacophony of color in the sky, with hundreds of kites aloft above the National Mall. The festival celebrates the role of kites in world culture, featuring competitions, demonstrations, and activity stations for young and old. Events include a Hot Tricks showdown, featuring aggressive kite maneuvers and tricks, and the Rokkaku Battle, a Japanese tradition with hexagonal kites flown against one another in battle with the aim of cutting the opponent's string or grounding the opposing kite.

CAPITAL FRINGE FESTIVAL

Various locations, www.capfringe.org

Fans of experimental and avant-garde theater love Capital Fringe, a festival that began in 2005 to bring offbeat performance art to DC and to showcase the city's acting talent. In 2010, nearly 30,000 people attended the festival, which featured 715 performances of 137 productions in a span of two weeks. Shows range from comedy, dance, drama, and variety shows to one-acts, cabarets, and one-person shows. Tickets and a festival button must be purchased for performances, which are held at venues across the city. Tickets are available online. In the month leading up to the show, a Capital Fringe button often yields discounts on local performances that aren't officially part of the festival.

CAPITAL PRIDE FESTIVAL

Various locations, www.capitalpride.org

Capital Pride is the city's largest annual LGBT event, usually spanning the first full week of June and featuring numerous activities that include a parade, a street festival, and a pageant to crown Mr. and Ms. Capital Pride. The festival is organized by Capital Pride Alliance, a nonprofit organization that aims to celebrate the heritage of the gay community and promote tolerance and diversity. The city's gay pride event traces its roots to 1975, when activist Deacon Maccubbin, founder of the city's first gay book store, Lambda Rising, organized a one-day community block party on 20th Street, not far from Dupont Circle.

PASSPORT DC
Various locations, www.culturaltourism-dc.org

For the past four years, DC's Cultural Tourism office has organized Passport DC, a month-long celebration highlighting the city's vibrant international component. The most popular event of Passport DC is the Around the World Embassy Tour, held on a Saturday in May, when a number of embassies open their doors to visitors. Thirty-five embassies took part in the event in 2011, letting visitors stroll through their gates and view their public spaces. It's nearly impossible to see them all in a single day, given the size of the crowds that attend the event; many participants look at the list ahead of time and plot their route, aiming to see five or six embassies. Other Passport DC activities include an open house of European Union embassies on a separate weekend, an international children's film festival, and street fairs.

JOINT SERVICE OPEN HOUSE AND AIR SHOW
Andrews Air Force Base, Md., www.jsoh.org

Andrews Air Force Base, home to Air Force One and numerous military units, throws open its gates in May, usually the weekend of Armed Forces Day, for an open house and air show that features flight demonstration teams, military aircraft, stunt planes, and more. Normally, one of the military's top demonstration teams, either the Air Force Thunderbirds or the Navy's Blue Angels, participate in the show. "Joint" means that all military services take part; the Army, Navy, Air Force, Marines, and Coast Guard set up military hardware and aircraft for visitors to examine and explore.

MEMORIAL DAY EVENTS
Various locations, www.arlingtoncemetery.org, www.nationalmemorialdayparade.com, www.rollingthunder1.com

Memorial Day is celebrated in DC with remembrance and fanfare: Wreath ceremonies and speeches take place at the city's war memorials and cemeteries, including the Tomb of the Unknowns, the Marine Corps War Memorial, the Air Force Memorial, in and around Arlington National Cemetery, the Navy Memorial, the Vietnam Veterans Memorial, the World War II Memorial, and elsewhere. The National Memorial Day Parade takes place the afternoon of Memorial Day, featuring military units, marching bands, celebrities, and the true VIPs for the day, veterans who have served in conflicts from World War II to the present day. Also taking place that weekend in DC is Rolling Thunder, a gathering of more than 250,000 motorcycle riders, usually riding American-made Harley-Davidsons; the event is deemed to honor combat veterans, missing in action, and prisoners of war. While Rolling Thunder participants begin arriving in Washington the Friday before the weekend, their main ride takes place Sunday morning, traveling from the Pentagon to the National Mall, where the bikers hear speeches and celebrate the memories of the military fallen.

NATIONAL CHERRY BLOSSOM FESTIVAL
The National Mall and Tidal Basin, www.nationalcherryblossomfestival.org

The biggest annual event in Washington is its festival celebrating the blossoming of the city's famed Japanese cherry trees, a two-week event that usually coincides with the trees' peak bloom time. Nearly 4,000 ornamental cherry trees line the Tidal Basin and the Potomac River and stand on the grounds of the Washington Monument, gifts in 1912 from the mayor of Tokyo; the festival celebrates the ties between the United States and Japan. The event includes a parade, the crowning of a Cherry Blossom Queen, concerts, a 10K race, children's activities, and a Japanese street festival called Sakura Matsuri, with food, demonstrations, music, and vendors.

SHAKESPEARE'S BIRTHDAY OPEN HOUSE

Folger Shakespeare Library, 201 East Capitol St. SE, www.folger.edu

The actual date of Shakespeare's birth is unknown, but April 23 is widely accepted, since there's evidence he was baptized on April 26. Thus, on the Sunday closest to April 23, the world's foremost Shakespearean library holds an open house and birthday celebration for the Bard, with entertainment from the Elizabethan era that includes jugglers, jesters, dancers, and songstresses. The event includes activities as well, such as the ever-popular stage combat workshops; crafts, including shield and jewelry making; a portrait contest; and art events. Of course, there's birthday cake and general merriment along with performances from the Folger's stable of Shakespearean actors. This is also the only day the Folger's reading rooms are open to the public, a chance to see the library's Flemish tapestries and paintings of scenes from Shakespearean plays.

WASHINGTON INTERNATIONAL FILM FESTIVAL

Various locations, www.filmfestdc.org

This 25-year-old film festival celebrates movies made in countries around the world as well as American films, showing the works of nearly 100 filmmakers from France, South Korea, Denmark, China, and Iran. Screenings take place at venues across the city, including arthouse theaters, mainstream movie screens, museums, and institutes. Tickets for each movie usually cost less than $15; special screenings at places like the Lincoln Theatre and the French Embassy often cost more but come with perks like gala festivities at the Lincoln and a cocktail reception at the embassy.

WHITE HOUSE EASTER EGG ROLL

White House lawn, 1600 Pennsylvania Ave. NW, www.whitehouse.gov

The lottery is competitive for tickets to this annual event held on the White House lawn, traditionally on Easter Monday. Children 12 and under, many dressed in Easter finery, turn out for the event, which includes not only races to determine who can roll an egg with a spoon the fastest but also activities like egg decorating, egg hunts, magic shows, concerts, and games. The event is attended by the President and the First Lady, and numerous celebrities show up as well, many of whom read books to youngsters and perform for them. In 2011, nearly 30,000 people attended the Easter Egg Roll, a tradition that dates back to 1878 when Congress banned Easter egg rolling on its grounds and President Rutherford B. Hayes decided the White House's South Lawn would be the perfect venue for it.

WHITE HOUSE SPRING GARDEN TOURS

White House, 1600 Pennsylvania Ave. NW, www.whitehouse.gov

Tickets to tour the inside of the White House may be hard to score, but each spring the government opens the White House grounds to visitors for a weekend, allowing the public to stroll through and linger in the house's magnificent gardens, including the Jacqueline Kennedy Garden, the famous Rose Garden, site of many political announcements and speeches, the Children's Garden, and the South Lawn. The event is free, but a ticket is required. They are distributed first-come, first-served starting at 8 A.M. the day of the tours. For information on dates and times, check out the White House website. Historically, the gardens have been open in mid to late April.

SUMMER
DC JAZZ FESTIVAL

Various locations, www.dcjazzfest.org

The city celebrates its musical heritage the first few weeks of June with its Jazz Festival, an event that brings in more than 100 performers for shows at dozens of venues across the city. The Jazz Festival is a great time to hear local favorites as well as artists who arrive from out of town, including trios and solo performers from New Orleans and elsewhere. The Jazz Festival stretches beyond traditional jazz; groups like

ARTS AND LEISURE

Patrick Alban and Noche Latina add international flair. Concerts take place in the city's historic nightclubs as well as in parks for Jazz Under the Stars. Jazz 'N Families Fun Days is a weekend-long event that has hands-on activities for children such as story-telling, art workshops, and an instrument "petting zoo" as well as kid-friendly concerts.

INDEPENDENCE DAY

The National Mall

The nation's foremost birthday celebration happens on July 4 in Washington DC, an unforgettable experience enjoyed by a mass of humanity that flocks to the National Mall for a parade, live music, food, and fireworks, usually on one of the hottest days of the year. Events start in the morning, with a reading of the Declaration of Independence by historical reenactors, music, and a military color guard at the National Archives. A lavish parade takes place along Constitution Avenue, with high school and university marching bands, military units, the U.S. Army's period-dressed Fife and Drum Corps, floats, police motorcycles, and hundreds of community groups. The capstone event occurs after dusk: a massive fireworks display held near the Washington Monument, visible from many points in the city. *A Capital Fourth*, a concert with big-name stars and singing groups, precedes the fireworks on the U.S. Capitol's West Lawn. It is simulcast on certain area radio stations and television stations, so spectators not close enough to the Capitol can tune in on portable radios to enjoy the music during the fireworks, usually patriotic tunes played by the National Symphony Orchestra. The area near the West Lawn opens to the public at 3 P.M.; if you stake a claim there for the 8 P.M. concert, you can enjoy music and see the fireworks at the same time. Other great spots to see the fireworks include the hill in Arlington, Virginia, near the Netherlands Carillon and the Marine Corps War Memorial, the grassy hill by the Air Force Memorial in Arlington, and Gravelly Point, the spit of land north of Reagan National Airport, also in Arlington.

Independence Day fireworks light up the sky behind the U.S. Capitol building.

⚔ MILITARY PARADES

Fort McNair, http://twilight.mdw.army.mil;
Marine Barracks, 8th St. and I St. SW; Marine Corps
War Memorial, N. Marshall Dr., Arlington, Va.,
www.marines.mil/unit/barracks/

The pomp and pageantry of military parades take place in Washington on summer evenings, showcasing area military bands and performance teams. On designated Wednesday nights in May and June, the U.S. Army holds a Twilight Tattoo at Fort McNair, a historic post on DC's southwestern waterfront that serves as home to the National War College. Performers include the U.S. Army Band, known as "Pershing's Own," along with units from the service's 3rd Infantry Regiment, the U.S. Army Drill Team, and various Army musical groups. Seating is first-come, first served on bleachers. The city's most impressive military parade is held Friday nights in the summer at Marine Barracks, the Marine Corps's oldest post. Set amid the backdrop of historic buildings, the Marine Corps Band battles it out with the service's Drum and Bugle Corps, while units from the base display their precision drill maneuvers. Tickets are required for the event and can be obtained through the Marine Corps' website. To see the same Marine Corps units perform a shorter program in a more casual setting—bring a picnic blanket for seating—head to the grounds of the Marine Corps War Memorial in Arlington on Tuesday nights from late May to mid-August for a Sunset Parade. The performance begins at 7 P.M.

SCREEN ON THE GREEN

The National Mall, 877/262-5866

Summertime is ideal for watching a flick outdoors, and outdoor film festivals like Screen on the Green have filled the void left behind by the death of the drive-in movie. For four consecutive Mondays during the summer, sponsors show a popular or classic movie on a big screen set up on the National Mall. Viewers bring picnic blankets, drinks, coolers, food, and bug spray to enjoy this summertime ritual. Be prepared to hop up and wave your hands in the air for the HBO dance before the movie; it's a silly

ritual, and no one seems to know how it got started. Also, most attendees sit on blankets or low sand chairs; high camping chairs are to be avoided as they block the view for others.

SMITHSONIAN FOLKLIFE FESTIVAL

The National Mall, www.festival.si.edu

Held during the weeks preceding and following Independence Day, the Smithsonian's Folklife Festival is a party celebrating domestic and international culture, held on the National Mall between the Washington Monument and the U.S. Capitol and featuring musicians, artists, performers, craftspeople, and events highlighting the culture of a designated group or nationality. Each year the Smithsonian chooses at least three cultural themes to showcase; in 2011, Folk Life revelers heralded the culture of Colombia, the U.S. Peace Corps program, and the musical movement rhythm and blues. The festival features daily and evening programs. Events are free, and food, drink, and souvenirs are available for purchase.

SUMMER RESTAURANT WEEK

Various locations, http://washington.org/
restaurantwk/

Like its winter counterpart, Summer Restaurant Week was designed to increase attendance at the city's eateries during the slow month of August, drawing patrons to top restaurants with discount fixed-price meals. More than 100 restaurants participate in the event, offering a range of cuisine from new American and seafood to Italian, Greek, fine French, and more.

FALL

ADAMS MORGAN DAY FESTIVAL

18th St., www.adamsmorgandayfestival.com

Washington's most diverse neighborhood celebrates its cultural heritage the second Sunday of September with a street festival, music, dancing, arts, and food amid the colorful environs and buildings of Adams Morgan. Stages host a variety of musical acts, including salsa, Latin rock, American rock and roll, jazz, funk, soul, and Central and South American music as well as theater, poetry, and dance workshops. Food vendors showcase the melting pot of Adams Morgan, serving up *pupusas,* tamales, kebabs, and the old festival favorite, funnel cakes. A kids' pavilion offers entertainment for youngsters that includes painting and crafts.

BLACK FAMILY REUNION CELEBRATION
Washington Monument, www.ncnw.org

A one-day festival of African American family life and culture sponsored by the National Council of Negro Women, this festival brings food vendors, a health fair, seminars, and pavilions celebrating black heritage to the grounds of the Washington Monument. Performances by local and nationally recognized artists round out the day.

HALLOWEEN
Various locations

The traditional locus for Halloween antics in Washington is the corner of Wisconsin Avenue and M Street in Georgetown, which draws costumed revelers and partiers into the night for fun, frolicking, and mayhem in the neighborhood's bars and pubs and on the streets and city sidewalks. The city doesn't have formal Halloween activities; they just spontaneously occur. Across the city, parties spring up block to block. In Dupont Circle, the High Heel Drag Queen Race isn't to be missed. Usually held the Tuesday before Halloween, this event features drag queens in elaborate costumes "racing" (usually more like strutting) along 17th Street between Church and Q Streets. The race usually takes place around 9 P.M., but the crowds and the queens start gathering by 7 P.M.

THE MARINE CORPS MARATHON
Pentagon to Marine Corps War Memorial,
www.marinemarathon.com

The fifth-largest road race in the United States, the Marine Corps Marathon hosts 30,000 runners on a 26.2-mile run past the nation's most recognized monuments, starting at the Pentagon and winding through the streets of Virginia and Washington DC, before finishing at the Marine Corps War Memorial in Arlington. The event draws thousands of spectators who line the route, cheering on the athletes, who include wheelchair racers, military personnel, units in boots and utilities, and runners carrying flags or wearing costumes. In 2008 a particularly hardy Theodore Roosevelt, a mainstay of Nationals baseball games, finished the course in just over six hours—no small feat for a guy wearing a 40-pound bobble-head costume.

NATIONAL BOOK FESTIVAL
Various venues, www.loc.gov/bookfest

Cofounded by the former librarian and First Lady Laura Bush in 2001, the National Book Festival, sponsored by the Library of Congress, brings together authors and readers for a weekend in September to celebrate the written word. The festival includes book sales, signings, author presentations, and meet-and-greets with storybook characters. A state pavilion represents the literacy and library promotion programs of all 50 states, DC, and the U.S. territories, and publishers and book companies sell the works of the authors featured at the annual event. Among the most popular destinations is the "Let's Read America" Pavilion, with storytellers and children's book readings, and the Library of Congress Pavilion, which offers a glimpse into the library's vast vaults.

WHITE HOUSE FALL GARDEN TOURS
The White House, www.whitehouse.gov

In the fall, usually in late September, the White House allows visitors to tour its gardens to see such treasures as the magnificent Southern magnolias planted by Andrew Jackson in the 1830s, brought as saplings from his Nashville home, the Hermitage. The trees are the oldest plants on the grounds. Other sites on the tour include the Rose Garden, which is usually still in bloom late into the fall, and other flower beds. The Obama vegetable garden is not part of the formal tour, but it can be seen from afar on the South Grounds.

Recreation

Washington is a city tailor-made for outdoor sports and recreation, and it's no surprise that numerous fitness magazines have ranked it among the top cities in the country for fitness. DC's geography of wide, flat spaces coupled with hilly, rocky terrain above the Potomac River's fall line as well as copious trails make it a running and hiking paradise. Its water frontage, which includes both challenging white water as well as a vast tidal river, plays host to paddlers, kayakers, rowers, and sailors; and its climate, with all four seasons, including a winter freeze, allow for pickup games of softball in the summer and outdoor ice-skating on the historic C&O Canal in the winter. With its unmatched scenery and innumerable activities—beach volleyball near the Lincoln Memorial, Ultimate Frisbee on the National Mall, kickball in East Potomac Park, to name a few—it takes a resolute person to remain a couch potato in DC.

Running remains one of the top activities in the city, especially along the National Mall and the Potomac River, where wide, flat trails offer a safe landscape for easy running. The most popular loop is the two miles between the Lincoln Memorial and the U.S. Capitol. The city's largest running event, the Marine Corps Marathon, attracts roughly 30,000 runners each year. The event is nicknamed the "People's Marathon" because it requires no qualifying time and its relatively flat course (with the exception of the doozy of the hill from Rosslyn to North Arlington) makes for a great starter marathon. Cyclists also have an excellent selection of trails, with a city-wide favorite being Beach Drive in Rock Creek Park, which is closed to motor-vehicle traffic from Saturday at 7 A.M. to Sunday at 7 P.M. Swimmers can head to several local aquatics centers or outdoor public pools for a workout, including a rarely crowded 50-meter pool in

© PATRICIA KIME

Sailing is a local pastime on the Potomac.

ARTS AND LEISURE

East Potomac Park. Equestrians, regardless of skill level, can enjoy their hobby at the Rock Creek Park Horse Center. And hikers will find themselves fortunate to have numerous trails to choose from, ranging from easy flat loops to strenuous, hilly pathways over boulders. Rock Creek Park, one of the largest forested urban parks in the country, offers miles of trails. Great Falls and the C&O Canal National Parks, just 15 miles northwest of Washington, have awesome trails as well, in addition to serving as top spots for adventure sports like rock-climbing and white-water kayaking.

If you'd rather watch your sports than partake, Washington is a smorgasbord of spectator activities, with its National Football League franchise Washington Redskins ruling the headlines if not the hearts of Washingtonians. The team with the politically incorrect name dominated the league for a decade starting in the 1980s, going to the playoffs eight times and winning the Super Bowl three times. In 2005, Major League Baseball returned to Washington when the Montreal Expos moved to the city. The Nationals, or Nats, have earned a loyal and grateful following of fans who love spending a beautiful summer evening in a sparkling new stadium enjoying a half-smoke from the Ben's Chili Bowl kiosk. The most popular team in DC is currently the Washington Capitals, whose fans are unwavering in their love of superstar Alex Ovechkin and, surprisingly, the team's outgoing and friendly owner, Ted Leonsis. Leonsis also owns the city's two other major-league franchises, the Washington Wizards and Mystics men's and women's basketball teams. But pro sports aren't the only games in town to watch; Washington boasts four universities that field Division I sports teams. Popular spectator sports at the schools include basketball and lacrosse.

PARKS

One of the first things people notice about Washington is how green it is, its verdancy established by the 300-acre expanse of the National Mall and extending into every neighborhood. In 1791 city designer Pierre L'Enfant planned for parkland and open space as an integral part of city life, with the National Mall

© PATRICIA KIME

Runners enjoy the green space around the National Mall.

(originally a boulevard in L'Enfant's plan, but lined with trees and grassy areas nonetheless) serving as the center and 15 parks set at intersections of major avenues across town. This groundbreaking urban design was cemented by later city planners, most notably the 1901 McMillan Commission, which called for expanding the downtown's green space and even adding to it by building up land dredged from the Potomac River. Today, Washington is home to numerous parks, nearly all of which are federal lands and free to visitors. In addition to the parks around the Mall, including the oft-enjoyed East and West Potomac Parks, the city contains one of the country's largest urban parks, Rock Creek Park, a favorite used by an estimated 2 million people each year. As with the green spaces surrounding the National Mall, Rock Creek's nearly 2,000 acres of woods, fields, trails, creeks, and parkland are overseen by the National Park Service. In addition to its extensive trail system, this forested park has a nature center featuring ranger-led programs, a planetarium, an equestrian center, and roadways popular with cyclists. Its dense woods also hold nine Civil War fort sites and other points of cultural interest, including an old mill and several manor homes. The rangers assigned to Rock Creek Park stay fairly busy, since they are also responsible for overseeing a number of Washington neighborhood parks, including Dumbarton Oaks Park in Georgetown (a public park separate from the private formal gardens of Dumbarton Oaks mansion), Montrose Park, and Meridian Hill—enticing places featuring streambeds and meadows, fountains, hidden picnic spots, and playgrounds.

The banks of the Potomac also hold public lands favored by Washingtonians, and each has unique features. At Georgetown's new waterfront park, sightseers can enjoy a picnic while watching crew regattas on spring weekends; a few miles south along the river at Gravelly Point, visitors spend countless hours watching planes take off and land at Reagan National Airport.

In terms of sports parks, East Potomac Park is by far the most popular, featuring a golf course, a public swimming pool, tennis courts, and large grassy areas for playing soccer, lacrosse, and other field sports. East Potomac Park is a popular destination for fishing as well: Most anglers simply stand on the park's seawall and cast their lines into the water. The park is heavily used by families on Saturday and Sunday for all-day picnics and reunions.

CHESAPEAKE AND OHIO CANAL NATIONAL HISTORIC PARK AND TOWPATH

1057 Thomas Jefferson St. NW, 202/653-5190, www.nps.gov/choh
HOURS: Open dawn-dusk
Map 8

This historic waterway runs through the heart of Georgetown and stretches for nearly 185 miles to Cumberland, Maryland, its flat pea-gravel tow path popular with hikers, runners, bikers, walkers, and the stroller brigade on the 13-mile segment that passes through the city from Georgetown past the great cliffs of the city's palisades and upriver to Great Falls. Built between 1828 and 1850, the canal, which has 74 locks, was constructed to transport coal, lumber, grain, and other goods around the Potomac River's major obstacles, including Great Falls. The C&O technically was doomed to failure from the start. The day John Quincy Adams turned the ceremonial spade starting its construction, the Baltimore and Ohio Railroad laid the cornerstone for its new venture, a train track to Cumberland, Maryland. Of course, no one knew which technology would be more successful at the time.

The towpath offers spectacular natural views of the region, while the waterway remains a popular place to paddle kayaks and canoes. In Georgetown and at Great Falls Tavern, the National Park Service manages information centers and maintains barges for mule-drawn rides on the canal. These trips, narrated by rangers in period dress, offer a glimpse into the area's Victorian era history. The boat rides last about an hour and are held three times a day, Wednesday through Sunday, from late spring until mid-October. Cost is $8 adults, $6 over age 61, and $5 ages 4–11.

ARTS AND LEISURE

DUMBARTON OAKS PARK

31st St. and R St. NW, 202/426-6841, www.doaks.org

HOURS: Open dawn-dusk

Map 8

Not to be confused with the private landscaped Dumbarton Oaks Gardens, this 27-acre park that borders the formal gardens is managed by the National Park Service. It is a natural landscape that contains native flora but also a number of landscape features that include stone bridges, ponds, waterfalls, and meadow trails, including one nicknamed "Lover's Lane," reflecting the park's favored status as a secluded spot for couples. A conservancy was formed in 2011 to restore the park to the state it was in when it opened (in the past few years it has become overridden by invasive vines). The park is still a favorite free place to enjoy nature in Washington.

EAST AND WEST POTOMAC PARKS

Ohio Dr. SW, 202/426-6841, www.nps.gov/nama

HOURS: Parks open 24 hours

Map 1 and Map 9

The wide, flat sidewalks and fields of East and West Potomac Parks draw a number of visitors, including sightseers; organized sports teams for soccer, lacrosse, kickball, rugby, and on occasion, polo; runners; and cyclists. West Potomac Park is the swath of green space that spans north from the Tidal Basin to Constitution Avenue and contains polo grounds; East Potomac Park runs south of the Tidal Basin down to Hains Point and is known for its recreation, featuring a tennis center, a golf course, a driving range, and a public swimming pool as well as picnic tables, benches, and thousands of feet of water frontage for fishing.

GEORGETOWN WATERFRONT PARK AND WASHINGTON HARBOR

K St. and 31st St. NW, 202/895-6070

HOURS: Open dawn-dusk

Map 8

A work in progress, the Georgetown Waterfront Park, also maintained by the National Park Service, is the last link in a publicly owned trail along the Potomac River from Cumberland, Maryland, to Mount Vernon, Virginia. This 11-acre park offers views of the Key Bridge and Kennedy Center, and it is the best spot in the city for watching crew regattas in the spring. Less than two years ago, this green space of trees, lawns, picnic benches, memorials, and fountains was a parking lot. Today, it is a popular spot for picnic lunches, photography, and to enjoy the water. The park's eastern section,

The Georgetown Waterfront Park is a popular recreation spot.

© PATRICIA KIME

ARTS AND LEISURE

currently under construction, will feature a fountain and steps leading down to the water for a better view of the regatta finish line, as well as a place to cool your feet on a hot day.

MERIDIAN HILL PARK

Bounded by 16th St., Euclid St., 15th St., and W St. NW, 202/462-7275, www.nps.gov/mehi

HOURS: Open dawn-dusk

`Map 7`

The hallmarks of the 12-acre Meridian Hill Park, referred to locally as Malcolm X Park, are its stupendous European-style fountain and Sunday afternoon entertainment—drum circles that draw neighborhood percussionists and dancers as well as myriad performance artists and acrobats. Meridian Hill is managed by the National Park Service and is the former site of John Quincy Adams's postpresidential home as well as Columbian College, precursor to George Washington University. It was transformed into a formal French and Italian Renaissance–style park in the early 1900s, when the Department of the Interior decided the city needed gardens to rival those of other great cities. Its fountain is among the city's grandest, a 13-basin cascade that ends in a vast reflecting pond of water lilies and fountains. The park contains a number of unusual statues, including sculptures of Dante, Joan of Arc, and James Buchanan. It is usually a place to enjoy sunshine and solitude, but on Sunday the place transforms into a lively entertainment venue, with a Sunday drum circle that has lasted more than 40 years. Drummers start gathering around 3 P.M. and play well past dusk; events usually wrap up by 8 or 9 P.M. The park is somewhat sketchy after dark, so it is best to leave once the crowds start thinning.

MONTROSE PARK

30th St. and R St. NW, 202/282-1063

HOURS: Open dawn-dusk

`Map 8`

A playground with swings—so hard to find nowadays and so much fun. Parents who aren't afraid of these now-deemed-dangerous contraptions love Montrose Park for its playground and lovely picnic areas. This enjoyable spot of

wilderness in Georgetown also has trails that climb high above a gorge of Rock Creek Park, and it is a popular spot for dog owners to exercise their pets off-leash. Technically this isn't permitted, but it seems that everyone is agreeable to it as long as dogs are well-behaved.

ROCK CREEK PARK

3435 Williamsburg Lane NW, 202/895-6000, www.nps.gov/rock

HOURS: Open dawn-dusk

`Map 9`

One of the largest urban forested parks in the country, Rock Creek Park is home to white-tailed deer, red and gray foxes, coyotes, squirrels, raccoons, chipmunks, and hundreds of bird species. It is a 2,700-acre space overseen by the National Park Service and is the single most popular hiking and biking destination within city limits. Rock Creek Park is heavily forested, spanning the fall line that runs between the Atlantic coastal plain and the piedmont. Thus the northern part of the park is rocky, with steep canyons and hillsides, and the lower section, closer to the city, fans out into broad flat land as Rock Creek empties into the Potomac River. Rock Creek Park has miles of hiking and biking trails, including a well-graded eight-mile loop that starts and ends at the Nature Center and crosses through a nearly unbelievable stretch of urban wilderness. Another top destination, especially for weekend bikers and Rollerbladers, is Beach Drive, a portion of which is closed from Saturday morning at 7 A.M. until Sunday evening at 7 P.M. Rock Creek Park has a popular Nature Center that hosts ranger-led activities, an Equestrian Center that conducts outings for riders of all experience levels, tennis courts, a golf course, and historic sites like Civil War fortifications and Peirce Mill, a scenic 1820s structure that operated as a gristmill until 1892. Although the park is very popular, it also is huge, and there are long stretches of trail that are isolated and remote. For safety reasons, if you plan to hike or jog, consider using the park with a friend, either two-legged or a large four-legged one, especially if you are female.

◖ THEODORE ROOSEVELT ISLAND

George Washington Parkway between Key and
Roosevelt Bridges, www.nps.gov/this
HOURS: Open dawn-dusk
Map 9

The magic of Roosevelt Island lies with the
surprise that comes at the end of the hiking
trail. Cross the footbridge and hang a left onto
the loop trail rather than following the sign
that indicates a memorial to the right. The left
route takes you on a path that circles the island, an easy 1.5-mile walk through the woods
and swampland, complete with a boardwalk
and viewing spots over the marshes. Along
the way you might see deer, ospreys, or eagles.
Keep going until you are almost back where
you started, and you'll find a secluded treasure built to honor the nation's 26th president.
Roosevelt Island is unique in that while it looks
like it has been forested and secluded for years,
it once contained a mansion belonging to one
of Virginia's oldest families and was mainly
open fields and farmland. Any trees that grew,
like nearly all of them in Washington, were
felled during the Civil War. The island also
housed a Union field hospital during the war.
When the government decided to dedicate a
monument to Theodore Roosevelt, long considered the first environmental preservationist
U.S. president, the island was restored to its
natural deciduous forest habitat by Frederick
Law Olmsted, who planted nearly 30,000 trees
and removed all nonnative species.

GARDENS
◖ DUMBARTON OAKS

1703 32nd St. NW, 202/339-6401, www.doaks.org
HOURS: Gardens Mar. 15-Oct. 31 Tues.-Sun. 2-6 P.M.,
Nov. 1-Mar. 14 Tues.-Sun. 2-5 P.M.; museum year-round
Tues.-Sun. 2-5 P.M.; closed national holidays and
Christmas Eve
COST: Garden Mar. 15-Oct. 31 $8 adults, $5 seniors and
under age 13; free Nov.-Mar. 14; museum free
Map 8

This landmark is known mainly for its captivating formal gardens, but the home at the
site also holds a vast collection of Byzantine
and pre-Columbian art and is a work of art

in itself—an 1801 manor home featuring a
painted beam ceiling and mural of El Greco's
The Visitation. The house museum is free, an
indication that the real treasure here for visitors is the garden, straight out of the pages of
Frances Hodgson Burnett's *The Secret Garden.*
Awash in the spring and summer with color
and fragrance, the garden features numerous
"rooms," each with a theme or surprise. The
grounds' landscape architects intended the visitor to discover various themes on beauty, from
the vast rose garden and wisteria vines drip-
ping with blooms to towering Southern magnolias and a warm inviting orangery filled with
tropical plants. In addition to the museum and
gardens, the facility is also a research center for
Harvard University, devoted to the exploration of early civilizations as well as landscape
and garden studies. Harvard's center was built
on a foundation of art collected by onetime
homeowners Robert and Mildred Bliss, who
donated the home and its collection to the
university in 1940. Robert Woods Bliss was a
foreign-service officer and U.S. ambassador to
Argentina; he married Mildred Barnes, heiress
to the Fletcher's Castoria fortune, whom he
met when his father wedded her mother.

SMITHSONIAN GARDENS

Bounded by 9th St., 12th St., Jefferson Dr., and
Independence Ave. SW near the Castle grounds,
202/633-2220, www.gardens.si.edu
HOURS: Open 24 hours, except the Enid Haupt
Garden, which is gated and open dawn-dusk
Map 2

Spring through fall the Smithsonian Gardens
are in bloom, with landscape architecture that
ranges from the formal, like the manicured
Enid A. Haupt Garden, to the rambling, such
as the natural habitats at the National Museum
of the American Indian. The Haupt Garden
and the Kathrine Dulin Folger Rose Garden
near the Smithsonian Castle feature colorful
beds and borders, perennials, annuals, and
heirloom and vintage roses as well as cast-
iron fountains and furnishings. The Museum
of the American Indian's landscape is like a
mini break in the Virginia countryside, with

more than 150 species of plants and water features from the mid-Atlantic Piedmont region, where trees like oaks, pines, and magnolias thrive near meadows and cropland, and pawpaws and birch loom over wetlands. The Mary Livingston Ripley Garden near the Arts and Industries Building is an olfactory delight: Named for the wife of the Smithsonian's eighth secretary, it was designed as a fragrance garden, containing a variety of blooming plants and shrubs.

OLMSTED WOODS AND
THE BISHOP'S GARDEN

National Cathedral, 3101 Wisconsin Ave. NW, 202/537-6100

HOURS: Open dawn-dusk

Map 9

The 59 acres surrounding the National Cathedral are a gardener's treasure, designed by Frederick Law Olmsted to evoke a sense of the grounds of walled medieval cathedrals. The Bishop's Garden hosts the practical and the decorative—two herb gardens, a rose garden, perennial borders, and a delightful stone gazebo with a slate roof called the Shadow House. The Olmsted Woods is a five-acre forest of red oaks, beeches, and other native trees bisected by a meandering stone footpath. It also contains a restored outdoor amphitheater and a contemplative circle, a peaceful spot to reflect and enjoy the natural landscape.

BICYCLING

The variety of terrain found in the Washington region appeals to serious cyclists as well as to the casual day tripper, with an extensive selection of recreational trails ranging from moderately challenging to easy. Cycling on city streets is a bit tricky; a few have designated bike lanes, but Washington's drivers, including the trained Metrobus professionals, are challenged when it comes to sharing the road with two-wheeled vehicles. DC definitely isn't Amsterdam when it comes to coexisting with bike traffic. Riders must take extreme care even in bike lanes.

Fortunately, the city has a great number of trails with varying surfaces for road cyclists, one-speeds, and hybrid bikes—miles of surface that wind along the Potomac River, up to the Maryland suburbs, south to Mount Vernon, and west to Virginia's horse country and Maryland's farmland. Fit bikers seeking a challenge enjoy taking on the streets and hills of Arlington, Virginia, or riding the 45-mile rails-to-trails W&OD Trail to Purcellville, Virginia. A dream trip for the casual cyclist is a sunny day and a jaunt along the Potomac River next to the George Washington Parkway to Reagan National Airport and back. The rule of thumb is that if you're cycling within view of water and east, the trail is likely to be flat; head north and west on any trail that's not a former railroad bed and you'll encounter some serious hills.

One of the best ways to see the memorials and monuments, other than walking them, is by bike. The National Mall and adjacent parks have a number of off-road multiuse pathways as well as lesser-used roadways for sightseeing by bicycle. Crowds are usually manageable, so maneuvering a bike on the sidewalks is easy and acceptable. The terrain is flat, and the scenery is magnificent. Cycling is the best way to see lesser-known parts of this area, including the George Mason Memorial, off the beaten

© PATRICIA KIME

Bishop's Garden

ARTS AND LEISURE

path in East Potomac Park, and the tip of Hains Point, a finger of land with views of the Potomac, historic Fort McNair, the National War College, and the Washington Channel.

Bikes are allowed on Metro trains during nonpeak hours and all day Saturday and Sunday, ideal for the rider who wants to get closer to trail access points before starting a trip. Each Metrobus has a bike rack as well, so there's practically no place in DC or the suburbs that's off-limits to cyclists.

The city's biking community has formed advocacy groups aimed at promoting cycling for healthy living and as a commuter choice. The Washington Area Bicyclist Association (www.waba.org) has lobbied the city for more bike lanes and wider recognition of two-wheeled commuters, and the website www.bikewashington.org provides maps and information on cycling in and around the city.

Trails

◖ CAPITAL CRESCENT TRAIL
The Key Bridge and Water St., www.cctrail.org
Map 8

One of the area's most popular trails, the Capital Crescent is a former railroad bed, once home to the Georgetown branch of the Baltimore and Ohio Railroad, with a slow gradient rising from the city to Bethesda, Maryland, passing alongside the Potomac River, over historic railroad bridges, winding through woods, and past the manicured lawns of upscale suburbs. The trail is paved for nearly 11 miles, and in some spots features an adjacent stone-dust trail for runners. Past Bethesda, it is surfaced in crushed stone, a three-mile addition that goes to Lyttonsville, Maryland.

CHESAPEAKE & OHIO CANAL TOWPATH
1057 Thomas Jefferson St. NW, 202/653-5190, www.nps.gov/choh
Map 8

Originally designed as a path to accommodate the mules that towed barges along the C&O Canal, this trail runs for nearly 184 miles from Georgetown to Cumberland, Maryland, passing through Harpers Ferry, West Virginia, and

a number of small towns before its end. This is the one trail in DC where having a hybrid or mountain bike with wide tires is preferable to a sleek street bike; the trail is mostly gravel or hard-packed dirt. Road cyclists tend to use the Capital Crescent Trail, which parallels the C&O Towpath for roughly three miles from Georgetown to Fletcher's Boathouse in western DC. The Capital Crescent Trail then heads north about half a mile west of the boathouse while the towpath continues westward. In the first 15 miles, the trail passes seven locks as well as Great Falls Tavern, a preserved historic tavern and ranger station with hiking trails, restrooms, and water.

MOUNT VERNON TRAIL
On the Virginia side of the Potomac River from Roosevelt Island to Mount Vernon
Map 9

The 18-mile Mount Vernon Trail is one of the area's most scenic, a broad paved swath that runs along the Potomac River past Reagan National Airport, through historic Alexandria, and onto Mount Vernon, George Washington's home, after passing over and through marshland and deciduous forests. The course is mainly flat and has numerous stopping points for food, water, and breaks. Its only downside is that it's extremely crowded on weekends, especially between the city and the Woodrow Wilson Bridge seven miles south, and for some reason, road cyclists often like to pretend they are on the Tour de France while riding this route regardless of how busy it is. After the bridge and south to Mount Vernon, the crowds ebb, but the terrain becomes slightly hillier and curvier.

WASHINGTON & OLD DOMINION TRAIL
S. Glebe Rd. and Four Mile Run, Arlington, Va., www.wodfriends.org
Map 9

Within reach of Washington via a connector trail called the Custis Trail, the 45-mile W&OD Trail passes through the Virginia suburbs into the state's horse country, with numerous stops along the way for refreshments and diversions. This trail is paved its entire length with a parallel soft trail farther west to accommodate horses. Fun stops along the way for meals include the **Vienna Inn** (www.viennainn.com) in Vienna, a dive that serves delicious chili dogs and cold beer, and the upscale **Magnolia's** (www.magnoliasmill.com) in Purcellville at the trailhead for a celebratory end-of-the-ride glass of wine (provided you aren't biking all the way back to Washington that day). The trail meanders through backyards, forgotten railroad towns, and remote depots—truly a national treasure.

Bike Rentals

BIKE AND ROLL

Union Station, 50 Massachusetts Ave. NE, 202/842-2453, www.bikethesites.com

`Map 5`

An outlet that offers guided tours of the city as well as bike rentals, Bike and Roll has two locations in the city as well as one in Alexandria, Virginia, and offers a selections of Trek bicycles, including comfortable hybrids, performance bikes, road bikes, children's sizes, and bicycles built for two. Prices vary, with one-speed cruisers running $25 per day to road cycles costing $55 per day. Bike and Roll also rents jogging strollers, mobility scooters, and wheelchairs. All bike rentals come with a U-lock, handlebar bag, map, helmet, and tire-changing kit.

CAPITAL BIKESHARE

12th St. and Independence Ave. SW and other various locations around the city, www.capitalbikeshare.com

`Map 2`

The bikes aren't sexy at Capital Bikeshare; they resemble nonmotorized mopeds, but the concept is catching on around town: Riders become members for a day, five days, a month, or a year, with fees prorated for each, and receive a code they enter at one of Bikeshare's numerous stations across the city to unlock a bike. They can then use it for 30 minutes for free and pay a user fee for additional minutes. They can drop their ride off at any Bikeshare station near their destination. The program is geared more for commuters and city-dwellers running errands, but I've seen visitors grab a bike from a kiosk near their hotel and take it to neighborhoods like Georgetown or Logan Circle, areas not conveniently served by Metro Rail.

© C. DEAN KIME

Capital Bikeshare has rental kiosks throughout town.

ARTS AND LEISURE

THE BOATHOUSE AT FLETCHER'S COVE

4940 Canal Rd. NW, 202/244-0461,
www.fletcherscove.com

Map 9

Open from roughly mid-March to mid-October, the Boathouse at Fletcher's Cove rents bicycles for use on the Capital Crescent Trail or C&O Canal Towpath. It carries Giant 21-speed hybrids, Sun single-speed cruising bikes, and children's bikes in 20- and 24-inch sizes. Helmets are available on request at no additional charge; anyone age 16 and under is required by law to wear a helmet in DC.

THOMPSON BOAT CENTER

2900 Virginia Ave. NW, 202/333-9543

Map 8

Thompson Boat Center is primarily what the name implies: a boathouse for boat rentals, but it also rents bikes and is conveniently located near trails to the National Mall as well as Rock Creek Park. Bike selection is limited, however, to one-speed cruisers and multispeed hybrids, which are an unusual seven-speed rather than the standard 21-speed mountain bike many riders are accustomed to. A few children's bikes are also available for rent, although the limited number means they are often gone by midday. Bikes rent for $28 per day.

SWIMMING

WILLIAM H. RUMSEY AQUATICS CENTER

635 N. Carolina Ave. SE, 202/724-4495

HOURS: Daily from 6:30 A.M., closing time varies; lap-swim only Mon.-Fri. 6:30-7:30 P.M.

COST: Free for DC residents; $7 day pass others

Map 5

Located roughly one block from the Eastern Market Metro stop, this aquatics facility with indoor and outdoor pools is a bit of a haul from Capitol Hill hotels but is well-suited for those who need to get their laps in. Rumsey Aquatics Center has friendly staff, suitable hours with morning and evening lap swim times, and serviceable locker rooms at an affordable price. Its location near the Market is ideal for picking up an after-swim snack or coffee.

SPECTATOR SPORTS

Is Washington's lack of overzealous fanaticism for its sports teams a factor in the population being tolerant of losing teams, or is it just that most of its residents are from somewhere else, already devoted to their hometown clubs and unable to make the switch? Either way, it makes the city an interesting sports-watching environment, where it's fairly easy to get tickets, and you can wear a jersey of the opposing team—or any other sports jersey, for that matter—and no one blinks an eye. Washington fans seem to be less enthusiastic about their sports teams than other cities its size, with the exception, perhaps, of the Capitals, whose fans' ardor does compare favorably with the frenzied joy Philadelphia has for its football team or Chicago has for its Cubs. But maybe that's because the Caps have made the playoffs for the last four years, and the Capitals' star, Alex Ovechkin, has slap-shot his way into Washingtonians' hearts.

The city has no shortage of spectator sports, and many residents clearly remember the glory days of the Washington Redskins, the early 1980s to the 1990s, when the team won three Super Bowls in the span of 10 years. Fans wait anxiously each year to see if the team can lift itself out of the doldrums it has endured since 1993. In the past 18 years, the team has had eight head coaches and only three playoff-game wins. For baseball, fans wildly welcomed the Nationals in 2005 when the team, formerly the Montreal Expos, brought baseball back to Washington, taking to the field at Robert F. Kennedy Stadium on April 14, 2005, to defeat the Arizona Diamondbacks. The team has continued to have a so-so record, but its beautiful new stadium, on the banks of the Anacostia River, continues to draw crowds seeking an enjoyable way to spend a summer evening in the nation's capital. DC United, the city's Major League Soccer team, has won its league championship four times since the team was established in 1996, and the team continues to draw new fans and fresh players each year. Basketball is one of the city's most popular spectator activities, mainly because the city has a wealth of top-notch teams, including its NBA Wizards and WNBA Mystics as well at its high-performing collegiate teams, including the Georgetown Hoyas, George Washington Colonials, American Eagles, and nearby Maryland Terrapins.

Tickets for nearly every sporting event, with the exception of the Caps games, are fairly easy to obtain, either by directly contacting box offices or going through the team's approved ticket brokers. In many cases, tickets also can be found on Craigslist for face value—especially Redskins tickets; unfortunately, the more the team loses and its owner angers the fans, the less the fans are willing to traipse out to Landover, Maryland, to sit in the freezing cold and pay for expensive food.

Baseball
WASHINGTON NATIONALS
1500 South Capitol St. SE, 202/675-6287, www.nationals.com

`Map 9`

The "Nats," as the Nationals are known locally, are the city's newest pro sports franchise, moving to Washington in 2005 from Montreal, where they were the Expos. The team is part of the National League East, which includes the Atlanta Braves, the Florida Marlins, and the Philadelphia Phillies. Baseball didn't originate in DC with the Nationals; the city was home to the Washington Senators (which sometimes went by the name Nationals and the nickname "Nats") from 1901 to 1960, before the team left DC to become the Minnesota Twins. There was also a Senators team in Washington 1961 to 1971, which moved to Texas to become the Texas Rangers, but by and large that team was forgettable. In the early 2000s, when Montreal's fan base began shriveling, Major League Baseball considered revoking the team's franchise, but Washington had been clamoring for years for a major league team despite the protestations of the Baltimore Orioles, whose American League East team plays 40 miles away. In late 2004 the league decided to move the Expos to Washington and change the team's name.

The Nationals played their first three seasons at Robert F. Kennedy Stadium in southeast DC, while the city built the team's new home, Nationals Park, completed in 2008, near the Anacostia River in southeast Washington. Nationals Park has become a fan favorite for its excellent sightlines, views, open layout, and variety of concessions as well its amusements geared toward the fans, including the fourth-inning Presidents' Race, during which four costumed and foam-headed figures—George Washington, Abraham Lincoln, Thomas Jefferson, and Theodore Roosevelt—run the bases. In the four years since the race has been held, Teddy has never won, although he has come close, once being tripped at the finish line by the Baltimore Orioles Bird mascot. Teddy may be an all-around loser on the race course, but he's a fan favorite.

The Nationals have yet to make it to the playoffs: In their first season in Washington, they went 81 and 81, the best record they've had since their move. From 2006 to 2010 they have not had a winning season. Since 2005 their best record was in 2007, with 73 wins and 89 losses. Still, Washington has embraced the team as well as a number of players on the roster, including former Virginia Cavalier third baseman Ryan Zimmerman, right fielder Jayson Werth, former Oriole Jerry Hairston Jr., and, barring further injury, pitcher Stephen Strasburg.

Basketball
WASHINGTON MYSTICS
Verizon Center, 601 F St. NW, 202/661-5000, www.wnba.com/mystics

`Map 3`

The Mystics are the city's women's professional basketball franchise, playing in the WNBA's East Conference. The team was founded in 1998, a year after the association was established, and it quickly amassed a following, winning league attendance records for seven of the 13 years of its existence. Performance on the court has been less successful, however. The team has had three winning seasons and has made it to the playoffs six times, winning the conference semifinals once before losing in the conference finals to New York in 2002. Fans have great hopes for the Mystics in 2011, since they ended the 2010 season with their strongest record ever, 22 wins and 12 losses, before losing to Atlanta in the semifinals. A new team look, adopted in 2011 at the same time as the Washington Wizards brought back its red, white, and blue color scheme, has fans hoping that all three professional sports teams based in the Verizon Center can "Rock the Red," as the NHL Capitals team has coined its rallying cry. A number of all-stars have played for the Mystics, including Olympian Nikki McCray, Tennessee Volunteer Chamique Holdsclaw, former Duke University star Alana Beard, and Maryland's Crystal Langhorne. The Mystics are coached by Trudi Lacey, who played for North Carolina State.

WASHINGTON WIZARDS

Verizon Center, 601 F St. NW, 202/661-5000, www.nba.com/wizards

Map 3

The Wizards' move to Washington was a long and gradual one, a story that has the team starting as the Baltimore Bullets and playing in Charm City from 1963 to 1973 before moving to an outer suburb of Washington DC and calling themselves the Capital Bullets for a year before renaming themselves the Washington Bullets. By then, their most famous player to date, Wes Unseld, was already rocking the court, having been named Rookie of the Year and Most Valuable Player, joining Gus Johnson in taking the team to the NBA Finals in 1971. They went to the finals again in 1975 and lost, finally winning an NBA Championship in 1978. The team has had its share of ups and downs, but it is enthusiastically embraced by its fans for a number of reasons, notwithstanding the team's move to the newly built MCI Center (now the Verizon Center) in 1997, a change that heralded the complete makeover of the city's downtown area. In 1995, owner Abe Pollin also changed the team's name, mainly because the city at the time was known as the murder capital of the country, and the term *bullet* evoked this violent trend. A contest was held to rename

The Washington Wizards play at the Verizon Center.

DANIEL LOBO – DAQUELLAMANERA.ORG

the team, and none of the choices for the final vote were relevant to Washington, including Wizards, Sea Dogs, Stallions, and Dragons. The team adopted new colors as well, and both Pollin's teams, the Capitals and the Wizards, sported blue, black, and gold uniforms. After Pollin's death in 2009, the Wizards were purchased by Ted Leonsis, who by then owned the Capitals and the Mystics. In 2011, Leonsis revived the red, white, and blue color scheme for the Wizards, a move that has fans calling for another name change as well. The Wizards play in the Eastern Conference of the Southeast Division.

Football
WASHINGTON REDSKINS
1600 FedEx Way, Landover, Md., 301/322-8026, www.redskins.com

Map 9

Hope springs eternal for Redskins fans, who root each year for their beloved team only to have their dreams dashed by the end of the season, or, in typical Redskins fashion, by the end of a game after being in the lead well into the third quarter. The Redskins are one of pro football's oldest teams, founded originally in Boston in 1932 as the Boston Braves and changing its name a year later to the Boston Redskins. The team moved to Washington in 1937.

The Redskins play in the East Division of the National Football Conference. They have played in five Super Bowls and won three, and during the early years of professional football, from 1932 to 1945, they participated in five championship games and won two. The list of famous men associated with the team's signature burgundy and gold includes not only record-setting players but legendary coaches as well. Hall of Famers George Allen and Joe Gibbs are remembered for their abilities to form cohesion with their unique rosters—Allen took the Redskins to the playoffs five times and to the Super Bowl once with a group of seasoned veterans nicknamed "The Over-the-Hill Gang," which included such standouts as Billy Kilmer, Richie Petitbon, Jack Pardee, and others, and Gibbs drew the improbable

fortune of being hired at the same time the team landed an eye-popping roster of young up-and-comers, including Art Monk, Mark May, Russ Grimm, and Dexter Manley, and later Darrell Green and Charles Mann, while veterans John Riggins and Joe Theismann hit their career peaks. The coming-together of these teams, combined with Gibbs's fearless coaching, led the Redskins to dominate the playoffs in the 1980s and early 1990s and win three Super Bowls.

Since roughly 1993, however, life hasn't been so rosy for the Redskins. The team has made the playoffs only three times since Gibbs retired, the first in 1992 (he returned to coach the Redskins for four seasons from 2004 to 2007). Superstitious fans think this poor string of luck is a curse for playing outside the city: The Redskins' stadium, FedEx Field, lies in suburban Maryland, a 90,000-plus-seat venue universally derided by fans as soulless, expensive, and hard to reach. The stadium, originally named for previous owner Jack Kent Cooke, opened in 1997; the team previously played at Robert F. Kennedy Stadium near the Anacostia River in southeast Washington. But seriously, for the most part, fans place the blame for the team's woes squarely on owner Daniel Snyder and his front office. Snyder, a self-made billionaire who made his money in marketing and acquisitions, has turned the Redskins into the second most valuable franchise in the NFL, on the heels of gridiron rivals the Dallas Cowboys. Among the ways Snyder has raised revenue was selling the naming rights to the stadium to FedEx for $207 million. He increased the stadium's size, adding amenities to its expensive club level to draw fans and businesses to purchase the pricier seats. And he started charging fans for prime tailgating spots. Among his most unpopular decisions was a 2009 edict banning all signs from FedEx Field, ostensibly because the franchise "didn't want anyone to be injured" by them, but after showing a pattern of booting people out of the stadium for hoisting anti-Snyder signs, the reason was clear: He didn't want to read anything negative about himself or his organization inside the stadium.

The controversy about the team's name continues, although less so since the U.S. Supreme Court refused to hear a case about it brought by several Native American groups who deem it offensive. Unlike other teams' names associated with Native Americans, like the Florida State Seminoles, which honors one of the state's Native American groups, or the Atlanta Braves, who named their team after young Native American warriors, "Redskins" stands out mainly because Native Americans say it was a term used to describe the scalps of their ancestors brought in by bounty hunters or kept as trophies by settlers during the founding of the colonies. The team argues that the name no longer has a link to that meaning, and given the its storied history, has established a brand recognized for honor and tradition. Either way, a U.S. Court of Appeals decision in 2009 denied the claim, saying the group hadn't filed its lawsuit in a timely manner, and the name has stayed.

Ice Hockey
WASHINGTON CAPITALS
Verizon Center, 601 F St. NW, 202/266-2200, www.capitals.nhl.com
Map 3

The seasons between 2007 and 2011 have been crushing for Washington's ice hockey fans; the National Hockey League's Capitals have made it to the playoffs all four years only to have their Stanley Cup dreams dashed either in the first round or smacked down in the heartbreaking second round. Still, it's practically a miracle the team is the city's most popular sports team, as Washington has no strong ice-hockey tradition. It is not a major sport played by any area high schools or colleges—heck, the Potomac River barely freezes over some years. But the Caps have captured Washington's imagination, not bad for a team whose main star is proudly Russian (Alex Ovechkin). The Capitals have won their conference once, in 1998, losing the Stanley Cup to the Detroit Red Wings that year. They have never won the cup, although "winning a sports championship" is on owner Ted Leonsis's lifetime bucket list. A number of Hall of Fame players have worn the Cap's uniform,

including Mike Gartner, Rod Langway, Larry Murphy, Scott Stevens, and Dino Ciccarelli. The Caps play at the Verizon Center, where games sell out frequently and the fan-base is known for being among the NHL's loudest.

Soccer
DC UNITED
2400 East Capitol St. SE, 202/587-5000, www.dcunited.com
Map 9

It must be hard to be DC United: The team is the city's most successful in its league, having won two U.S. Open Cups and four Major League Soccer Cups since its establishment in 1995, and still, mainstream Washington forgets about them. Yet DC United has a loyal and vocal fan base, with three fan clubs and one of the league's highest attendance records. In addition to its domestic success, the team has made a name for itself on the international stage, participating in 2005 in the Copa Sudamericana and making its round of 16, and playing and beating UK teams Chelsea and Celtic FC. Notable players for DC United include Jaime Moreno, Eddie Pope, and Marco Etcheverry. The team plays in Robert F. Kennedy Stadium, located on Metro's Orange and Blue lines.

WATER ACTIVITIES
George Washington chose the city's site for a number of reasons, not the least of which was that it lay at the confluence of two rivers with lovely views of a grand river and a tidal marsh and access to transportation by water. Georgetown was already a thriving tobacco port; Washington envisioned a city where agricultural goods would be carried in from across the mid-Atlantic and floated down-river to destinations along the East Coast and across the ocean. When the river silted in and Georgetown declined as an economic powerhouse, the waterway fell into disuse, becoming a dumping ground for human and industrial waste and garbage and a ready receptor for agricultural runoff upstream. It frequently became a source of a disease and illness: A

typhoid outbreak during the Civil War killed Abraham Lincoln's son Willie and other Washingtonians. By the 1950s, mass fish kills were occurring in the river, and the *Washington Post* described the Potomac River as an "open sewer." Algae blooms often turned the surface fluorescent green in the summer, and in the 1960s, President Lyndon Johnson declared it "a national disgrace." Fortunately, the bad press (and smell) sparked a movement to clean up the river. While it still has a long way to go, it has become a place for recreational boating and fishing, where people have no qualms about plying its waters or eating the fish they catch in it.

Among the boating activities on the river are kayaking and canoeing on all portions of the river and sailing south of the 14th Street Bridge. During the summer, the occasional water-skier or personal watercraft user will take to the water, but there's no place in town to rent them; you'll have to bring your own. Area high schools and colleges use the river heavily in the spring and fall for rowing, and recreational motor boat users tie up in the river around Georgetown all summer long for a day of relaxation. Fishing has returned to the area's waterways as well, and anglers usually heading upstream above the city to catch bass, bluegill, and crappie. Along the city seawalls and shorelines, it's not uncommon to see someone reeling in a catch. And although it still doesn't earn an A rating for cleanliness, people do swim in the Potomac, although it's not advised, not so much because of the pollution but for the dangerous currents that run under the seemingly placid surface.

Fishing
THE BOATHOUSE AT FLETCHER'S COVE
4940 Canal Rd. NW, 202/244-0461,
www.fletcherscove.com
Map 9

Anglers enjoy Fletcher's Cove, where they can purchase a fishing license, rent a rowboat, buy tackle and bait, and hit a great fishing hole, Fletcher's Cove, known for its striped bass, shad, perch, and, as in the rest of the Potomac

River, the much-hated snakehead. Fletcher's also rents kayaks and canoes: individual kayaks for $10 per hour, double sit-in kayaks for $17 per hour, and canoes that can be fitted with an extra cushion for a third seat for $12 per hour. Places to explore near Fletcher's include the C&O Canal and the Potomac River, which, in this area, has small inlets and beaches.

Kayaking and Rowing
JACK'S BOATHOUSE
3500 K St. NW, 202/337-9642,
www.jacksboathouse.com
Map 8

The folks at Jack's Boathouse have a reputation for being "chill," although they seem to be a little too laid-back for a service company. They only answer the phone when they're near it, they don't return phone messages (why bother having a machine?), and they don't respond to emails. And if there's a small craft warning 40 miles away on the Chesapeake Bay, they might just decide not come in to work that day, even if they have customers waiting. Still, they do rent kayaks and canoes from a lovely new dock right under the Key Bridge, and their guides conduct the city's only 90-minute guided twilight kayak tour, a cool adventure where paddlers float past Kennedy Center and view the monuments and Roosevelt Island before heading upriver past the Key Bridge to the relative solitude of the tree-lined Potomac River, checking out a small island and looking for herons, egrets, or if they're lucky, a bald eagle.

THOMPSON BOAT CENTER
2900 Virginia Ave. NW, 202/333-9543
Map 8

Thompson Boat Center rents mainly kayaks and canoes, single kayaks for $10 per hour, double sit-in or sit-on-top ocean kayaks for $17 per hour, and canoes that can hold up to three people for $12 per hour. Thompson is the only place in the city to rent a rowing shell, but there's a catch: You must be certified through the Boat Center to rent one. No, rowing for your Stotesbury Cup–winning high school or college varsity team doesn't count. However,

© PATRICIA KIME

rowers on the Potomac

for experienced rowers, the certification class is shorter than it would be for beginners. Single sculls are available for $16 per hour, doubles for $26 per hour, and both parties must be certified. Scenery near Thompson's includes an area of the Potomac River from the Roosevelt Bridge north past Key Bridge, including views of Kennedy Center, Georgetown, and Roosevelt Island.

Sailing
WASHINGTON SAILING MARINA

1 Marina Dr. at Daingerfield Island, 703/548-9027, www.washingtonsailingmarina.com

Map 9

The Washington Sailing Marina is the area's largest marina, with floating slips, rack space, and dry storage for boats, sailing lessons for youths and adults from beginner to intermediate on Flying Scots and Sunfish sailing dinghies, and summer camps. It is home to a number of sailing groups, including the Potomac River Sailing Association, which holds regattas throughout the year, as well as the Georgetown Sailing Team, the American University Sailing Team, and a Sea Scouting crew. Available boat rentals include 19-foot

Flying Scots for $23 per hour (minimum two hours) and Aqua Finn sailboats for $15 per hour. Proof of sailing certification is required for rentals; otherwise, prospective renters can take a sailing test at the marina to qualify. The range for rented boats from the marina spans from the 14th Street Bridge to Old Town Alexandria.

Boating Supplies and Facilities
WASHINGTON MARINA

1300 Maine Ave. SW, 202/554-0222, www.washingtonmarina.com

Map 9

Out-of-town boaters needing supplies, parts, gas, or a transient slip to dock for the night will find them at Washington Marina in the Washington Channel. The channel has several marinas and is home to the DC Fire Department's rescue fleet as well as the former presidential yacht *Sequoia*. Washington Marina is conveniently located closest to the monuments and memorials for daytime sightseeing. Sailboats needing mast clearance can check out James Creek Marina (www.jamescreekmarina.com), nearby on the Anacostia River.

GYMS AND HEALTH CLUBS
FITNESS FIRST
1075 19th St. NW, 202/659-1900,
www.fitnessfirstclubs.com
HOURS: Mon.-Thurs. 5 A.M.-11 P.M., Fri. 5 A.M.-10 P.M.,
Sat.-Sun. 8 A.M.-8 P.M.
COST: Day pass $19
Map 4

For a decent workout at a lower price, Fitness First offers nearly any class you could want, including Pilates, spinning, yoga, Zumba, aerobics, belly dancing, boot camp, and cycling, and also has cardiovascular equipment, free weights, and weight machines. It also has a sauna and steam room as well as locker rooms equipped with hair dryers.

NATIONAL CAPITAL AREA YMCA
1711 Rhode Island Ave. NW, 202/862-9622,
www.ymcadc.org
HOURS: Mon.-Fri. 5:30 A.M.-10:30 P.M.,
Sat. 8 A.M.-6:30 P.M., Sun. 9 A.M.-5:30 P.M.
Map 6

The National Capital Area YMCA has an indoor pool, squash courts, basketball courts, and a rock-climbing wall as well as a gym with cardio machines, free weights, and Nautilus equipment. The indoor track is a bonus for wimps like me who hate running in the cold but don't like treadmills either. The Y also offers a full complement of classes.

RESULTS THE GYM
315 G St. SE, 202/234-5678, www.resultsthegym.com
HOURS: Mon.-Fri. 5 A.M.-11 P.M., Sat.-Sun. 7 A.M.-9 P.M.
COST: Day pass $19
Map 5

Housed in an 1887 building that served as one of the District's first schools for African American children, Results is among the largest and most comprehensive fitness facilities in the city, with 65,000 square feet devoted to basketball, volleyball, squash, indoor rock climbing, aerobics, yoga, and more. Cardio machines are found on three different levels, including a room devoted exclusively to treadmills. Locker rooms are what you would expect of a gym that draws its membership from the Capitol Hill neighborhood, a soothing spa experience with towel service, toiletries, steam and dry saunas, and hot tubs.

GUIDED TOURS
A guidebook is handy, but sometimes a city's secrets are best discovered on a tour with someone who can share Washington's intimate details, its history or hidden places, and its many neighborhoods with their own stories to tell. While Washington DC doesn't have a single one-stop shop for information on tickets and tours, Destination DC (901 7th St. NW, 4th Fl., 202/789-7000, www.washington.org), the former Washington DC Convention and Tourism Corporation, publishes a guide to the capital as well as maps, which can be ordered by mail ahead of your visit through its website or picked up at the its downtown office. An information desk at Union Station also has pamphlets on various opportunities and assistants to help you decide which tour fits your schedule and interests. Washington is known as a very walkable city, but visitors also tend to overdo it, getting tired rushing from one famous site to another. Bus and vehicle tours provide an opportunity to rest your feet and get your bearings. Along the way you'll likely learn a thing or two you never knew about DC. The city also has a number of unusual ways to enjoy the monuments and memorials: on a bike, a Segway, or a World War II–era amphibious assault vehicle called a "duck."

BIKE AND ROLL
Union Station, 50 Massachusetts Ave. NE; 1100 Pennsylvania Ave. NW; 1 Wales Alley, Alexandria, Va.; 202/842-2453, www.bikethesites.com
COST: Tours from $40 adults, $30 children
Map 5

The sights of Washington are easily explored by bike, and Bike and Roll takes group no larger than 15 on two- and three-hour tours from any of its three locations, with guides leading bike hikes of easy to moderate intensity. Tours are available from roughly mid-March to mid-December and use Trek bicycles. The night bike tour is popular, a chance to see the monuments after dark and not worry too much about weaving in and out of the crowds.

CITY SEGWAY
624 9th St. NW, 877/734-8687 or 202/626-0017, www.citysegwaytours.com/washington-dc
COST: Tours from $60
Map 3

An international company runs City Segway, with similar tours in Munich, Vienna, and Paris as well as a handful of U.S. cities. If you can get past the nerd factor of riding a Segway (most teenagers snicker about these two-wheeled vehicles, until they ride one), you'll find you can cover a vast area without breaking a sweat. The company offers two- and three-hour tours two or three times a day; participants listen to their guides through headsets, learning about sites along the National Mall and throughout the city. The last tour of the day is particularly popular, a chance to see a bit of the city in the daytime and enjoy sunset and the evening as the lights come on. Riding a Segway is easier than riding a bike—it takes about two minutes to learn.

DC BY FOOT
1740 18th St. NW, Suite 304, 202/370-1830, www.dcbyfoot.com
COST: Free; tips greatly appreciated
Map 6

DC By Foot has an interesting business model: Guides are informative, funny, and helpful, they show up at a certain time and place daily to take whomever is there on a walking tour, and they work for tips only. Tours include topics like "More Than Just Monuments," "Lincoln's Assassination," and Arlington Cemetery. Guides willingly answer questions, provide follow-up, and spend just over an hour touring the sights, mixing facts with factoids to keep the group alert and interested, and all have a certain storytelling prowess that is the mark of a good tour guide. And yet they work only for tips, and it works: DC By Foot is one of the most popular guide services in the area.

DC DUCKS
Union Station, 50 Massachusetts Ave. NE, 202/633-2214, www.dcducks.com
COST: $35 adults, $25 children
Map 5

Tours in World War II amphibious vehicles have become ubiquitous in cities lucky enough to have a navigable waterfront, but this doesn't mean a tour on a "duck"—a nickname for the vehicle's original designation, DUKW—is any less fun. These white trucks with bright yellow awnings carry visitors throughout the city's streets, guided by conductors that are part historian, part stand-up comic. The tours pass nearly all the city's famous sites before splashing into the Potomac River for a 20-minute ride to National Airport. Look online to buy discount tickets.

ODYSSEY CRUISES
6th St. and Water St. SE, 888/741-0281, www.odysseycruises.com
COST: Varies; lunch, brunch, and dinner cruises
Map 9

The low profile of the Odyssey fleet allows the company's boats to fit underneath all the Potomac River's bridges, including Memorial Bridge, which means that a dinner cruise aboard an Odyssey vessel will afford you a look at DC's monuments at night instead of a standard cruise to Old Town Alexandria and back (which is nice too, but not what many people come to DC to do). Dinner cruises in cities are inherently designed for visitors, and from experience, they usually don't have the best food or wine, and the Odyssey is typical in this area. But if you go with an attitude that you'll have a good time and maintain low expectations for the food and service, you can have a surprising amount of fun. One tip: Consider getting a reservation for July 4; the river is a great place to be during the spectacular fireworks show.

OLD TOWN TROLLEY TOURS
Union Station, 50 Massachusetts Ave. NE, 202/832-9800, www.oldtowntrolley.com
COST: $35 adults, $25 under age 11, free under age 4, good for two days with certain restrictions
Map 5

For a hop-on, hop-off option that takes riders

© DESTINATION DC

A DC Ducks tour passes the U.S. Capitol.

to Georgetown and the National Cathedral, Old Town Trolley tours offers a "green loop" option that traverses Embassy Row to the National Zoo and through Georgetown. Riders also have access to the other Old Town loops, including tours of the National Mall area and a ride to Arlington Cemetery (although not through the cemetery). Operators serve as tour guides, and some are very knowledgeable, although don't necessarily believe everything they say. Some seem to be full of what Queen Victoria referred to as "blarney." Look online for discount tickets.

OPEN TOP TOURS, GRAY LINE

Union Station, 50 Massachusetts Ave. NE, 202/289-1995, www.graylinedc.com
COST: $35 adults, $18 children, good for 24 hours
Map 5

In October, 2011, a DC staple, Tourmobile, a retro, open-air tram service that navigated the area around the Mall for 42 years folded, leaving a hole in the range of choices for personally narrated hop-on, hop-off tours of the city. Tourmobile wasn't cheap, but its fares, just slightly below Gray Line's ubiquitous double-decker Open Top Tours, were good for two days. Until the National Park Service, which contracted with Tourmobile, comes up with an alternative, Open Top Tours by Gray Line are an acceptable, albeit pricey hop-on, hop-off alternative, but you won't find much personal service and witty repartee while riding. The canned tours emitting from the buses' speakers aren't always in sync with the view, and the buses don't always show up when you want them. Still, they are a good way to familiarize yourself with the lay of DC's land, to figure out what you might want to return to later, or simply to get between sites without wearing out your feet.

WASHINGTON WALKS

819 G St. SW, 202/484-1565, www.washingtonwalks.com
COST: Varies, tours from $15.
Map 9

Visitors and locals alike enjoy the tours by Washington Walks, a company that takes the time to explore the city's neighborhoods

ARTS AND LEISURE

or sights with groups, educating them in a way that's usually more informative and better researched than fly-by-night tour guides. The company's "Get Local Saturdays" highlight a different neighborhood or theme each week, with two-hour tours exploring places like Petworth, the history of John Philip Sousa in DC, or K Street's modernist architecture. The most popular tours for visitors are "Monuments by Moonlight" and the "Most Haunted Houses" tour. The company also hires out private guides for individualized tours.

OTHER RECREATION
Bowling
LUCKY STRIKE LANES
701 7th St. NW, 202/347-1021, www.bowlluckystrike.com
Map 3

The over-21 set rocks the lanes and the lounge after 8 P.M. at Lucky Strike, a lounge–bowling alley designed more for fun than fitness, with several bars, 14 lanes, 10 projection screens, and a high-end sound system. Those under the drinking age are allowed to venture inside and bowl some games before 8 P.M. Patrons report long lines for a lane. If good music and fun is what you seek, you might be better off going to a trendy bar nearby. If you happen to have a military identification card, the best bowling alley close to Washington is at Fort Myer (703/528-4766) in Arlington, Virginia, with a bowling center and a cheap snack bar.

Golf
Washington is home to some of the country's finest private courses, including the Congressional Country Club, host of the 2011 U.S. Open, as well as the Washington Golf and Country Club and Army Navy, whose Arlington and Fairfax, Virginia, courses were preferred by President Clinton during his presidency; he continues to frequent them today when he's in town. The city has a number of golf courses open to the public as well. Greens fees are surprisingly affordable, and though the grounds aren't quite as groomed as you'd find at Congressional, they'll do for a day of fun under the sun. All three venues rent clubs.

EAST POTOMAC PARK
972 Ohio Dr. SW, 202/554-7660, www.golfdc.com
COST: 18 holes $27 Mon.-Fri., $31 Sat.-Sun., 9 holes $10, $13, or $18 Mon.-Fri., $13, $16, or $21 Sat.-Sun., depending on the course
Map 9

The courses at East Potomac Park are a bit worse for wear, but they offer great views of the Washington Monument and the Jefferson Memorial as well as the Potomac River and the planes landing at Reagan National. The weather on the course, especially down near Hains Point, can be windy, challenging even the best driver to adjust his or her aim. The staff at the driving range is friendly and willing to offer tips and advice as well as their insight regarding the greens. There's a miniature golf course here as well.

LANGSTON GOLF COURSE
2600 Benning Rd. SE, 202/397-8638, www.golfdc.com
COST: 18 holes $24 Mon.-Fri., $30 Sat.-Sun., 9 holes $17 Mon.-Fri., $22 Sat.-Sun.
Map 9

A historic course built in 1939 for African American golfers, Langston is a small urban golf course wedged between Robert F. Kennedy Stadium and the Anacostia River, a relatively flat course that's difficult to lose a ball on and is well-regarding by everyone who plays it. This isn't a neighborhood secret; area golfers use Langston frequently. Newcomers to the city don't tend to know about it because it is in a somewhat downtrodden section of town. The back nine, in fact, can be a little sketchy. But the prices are right, the greens are in relatively good shape, and the clubhouse grill serves food at decent prices.

ROCK CREEK GOLF COURSE
6100 16th St. NW, 202/882-7332, www.golfdc.com
COST: 18 holes $20 Mon.-Fri., $25 Sat.-Sun., 9 holes $15 Mon.-Fri., $20 Sat.-Sun.
Map 9

Rock Creek is nearly the cheapest game in

town, but golfers get what they pay for. The greens are among the worst of the three public courses described here, and while the course is challenging (*Golf Digest* magazine named it one of the best places to play in 2008), its woodsy back nine is difficult to maneuver. There may be a reason for the natural state of the greens: Audubon International recognized it for its environmentally friendly maintenance practices, a boon to wildlife like deer, raccoons, foxes, and hawks but not for golfers, who may not like losing their balls in holes or driving from tees that have no grass.

Ice Skating
SCULPTURE GARDEN ICE RINK
National Gallery of Art on the National Mall between 7th St. and Constitution Ave., 202/216-9397, www.nga.gov/ginfo/skating.shtm

HOURS: Weather permitting, mid-Nov.-mid-Mar. Mon.-Sat. 10 A.M.-11 P.M., Sun. 10 A.M.-9 P.M.

COST: $7 adults, $6 over age 49, students, and under age 13

Map 2

A smallish rink in the heart of a large, landscaped garden filled with art, the seasonal ice rink at the National Gallery of Art is a unique urban experience, drawing skaters of all ages to enjoy a sport that few are really good at but hundreds are willing to try. Skates are available for rent, and the garden also offers lockers. If you have your own skates, bring them; you'll save money and are guaranteed that the edges will be better than the rental skates regardless of when you last had them sharpened. Your ticket (a sticker, in this case) buys a two-hour block of time to enjoy the ice, twirling, spinning, and dodging kamikaze kids. Evening skate is colder but significantly less crowded. Access to the rink and the Pavilion Café, which stays open late as well selling hot chocolate, coffee, and food, is through the Constitution Avenue and Madison Drive entrances at 9th Street.

Tennis
The city has a number of free tennis courts. For information on locations, schedules, and reservations, check out the city's Department of Parks and Recreation (www.dpr.dc.gov).

EAST POTOMAC TENNIS CENTER
1090 Ohio Dr. SW, 202/554-5962, www.eastpotomactennis.com

Map 9

The public Tennis Center at East Potomac Park has five indoor hard courts available for play year-round as well as 10 clay courts open May through November and outdoor hard courts available by reservation. Fees are charged to use the courts; at the time of this writing the center was in the process of revamping its fee schedule.

ROCK CREEK PARK TENNIS CENTER
16th St. and Kennedy St. NW, 202/722-5949, www.rockcreektennis.com

COST: Hard courts $12 per hour Sat.-Sun., $10 per hour Mon.-Fri. 7 A.M.-6 P.M., $12 per hour 6-11 P.M.; clay courts daily $18 per hour

Map 9

Rock Creek Tennis Center is the home of the Legg Mason Classic, and it is a popular venue, with hard- and soft-surface courts for public use. Reservations are required April through October, and the center has rackets for rent for those who've left them at home. A full-service pro shop offers lessons and services like stringing. The center also offers clinics and private lessons.

ARTS AND LEISURE

SHOPS

Shopping in DC can be haute or cool, high-end or bargain basement, St. John and pearls or boho and Birkenstocks. The city and its environs have nearly every top department store and retail chain but also offer a significant number of boutiques and homegrown emporiums where shoppers can discover the alluring or unique. Historically, DC has been a destination for antiques, art, home decor and furnishings, jewelry, books, and political memorabilia, and in the main shopping arenas you'll find countless opportunities to browse these specialties. In the past decade, the city has also cultivated a fledgling boutique industry aimed at tempting fashionistas to shop locally for memorable clothes, fabulous shoes, and matchless accessories. The city is still not considered a fashion powerhouse by any stretch, but its young residents and international population have helped increase Washington's focus on style, and the demand has spurred growth of numerous small businesses.

Georgetown remains the one-stop neighborhood for meeting any shopper's desires: The area's major thoroughfares, M Street and Wisconsin Avenue, are lined with stores, from independent boutiques carrying current styles to unique furniture stores, antiques shops, and home accessories warehouses selling everything from traditional American and European furniture to the latest creations of master woodworkers. On weekends at the height of the day, Georgetown is jammed with crowds, mainly visitors, who flock to its storefronts as well as its restaurants and pubs. Just over a mile

© PATRICIA KIME

HIGHLIGHTS

LOOK FOR ◖ TO FIND RECOMMENDED SHOPS.

◖ **Best Antique Furniture:** Visitors hoping to carry home a bit of 18th- or 19th-century Washington may find it at **Susquehanna,** known for its fine American and British antique furniture and decorative arts (page 191).

◖ **Best Shop for Browsing Antique Art:** Three stories of art are crammed into a corner row house at **L'Enfant Gallery** in Georgetown (page 192).

◖ **Best Museum Shop:** One just isn't enough at **The National Gallery of Art,** with three gift shops dedicated to books, art supplies, children's toys and games, jewelry, and art-themed accessories (page 195).

◖ **Best Book Store:** The fiercely independent **Politics and Prose** is more than a bookstore; it's the premier spot for DC book signings, discourse, and community relations (page 195).

◖ **Best Flea Market:** The Sunday flea market at **Eastern Market** is hard to beat for jewelry, vinyl LPs, crafts, handmade furniture, and unique gifts at reasonable prices (page 201).

◖ **Best Tacky, Quirky, and Quixotic Gifts:** The supply of gag gifts, amusing greeting cards, candy, cocktail napkins, and games is top-notch at **Chocolate Moose** (page 205).

◖ **Best Place for the Perfect Bauble:** Washington favorite **Tiny Jewel Box** boasts three floors of coveted designer and vintage jewelry (page 205).

◖ **Best Store for Kids:** The gadget selection at the **Spy Museum Store** will satisfy amateur sleuths, but the prices often prompt parents to perform a disappearing act (page 207).

◖ **Best Consignment Shop:** The once-loved designer duds of Washington doyennes end up searching for a new owner at **Secondi** (page 211).

© PATRICIA KIME

Eastern Market buzzes during Sunday flea markets.

away, the scene at Dupont Circle trends more local: Shops range from high-end retailers south along Connecticut Avenue to the fun, funky, and unusual closer to the traffic circle. Another favorite haunt for Washingtonians is the Capitol Hill area: The Sunday flea market at Eastern Market draws a lively crowd, with more than 100 vendors who hawk crafts, jewelry, art, clothing, handbags, beads, and more. The Capitol Hill area also has a number of neighborhood stores carrying home goods, accessories, and gifts. If you've come to DC for a high-end shopping fix, you'll be able to meet that yen as well, but you'll need to head farther afield from the city center, either to northernmost Wisconsin Avenue and into Chevy Chase, Maryland, with the home stores of Dior, Gucci, and Cartier as well as department stores such as Barneys New York Co-op, Saks Fifth Avenue, Neiman Marcus, and Bloomingdale's, or into the Virginia suburbs, including nearby Arlington, with its small but convenient mall accessible by Metro, or to Tysons Corner near McLean, Virginia, home to the area's largest shopping mall, the grand-daddy of them all, Tysons Corner Center, as well as its upscale neighbor, Tysons Galleria, which combined have more than 400 stores under two roofs.

SHOPPING DISTRICTS
Downtown

Downtown Washington isn't a place for des-tination shopping, although it has a number of stores sprinkled throughout, perfect for browsing if you find yourself in the area. The National Press Club Building near the cor-ner of 14th Street and F Street NW, at one of two primary shopping loci, has a number of apparel stores on its first floor and several shoe and jewelry stores nearby. The neighbor-hood also boasts a fine tobacco shop and the city's premier French lingerie boutique. The other focal point for downtown shopping is Gallery Place near the Verizon Center. Here you'll find common retail outlets like Urban Outfitters and Bed Bath & Beyond. But just a couple of blocks west on F Street are some unique shops, including Mia Gemma, home to original handcrafted jewelry and designs, and Peruvian Connection, featuring alpaca scarves, ponchos, sweaters, and jewelry as well as other interesting stand-alone shops. This area contains several museums with noteworthy museum shops, including the International Spy Museum and the National Portrait Gallery.

Capitol Hill

The stores on Capitol Hill are centered largely in one of two places: inside the vast expanse of Union Station or in and around Eastern Market, the city's Victorian-era enclosed pub-lic market, built in 1873 and recently reopened following a devastating fire in 2007. Union Station contains many stores found in a typi-cal suburban shopping mall, including Ann Taylor, Victoria's Secret, and White House/Black Market, but it also features a smatter-ing of unique shops for crafts, jewelry, and

accessories. Eastern Market, although small compared with markets found in other large American cities, houses butchers, fishmongers, florists, bakeries, and several breakfast and lunch counters. On weekends, the fun spreads outside the brick facade. Spring through fall, the area features a farmers market on Saturday and a flea market year-round on Sunday. The neighborhood also has a few independent shops, doing business out of tiny row houses along the neighborhood's narrow streets.

Dupont Circle

On Connecticut Avenue closer to K Street are a number of high-end clothiers and boutiques such as Thomas Pink and Brooks Brothers men's clothiers, Burberry and Ann Taylor, Washington's own Rizik's for women's wear, and jewelry retailers. Head north toward Dupont Circle and the climate changes, becom-ing more free-spirited and imaginative with vin-tage shops, art galleries, bookstores, and retro jewelry stores—a place to stock up the closet or the home or find fun gifts for friends.

Adams Morgan and U Street

Adams Morgan is known for its nightlife, but it has a handful of family-owned businesses and shops, including some haunts to find an-tique housewares, vintage and funky clothing, collectibles, gifts, and international markets. On U Street, stores seem to come and go, but a number have established a firm foothold in this now "officially arrived" neighborhood, fea-turing cool boutiques, vintage apparel, crafts, cards, and unique housewares.

Georgetown

The city's most popular shopping destination, with charming storefronts in 18th and 19th century buildings, has a range of choices that can occupy a shopper's entire day, and that's not counting side trips to little places off the beaten path or walking down neighborhood streets for a peek at how Washington society lives. (3307 N Street NW, just two blocks west of Wisconsin Avenue, was the home of John F. Kennedy before he moved into the White

Georgetown is the city's most popular place to shop.

House.) From apparel and antique prints to home goods, furniture, and landscaping ornamentation, this upscale neighborhood has something for everyone, including collectors of fine art and fashion, bargain hunters looking for a Louis Vuitton knockoff from a sidewalk vendor (just up Wisconsin Avenue on the right), and teenagers seeking to find something to take home as a reminder of their trip. Plan to spend at least half the day here and to have a meal—this part of the city is also replete with dining options, from tavern food to fine cuisine.

Greater Washington DC
FRIENDSHIP HEIGHTS AND CHEVY CHASE, MARYLAND

The desire to max out the credit cards can be met on North Wisconsin Avenue, where the road leaves the District of Columbia and enters Maryland, home to a quarter-mile stretch that includes posh shops and swanky stores like Tiffany, Vera Wang, and Saks Jandel, a locally owned store for couture from Valentino,

Yves Saint Laurent, and the like. The neighborhood definitely draws the high rollers: Area anchor stores include Bloomingdale's, Neiman Marcus, and Saks Fifth Avenue. But the budget-conscious and shopping-savvy also find a deal here: The neighborhood has a Loehmann's, one of the area's best for sunglasses, handbags, and designer denim, as well as swimsuits in season.

VIRGINIA SUBURBS

If you still haven't found what you are looking for, shoot over the Potomac River to Virginia to check out the shopping scene. Fashion Centre at Pentagon City is manageable, with enough shops to satisfy a short shopping spree. The mall's main stores are Nordstrom and Macy's, with nearly 100 stores between, including Sephora and MAC cosmetics, Steve Madden and Clarks shoes, Armani Exchange, Michael Kors, and Cache clothiers, and more. The mall is on the Yellow and Blue Metro lines and is easily accessible from the city. During the week, tour buses drop their groups off for a morning or afternoon of shopping, yet these times are actually preferable to visiting on the weekend, when the stores are crowded and the Macy's, in particular, gets messy. But if 100-plus stores aren't enough and you're still seeking the true "shop till you drop" experience, a visit to Tysons Corner in McLean, Virginia, is a requirement. The area's two malls are currently only accessible by car, although a new Metro line is expected to be completed to the area in 2013. Tysons is home to the region's largest mall, Tysons Corner Center, with more than 300 stores, a 16-screen movie theater, and about two dozen restaurants. At Tysons, shoppers can browse through a two-story L. L. Bean, visit the nation's first Apple store, shop at the country's first Mango outlet, and spend hours at Bloomingdale's and Nordstrom. Just across a major thoroughfare from that mall lies the upscale Tysons Galleria, which locals often refer to as Tysons II. It contains a Macy's as well (less crowded, with more attentive staff than most), a Saks Fifth Avenue, Neiman Marcus, and high-end boutiques that include Cartier, Chanel, DeBeers, and Coach.

© DESTINATION DC

Antiques

THE BRASS KNOB

2311 18th St. NW, 202/332-3370,
www.thebrassknob.com
HOURS: Mon.-Sat. 10:30 A.M.-6 P.M., Sun. noon-5 P.M.
Map 7

Owners of old houses know where to go for a replacement ceramic doorknob or an original Georgian mantle: the Brass Knob, a dealership that specialized in antiques and architectural salvage. The store carries mainly hardware and special touches from former homes and office buildings across DC, including door hardware, vintage bath accessories and fixtures, iron work, leaded glass windows, and lighting.

CHRIST CHILD SOCIETY OPPORTUNITY SHOP

1427 Wisconsin Ave. NW, 202/333-6635,
www.christchild.org
HOURS: Sept.-Dec. and Mar.-June Mon.-Sat.
10 A.M.-4:30 P.M., Sun. noon-4 P.M.; Jan.-Feb. Mon.-Sat.
10 A.M.-5 P.M.; July-Aug. Mon. 10 A.M.-4 P.M., Tues.-Sat.
10 A.M.-5 P.M.
Map 8

A consignment shop whose mission is to support a charity that helps indigent children, the Opportunity Shop has two floors brimming with estate jewelry, silverware, china, and crystal stemware along with some furnishings and decorative arts. On any given day, shoppers will find Lalique and Waterford crystal, sterling and silver-plate chargers, Oriental rugs, designer handbags, and more. Since the stock turns over quickly (antiques like a Revereware punch bowl and silver biscuit warmer don't stay on the shelves for long), this store has become a monthly habit for many Washington interior designers and antiques lovers.

GOODWOOD

1428 U St., 202/986-3640, www.goodwood.com
HOURS: Mon.-Sat. noon-7 P.M., Sun. noon-5 P.M.
Map 7

What exactly is GoodWood? Is it a furniture store, a vintage clothing store, a home accessories shop? Yes, and more. This shop, one of the pioneers on U Street, sells antique and vintage furniture, books, frames, jewelry, candles, and even clothing, all artfully placed and so beautifully displayed that it is hard not to want to buy everything. Browsing is an adventure, and for the design-challenged, the entire place is a lesson in furniture repurposing and placement. It will make you think twice about wanting to get rid of Grandma's hand-me-down dresser.

MARSTON LUCE

1651 Wisconsin Ave. NW, 202/333-6800,
www.marstonluce.com
HOURS: Mon.-Sat. 11 A.M.-5 P.M.
Map 8

A glimpse in the window at Marston Luce indicates more of the loveliness found inside: a couple of French antique chairs, a 10-foot-tall shutter from a Provence farmhouse, a piece of limestone statuary. Marston Luce carries French and Swedish antiques, including lighting, mirrors, and furniture. Selections range from the fine, like an early-19th-century Empire pier table, to the comfortable, like an 1800s pine trestle table. The store also carries a number of garden decorations such as terra-cotta bowls and antique statuary.

MILLENNIUM DECORATIVE ARTS

1528 U St. NW, 202/483-1218,
www.milleniumdecorativearts.com
HOURS: Thurs.-Sun. noon-6 P.M.
Map 7

Fans of midcentury modern furniture and accessories can find them at Millennium Decorative Arts, minus the price tag that is now tacked onto this much-in-demand style. Stock turns over quickly at this shop, popular with 20-somethings for furnishing their condos as well as architects and collectors. Those who crave an Eero Saarinen tulip chair or a patio dressed with a Salterini dining set should stop here. You might not find the brands named, but you'll certainly find something similar. Or, if you are lucky, you may stumble on the real deal.

RANDOM HARVEST

1313 Wisconsin Ave. NW, 202/333-5569,
www.randomharvesthome.com

HOURS: Mon.-Sat. 11 A.M.-6 P.M., Sun. noon-6 P.M.

Map 8

New mingles with old at Random Harvest, a furniture and home decor store with four locations across the region that sell antique, vintage, and new furniture and accessories and also offers design services. Among the most popular sellers are vintage club chairs and sofas clad in white muslin, ready to be reupholstered or used as-is, and 19th-century French wardrobes and sideboards. Each store contains a photo album of furniture offered at the others, so there is need to dash around town if you are looking for a specific item. Also, if they don't currently have what you want, they'll take your name and email you if something new comes in.

◖ SUSQUEHANNA

3216 O St. NW, 202/333-1511,
www.susquehannaantiques.com

HOURS: Mon.-Sat. 10 A.M.-6 P.M.

Map 8

If you've been inspired by a home tour of Dumbarton House or Mount Vernon and want to own your own piece of American history (or English as well), Susquehanna sells fine 18th- and 19th-century furniture, oil paintings, and antiques, mostly American, with some Revolutionary War–era British and European pieces tossed into the mix. Owner David

© PATRICIA KIME

Susquehanna, in Georgetown, is a must for antiques connoisseurs.

Friedman has operated his Georgetown store for nearly 30 years, scouring the Eastern Seaboard for some of the country's best antiques; recently, his collection included several original Windsor chairs, a George III chest-on-chest, case clocks, and fine portraits. The store also sells gilt-wood frames. Prices are comparable to dealers across the region—a welcome relief in a neighborhood that marks everything up simply because you found it in Georgetown.

Arts and Crafts

APPALACHIAN SPRING

East Hall, Union Station, 50 Massachusetts Ave. NE, 202/682-0505, www.appalachianspring.com

HOURS: Mon.-Sat. 10 A.M.-9 P.M., Sun. noon-5 P.M.

Map 5

Pricey but loaded with unique gifts and accessories not found elsewhere in Washington, Appalachian Spring features crafts—hand-blown glass, jewelry, turned wooden bowls, pewter, jewelry boxes, pottery, and other decorative items—produced by American artists, primarily from the Appalachia region, along the mountains from Maine to northern Alabama. The store was established in the late 1960s in Georgetown and has five locations. The Union Station locale is notable for its large size and placement, just off the train station's magnificent East Hall. President Bill Clinton used to shop here each Christmas when he resided at the White House.

INDIAN CRAFT SHOP

1518 C St. NW, 202/208-4056,
www.indiancraftshop.com

HOURS: Mon.-Fri. 8:30 A.M.-4:30 P.M., third Sat. of each month 10 A.M.-4 P.M.

Map 4

Works of art handcrafted by Native Americans are as close as the Department of the Interior, whose Indian Craft Shop has been selling goods made by the country's indigenous population for more than 70 years. The store's stunning array of merchandise, at any given time produced by roughly 45 of the country's 565 registered Indian tribes, includes carvings made from walrus tusk, baskets, blankets and textiles, turquoise jewelry, and sculptures. The shop is a throwback, a work of historic preservation in itself, featuring original murals from 1938. To get to the store, visitors must pass through security; be prepared to open your handbag for inspection.

◖ L'ENFANT GALLERY

1442 Wisconsin Ave. NW, 202/625-2873,
www.lenfantmoderne.com

Map 8

On a recent visit to L'Enfant Gallery, two tiny sketches hung cockeyed on a wall amid huge oil paintings and just above another set of prints and paintings stacked against the wall. Just getting a close look was an exercise in contortion—one slip and the viewer would bump into an antique dresser or knock over another pile of paintings. But yes, on close inspection, they were Picassos, and they weren't cheap. But there they were, for sale amid the thousands of paintings stuffed into three floors of a cramped corner row house in Georgetown. L'Enfant Gallery has the feel of a thrift shop but the quality of a fine gallery. The prices aren't at all thrift-store (the

owners definitely know the value of a Picasso or of students of Canaletto), but the experience of the hunt is.

OLD PRINT GALLERY

1220 31st St. NW, 202/965-1818,
www.oldprintgallery.com

HOURS: Tues.-Sat. 10 A.M.-5:30 P.M.

Map 8

Georgetown's Old Print Gallery contains a vast collection of American and European prints and maps, spanning the 17th century to today. It also carries political cartoons, historic documents, lithographs, and engravings, many with historical themes. Recently the gallery has expanded its modern and contemporary collection, now offering a broader range of 20th- and 21st-century printmakers. The shop sells everything unframed, a state desired by collectors, who prefer to examine a print's edges and back for flaws and imperfections. The shop offers custom framing as well, with a discount if the item to be framed was purchased at Old Print Gallery.

THE PHOENIX

1514 Wisconsin Ave. NW, 202/338-4404,
www.thephoenix.com

HOURS: Winter Mon.-Sat. 10 A.M.-6 P.M., Sun. noon-5 P.M.; summer Mon.-Sat. 10 A.M.-6 P.M., Sun. 1-6 P.M.

Map 8

This Georgetown shop is a place to dress yourself and your home, featuring a selection of women's clothes from makers like Eileen Fisher and Lilla P in addition to Mexican art, jewelry, and accessories. Its folk and fine art catalog focuses on works from Oaxaca and Mexico City; the housewares selection includes handcrafted polished pewter and stainless steel, ceramics, and silver.

Bath and Beauty

BEAUTY 360

1350 Connecticut Ave. NW, 202/331-1725,
www.beauty360.com
HOURS: Mon.-Fri. 10 A.M.-7 P.M., Sat. 10 A.M.-6 P.M.
Map 6

CVS threw itself into the beauty-product retail market in 2008, opening the Connecticut Avenue storefront of Beauty 360 and another prototype in Mission Viejo, California, to sell small lines of cosmetics as well as skin and hair-care products. Today, the upscale store can be found in 25 locations, but only two of them are outside the Golden State. Beauty 360 carries niche beauty brands such as Laura Geller, Paula Dorf, and Borba and provides a number of services, including makeup application, express facials, and mini manicures. Customers wanting more budget-friendly beauty products can find them next door at the regular CVS.

BLUE MERCURY

1619 Connecticut Ave. NW, 202/462-1300,
www.bluemercury.com
HOURS: Mon.-Sat. 10 A.M.-8 P.M., Sun. 11 A.M.-6 P.M.
Map 6

Spa products from Bliss, Creed, and Trish McEvoy are top sellers at Blue Mercury, but this small chain also carries a full line of makeup from Bobby Brown, Laura Mercier, and Nars as well as offering massages, waxing, and facials. Given the competition in the market (Sephora stores sell Laura Mercier and BB products, and other places in DC carry Bliss), the sales staff at Blue Mercury could stand to be more service-oriented with less attitude.

CELADON SPA

1180 F St. NW, 202/347-3333, www.celadonspa.com
HOURS: Mon., Wed., and Fri. 8:30 A.M.-6 P.M., Tues. and Thurs. 8:30 A.M.-7 P.M., Sat. 8:30 A.M.-4:30 P.M.
Map 3

Conveniently located for nine-to-fivers to duck in for a manicure, wax, or relaxing massage, Celadon is a luxurious space for being pampered or getting groomed. Services include

COURTESY CELADON SPA

Celadon Spa

haircuts and color, facials, therapeutic and deep-tissue massage, exfoliating body wraps, manicures, pedicures, and hot and flexible waxing. The spa also carries a wide array of beauty products, including an organic line, as well as a fragrance line of candles and diffusers so you can prolong that spa experience at home.

THE GROOMING LOUNGE

1745 L St. NW, 202/466-8900,
www.groominglounge.com
HOURS: Mon.-Fri. 9 A.M.-7 P.M., Sat. 9 A.M.-6 P.M., Sun. 10 A.M.-5 P.M.
Map 4

The Grooming Lounge is a high-end salon for men. Stylists will actually make suggestions on haircuts, customers are asked whether they want a beverage during their stay (tea, coffee, scotch, water?), desk clerks pedal the incredible selection of products from Kiehl, Jack Black, and the company's own line, and clients can receive nearly any grooming service they need, from the store's signature hot lather shave to business manicures, massages, waxes, and facials.

Books and Music

BARTLEBY'S BOOKS

1132 29th St. NW, 202/298-0486,
www.bartlebysbooks.com

HOURS: Mon.-Sat. 10:30 A.M.-4:30 P.M., Sun. noon-4 P.M.

Map 8

Specializing in history and law books but with an extensive collection of first editions and rare books, Bartleby's is perfect for lingering, a well-shelved store for antiquarian books and unique prints in a light-filled setting. Some books are behind glass: precious volumes that include a first edition of *Huckleberry Finn* or an original *Island of Dr. Moreau* by H. G. Wells. The shop's Americana area features sections on each state. Other subjects covered include military history, the Civil War, and an expansive Britain collection.

CAPITOL HILL BOOKS

657 C St. NW, 202/544-1621, www.capitolhillbooks.com

HOURS: Mon.-Fri. 11:30 A.M.-6 P.M., Sat.-Sun. 9 A.M.-6 P.M.

Map 5

Not for the allergy-prone, claustrophobic, or wheelchair-bound, Capitol Hill Books is a book scavenger's paradise, a fire hazard of used tomes crammed into a DC row house that spans the Dewey decimal system of subjects. Great piles of books are stacked or shelved, organized by subjects labeled with scrap paper taped nearby. The primarily hardback inventory includes a wide selection on military and politics and a significant number of picture books at reasonable prices. The foreign-language section can be found in the bathroom, and the scant science fiction section and outdoor writing is located in the timeworn basement that looks like it might collapse under the weight of the piles upstairs.

CROOKED BEAT RECORDS

2116 18th St. NW, 202/483-2328,
www.crookedbeat.com

HOURS: Mon. 1:30-8:30 P.M., Tues.-Sat. noon-9 P.M., Sun. noon-7 P.M.

Map 7

My knowledge of cutting-edge music disappeared a few years after this store's namesake song, "Crooked Beat," showed up on a Clash LP, but I know enough to realize this record store is a punk and indie-rock nirvana, selling

Kramerbooks & Afterwords offers shoppers a chance to enjoy snacks and coffee in between book-browsing.

DANIEL LOBO – DAQUELLAMANERA.ORG

mostly new and vintage vinyl as well as CDs cut by the well-known and local favorites. Crooked Beat has both new and used merchandise, not necessarily limited to its target genre: Recent top sellers include Radiohead, Arcade Fire, and Kanye, but the post–hardcore and punk set will find plenty of Fugazi and Dirt Bombs. The staff is willing to help get you up to speed and won't make you feel like an idiot for skipping a few decades.

KRAMERBOOKS & AFTERWORDS

1517 Connecticut Ave. NW, 202/387-1400, www.kramers.com

HOURS: Sun.-Thurs. 7:30 A.M.-1 A.M., Fri.-Sat. 24 hours

`Map 6`

Launched the year of the Bicentennial, Kramerbooks & Afterwords was Washington's first combination bookstore and café; after all these years, it is going strong for the very reasons it was a hit in the first place: good books, decent food, coffee, and camaraderie. Most days the place has live music in the evenings; this isn't a place where you can find a cozy quiet nook and curl up with your latest find. But you can get a beer and a bite to eat, as well as perhaps a date—Kramerbooks has a long-standing reputation as a pick-up spot. As for the books, its collection leans toward popular fiction and book-club paperbacks, but it does carry other subjects, with travel and political books ranking among the top sellers.

MELODY RECORD SHOP

1623 Connecticut Ave. NW, 202/232-4002, www.melodyrecords.com

HOURS: Daily 10 A.M.-9 P.M.

`Map 6`

Melody carries more CDs and DVDs than it has vinyl, but it has been a record store since 1977, so the name stays. Well-organized, it has a wide selection of music—jazz, pop, rock, classical, opera, blues, and folk—and a decent library of international music, mostly at discount prices. The store also carries electronics.

◖ THE NATIONAL GALLERY OF ART

4th St. and Constitution Ave. NW, 202/737-4215. www.nga.gov

HOURS: Mon.-Sat. 10 A.M.-5 P.M., Sun. 11 A.M.-6 P.M.; closed Christmas Day and New Year's Day

`Map 2`

The National Gallery of Art's three gift shops contain an extensive collection of art books, from expensive, heavy coffee-table books on artists and the gallery to works of nonfiction about art and art-related topics. It also features a nice selection of children's books and both nonfiction and fictional works on artists as well as activity books and art supplies. Postcard books make a nice takeaway, as do the shops' array of note cards depicting some of the gallery's best-known works.

◖ POLITICS AND PROSE

5015 Connecticut Ave. NW, 202/364-1919, www.politics-prose.com

HOURS: Mon.-Sat. 9 A.M.-10 P.M., Sun. 10 A.M.-8 P.M.

`Map 9`

As an institution, political book stores tend to lean red or blue, with very few attempting to strike a balance. Politics and Prose is the rare exception, a place where local authors like Seymour Hersh and Jim Lehrer speak and sign books, where well-known public servants Condoleezza Rice and Bill Clinton have met with patrons, where more than half the 2011 Pulitzer Prize winners visited within

Politics and Prose caters to an array of political mindsets.

© PATRICIA KIME

the year. Founded in 1984 by Washington residents Barbara Meade and Carla Cohen, Politics and Prose is a top destination, where the city's cognoscenti stock their libraries, enjoy a cappuccino, and mingle with writers on the *New York Times* Best Seller list. Politics and Prose will start a new chapter this year: Following the death of Cohen in 2010, it was purchased by *Washington Post* journalist Bradley Graham and his wife, Lissa Muscatine, who have promised to uphold the store's mission as a gathering ground for debate and exploration.

RED ONION RECORDS & BOOKS

1901 18th St. NW, 202/986-2718,
www.redonionrecordsandbooks.com
HOURS: Tues.-Fri. noon-7 P.M., Fri.-Sat. noon-8 P.M.,
Sun. noon-8 P.M., closed Mon.
Map 7

This basement store promotes the latest indie records and bands, but its strength lies in its collection of classics and old-school vinyl, some for sale at the same price they cost new—virtually unheard-of pricing given the current renewed interest in records. The bookstore part

of the shop loses out to the urge to flip through racks of records. Recently seen at the store was a copy of *Dark Side of the Moon* for less than $7. On eBay it often sells for more than $20. Look carefully for this tiny store, identified by a tiny sign.

SECOND STORY BOOKS

2000 P St. NW, 202/659-8884,
www.secondstorybooks.com
HOURS: Daily 10 A.M.-10 P.M.
Map 6

Some used book stores are indiscriminate, hawking everything their owner has picked up at estate sales. Others are known for their rare books and curated collections. Second Story is a bit of both, with manuscripts ranging from the unusual to well-thumbed paperbacks. A rare book room houses first editions and antiquarian publications; the main room spans the range of fiction and nonfiction, textbooks, and obscure subject matter crossing a university's spectrum. Outside, at any time of year, patrons scour boxes containing cut-rate books. The store also sells used records and CDs.

Clothing and Accessories for Men

JOS. A. BANK CLOTHIERS

Union Station, 50 Massachusetts Ave. NE,
202/289-9087, www.josbank.com
HOURS: Mon.-Sat. 10 A.M.-9 P.M., Sun. noon-6 P.M.
Map 5

If the prices at J. Press or Brooks Brothers don't suit your budget but the style appeals, Baltimore's own Jos. A. Bank Clothiers has stores across the region (the flagship is on East Pratt Street in Charm City, just 45 minutes away), carrying traditional men's garb—khaki pants, wool suits, summer poplin sport coats, oxford shirts, and ties of nearly every hue and tone. Jos. A. Bank is where new arrivals to Washington stock up for their new lives in the working world. There always seems

to be a sale going on; if you find something full-price, wait a week or so and it will likely be marked down. Get on their mailing list to receive monthly coupons and deals.

J. PRESS

1801 L St. NW, 202/857-0120, www.jpressonline.com
HOURS: Mon.-Sat. 9:30 A.M.-6 P.M.
Map 4

Clothier to male Georgetown students, older men, and preppies across the region, J Press, with stores in DC, New Haven, Connecticut, New York City, and Cambridge, Massachusetts, carries the gamut of traditional conservative men's wear, from madras shorts and neckties to seersucker and wool suits and formal attire.

DANIEL LOBO – DAQUELLAMANERA.ORG

pink shirts on display in the window of Thomas Pink

The shop prides itself on having served clients for more than 100 years, bearing the feel of Brooks Brothers' flagship store before that clothier's stores became ubiquitous at malls. In addition to expertly sewn suits and fine sport coats and jackets, J. Press offers in-house tailoring and a "made to measure" service for custom-made attire.

THOMAS PINK

1127 Connecticut Ave. NW, 202/223-5390, www.thomaspink.com

HOURS: Mon.-Wed. and Fri. 10 A.M.-7 P.M., Thurs. 10 A.M.-8 P.M., Sat. 10 A.M.-6 P.M., Sun. noon-5 P.M.

Map 4

With stores in just 14 cities in the United States, London-based Thomas Pink sells shirts: high-end traditional business and casual shirts in myriad colors. The store is located in the Mayflower Hotel's former venerable Town & Country Lounge, with decor designed to call to mind a London town house. The shop features herringbone granite floors, black leather

club chairs with pink trim, and display cases designed like fine English antiques. In addition to its kaleidoscope of shirts, Thomas Pink carries men's accessories and necessities like neckties, boxer shorts, and cuff links. It also features a selection of women's shirts. Look for after-Christmas sales to get the best buys on these tailored goods.

UNIVERSAL GEAR

1529 14th St. NW, 202/319-0136, www.universalgear.com

HOURS: Sun.-Thurs. 11 A.M.-10 P.M., Fri.-Sat. 11 A.M.-midnight

Map 6

A store for fashion-obsessed men, the cavernous Universal Gear carries the trendiest men's wear, with labels from Diesel, 7 for All Mankind, Citizens of Humanity, and True Religion. It also has a remarkable assortment of athletic wear at reasonable prices and its own line of T-shirts, shorts, and cashmere sweaters. Among the store's biggest sellers is its extensive undies collection, with briefs on display in the windows and throughout the shop worn by giggle-worthy amply endowed mannequins.

URBAN OUTFITTERS

737 7th St. NW, 202/737-0259, www.urbanoutfitters.com

HOURS: Mon.-Sat. 10 A.M.-10 P.M., Sun. 11 A.M.-9 P.M.

Map 3

The second floor of the Chinatown Urban Outfitters is devoted to men's apparel, but in Urban Outfitter's world, "men" means roughly the ages of 15 to 22, and specifically, fans of indie rock and hipster apparel—fatigue pants, graphic T-shirts, jackets, slouchy shorts—perfect accoutrements for Timberland boots in the winter and brown flip-flops in the summer. The first floor carries women's clothes and housewares; books and accessories are scattered throughout; and apartment goods and sales racks take up nearly the entire top floor.

Clothing and Accessories for Women

BETSEY JOHNSON

3029 M St. NW, 202/338-4090,
www.betseyjohnson.com

HOURS: Mon.-Fri. 11 A.M.-7 P.M., Sat. 11 A.M.-8 P.M.,
Sun. noon-6 P.M.

Map 8

Tulle, lace, and floral prints reign supreme
at Betsey Johnson, a trendy apparel store catering to the fresh-faced, young, and super-
feminine. This relatively small boutique has
a surprisingly large selection of dresses, shoes,
handbags, and accessories, showcased in pink-
and-white sweetness. The small secret garden
in the back of the store carries the theme outdoors in the spring. Accessories and bags carry
more of the designer's punk zing with them, in
edgier prints and vibrant tones.

BETSY FISHER

1224 Connecticut Ave. NW, 202/785-1975,
www.betsyfisher.com

HOURS: Mon.-Wed. 10 A.M.-7 P.M., Thurs.-Fri.
10 A.M.-8 P.M., Sat. 10 A.M.-6 P.M., Sun. noon-4 P.M.

Map 6

The city's power women shop for feminine
twists on career and daytime clothing at Betsy
Fisher, a boutique that showcases American,
French, and Italian designers, carrying impeccably made suits, separates, dresses, shoes, and
accessories. The attentive and knowledgeable
staff will help dress you from head to toe for any
occasion. A few times a month, the store hosts
trunk shows and events at cocktail hour, which
can be fun but dangerous to the credit card balance. Merchandise sells quickly and turns over
often: sizes 4–8 often sell out within days.

COUP DE FOUDRE LINGERIE

1001 Pennsylvania Ave. NW, 202/393-0878,
www.coupdefoudrelingerie.com

HOURS: Mon.-Sat. 11 A.M.-6 P.M.

Map 3

Guillaume Tourniaire, the designated "romance
concierge" at the Willard InterContinental,
loves directing his female clients to Coup de
Foudre, a French lingerie shop that carries
high-end, lacy, lovely bras and panties as well
as undergarments for daily wear. The French
saleswomen are all well-informed regarding
bra sales and fittings, and co-owner Francoise
David is reportedly remarkable at helping
women correctly size themselves. Fittings are
by appointment only.

FILENE'S BASEMENT

1133 Connecticut Ave. NW, 202/872-8430,
www.filenesbasement.com

HOURS: Mon.-Sat. 9:30 A.M.-8 P.M., Sun. noon-5 P.M.

Map 4

You may hit the jackpot here or you may not;
this location is smaller than other area Filene's
Basements but it often carries high-quality
clothing at decent prices. I'm not very good at
stores where you have to scavenge, but if this
type of store appeals to you, Filenes carries
loads of items, numerous brand names, and
many different styles. This location seems less
picked-over and neater than the others most of
the time. The Filene's at 529 14th Street NW
has a surprisingly large selection of petite clothing, a boon to the height-challenged among us.

NANA

1528 U St. NW, 202/667-6955, www.nana.com

HOURS: Mon. and Wed.-Fri. noon-7 P.M.,
Sat. 11 A.M.-5 P.M., Sun. noon-5 P.M., closed Tues.

Map 7

The compelling mix of new and vintage items
at Nana is the work of maven Jackie Flanagan,
a former corporate worker bee who opened a
shop in 2003 aimed at providing a fun, funky
clothing establishment that appealed to patrons and residents of this übercool neighborhood. The effect is a sassy clothing store
that carries contemporary clothing with bohemian and retro bents. Lines include Dagg and
Stacey, Dear Creatures, and Preloved. Flower
children and fans of flowing casual are likely to
find numerous purchases here. The store also
now carries home accessories, kids clothing,

Elizabeth W perfume, and Fashion Doll hats and bags.

PERUVIAN CONNECTION

950 F St. NW, 202/737-4405,
www.peruvianconnection.com
HOURS: Mon.-Wed. and Fri.-Sat. 10 A.M.-6 P.M.,
Thurs. 10 A.M.-7 P.M., Sun. noon-6 P.M.
Map 3

Fans of the catalog will enjoy shopping at the company's flagship store, which carries fashions inspired by South American style, or at least a Hollywood vision of a vaquero—romantic mid-calf skirts, draping sweaters, flowing shirts, and muted colors—as well as some hand-knit wares such as alpaca sweaters and coats. The store's selection is not as extensive as the catalog's but has a fair amount of Peruvian jewelry for purchase. The shop is crisp and well designed, and the helpful sales people know their products.

PROPER TOPPER

1350 Connecticut Ave. NW, 202/333-6200,
www.propertopper.com
HOURS: Mon.-Fri. 10 A.M.-8 P.M., Sat. 10 A.M.-7 P.M.,
Sun. noon-6 P.M.
Map 6

Thanks to Princess Kate and Carrie Bradshaw, we've been reminded what a fascinator is—the hat that ladies at Proper Topper never forgot. This store, which carries hats, headbands, and felts, also sells handmade jewelry, books, soaps, scarves, household items, and adorable albeit high-priced children's clothes. The store is small and loaded with unique gifts and hard-to-find items as well as business gear for the traveler, including umbrellas, wallets, and passport holders.

RIZIK BROTHERS

1100 Connecticut Ave. NW, 202/223-4050,
www.riziks.com
HOURS: Mon.-Sat. 9 A.M.-6 P.M., Thurs. 9 A.M.-8 P.M.
Map 4

Rizik's has been selling Washington evening wear, wedding gowns, bridal party dresses, and high-end fashions for more than 100 years,

carrying brands like Christian Lacroix, Escada Sport, and scrumptious Carmen Marc Valvo to wear to all the city's galas, events, dinners, and fund-raisers. The family-owned store suffers from its popularity as a destination for evening wear; many Washingtonians forget that it's also a great shop for sophisticated suits and separates, winter coats, and more. In days past, purchases at Rizik's were delivered by bicycle messenger; today, if you have something tailored or don't want to carry a new purchase out, it can be sent by car and driver to your home or hotel.

RUE 14

1803 14th St. NW, 202/462-6200, www.rue14.com
HOURS: Tues.-Fri. noon-7 P.M., Sat. 11 A.M.-7 P.M.,
Sun. noon-6 P.M., closed Mon.
Map 7

Rue 14 carries the latest trends without a budget-busting price tag. This second-floor boutique sells men's and women's clothing that leans toward the youngish, hipster side, with labels like BB Dakota, Free People, and Penguin. Owner Jiwon Paik-Nguyen told the *Washington Post* that her favorite designers are Marc Jacobs and Phillip Lim. "We want to cater to a mid-level price point but keep some of those designers' aesthetics," she said when the store opened in 2008. Several years later, it is still going strong, with fashion-forward dresses and separates as well as affordable denim.

URBAN CHIC

1626 Wisconsin Ave. NW, 202/338-5398,
www.urbanchiconline.com
HOURS: Mon.-Sat. 10 A.M.-7 P.M., Sun. noon-5 P.M.
Map 8

A large boutique slightly off the beaten path in Georgetown (a few blocks up from M Street, preferred by the wandering masses), Urban Chic carries a complete line of women's apparel and accessories as well as some men's clothing and shoes as well as jeans from makers like Paige, Joe's Jeans, and Citizens for Humanity and clothing from Anlo, Diane Von Fürstenberg, Tory Burch, and others. It also has some skin and beauty items, including a limited collection of Bliss products. The shop is larger than most Georgetown area boutiques and well-organized, with items spaced apart and well showcased. It also tends to be quiet, likely because of its location (recently overheard: "I always forget you guys are here; I never walk up Wisconsin"), which I consider a bonus.

WINK

3109 M St. NW, 202/338-9465, www.shopwink.com
HOURS: Mon.-Sat. 11 A.M.-7 P.M., Sun. noon-6 P.M.
Map 8

Located in a basement below a Steve Madden shoe store, the boutique Wink has a small but thorough collection of adorable dresses, jeans, sandals, and jewelry, with labels like Diane Von Fürstenberg, James Perse, and Ella Moss. On a recent trip, two 20-somethings were arguing over a pair of tangerine braided-leather sandals. The style is fun and flirty, but the store seems to trend toward the smallest sizes. I'm a size 4 on a good day, and I often feel like a cow when I'm in here.

ZARA

1025 F St. NW, 202/393-2810, www.zara.com
HOURS: Mon.-Sat. 10 A.M.-9 P.M., Sun. 11 A.M.-8 P.M.
Map 3

Fans of Swedish clothing powerhouse H&M love Zara, a Spanish chain that carries trendy, relatively inexpensive clothes for women, men, and kids. The F Street location is less picked-over than the one in Georgetown, featuring three floors of merchandise. Salespeople are friendly, if not overly helpful. Stock and style rotates every month (it's the corporation's business model), so if you see something you like, you'd better buy it: It won't be on the shelves the next time you stop by. Great buys at Zara include jackets and dresses, often knockoffs from designers' current collections.

window shopping at Zara

Flea, Food, and Farmers Markets

CAKELOVE

1506 U St. NW, 202/588-7100, www.cakelove.com

HOURS: Mon.-Fri. 8:30 A.M.-6 P.M., Sat. 10 A.M.-5 P.M.

Map 7

In 2002, Washington health care attorney Warren Brown left his legal career behind to jump-start Cakelove on U Street, a bakery specializing in cakes and tiny treats like cupcakes and éclairs. Nearly a decade later, with a Food Network show under his belt and numerous appearances as a speaker and on television talk shows, including *Oprah,* the country has one less lawyer. Brown has fended off competition from newcomer cupcake bakeries, but his strength lies in wedding cakes and his magical "crunchy feet," little cookie-cake tartlets topped with a dollop of buttercream and fresh fruit.

COWGIRL CREAMERY

919 F St. NW, 202/393-6880,

www.cowgirlcreamery.com

HOURS: Mon.-Fri. 7:30 A.M.-7 P.M., Sat. 11 A.M.-7 P.M.

Map 3

Two of the world's three Cowgirl Creamery shops are in Northern California. Washington is blessed with the third, an outpost that showcases the company's small but award-winning cheeses—several triple crème cheeses, seasonal selections, everyday table cheese, and fresh selections such as crème fraîche and cottage cheese. The shop also carries selections by other small producers and sells bread and wine to go along with your purchase.

DEAN & DELUCA

3276 M St. NW, 202/342-2500, www.deandeluca.com

HOURS: Café daily 7 A.M.-8 P.M., market daily 9 A.M.-8 P.M.

Map 8

This outlet of the New York City gourmet market features a tantalizing array of produce, meats, cheeses, flowers, baked goods, and fine wine housed in a former 1865 market building, with the feel of shopping in a public market like Eastern Market but with a single vendor and New York prices. Still, should you have the occasion to serve pâté, fine charcuterie, d'Affinois cheese, and California wine, or you want to pick up a special dessert for dinner (pies, crème brûlée, etc.), the selection is as mouthwatering as it is beautiful to behold. Dean & Deluca is a terrific spot to pick up a salad or sandwich for lunch. Seating is available year-round out on the brick patio, and the structure abuts the C&O Canal, a perfect spot for an impromptu picnic.

◖ EASTERN MARKET

225 7th St. SE, 202/698-5253,

www.easternmarket-dc.org

HOURS: Stall hours vary; generally Tues.-Fri. 7 A.M.-7 P.M., Sat. 7 A.M.-6 P.M., Sun. 9 A.M.-5 P.M.

Map 5

DC's oldest enclosed public market, Eastern Market's stalls showcase fresh fare: cut flowers, organic vegetables, hormone-free meats, seafood, pastries, and baked goods. On weekends the market is at its busiest. Crowds flock

© DESTINATION DC

Look for locally grown products at the Eastern Market.

to the Saturday and Sunday farmers market to purchase locally grown products such as organic cheeses, homemade sausage, seasonal vegetables, and unusual offerings that range from handmade soap to haggis produced in nearby Virginia, Maryland, and West Virginia. Sunday is flea market day with vendors selling art, clothing, housewares, jewelry, accessories, and antiques but focusing more on new goods and crafts than antiques and yard-sale finds— the Northeastern sense of the word.

FRESHFARM MARKET, PENN QUARTER
8th St. NW between D St. and E St., 202/362-8889, www.freshfarmmarkets.com
HOURS: Thurs. 3-7 P.M.
Map 3

The region's farmers markets are all pricey, yet when the weather turns warm, they beckon after-work and weekend crowds with abundant produce, fresh-baked breads, and farm-raised meats. Having spent my high school years near Warrenton, Virginia, a walk through the stalls of these local growers is like a trip home; most of the vendors at Freshfarm are regional, from places like Warrenton, Upperville, and Purcellville, Virginia, Maryland's Eastern Shore, and the mountains of West Virginia. Depending on the time of year, shoppers will line up for golf ball–sized berries; pungent, flavorful, ripe tomatoes; smooth brown eggs; and bunches of zinnias. At Red Apron Butchery, shoppers can purchase fine charcuterie—*soprasetta, tesa,* and other cured meats—for that special dinner at home.

GEORGETOWN FLEA MARKET
1819 35th St. NW, 202/775-3532, www.georgetownfleamarket.com
HOURS: Sun. 8 A.M.-4 P.M.
Map 8

The Georgetown Flea Market took a hit when it was forced to move to Arlington, Virginia, for a couple of years in the late 2000s, but it is back in its original digs, in the parking lot at Hardy Middle School across from Georgetown's recently renovated Social Safeway. Newcomers often compare the experience here to Eastern Market's "flea," but the two are of different ilk: Eastern Market is more of an arts bazaar and crafts fair; Georgetown flea is for browsers, bargain hunters, antiques shoppers, and fans of "junque." Legendary stories have spun from the Georgetown flea. A few years ago, a Washington midcentury modern dealer spotted two matching tables and bought them for $65; his hunch that they might be special proved true. They were rare prototypes by Isamu Noguchi. One sold for $132,000; the other the dealer loaned to the Noguchi Museum in New York.

Furniture and Home Decor

A MANO
1677 Wisconsin Ave. NW, 202/298-7200, www.amano.bz
HOURS: Mon.-Sat. 10 A.M.-6 P.M., Sun. noon-5 P.M.
Map 8

A Mano carries nearly everything to throw a fabulous dinner party or decorate your home and yard: unique Italian ceramics, French table linens, gourd lamps, granite statuary, cookbooks, crystal, flatware, handblown glassware, and numerous other accessories. Recent finds include a Piet Mondrian–style serving tray and a hand-painted butler's table featuring a perfect rendition of a Veuve Clicquot champagne label. Italian ceramica is imported direct; shop owner Adam Mahr travels the globe to find his distinctive inventory. Friendly service and the shop itself, crammed to the rafters with luxuries, contribute to the overall ambience and experience.

CADY'S ALLEY
3318 M St. NW., www.cadysalley.com
HOURS: Most stores Mon.-Sat. 10 A.M.-6 P.M., some stores also Sun. noon-6 P.M.
Map 8

Cady's Alley isn't a single shop; it's a cluster of

© PATRICIA KIME

Take a stroll down Cady's Alley in Georgetown.

high-end design and furniture stores set in a city block of historic industrial buildings, a cozy arrangement of stores designed to meet any homeowner's needs or dreams for form and function. While shops have turned over since Cady's Alley first started drawing customers at the end of the 1990s, the concept remains the same: modish furnishings, fashionable home goods, and impeccably designed goods for purchase and to inspire. Stores include Thos. Moser Cabinetmakers, Baker Furniture, Bulthaup, Poggenpohl, European kitchen designers, and Yves Delorme linens. Leopold's Kafe, on the alley, serves German specialties like schnitzel and bratwurst, charcuterie, and Sacher torte.

GINZA

1721 Connecticut Ave. NW, 202/332-7000,
www.ginzaonline.com
HOURS: Vary, generally Mon.-Sat. 11 A.M.-7 P.M.,
Sun. 11 A.M.-6 P.M., sometimes closed Tues.
Map 6

Ginza carries Japanese housewares and home furnishings, accessories, toys, and gifts,

including kimonos, scented candles and incense, futons, fountains, and rock gardens. Hello Kitty and Little Angry Girls items are best-sellers, as are bento boxes and teapots.

HOMEBODY

715 8th St. SE, 202/544-8445, www.homebody.com
HOURS: Tues.-Sat. 11 A.M.-7 P.M., Sun. 11 A.M.-6 P.M.
Map 5

A contemporary shop for furniture, accessories, and housewares, Homebody, across from the Marine Barracks on 8th Street, carries distinctive and unusual pieces at reasonable prices. Furniture is sized appropriately for condos or the Hill's small town houses, and housewares and accessories range from the practical (scented candles) to decorative arts, including Mexican folk art and Haitian ironwork, along with the quirky, such as hugging salt and pepper shakers or the Green Army Man candelabra recently purchased as a Christmas gift for the nephew obsessed with militaria.

HOME RULE

1807 14th St. NW, 202/797-5544, www.homerule.com
HOURS: Mon.-Sat. 11 A.M.-7 P.M., Sat. noon-5:30 P.M.
Map 7

The colorful storefront of Home Rule indicates what lies within: a fun array of housewares, kitchen gadgets and goods, bath items, and decorations, some that have a purpose and others that exist purely for whimsy—look no farther if you need a Virgin Mary toast stamp. Home Goods carries Cuisinart cookware and octopus dish scrubbers, onion goggles, and Pac-Man silicone oven mitts. When ringing up your purchases, note the mosaic countertop at the register; it is made from the glass of storefronts smashed in the neighborhood's 1968 riots.

MULEH

1831 14th St. NW, 202/667-3440, www.muleh.com
HOURS: Tues.-Sat. 11 A.M.-7 P.M., Sun. noon-5 P.M.,
closed Mon.
Map 7

Muleh is home to a gallery of Asian-inspired goods that include furniture, clothing, and accessories, many made from natural materials like bamboo, rattan, and reed. Some of the pieces are one of a kind, and the store's owners know how to showcase them. At Muleh, you can shop for your wardrobe and furnish your house at the same time, color coordinating your new Vivienne Westwood dress with a Kenneth Cobonpue split rattan and stainless steel chair.

VASTU

1829 14th St. NW, 202/234-8344, www.vastu.com
HOURS: Tues.-Sat. 11 A.M.-7 P.M., Sun. noon–5 P.M., closed Mon.
Map 7

The shop's name is short for an ancient Hindu philosophy of design and alignment in which architecture and building elements affect the state of mind. Certainly the display of beautiful Eames chairs, pedestal tables, and streamlined sofas appeal to Vastu customers, who frequent this store, in a former nightclub space, to get their fill of contemporary modern furnishings. The store itself is stylish and sophisticated, almost so perfect it hurts. Vastu carries artwork to dress up bland walls and also sells nearly 15 styles of EcoSmart ventless fireplaces.

WOVEN HISTORY & SILK ROAD

315 7th St. SE, 202/543-1705, www.wovenhistory.com
HOURS: Tues.-Sun. 10 A.M.-6 P.M.
Map 5

What began as a vendor stall in Eastern Market has taken over two row houses on Capitol Hill: Woven History, a store that specializes in tribal rugs from Afghanistan and Tibet, and Silk Road, a gift shop of antiques, clothes, art, and jewelry from the Middle and Far East. The heavy scent of dyed wool hangs over both stores, adding an air of excitement to the hunt for a colorful, handmade, vegetable-dyed Turkman, Hazara, or Tibetan carpet. Fine woven rugs can also be found in a variety of sizes. Many of the floor coverings are woven by exiled Tibetans living in Nepal and Afghan refugees in Pakistan; Owner Mehmet Yalcin, a Harvard-educated doctor of Inner Asian and Altaic studies, is a member of Cultural Survival, a Massachusetts-based nonprofit that assists these groups and aims to discourage the sale of rugs made with child labor.

Gifts and Jewelry

AMERICA!

Union Station, 50 Massachusetts Ave. NE,
202/842-0540, www.americastore.com
HOURS: Mon.-Sat. 10 A.M.-9 P.M., Sun. noon–6 P.M.
Map 5

The America! shop is the place to go for those CIA and FBI T-shirts that visitors love, along with a cherry blossom snow globe or a coffee cup featuring the Presidential Seal or the president's likeness. Not all the items are schlock; in the winter, the store carries current and previous White House Christmas ornaments, created by the White House Historical Foundation. Year-round, shoppers will find an assortment of books on Washington landmarks and history as well as patriotic-themed decorative throw blankets and accent pillows.

BEADAZZLED

1507 Wisconsin Ave. NW, 202/265-2323,
www.beadazzled.net
HOURS: Mon.-Sat. 10 A.M.-8 P.M., Sun. 11 A.M.-6 P.M.
Map 8

Beginning and experienced jewelry makers alike enjoy this store, which carries an array of beads, glass, semiprecious stones, and gems as well as ready-made earrings, necklaces, bracelets, and other baubles. Beading can be an expensive hobby: Items such as Czech seed beads or sterling silver cost $4–5 each. The shop also carries Hindu and Buddhist statuary as well as netsuke, small Japanese figurines. Pamphlets on beginner jewelry making are available, and helpful employees will guide you on purchasing and putting together your creation. Classes are offered on weekends.

◖ CHOCOLATE MOOSE

1743 L St. NW, 202/463-0992,
www.chocolatemoose.com

HOURS: Mon.-Sat. 10 A.M.-6 P.M.

Map 4

It took me years to find a decent card shop in DC—you know, those laugh-out-loud ones that are actually funny without having to resort to bodily-function jokes? And here it was all along, in the guise of a candy store. Well, not exactly a candy store: Chocolate Moose is like a refined Spencer's Gifts, thankfully minus the black lights and Day-Glo posters. This store has Obama paper dolls, very fun moose and pig poppers for shooting projectiles at office mates, jewelry for big and little kids, wind-up toys, and more. And it sells candy—Belgian chocolates, bulk candy, lollipops, and gift bags of the sweets.

JR CIGAR

1730 L St. NW, 202/296-3872, www.jrcigars.com

HOURS: Mon.-Fri. 9 A.M.-6:30 P.M.,
Sat. 10 A.M.-11 P.M., closed Sun.

Map 4

It calls itself "the world's largest cigar store." I can't prove it, but it does look like a Wal-Mart of cigars, featuring a dazzling array of smokes from all over the world: 200 brands of cigars and pipe tobacco from foreign shores such as Tanzania and Sumatra. The deep rich scent of this place makes a visit worthwhile, even for nonsmokers like me who simply appreciate the scent of fresh tobacco. JR offers monthly deals and hosts special events, including visits from Playboy playmates. In addition to its tobacco products, the shop also carries handsome humidors, cigar cutters, lighters, and other smoking paraphernalia.

MIA GEMMA

933 F St. NW, 202/393-4367, www.miagemma.com

HOURS: Mon.-Fri. 11 A.M.-6 P.M., Sat. noon-5 P.M.

Map 3

Limited-edition and one-of-a-kind American and European designs can be found at Mia Gemma, a cozy storefront containing a dazzling assortment of gold, silver, and gems at price ranges that appeal to teenagers making a big purchase for a girlfriend, running up to pricey baubles for wives, girlfriends, mistresses, and selves. The store carries a unique assortment of engagement rings and wedding bands as well, with an option to purchase loose stones and have a design custom-made.

◖ TINY JEWEL BOX

1147 Connecticut Ave. NW, 202/393-2747,
www.tinyjewelbox.com

HOURS: Mon.-Sat. 10 A.M.-5:30 P.M.

Map 4

Washingtonians have fallen for Tiny Jewel Box's slogan: "If it's not special, it's not here." This store (once tiny, really), is multiple stories of new, estate, and antique jewelry, a go-to shop for engagement rings, wedding bands, designer jewelry, unusual pieces, and fine watches. Featured designers include David Yurman, Ten Thousand Things, and Mark Patterson. The shop also carries fine gifts and home accessories—handbags, crystal, vases—perfect for hostess gifts and bridal parties. Mid-April through Mother's Day, Tiny Jewel Box has its once-a-year sale, with savings from 10 to 70 percent on most items in the store.

Tiny Jewel Box

© PATRICIA KIME

Kids' Stores

KID'S CLOSET

1226 Connecticut Ave. NW, 202/429-9247,
www.kidsclosetdc.com

HOURS: Mon.-Fri. 10 A.M.-6 P.M., Sat. 11 A.M.-5 P.M., Sun. noon-4 P.M.

Map 6

The appeal of Kid's Closet is not having to schlep to a mall to pick up affordable and practical baby and children's clothes from some of the favorite makers of sturdy and cute children's apparel like Carters, OshKosh, and a personal favorite, Little Me. This well-organized store also carries toys and gifts for new arrivals as well as accessories like headbands and tights for baby girls. Look for sales and special items during holiday seasons, like cute Halloween costumes and nice Christmas dresses and cardigans.

PICCOLO PIGGIES

1533 Wisconsin Ave. NW, 202/333-0123,
www.piccolo-piggies.com

HOURS: Mon.-Sat. 10 A.M.-6 P.M., Sun. 11:30 A.M.-5 P.M.

Map 8

One of the nicest things about Piccolo Piggies is that the store sells dresses for girls up to preteen that are sweet and cute for young ladies, unlike the current retail trend of marketing hip and provocative apparel to this age group. The place is brimming with adorable, albeit expensive, baby and children's wear from makers like Lilly Pulitzer, Burberry, and other European and American designers. The light-filled white and pastel shop also carries accessories, toys, and layette items such as the sweet Cloud B Sleep Sheep, a plush toy that

MUSEUM SHOPPING

Inside the city's museums is a shopping bonanza: stores with special treasures, unique art, jewelry, clothing, and one-of-a-kind finds from across the country and around the globe. Even the most shopping-challenged are likely to find a gift for that hard-to-please friend or relative on their list at one of these spaces. Two museum stores top my list for distinctive gifts: the **Spy Museum Store at the International Spy Museum** for neat toys and gadgets that enthrall kids, and the **National Gallery of Art** for its lovely array of note cards, books, posters, toys, and games.

Many of Washington's museum shops sell jewelry based on their collections (or completely copied, in the case of a Hope "Diamond" pin), or clothing and home decor items gleaned from their subject matter. One sure to amuse youngsters for hours is the **National Air and Space Museum Shop**—go ahead, buy the freeze-dried astronaut ice cream, it's practically a Washington childhood rite of passage – and they also enjoy the **National Museum of Natural His-**

tory, with its vast array of stuffed animals, toys, stickers, books, and kid-friendly wares. At the **National Museum of American History,** shoppers will find wares with a historic bent, including presidential tchotchkes, copies of America's great documents, prints, and more. Under pressure from a Vermont congressman, this museum has recently embarked on a program to provide more American-made items in its store. Another often overlooked shop is the National Museum of African Art's store, with a striking array of woven baskets, wall hangings, and other African-made home accessories you won't find elsewhere.

There's no tax on purchases at government-owned museums. Also, many of the items at the major museums can be purchased online if you choose not to get them during your visit, but be aware that not every item in every museum is available on the Web. And special places, like the **National Museum of African Art** and the **Textile Museum,** both of which carry lovely gifts and unique items, have very few of them for sale online.

SHOPS

lulls a baby to sleep with a selection of sounds found in nature.

◖ SPY MUSEUM STORE

International Spy Museum, 800 F St. NW, 202/393-7798, www.spymuseum.org
HOURS: Vary
Map 3

Decoder rings, invisible ink, fingerprint kits, spy movie trivia games, and listening devices are all part of the fun at this shop for wannabe spies and kids of the covert. The store also has a great selection of *Spy vs. Spy* paperbacks, T-shirts, and reproduction buttons and posters from *MAD* magazine's heyday. But this place isn't just for kids. Adults will enjoy perusing the thorough book selection, Cold War memorabilia, music selection, and clothing. If spy-next-door Anna Chapman's popularity is any indication, the world loves a well-dressed, well-accessorized spy.

© PATRICIA KIME

The Spy Museum Store is fun for kids of all ages.

Pet Supplies and Grooming

DOGGIE STYLE

1825 18th St. NW, 202/667-0595, www.doggiestylebakery.com
HOURS: Mon.-Wed. 11 A.M.-7 P.M., Thurs. noon-8 P.M., Fri.-Sat. 11 A.M.-7 P.M., Sun. noon-6 P.M.
Map 7

The edgy name fits the neighborhood at this bakery, shop, and grooming locale for dogs. The place specializes in environmentally friendly products for your pooch, selling all-natural pet foods and baked treats, chemical-free shampoos and grooming products, and a selection of toys, apparel, and accessories— bowls, leashes, collars—mainly made in the United States and determined to be free of contaminants such as lead or harmful chemicals. The store also offers full-service grooming.

THE DOG SHOP

1625 Wisconsin Ave. NW, 202/337-3647, www.dogshop.com
HOURS: Mon.-Fri. 8:30 A.M.-8 P.M., Sat. 9 A.M.-5 P.M., Sun. 11 A.M.-4 P.M.
Map 8

This store is geared mainly to providing goods and services for your pooch, carrying a variety of products such as food, treats, collars, leashes, and toys, all deliverable to your home. Dog owners can even call ahead and have items taken out to them curbside or delivered the same day. The Dog Shop has grooming and training services, an off-site boarding facility, and a self-serve washtub for do-it-yourself owners. Monthly events include dog adoptions and socialization groups.

Shoes

COMFORT ONE
716 7th St. NW, 202/783-1199,
www.comfortoneshoes.com
HOURS: Mon.-Sat. 10 A.M.-9 P.M., Sun. 11 A.M.-7 P.M.
Map 3

Homegrown Comfort One was founded in Alexandria, Virginia, in 1993, a store dedicated to providing patrons with stylish shoes that actually feel good. Naturally, Comfort One sells the usual Doc Martens, Birkenstocks, and Ecco but also includes brands like Earthies, Mephisto, and Dana Davis. Comfort One has 26 locations throughout the area, with six alone within the city limits. Look for it also at The Fashion Centre at Pentagon City.

HU'S SHOES
3005 M St. NW, 202/342-0202,
www.shop.husonline.com
HOURS: Mon.-Sat. 10 A.M.-7 P.M., Sun. 1-5 P.M.
Map 8

An exotic collection of pumps, wedges, flats, and sandals from Marc Jacobs, Lanvin, Miss Trish, Brian Atwood, and other top-end designers as well as lesser-known up-and-comers can be found at Hu's, a shoe boutique that specializes in trendsetting fashions. Owner Marlene Hu Aldaba has carefully crafted a nearly museum-worthy collection, beautifully displayed in a well-lit, welcoming environment. The staff is friendly, helpful, and always willing to strike up a conversation regardless of what you are wearing and whether you look like you can afford their $500-plus products—a rarity in upscale boutiques that should be standard across the board.

SASSANOVA
1641 Wisconsin Ave. NW, 202/471-4400
HOURS: Mon.-Wed. and Fri.-Sat. 10 A.M.-6 P.M.,
Thurs. 10 A.M.-7 P.M., Sun. noon-5 P.M.
Map 8

Way cute shoes: Sassanova's selection of flats, espadrilles, wedges, sling backs, and booties from Kate Spade, Tory Burch, Moschino Cheap and Chic, and others is drool-worthy, a collection sure to please any shoe lover. The store also carries handbags, jewelry, accessories, and a small but adorable collection of children's wear, including teeny shoes. The small row house is comfortable, with chairs for those trying on shoes as well as their weary shopping companions.

Shopping Centers

THE FASHION CENTRE AT PENTAGON CITY
1100 S. Hayes St., Arlington, Va., 703/415-2400,
www.simon.com/Mall/?id=157
HOURS: Mon.-Sat. 10 A.M.-9:30 P.M., Sun. 11 A.M.-6 P.M.
Map 9

This light and airy shopping center is a favorite for locals simply for its convenience, right on the Metro line and near several major highways. Stores include Macy's and Nordstrom, with a variety of high-end cosmetics stores, including Sephora and MAC, and mid-level retailers Gap, J. Crew, Abercrombie & Fitch, Talbots, Ann Taylor, Jos. A. Bank, and American Eagle. It was in the first-floor food court, just at the bottom of the escalator, where the FBI first approached Monica Lewinsky to inquire about her relationship with President Clinton. Her "friend" Linda Tripp was there too.

GALLERIA AT TYSONS CORNER
2001 International Dr., McLean, Va., 703/827-7730,
www.tysonsgalleria.com
HOURS: Mon.-Sat. 10 A.M.-9 P.M., Sun. noon-6 P.M.
Map 9

Tysons Corner Center's swankier sister, the Galleria at Tysons Corner is a high-end shopper's mecca containing a number of stand-alone stores of American and European

The Fashion Centre at Pentagon City is a popular shopping destination for locals.

designers as well as anchor stores like Neiman-Marcus and Saks Fifth Avenue. This place is never crowded, even at Christmas time, and the stores do a brisk business, but nothing is ever out-of-place, nor is anyone—the clientele, the salespeople—harried. Nicole Miller, Betsey Johnson, Ralph Lauren, Carol Mitchell, and Michael Kors all have stores here, along with Burberry, Anthropologie, Versace, and Vineyard Vines.

MAZZA GALLERIE

5300 Wisconsin Ave., 202/966-6114, www.mazzagallerie.com

HOURS: Mon.-Fri. 10 A.M.-8 P.M., Sat. 10 A.M.-7 P.M., Sun. noon-6 P.M.

Map 9

Five miles up Wisconsin Avenue from Georgetown, this upscale shopping complex is the main anchor for a bevy of high-end retailers in the neighborhood, catering to an older, wealthy clientele. Anchor stores inside the Gallerie include Neiman-Marcus and Saks 5th Avenue Men's Store; small shops include Ann Taylor, Williams-Sonoma, and a handful

of jewelry and luggage shops. There's also a seven-screen movie theater. Across the street is a Stein Mart, and north on Wisconsin Avenue are a host of stores, including Anthropologie, Gap, Banana Republic, Louis Vuitton, Tiffany & Co., and Barneys Co-op.

TYSONS CORNER CENTER

1961 Chain Bridge Rd., McLean, Va., 703/893-9400, www.shoptysons.com

HOURS: Mon.-Thurs. 10 A.M.-9:30 P.M., Fri.-Sat. 10 A.M.-10 P.M., Sun. 10 A.M.-8 P.M.

Map 9

There doesn't seem to be a store that Tysons doesn't have. Under one roof, Virginia's largest mall has roughly 300 retailers, more than 20 restaurants, a mammoth food court, a 16-screen movie theater, and *two* Starbucks—clearly the place is so big that one is not enough. Yet despite its size, it doesn't feel overwhelming; maybe I think this because I grew up with it, watching it morph from a small one-hall indoor shopping center into its present-day conglomeration. Unique shops include a Lego store, Mango, Jessica McClintock (for all things prom), Lord & Taylor, L. L. Bean (with a two-story waterfall and a fresh fish pond), and Coldwater Creek.

UNION STATION
50 Massachusetts Ave. NE, 202/289-1908, www.unionstation.com
HOURS: Mon.-Sat. 10 A.M.-9 P.M., Sun. noon-6 P.M.
Map 5

A beautiful historic space containing stores found in any suburban mall, Union Station still has a few gems, including Appalachian Spring, a high-end craft store near the rear of the East Hall that specializes in art glass, exquisite paperweights, turned cherrywood salad bowls, jewelry, and American-made crafts. Prepubescent teenage girls will go gaga for LittleMissMatched, an apparel and accessories store that features scarves, socks, dresses, clothes, and bedding in an eye-popping array of colors and patterns. Souvenirs, both the schlock and the acceptable, can be found in I Luv DC, America!, and Life on Capitol Hill stores.

Stationery

THE PAPER SOURCE
3019 M St. NW, 202/298-5545, www.paper-source.com
HOURS: Mon.-Sat. 10 A.M.-9 P.M., Sun. 11 A.M.-7 P.M.
Map 8

The numerous racks of sheet wrapping paper are a sight to behold at The Paper Source. It's a close second to the paper stores of Florence, with reams of paper featuring rich textures and patterns. Many of the floral papers are imported from Europe, and the graphic patterns come from Japan. The store has stock stationery and cards and offers custom-order personalized notes, invitations, and stationery. For creative types it also offers a full array of components for designing your own correspondence or personalizing scrapbooks. The shop also features a neat selection of gifts and diversions for youngsters shopping with their paper-addicted parents.

PULP
1803 14th St. NW, 202/462-7857, www.pulp.com
HOURS: Mon.-Sat. 11 A.M.-7 P.M., Sun. 11 A.M.-5 P.M.
Map 7

The Washingtonian who always has the funniest greeting card, the perfect pick-me-up gift, lovely journals, and miscellanea likely found it at Pulp, a vast card store in the trendy U Street–Cardozo corridor. Cards run the gamut from G-rated to NC-17; the shop also has a large selection of cards and items catering to the LGBT community. Paper stock aside, Pulp also features unusual and racy gifts, graphic T-shirts, and novelty items like Cat Butt Gum and cases for feminine products that bear amusing slogans. It's definitely a store full of things you don't think you need until you see them.

THE WRITTEN WORD
1926 17th St. NW, 202/223-1400, www.writtenword.invitations.com
HOURS: Tues.-Fri. 11 A.M.-6 P.M., Sat. 11 A.M.-5 P.M.
Map 7

It has been a long time since I've ordered wedding invitations, but the folks at the Written Word, who have an antique letter press in their basement shop, can tell you the difference between engraved, letter pressed, or thermographed invitations. The store specializes in invitations, personalized stationery, and announcements, and it carries my old school favorite, Crane paper, with its thick textured feel and resistance under a fine pen, along with perfect Kate Spade stationery, crisp and just so. If you need a card, gift bag, or wrapping paper, they have those too.

Vintage

MEEPS AND AUNT NEENSIES VINTAGE FASHIONETTE

2104 18th St. NW, 202/265-6546, www.meeps.com

HOURS: Mon.-Sat. noon-7 P.M., Sun. noon-5 P.M.

Map 7

Meeps trends more to the look of *That '70s Show* than it does vintage couture, with racks that actually contains jumpsuits and polyester pantsuits. The men do better here, with a wide selection of suits and shirts that can meld nicely into any contemporary wardrobe. Meeps is hit or miss, and the times I've visited it has been more of the latter. Still, this place has some finds: On a recent trip, I noted a lovely short 1950s cocktail dress and a seersucker shirt dress.

SECONDHAND ROSE

1516 Wisconsin Ave. NW, 202/337-3378, www.secondhandrose.com

HOURS: Mon.-Sat. 11 A.M.-6 P.M., closed Sun.

Map 8

This quirky little shop, in the second story of an inauspicious town house, specializes in designer merchandise and is known mainly for its shoe and bag selection, including Christian Louboutin, Ferragamo, Chanel, and Marc Jacobs.

As a consignment store, it enforces rigorous standards regarding wear and age, so much of the merchandise appears to be in excellent condition. Prices are roughly one-third of retail.

◖ SECONDI

1702 Connecticut Ave. NW, 202/667-1122, www.secondi.com

HOURS: Mon.-Tues. 11 A.M.-6 P.M., Wed.-Fri. noon-7 P.M., Sat. 11 A.M.-6 P.M., Sun. 1-5 P.M.

Map 6

Oh, I love that…and that…and that! It's nearly impossible to go into Secondi and not see something you could picture in your closet, with its selection of designer suits, handbags, evening wear, and separates. The store specializes in like-new high-end merchandise from labels like Chanel, Kate Spade, Helmut Lang, and newer retailers—Banana Republic, White House/Black Market, and J. Crew. Secondi generally lives up to its aim, though like any consignment shop, it has a generous amount of duds and lifeless attire that seem destined for Goodwill. Prices are high, but for vintage evening wear, classic dresses, and well-cared-for designer shoes and bags, they may be worth the money.

© PATRICIA KIME

Secondi specializes in like-new, high-end merchandise.

HOTELS

Washington has no shortage of hotel rooms. From pricey suites with stunning views to a budget-friendly double hostel room with shared bath three blocks from the Smithsonian's American Art Museum, the city offers accommodations for nearly every type of traveler: couples seeking a romantic getaway, a family enjoying their spring break, cash-strapped students, and business travelers needing a temporary home near public transportation. Within the city proper, Washington has 29,000 hotel rooms, with roughly 66,000 more scattered across the region. Some of the city's finest—and most expensive—hotels naturally are located near the city's prominent landmarks, either in Foggy Bottom near the White House, on Capitol Hill, or along Georgetown's historic streets. Many offer extensive views, upscale amenities, and posh decor within walking distance of the major sightseeing areas and the prime businesses districts, and they cater to those willing to pay a premium for proximity. Still, a few relative bargains can be found in these neighborhoods, including inns with fewer amenities, historic B&Bs, and hostel options. Farther afield, both in the city and across boundaries in Virginia and Maryland, travelers will find less expensive options, many conveniently located near Metro stops and just a quick trip from the downtown sites. Families seeking lower-priced accommodations with kid-friendly amenities are often drawn to these close-in suburbs, with their selection of megahotels as well as low-rise motels and affordable inns. But business travelers often choose to stay in these areas as well, mainly because they are

HIGHLIGHTS

LOOK FOR ◖ TO FIND RECOMMENDED HOTELS.

◖ **Best Deal:** Quiet and convenient, with kitchenettes and prices perfect for an extended stay, the **George Washington University Inn** is a budget pleaser, if you're lucky enough to snag a reservation (page 220).

◖ **Most Historic Hotel:** It's a toss-up between **The Renaissance Mayflower** (page 222) or the **Willard InterContinental** (page 223) – the only city hotels that make the National Park Service's official National Register of Historic Places travel itinerary.

◖ **Best Views:** The west- and south-facing rooms at the **W Hotel Washington DC** overlook the White House, the National Mall, the Washington Monument, and the Lincoln Memorial (page 222).

◖ **Best Boutique Hotel:** Minimalist urban chic and perfectly located near the U.S. Capitol, the **Hotel George** is cool without being cold (page 224).

◖ **Best Hotel to See-and-Be-Seen:** Celebrities favor **The Four Seasons** whether they are in town to star in a concert, enjoy the sights, or lobby for a cause (page 230).

© PATRICIA KIME

Hotel George

HOTELS

---

close to outlying government offices and businesses as well as area airports.

As a crossroads of the rich and powerful, Washington has its share of luxury hotels: destinations like the Forbes five-star Four Seasons, the Mandarin Oriental, the Ritz-Carlton, and the St. Regis, properties known for pampering guests with opulent settings, extraordinary service, and fine amenities. The city also has a number of historic hotels, edifices that are not only historic buildings in themselves but where history was made, either in their restaurants or small smoke-filled rooms or within a bed chamber: resorts like the Hay Adams, the lodging choice in the 1920s for pilots Charles Lindbergh and Amelia Earhart and home for the Obamas in the two weeks leading up to the 2009 inauguration.

The historic Mayflower hosted FBI director J. Edgar Hoover for lunch daily for 20 years, and it was where Franklin Roosevelt dictated his inaugural speech with its famous phrase, "the only thing we have to fear is fear itself." The Willard hosted the 1861 Peace Conference, an effort aimed at staving off the Civil War, and hosted Julia Ward Howe, who wrote the words to "The Battle Hymn of the Republic"

PRICE KEY

$ Less than $150 per night
$$ $150-250 per night
$$$ More than $250 per night

in one of its guest rooms. In the past decade, the Kimpton hotel group has scooped up a number of existing small properties in Washington and upgraded them into sleek boutique hotels, quickly becoming a hotel powerhouse in the city for its upscale lodgings and emphasis on service. Kimpton hotels include the well-placed Hotel George on Capitol Hill and the Hotel Monaco adjacent to the Verizon Center. Georgetown is home to a number of small homegrown hotels, including the Georgetown Inn and the Georgetown Suites. Ecoconscious visitors will have to go across the Potomac River to Arlington to find a LEED-certified hotel, but the Carlyle Suites near Dupont Circle does its best to be green in an existing space, investing in energy certificates to ensure that the entire hotel runs on wind power and establishing an extensive hotel recycling program. For those without any cash to spare, the city also has some lower-cost options, including several youth hostels and a number of clean yet dated family-run hotels. In some neighborhoods covered by this guide, no lodging options may exist, but the neighborhoods are so close together that it is likely you'll find a hotel within a 10-block radius of where you want to stay.

CHOOSING A HOTEL

Location and luxury appointments are the driving factors in hotel rates in Washington, just as in most major cities. Generally, the closer you are to any of the white marble buildings that define the city's skyline, the more you'll pay. If this is a once-in-a-lifetime trip, consider splurging on a place with the view or the historic hotel with Washington charm. You might regret the lightness of your wallet, but you won't forget the experience of being a part of this capital city. If you decide to stay downtown near the U.S. Capitol or the White House, you will have an array of options, from properties run by the large chain hotel corporations to smaller boutique properties and a handful of small independently owned operations. Regardless, make sure to ask about parking if you plan to arrive

by car. Very few hotels in the city offer free parking, and fees can be steep, often tacking $25 or $35 per day onto your bill. Be sure to understand your hotel's policies on valet parking, pickup, and payment requirements; parking fees are among the biggest sources of complaints that Washington hoteliers receive from customers.

To experience Washington like a native, consider booking a room in Georgetown or Dupont Circle. Both offer accommodations in restored row houses or historic low-rises, situated among shops, restaurants, and nightspots favored by Washingtonians. Dupont Circle offers wider access to the city by public transportation since it has its own Metro stop. If you are still undecided as to where you want to stay, take a look at what's on your itinerary and simply choose a place near where you plan to visit or near a Metro stop. What you're likely to find is that Washington is so small that if you stay downtown on Capitol Hill or in Georgetown, Dupont Circle, Adams Morgan, Foggy Bottom, and Arlington, Virginia, you can be at the Smithsonian Metro stop in less than a half an hour. Be aware that if you elect to stay in the highly touted new development called National Harbor in Prince George's County, Maryland, just south of DC, or in Alexandria, Virginia, these areas offer upscale lodgings and waterfront views but can be up to 40 minutes away by car.

Finding a hotel deal in Washington can be a challenge. Hotels have no set rates, but generally, rates tend to be lower on weekends and holidays, and they also dip in late July and August and again in January and February. If you want to get a great rate, first check out the usual Internet bargain-hunter sites, including Hotwire.com and Priceline.com, and glance at the city's official tourism website, www.washington.org, which often features hotel specials and package deals. Take note of your own credentials before booking: Are you traveling for business or for the government? Are you in the military, or do you have a military ID card? Do you have membership in an auto club or have benefits through a frequent-flyer or car-rental program? You may be eligible for a discount. Don't be shy about asking for one even if you don't think you qualify. It never hurts to ask.

The rates listed here are based on spring-season rates—the highest charged by all DC hotels—but are also for a weekend stay. Rates are usually higher during the week, so if you are traveling to DC for a weekday meeting, you might pay a slightly higher rate.

The National Mall East   Map 2

The advantage to staying near the National Mall is the proximity to the city's main monuments, memorials, and the Smithsonian. The disadvantage is that the neighborhood lacks dining and shopping options; guests who stay here must hop on the Metro or take a cab to enjoy the wide range of restaurants, stores, and night-time entertainment venues in the city. Yet visitors are still drawn to the area for a few reasons, including the luxury and waterfront views at Mandarin Oriental and the convenience and business-friendly environment at the L'Enfant Plaza Hotel.

L'ENFANT PLAZA HOTEL $$

480 L'Enfant Plaza SW, 202/484-1000, www.lenfantplazahotel.com

Well-placed in an office complex above the L'Enfant Plaza Metro Station, this hotel's biggest draw is its location just blocks from the Mall. Guest rooms are clean and feature the basics—a hair dryer, a TV, an ironing board—and, reportedly, extremely comfortable beds. But the entire hotel has an air of being dated, which exudes from the laminate furniture and fading wallpaper. It is a full-service hotel with a restaurant and bar, a swimming pool, a business center, and a fitness center, a rarity in this area. L'Enfant Plaza Hotel is pet-friendly, with a generous weight limit—a bonus for owners of large dogs. Dining options in the hotel include the American Grill and the Foggy Brew Pub, which you'll likely patronize unless you don't mind hopping a cab or the Metro for food; the only nearby restaurant options besides those in the hotel are at the Mandarin Oriental.

MANDARIN ORIENTAL $$$

1330 Maryland Ave. SW, 888/888-1778, www.mandarinoriental.com/washington

The Mandarin Oriental is one of the city's most luxurious hotels, an Asian-themed getaway with nearly 400 guest rooms decorated by the principles of feng shui, aimed at pampering guests and maximizing their comfort. The hotel's location, overlooking the Tidal Basin and the Jefferson Memorial, make it the ultimate stay during the city's Cherry Blossom Festival, as many guest rooms overlook the trees—and the crowds—below. The Mandarin Oriental is within walking distance of the monuments on the eastern

Mandarin Oriental towers over a business district in a prime locale.

half of the Mall as well as the U.S. Holocaust Memorial Museum; otherwise, guests will find the hotel's neighborhood quite dull, a business setting that clears out at night and has no nightlife or eateries. But the hotel has many amenities of its own, including CityZen, one of the city's finest restaurants for foodies, as well as a 50-foot heated lap pool, a spa and fitness center, and a private gallery containing museum pieces on loan from the Smithsonian.

Downtown   Map 3

DC's downtown area, encompassing the Penn Quarter and Chinatown neighborhoods, is as close as the city gets to 24-7 living, with museums, movie and stage theaters, upscale restaurants, stores, bars, and lounges. A stay in this area is a truly urban experience, and the hotels are all within close proximity of the pulsing beat, flashing neon, and fun spirit that defines this area after dark.

COURTYARD WASHINGTON CONVENTION CENTER $$

900 F St. NW, 202/638-4600 or 800/393-3063, www.marriott.com/hotels/travel/wascn-courtyard-washington-convention-center
Located in the former Riggs Bank building, constructed in 1891, this hotel is in many ways a typical Courtyard by Marriott: basic furnishings, an indoor pool and hot tub, and

BEST HOTELS FOR FAMILIES

A trip to Washington is a pilgrimage for many families, and fortunately, the city is replete with hotels that cater to this demographic. As any parent knows, choosing a hotel that's close to restaurants and attractions and near the Metro is paramount; if it has a pool, a refrigerator, and breakfast on-site, even better. Here are a number of accommodations that will make your family's visit to Washington enjoyable.

Located near the Spy Museum, a couple of Metro stations and a bevy of restaurants, the **Courtyard Washington Convention Center** is located in a cool old bank building and has something to please everyone, with a pool and a whirlpool, a fitness center, an in-house breakfast spot, and a Gordon Biersch Brewery.

Kids love the room service and swimming pool at the **Embassy Suites** near the Convention Center; parents love paying for one room, tucking their children into the pullout sleeper sofa, and closing the door.

It's hard to tell kids you won't pay the exorbitant prices for the Pez in the minibar at the **Hotel Helix.** So take advantage of the Bubbly Hour (champagne served gratis in the afternoon) and spring for the candy; you'll get years of enjoyment listening to the "Remember that cool hotel we stayed at with the bunk beds and the Pez?"

With space to romp and roam and a huge swimming pool open during the summer, the **Omni Shoreham** is a kid-pleaser. The Omni's Sensational Kids program gives children backpacks filled with games and books and provides child-friendly menus. Also, the hotel is just a short distance from the National Zoo, a great place to take early risers, as the animals are "morning people" too.

The budget-conscious will enjoy the **Residence Inn Courthouse** in Arlington, Virginia, directly on Metro's Orange Line and which offers one- and two-bedroom suites at reasonable rates. Couple the spacious guest rooms with amenities like a swimming pool and nearby restaurant choices, and your family will quickly settle into this space, just 13 minutes by Metro from the Smithsonian Station.

a bistro to grab breakfast before heading out for the day. But in other ways this Courtyard is not so run-of-the-mill. The Gordon Biersch Brewery on the first floor provides room service, a concierge is on hand to help guests find their way, and the manager hosts a wine-and-noshes happy hour during the week. The convenient location—in the heart of downtown just two blocks from the Verizon Center, close to the Metro, and near the International Spy Museum, the National Museum of Crime and Punishment, and the National Portrait and American Art Galleries—is this property's biggest asset. But it can also be something of a drawback regarding noise: Patrons party at nearby bars late into the night. Guest rooms are city-small, and if you don't like noise, ask for an inner room; you'll sacrifice a neighborhood view, but it will be quieter.

DONOVAN HOUSE ⑤⑤⑤

1001 14th St. NW, 202/737-1200 or 800/383-6900, www.thompsonhotels.com

As retro-cool as a planned remodel for Don Draper's office circa 1969, Donovan House caters to fans of Danish egg chairs, leather swings, and glass coffee tables, a property managed by Thompson Hotels aimed at drawing a young hip crowd or those who still think they fall into that demographic. Guest rooms are of minimalist design but have two notable features: dark leather canopy beds that define the sleeping space, and lighted, nautilus-shaped plastic showers that extend into seating area. Hotel amenities include Sferra sheets, a rooftop pool that transforms into an überchic lounge area at night, and a fitness center.

THE ELDON ⑤⑤⑤

933 L St. NW, 202/540-5000 or 877/463-5336, www.eldonsuites.com

A relatively new property in an up-and-coming neighborhood, the Eldon is one of the lodging pioneers near the Washington Convention Center, an all-suite hotel with guest rooms the size of apartments (none smaller than 650 square feet) geared to family vacationers and long-term business travelers. In this hotel, guests won't be bothered by hordes of touring school groups; it doesn't cater to them. Guest rooms are decorated in shades of burnt orange, beige, and cream, and interiors are dominated notably by stone and granite; most guest rooms have tile floors with a few area rugs. Little luxuries include complimentary breakfast, in-room robes and slippers, showers with side massage jets, and full-size refrigerators and dishwashers.

EMBASSY SUITES HOTEL DC CONVENTION CENTER ⑤⑤

900 10th St. NW, 800/362-2779 or 202/739-2001, www.washingtonconventioncenter.embassysuites.com

The Embassy Suites Hotel near the Convention Center has everything a family wants in a hotel: complimentary hot breakfast, convenient location near museums and the Metro, a pool, snacks and drinks in the afternoon, and the all-important door between the bedroom and the living area that holds the pull-out couch and dining table. Guest rooms have flat-screen TVs, tables, chairs, microwaves, and mini refrigerators as well as easy chairs, couches, and pull-out sofas. The on-site restaurant, Finn & Porter, serves steaks, seafood, salads, and other American choices, and also provides room service throughout the evening.

GRAND HYATT WASHINGTON ⑤⑤

1000 H St. NW, 202/582-1234 or 800/233-1234, www.grandhyatt.washington.com

The Grand Hyatt is one of the largest hotels downtown, with 888 guest rooms and views that overlook either the hotel's 13-story atrium or the city. A player piano provides background music beside a waterfall in the soaring center court; guests also can choose to linger by the seasonal fire at Cure Bar. The Hyatt is conveniently located directly over Metro Center, the system's major hub. Guest rooms are decorated in shades of beige, gold, and brown with dark furniture and feature bathrooms with granite

HOTELS

counters and marble touches. The hotel also has a sports bar that pays homage to DC's sports teams, a place that fills up after games at the nearby Verizon Center.

HAMPTON INN CONVENTION CENTER ⑤⑤

901 6th St. NW, 202/842-2500 or 800/426-7866, www.washingtondc.hamptoninn.com

Development has been slow around the Washington Convention Center, which opened in 2003, but in the past couple of years, change is finally coming to this once beleaguered neighborhood. Among the new construction is the Hampton Inn, a sparkling new property that features a saltwater aquarium in its brightly lit lobby, an indoor pool, a cardio room, and all-day coffee. Guest rooms in this nonsmoking 228-room hotel are decorated in shades of beige and brown and include free Internet access, lap desks, and 32-inch flat-screen TVs.

HOSTELLING INTERNATIONAL WASHINGTON DC ⑤

1009 11th St. NW, 202/737-2333 or 800/909-4776, www.hiwashingtondc.org

For backpackers, students, and travelers on a budget, this hostel is considered the top choice in the city, with 250 beds, updated bathrooms, a kitchen, a coin-operated laundry, dining areas, and lounge rooms with TV and free Internet access. Located near several Metro stops as well as downtown museums, restaurants, and a few bars, the hostel attracts groups of all ages who love it for its cost, decent breakfast, and surprisingly, the range of activities offered through its program office, including free walking tours of the monuments, a pub crawl of Dupont Circle nightspots, and trivia contests at a nearby Irish pub.

HOTEL MONACO ⑤⑤⑤

700 F St. NW, 202/628-7177 or 800/649-1202, www.monaco-dc.com

What's old is new again at the Hotel Monaco, a Kimpton Hotel housed in an all-marble building on the site of a former hotel. The hotel's gorgeous all-marble facade, breathtaking

Hotel Monaco, near the Verizon Center

© PATRICIA KIME

at night, was the General Post Office in the 1800s and home to the U.S. International Trade Commission for most of the 1900s. In 2002 the San Francisco–based Kimpton group took over the property and refurbished it into the luxurious Hotel Monaco, noted for its large guest rooms (some with 15-foot ceilings) and eclectic style, featuring vibrant colors, modern and traditional furniture, Spanish art, and bold patterns. Interior guest rooms overlook the center courtyard and restaurant; the Monte Carlo rooms on the third floor, reportedly favored by visiting basketball teams, are twice the size of the regular guest rooms. The free Kimpton guest loyalty program gives guests free wireless Internet access, a voucher for the minibar, and other perks. The hotel also offers fresh-baked cookies, afternoon drinks, and pet-friendly amenities like dining bowls and treats.

JW MARRIOTT ⑤⑤⑤

1331 Pennsylvania Ave. NW, 202/393-2000 or 800/228-9290, www.marriott.com/wasjw

This property languished in the 1990s, with

a central atrium pretty enough to serve as a set for the 1987 movie *Broadcast News* but not keeping up with newcomers like the W Washington a few doors down. But a $40 million renovation in 2009 altered the interior significantly: It has the same bones as before but has definitely become more 21st-century, with lobby and public areas featuring leather-covered columns, wood paneling, and platinum ceiling inlays. Guest rooms are updated as well, decorated in muted shades of red and gold and featuring high-backed desk chairs and technology that allows guests to check their email on their TV sets.

MORRISON CLARK INN $$

1015 L St. NW, 202/898-1200, www.morrisonclark.com

A property that catches the eye of anyone walking by for its Chinese-style porch and roof that spans the facade of two Civil War-era town houses, the Morrison Clark Inn is an anomaly on L Street, a manor set among office buildings and parks two blocks from the Washington Convention Center. The inn has 54 guest rooms and suites that retain their original features, including high ceilings and ornate crown moldings, rich upholstered pieces, and antique bedding and furniture, much of it true to Victorian style. Public areas feature marble floors and fireplaces, 12-foot mahogany mirrors, and 19th-century

Morrison Clark Inn, a National Trust Historic Hotel of America

art. Complimentary Internet access, coffee, turndown service, and shoeshine is included in the room rates. The Morrison Clark is on the National Register of Historic Places; it once served as a military club offering low-cost lodging to service members.

Foggy Bottom

Map 4

Although it is primarily a business district, Foggy Bottom is one of the most convenient places to stay in Washington, close to sights and museums, recreation, and restaurants. And because it is home to major government offices, including the State Department, the White House, and daytime destinations, it is quiet at night yet not so empty that visitors feel unsafe. Not surprisingly, the area is home to several of the city's most elegant hotels, favored by visiting dignitaries, business executives, and those willing to pay a premium for luxury.

CAPITAL HILTON $$

1001 16th St. NW, 202/393-1000 or 800/445-8667, www.capital.hilton.com

Its proximity to the White House and K Street draw business travelers to the Capital Hilton, a newly renovated 544-room hotel that features updated decor and furniture, a lovely Federal-style lobby with mahogany columns, and the amenities guests want, including spacious guest rooms (some with wet bars), a top-notch concierge, and a bar and restaurant that stay open late. Three suites have patios, and some of the corner rooms have a partial view of the White House. The drawback to this hotel is the nickel-and-diming price schedule. If you are not at least a Hilton Honors Silver member, expect to pay at least $15 per day for the gym, the business center (charged by the hour), Internet access, and parking. The parking fees are understandable, given its location, but the added fees for amenities that don't cost the hotel that much to provide are annoying.

GEORGE WASHINGTON UNIVERSITY INN $$

824 New Hampshire Ave. NW, 202/337-6620 or 800/426-4455, www.gwuinn.com

Favored by business travelers and families, the guest rooms at the George Washington University Inn contain the comforts needed for a long-term stay: two full-sized or king beds, toiletries, a microwave, a mini fridge, and a coffeemaker in the regular guest rooms or kitchenettes in the larger guest rooms and suites. The inn is located on a quiet street at the edge of the university and just a block from the Foggy Bottom Metro Station, and it is also not far from Kennedy Center. All guest rooms feature complimentary Wi-Fi, flat-screen TVs, and free access to a nearby fitness center.

HAY-ADAMS HOTEL $$$

1 Lafayette Square NW, 202/638-6600 or 800/853-6807, www.hayadams.com

Barack Obama and his family lived at the Hay-Adams for several weeks before his inauguration in 2009, mainly because Blair House, the presidential guesthouse where presidents-elect usually stay for a few days before taking the oath of office, was already booked. Of the historic hotels in DC, why did the Obamas choose this one? Its location in their new neighborhood afforded them great views of their future home, and it definitely was the most convenient: They moved into neighboring Blair House on January 15 and into the White House on January 20. The Hay-Adams on Lafayette Square has hosted luminaries and legends for more than 83 years, including Ethel Barrymore, Sinclair Lewis, Amelia Earhart, and Charles Lindbergh. Named for the powerful

Hay-Adams Hotel

© PATRICIA KIME

men who lived in homes on the site (Lincoln's Secretary of State John Hay and journalist and historian Henry Adams), the Hay-Adams has a classic historic feel; guest rooms are richly decorated in fabric and fine wallpapers and feature plush upholstered furniture, luxurious Frette linens, and marble bathrooms. Public areas are not spacious but are beautifully decorated and boast Old World charm; the lobby is vaguely reminiscent of a famous hotel lobby in Paris, and the Off the Record bar brings to mind a few establishments at fine hotels in London. If the Hay-Adams doesn't fit your style or budget, consider stopping in for a drink: The gin with house-made tonic is among the city's best.

HOTEL LOMBARDY $$

2019 Pennsylvania Ave. NW, 202/828-2600 or 800/424-5486, www.hotellombardy.com

The public rooms at the Hotel Lombardy in DC are distinctly northern Italian in style, with ornate wallpaper, dark wood paneling, crystal chandeliers, and shuttered doorways. Elegant and comfortable, this hotel welcomes guests to linger in the Café Lombardy and Venetian

Room lounge, where you're likely to overhear many languages being spoken by foreign diplomats and World Bank visitors, who favor the hotel. Guest rooms are decorated in off-white and touches of color and feature original artwork. Some have kitchens and eating areas.

ONE WASHINGTON CIRCLE HOTEL ⓢⓢ

1 Washington Circle NW, 202/872-1680 or 800/424-9671, www.thecirclehotel.com

Centrally located near K Street, the White House, and Georgetown, One Washington Circle also attract business travelers and families, with large guest rooms and suites, some with full kitchens. Guest rooms are decorated in contemporary style; a few have walkout balconies and views of Washington Circle and the neighborhood. The hotel also features an outdoor pool, a fitness center, and an on-site restaurant; Internet access is complimentary. If you have business with George Washington University, tell the front desk when you make a reservation, as GW guests often receive a discount on room rates.

PARK HYATT ⓢⓢⓢ

1201 24th St. NW, 202/789-1234 or 800/778-7477, www.parkhyattwashington.com

Simplicity is the style at the Park Hyatt, a modern hotel decorated in American folk style that favors clean lines and minimalist design. The scheme is as much form as it is function: Park Hyatt offers hypoallergenic guest rooms with reduced airborne particles and irritants. The style of the guest rooms, from the wood blinds to the sleek Windsor chairs and open soaking tub with a rain shower, make it a challenge for a speck of pollen or a dust mite to find a perch. The Park Hyatt houses the Blue Duck Tavern, one of the city's top restaurants, and also features a Tea Cellar, an indulgence for tea lovers featuring a humidor to preserve the property's unique collection of rare teas. Amenities include a bicycle valet program, where guests can borrow a bike, a helmet, a map, and bottled water to explore the nation's capital, as well as an indoor pool, a whirlpool, and a full-service spa.

HOTELS

BEST MONUMENT VIEWS

You've come to see Washington's iconic buildings, and for a price, you can stare at them out your hotel window, although you'll pay a premium to stay on the side with the view at any hotel that offers one. Many hotels near the National Mall offer panoramic views of the city's most famous sites, starting with the trendy **W,** with its rooftop lounge and guest rooms that offer commanding views of the White House, Lincoln Memorial, and Washington Monument. Next door and two doors over, the **Willard InterContinental** and **JW Marriott** offer the same vista, just slightly farther from the White House and, in the case of the JW Marriott, a better view of the U.S. Capitol.

At the **Hay-Adams** you can gaze at the scenery while appreciating the city's symmetry and historic design: The Hay Adams has nearly direct unobstructed views of the White House across Lafayette Square, and beyond it, the Washington Monument and the Jefferson Memorial, both of which are aligned with the presidential mansion.

The Capitol Dome is hard not to miss from many of the hotels along the National Mall, but the **Hyatt Regency Washington on Capitol Hill** offers a nearly straight view up New Jersey Avenue of this magnificent structure.

For panoramic views that include the Tidal Basin, the Jefferson Memorial, the Lincoln Memorial, the World War II Memorial, the Potomac River, Arlington House, and Arlington National Cemetery, a west-facing guest room in the **Mandarin Oriental** offers some of the best vantages in the city. Even if you don't land a room with that view, the other guest rooms in this nine-story hotel overlook the Potomac, east Potomac Park, and scenery that includes Reagan National Airport.

◖ THE RENAISSANCE MAYFLOWER $$$

1127 Connecticut Ave. NW, 202/347-3000 or
800/228-7697, www.renaissancemayflower.com

The Mayflower is one of Washington's historic
hotels: the site of Calvin Coolidge's inaugural
ball (which the president did not attend because he was mourning his son's death), where
Franklin Delano Roosevelt lived before he
moved into the White House, and where Harry
Truman announced his decision to run for the
presidency in 1948. More recently, Room 871
was the site of a now-infamous tryst between
former New York governor Eliot Spitzer and a
pricey call girl. This Marriott property features
657 guest rooms, including 74 suites, lavishly
decorated with upholstered walls, silk draperies, and carved mantels. A new bar is set to
open in 2011, replacing the hotel's venerable
Town & Country Lounge. No word on the
decor or feel of the new space, but it will have
at least one holdover from the clubby old bar:
master Sam Lek, who has been serving up some
of the city's best cocktails since well before
cocktails made a comeback. January 20 is a
special day at the Mayflower; in the past, staff
and guests have reported strange sightings—
lights flickering, an elevator that won't work,
glasses of wine discovered in public areas that
were not being used; fans of the paranormal
believe the ghost of Calvin Coolidge returns
to the hotel each present-day inauguration date
because he missed his own party.

SOFITEL LAFAYETTE SQUARE $$$

806 15th St. NW, 202/730-8800 or 800/763-4835,
www.sofitel.com

At the French-owned Sofitel Lafayette Square,
great attention is paid to the small details, like
the flattering lighting in the bathrooms, natural sunlight flooding the guest rooms through
large windows (nearly floor-to-ceiling on the
second and third floors), comfortable king
beds with down comforters, and attentive
staff. Furnishings are modern and sleek; the
hotel has a distinctly European feel and is well-
placed just a few blocks from the White House.

Ask for a room facing 15th or H Streets; otherwise you'll be staring into an alleyway. The
L'Occitane en Provence bath products are a
nice bonus.

THE ST. REGIS $$$

923 16th St. NW, 202/638-2626, www.stregis.com/
washingtondc

With its $40 million makeover in 2008, the
St. Regis Washington has remained at the top
of its game, a landmark hotel not far from the
White House that prides itself on its lovely
spaces, impeccable service, and fine appointments. The St. Regis boasts 182 guest rooms,
including 25 suites, with plush bedding, TVs
hidden in built-in armoires, wine refrigerators,
and TVs in the bathrooms disguised behind
mirrors. Service is impeccable; the staff aims
to make every guest feel special.

◖ W HOTEL WASHINGTON DC $$$

515 15th St. NW, 202/661-2400,
www.starwoodhotels.com/whotels

Since it opened in the former Hotel Washington
in 2009, the W Washington has been over-
shadowed by the buzz over its cocktail lounge,
POV, that draws the well-heeled to its rooftop terrace. When POV opened it reportedly
caused a stir with the Secret Service, mainly
for its direct views of the White House lawn
and helicopter pad (the Hotel Washington was
also known for its rooftop bar featuring the
same stunning views with the same security
concerns). The W has its own unique allure,
mixing the brand's signature "so hip it hurts"
decor with the historic touches of the previous occupants. As with all W properties, guests
enter the hotel through the Living Room (the
lobby), where they are greeted by fit young
assistants and the beat of electronica playing
over the sound system. In the evenings, this
area turns into a cocktail bar with pulsing DJ-
driven music. The hotel's 317 guest rooms are
equipped with sleek, modern furnishings and
are decorated in cool tones—whites, grays, and
blues. Some feature digital fireplaces and views
of the Washington Monument, the Lincoln

and Jefferson Memorials, and the Potomac River. The W Washington also has the city's only Bliss Spa.

◖ THE WILLARD INTERCONTINENTAL ❸❸❸

1401 Pennsylvania Ave. NW, 202/628-9100 or 800/827-1747, www.washingtonintercontinental.com

The staff at the historic Willard is quick to point out their hotel's historic heritage and Washington clout, but it is no wonder: The Willard is where a fire one evening in 1922 forced the evacuation of its 500 guests, including long-term resident Vice President Calvin Coolidge, John Philip Sousa, four senators, and numerous members of congress and captains of industry. At the Willard in 1861, Julia Ward Howe penned "The Battle Hymn of the Republic," and in 1963, Martin Luther King polished his "I Have a Dream" speech. Presidents Lincoln and Coolidge lived here for

brief periods as well. "If you want to give an impression that you mean serious business, you stay at the Willard," says concierge Guillaume Tourniaire. An inn has been operating on this site since 1816; the current building was constructed in 1904. Guest rooms in this Second Empire–style building are opulently furnished with Federal and Edwardian reproduction furniture, as are the public spaces, including the Round Robin Bar, a watering hole favored by Walt Whitman, Mark Twain, Ulysses S. Grant, and Abraham Lincoln. Guest rooms along Pennsylvania Avenue offer views of the Washington Monument, the Ellipse, and the National Mall. The Jenny Lind Suite is the hotel's most requested guest room for romance; tucked under the mansard roof, this three-room space features a bedroom with a canopy bed and vaulted ceiling and direct views of the Washington Monument from the two-person soaking tub.

HOTELS

© PATRICIA KIME

The Willard InterContinental's architecture style is just as impressive as its list of former guests.

Capitol Hill Map 5

HOTELS

The Capitol Hill neighborhood bustles in the daytime and falls fairly quiet at night, with the sounds of laughter and music occasionally drifting from the area's bars and restaurants on the wind. Most lodgings on Capitol Hill are chain hotels found on the Senate side and favored by business travelers; a few bed-and-breakfasts and suite hotels are located on the eastern side of the dome, closer to the neighborhood's busy eateries and bars.

APPLE TREE INN $$

5th St. and Constitution Ave. NE, 202/328-3510, www.bedandbreakfastdc.com

The Apple Tree Inn provides all the comforts of home—a spacious bedroom with a private bath, a living room, a den, and a private courtyard to enjoy morning coffee—because it is someone's home, specifically, Simon and Robyn Hinson-Jones's. A Victorian row house bed-and-breakfast with just one guest room, a stay at the Apple Tree Inn is a chance to see what it's like to live in one of the city's finest neighborhoods. The Apple Tree Inn row house, built in 1881, features many fine architectural details, including fireplaces, pocket doors, 12-foot ceilings, and carved woodwork and moldings. The well-decorated guest suite contains a queen-sized brass bed, a hallway bath exclusively for use by the guests, and a TV. A hot breakfast is served daily by the hosts. The Hinson-Joneses require a two-night minimum. Visitors with allergies should be aware that there is a dog and a cat on the property, but neither is allowed in the guest suite.

CAPITOL HILL SUITES $$

200 C St. SE, 202/543-6000, www.capitolhillsuites.com

For the feel of living in the neighborhood, the Capitol Hill Suites, located a block from the House Cannon Office Building and the Capitol South Metro, offers its guests functional apartment-style accommodations with kitchenettes, desks, and complimentary Internet access in the guest rooms. Favored by business travelers, the Capitol Hill Suites is suited to travelers seeking simple lodgings. Most of the suites are studio-style rooms; those wanting more space or a door between the living room area and a bedroom will need to reserve a deluxe suite. Continental breakfast is included in the room rates, and the hotel offers discount rates for weekend stays. If you arrive in DC by car, be aware that this hotel and nearly every other on Capitol Hill charges more than $30 per day for parking.

◖ HOTEL GEORGE $$$

15 E. St. NW, 800/576-8331 or 202/347-4200, www.hotelgeorge.com

Luxurious, sleek, and chic, Hotel George, originally built in 1929 and purchased by the Kimpton Hotel Group in 2003, pampers its customers, from its wine hour held each weekday in its artfully designed lobby to its complimentary in-room yoga program featuring 24-hour yoga on each room's 32-inch flat-screen TV and a yoga basket with essential yoga equipment. The George has long been one of Washington's top hotels and meeting spots, located near the Capitol on the Senate side and featuring one of the city's finest restaurants, Bistro Bis. Kimpton Hotels are known for luxury; the George is no exception. The hotel boasts a large modern art collection, attentive staff, well-stocked minibars, plush robes, and luxury linens. It also has a favorable pet policy with no restrictions on weight or size.

HYATT REGENCY WASHINGTON ON CAPITOL HILL $$$

400 New Jersey Ave. NW, 202/737-1234 or 800/311-5192, www.washingtonregency.hyatt.com

With an ideal location for travelers on business to the Capitol, the Hyatt Regency features everything you expect from Hyatt, including a huge atrium lobby with several bars and a grill, an indoor heated lap pool, quality workout facilities, conference and meetings spaces, business lounges, and a whopping 834 guest rooms, including amply sized doubles as well as king, deluxe, and executive suites. Furnishings are modern, and guest rooms are decorated in neutral shades of gold and brown. Unless you are a member of Hyatt's frequent-stay program, however, be prepared to pay for extras such as breakfast, Wi-Fi, and one of the biggest budget-busters in Washington, parking, which can cost up to $40 per night.

LIAISON CAPITOL HILL ●●

415 New Jersey Ave. NW, 202/638-1616, www.affinia.com

Once a favorite among budget-conscious business travelers when it was the Holiday Inn on the Hill and still a relative bargain in the neighborhood, the Liaison Capitol Hill is now an Affinia Hotel property featuring a contemporary design, a wannabe W of sorts, only warmer, since the hotel's dark, moody, and oh-so-hip lobby and guest rooms are decorated in shades of brown and warm red rather than the W's signature grays, purples, and blacks. As with most hotels on Capitol Hill, the location is ideal for business travelers as well as sightseers. Little luxuries include an in-room pillow menu and a seasonal rooftop pool. A large perk at the Liaison is its in-house restaurant, Art & Soul, offering upscale (and pricey) takes on Southern cuisine from Oprah Winfrey's former chef Art Smith.

PHOENIX PARK HOTEL ●●

520 N. Capitol St. NW, 800/824-5419 or 202/638-6900, www.phoenixparkhotel.com

Reasonably priced for its incredible location adjacent to Union Station and a block from the Capitol Grounds, the Phoenix Park Hotel has distinct European style, with a small lobby,

© PATRICIA KIME

Phoenix Park Hotel

comfortably sized guest rooms, and a hallway leading to the Irish pub in the building on the first floor. Guests can probably guess what the interior promises by the Irish flag flying over the circular drive. The lobby boasts a massive landscape of an Irish castle and lake and a fanciful china cabinet displaying the hotel's collection of Waterford crystal. The property's 149 guest rooms feature king or queen singles or doubles, decorated with damask wallpaper and ornate European-style furniture. All guest rooms come with in-room coffee service, Irish bathrobes, umbrellas, and 32-inch flat-screen TVs; many have views of Union Station or the U.S. Capitol.

Dupont Circle

Map 6

Dupont Circle is one of DC's liveliest residential neighborhoods, with charming cafés, fine restaurants, shops, galleries, and a mix of people—young, old, gay, straight, artsy, brainy. This is the city's bohemian center. Lodging near Dupont is plentiful, ranging from large full-service business hotels to intimate boutiques and reasonable bed-and-breakfasts, each within close proximity of the traffic circle that serves as the district's heart. The rest of the city is as close as your hotel's distance to one of the area's two Metro stops.

CARLYLE SUITES HOTEL $$$

1731 New Hampshire Ave. NW, 202/234-3200 or 800/944-5377, www.carlylesuites.com

Close to the shops and restaurants of Dupont Circle, the Carlyle Suites features a beautiful art deco lobby and 175 custom-decorated guest rooms with kitchens, Tempur-Pedic beds, and brightly colored upholstered furniture. Guests receive passes for a nearby health club, and laundry can be done on premises. The Carlyle Suites is pet-friendly—no extra fees for your pooch, but hotel managers ask you call ahead. Another bonus: The hotel has a handful of free parking spots for guests' use, a virtually unheard-of perquisite at city lodgings.

THE DUPONT AT THE CIRCLE $$$

1604 19th St. NW, 202/332-5251, www.dupontatthecircle.com

Located on a residential street just steps from Dupont Circle, the Dupont is a B&B in two 1885 Victorian row houses, with nine guest rooms, including several suites, filled with antiques and decorative touches that celebrate the home's era. All guest rooms have private baths and unique themes. The Lincoln Room contains a fireplace with a decorative tile surround and furnishings similar to those seen in the White House's Lincoln Bedroom. The Plum Suite takes up an entire floor, featuring a living room with a fireplace and a bedroom with a wrought-iron bed, a desk with an antique

chair, and stained-glass Tiffany-style lamps. Breakfast, included in the room rates, consists largely of fresh breads and rolls from a nearby bakery along with fruit, coffee, and juice.

HOTEL HELIX $$$

1430 Rhode Island Ave. NW, 202/462-9001, www.hotelhelix.com

A pop art property that isn't afraid of block color schemes, neon cabinetry, Barbie-doll throw pillows, and even bunk beds, this Kimpton property caters to fans of retro-chic, teenagers, and the young at heart, especially those who enjoy that they can buy Twizzlers in the minibar. The place is sassy, but the service is anything but: The staff is attentive and ensures that newcomers feel welcome and know about the hotel's perks, including a champagne hour in the afternoon and movies on the back patio. As with many Kimpton properties, Hotel Helix features some specialty guest rooms—a few with in-room exercise equipment, some with kitchens, and others with platform beds and bunks for families.

HOTEL PALOMAR WASHINGTON $$$

2121 P St. NW, 202/448-1800 or 877/866-3070, www.hotelpalomar-dc.com

The snazzy Hotel Palomar, a Kimpton property, has captured the spirit of the Dupont Circle neighborhood with its chic lobby adorned with decorative arts and guest rooms decked out in original art and zebrawood furnishings. The accommodations, accented with shades of magenta, blueberry, and grape, come equipped with an oversize work desk with built-in electrical outlets and ergonomic chairs. Specialty guest rooms include several Motion Rooms, containing in-room exercise equipment, and King Spa Suites, with two-person soaking tubs. Bathrooms feature deep sinks, granite countertops, and top-of-the-line toiletries. In-room coffeemakers are available on request. As a Kimpton property, the Hotel Palomar offers a complimentary wine reception in the evenings and packages catering to any furry companions guests may have along for the trip. The Hotel Palomar has an outdoor pool, open during the summer, and an on-site fitness center.

HOTEL ROUGE
1315 16th St. NW, 202/232-8000 or 800/368-5689, www.rougehotel.com

Appropriately named, red dominates the Hotel Rouge, from the deep red lobby with red tile floor and stainless steel accents and the red, gray, and stainless Bar Rouge to the red leather platform beds and red draperies in the guest rooms. Oddly, the minibars are bright orange, seemingly jacked from the flamboyant Hotel Helix, a Kimpton property less than a mile away. As with most hotels in this group, Hotel Rouge hosts a nightly wine hour (red wine and red beer) and is pet-friendly, providing beds, treats, bowls, and local tags for your companion. Room extras at Hotel Rouge include access to a small fitness center, complimentary coffee, and one night's free parking for red cars, a savings of more than $30.

HOTEL TABARD INN $$
1739 N St. NW, 202/785-1277, www.tabardinn.com

The Tabard Inn is a popular destination in DC for dining and brunch, but it is also a hideaway for city visitors, a 40-room hotel furnished with vintage finds and antiques. Named for the inn in Chaucer's *Canterbury Tales,* it has a comfortable lodge feel, with plastered or brick walls, heavy five-paneled doors, wrought iron beds, fireplaces, ceiling fans, and more. It actually served as a boarding house during World War II for Navy WAVES; a few guest rooms even have shared baths (and breakfast is included in the room rates, so perhaps it is more proper to think of it as a B&B than a hotel). Also, the rooms have no TVs, and the place has no elevator. But the public rooms feature cozy fireplaces, the restaurant is a top destination in the city for new American cuisine, and the bar features a menu replete with historic and creative cocktail recipes.

THE JEFFERSON $$$
1200 16th St. NW, 202/448-2300, www.jeffersondc.com

The 99-room Jefferson is one of Washington's finest hotels, built in 1923 as an upscale apartment, transformed into a hotel in the 1950s, and renovated in 2009, an architectural gem that pays tribute to the nation's third president (who also served as the country's first secretary of state). The elegant guest rooms pay homage to Jefferson's posts, featuring French and American reproduction furnishings, many with four-poster beds or leather upholstered headboards and footboards, drum tables, marble baths, and touches like fresh flowers, crystal vases, and fine woodwork. Such finery camouflages each room's technology upgrades, like TVs disguised with mirrors in the bathrooms and games and game consoles on request. Suites are themed according to Jefferson's many interests, including oenology, farming, and butterfly collecting. Decorative touches throughout the hotel include Jefferson-era maps and books, and even a few documents signed by Jefferson. When wandering through the public spaces, take note of the barrel skylight, rediscovered and restored in the most recent renovation. The Jefferson was recognized as one of the "World's Best" hotels by *Travel + Leisure* magazine in 2010.

MANSION AT O $$$
2020 O St. NW, 202/496-2000, www.omansion.com

If you prefer minimalism and clean lines, the Mansion at O is not for you. A string of late-1800s redbrick row houses connected by mysterious passages and secret doors, the Mansion is a museum, foundation, popular brunch destination, and secret hideaway, stuffed to the rafters with art, china, home furnishings, musical instruments, costume jewelry, record albums, linens, books, statuary, and more, most of it for sale. The 37 guest rooms and suites are decorated in unique themes and cater to guests' privacy and comfort, as long as guests have no issue with a decorating scheme seemingly forged in the mind of the Mad Hatter. One of the guest rooms is hidden behind a bookcase and comes with instructions on how to find it; the log cabin is a two-story suite with leather furniture, Remington bronze sculptures, and its own aquarium; a penthouse takes up an entire floor with a living room, a kitchen, two bathrooms, its own elevator, and numerous security cameras. Long-term stays are allowed, and the Mansion offers a number of business services, including conference rooms for guest use. The Sunday brunch at the Mansion is a big weekly draw, with live music and jam sessions. Diners are allowed to tour the property with their champagne to peek at the facility's nearly 100 rooms and all its stuff.

THE NORMANDY 💲💲

2118 Wyoming Ave. NW, 202/483-1350, www.doylecollection.com

The Normandy is a delightful 75-room boutique hotel that offers guests a sense of what it's like to live in Washington, located on a quiet street near a number of embassies but just a short walk from two major entertainment hubs: Dupont Circle, with its shops, restaurants, and bars, and Adams Morgan, with its all-night clubs and dance spots. Guest rooms are sumptuously decorated and surprisingly unfussy, given that many of them have toile wallpaper and rich draperies. Guest rooms feature free Wi-Fi access, flat-screen TVs, and Nespresso coffee machines as well as marble baths with Bath & Body Works toiletries.

THE TOPAZ 💲💲

1733 N St. NW, 202/393-3000, www.topazhotel.com

If modern and hip is your style but the color red doesn't suit you, bypass the Hotel Rouge and consider the Topaz, a Kimpton hotel whose decorating scheme is in jewel tones and whose theme is wellness. In the mornings, guests at this 99-room property can enjoy a complimentary energy drink during a Morning Power hour. A free yoga program—mats, instructional television channel, and New Age CDs—is available to all, and the truly committed can choose to stay in a Yoga guest room that features a yoga nook with a mirror and amenities such as music, mats, and magazines. The Topaz is located on a quiet street of row houses containing embassies, apartments, and other small hotels two blocks from the bustle of Dupont Circle.

WASHINGTON HILTON 💲💲💲

1919 Connecticut Ave. NW, 202/483-3000 or 800/445-8667, www.washington.hilton.com

A $140 million renovation has pumped new life into the Washington Hilton, a 1965 midcentury modern hotel that sits on nearly six acres on Connecticut Avenue between the busy K Street business corridor and the galleries, shops, and restaurants of Dupont Circle. Primarily a business hotel, the Hilton contains more than 1,000 guest rooms and studio suites decorated in shades of gold, taupe, and gray and features remodeled bathrooms with granite counters, cherry cabinetry, and Crabtree and Evelyn toiletries. Property highlights include a 25-meter

The Washington Hilton sits in a modern space near Dupont Circle.

© PATRICIA KIME

saltwater swimming pool, a courtyard and gardens with fire pits and fountains, and the International Ballroom, a 36,000-square-foot ballroom whose interior design seems straight out of a *Jetsons* cartoon. It's one of the region's largest ballrooms and the only one in the area able to serve hot dinners to 4,000 guests nearly simultaneously. If you are lucky enough to attend an event in this space, go, if only to enjoy the funky decor. While most people call the Washington Hilton by its proper name, some still refer to it as the "Hinckley Hilton." This is the site where Ronald Reagan was shot on March 30, 1981.

Adams Morgan and U Street   Map 7

HOTELS

Adams Morgan and U Street are neighborhoods known for their individualism, the former having grown into a global village of sorts, the latter preserving the history of DC's African American culture. Staying in this neighborhood is a chance to enjoy the local scene, to mix with a younger or international crowd, and to enjoy the city's eclecticism and soul.

ADAM'S INN 🏷️🏷️

1746 Lanier Place NW, 202/745-3600 or 800/578-6807, www.adamsinn.com

A gathering place for budget travelers from around the world, Adam's Inn features 25 guest rooms in two adjacent row houses and a carriage house, simply furnished with vintage and antique finds, some with private baths and some with a washstand in the room but shared baths down the hall. Rooms are spacious and air-conditioned; amenities include free Wi-Fi and the use of common rooms, including a garden patio, sitting rooms with televisions, and a guest kitchen with a refrigerator and a microwave. A simple breakfast of bagels, cereal, toast, and fruit is served daily. Adams Inn is about seven blocks from a Metro stop and within walking distance of the National Zoo; it's just four blocks from the heart of Adams Morgan nightlife along 18th Street NW.

BED AND BREAKFAST ON U STREET 🏷️🏷️

17th and U Street NW, 202/328-3510 or 877/893-3233, www.bedandbreakfastonustreet.com

A four-room guest house set in a brownstone, the Bed and Breakfast on U offers lodgings in a place where historically, there have been few. Guest rooms are spread out over two floors: The largest suite features a queen bed and a seating area and an additional living room space with pullout sofas, appropriate for a family. A queen bed with a large seating area is also on the second floor, and two queen rooms occupy the third floor. All guest rooms feature TVs and free wireless Internet; the hosts even provide a laptop for guest use. A continental breakfast is served in the morning, featuring rolls, breads, jams, fruit, juices, and boiled eggs.

SWANN HOUSE 🏷️🏷️🏷️

1808 New Hampshire Ave. NW, 202/265-4414, www.swannhouse.com

The gorgeous Swann House is a nine-room inn set in an 1883 Romanesque Revival mansion, a romantic spot where guests are pampered in their rooms, many of which have fireplaces, whirlpool baths, and private decks. All guest rooms have cable TV and telephones; Internet access is complimentary. The Il Duomo room is one of the property's most requested, set in the home's apex and featuring Gothic windows, cathedral ceilings, a skylight, and a fireplace along with a turreted bathroom with a gilded dome ceiling. Several guest rooms are more formal, with traditional furnishings expected in a bed-and-breakfast, such as four-poster beds and fireplaces; others have sleek lines and modern furnishings or unique themes, like the Asian Shanghai'daway, with ebony furnishings and an elegant travertine marble shower, or the Serengeti Suite, with rattan and beige accents.

WINDSOR INN $\textbf{\$\$}$
1842 16th St. NW, 202/667-0300,
www.windsor-inn-dc.com
A small budget inn that was once an apartment complex, the Windsor Inn has furnishings—and a lobby cat—that make it feel more homey than a hotel, with 1920s-era crown moldings, floor tiles, and vintage decor. Guest rooms feature beds, nightstands, a dresser, and a TV with cable and HBO. A continental breakfast is served daily, featuring pastries, fruit, coffee, juice, and cereal.

Georgetown   Map 8

Isolated from the rest of the city because it does not have a Metro station, Georgetown nonetheless is one of the most popular places to hang out, to walk down cobblestone streets and crooked brick sidewalks, to window shop and browse in stores, or to wander down a path alongside a historic canal. Georgetown is the place where visitors can feel the city's historic roots, its beginnings as a Southern tobacco port, and its prosperity through the years.

◖ THE FOUR SEASONS $\textbf{\$\$\$}$
2800 Pennsylvania Ave. NW, 202/342-0444 or
800/332-3442, www.fourseasons.com/washington
The luxury Four Seasons is the city's only Forbes five-star hotel, a property with 222 guest rooms, top-notch service, lavish appointments, and even a 1,650-piece contemporary art collection. The hotel underwent a $34 million makeover in 2008, opening just before President Barack Obama's inauguration and quickly reclaiming its spot as the preferred lodging in the city for Hollywood stars, music icons, and foreign diplomats. The staff is trained to cater to guests' every need, and the concierges are among the city's finest, well connected and able to obtain difficult-to-get tickets, private tours, and more. Guest rooms are spacious and stately, with views of Georgetown, the C&O Canal, or the property's landscaped courtyard. Furniture is traditional with modern lines; luxuries include fresh flowers, fine linens, and marble bathrooms with imported toiletries. Bourbon

Steak, in the rear of the hotel overlooking the canal, is one of the city's top restaurants and also draws a vibrant crowd nightly to its chic bar.

GEORGETOWN INN $\textbf{\$\$}$
1310 Wisconsin Ave. NW, 202/333-8900 or
800/368-5922, www.georgetowninn.com
Every university has one: a place where well-to-do parents stay when visiting their sons and daughters. The Georgetown Inn is the hotel of choice for Georgetown University alums and bill-payers, situated directly on Wisconsin Avenue among the neighborhood's bustling shops and vibrant bars. The inn occupies a collection of restored row houses, and its 95 guest rooms are decorated in a mix of 19th-century American reproduction furniture and comfortable upholstered pieces. Amenities on the property include an on-site fitness center and in-room spa services. Some guest rooms feature full baths with bidets, unusual in this part of the world, even for a city as international as DC.

GEORGETOWN SUITES $\textbf{\$\$}$
1111 30th St. NW and 1000 29th St. NW, 202/298-1600
or 800/348-7203, www.georgetownsuites.com
Popular with families and business travelers in Washington for extended stays, the Georgetown Suites is two properties: one at the edge of Georgetown, a quick walk to bustling M Street; the other closer to Washington Harbor, practically on top of the Whitehurst Freeway. The travelers I know prefer the former,

© PATRICIA KIME

one of Georgetown Suites's two properties

although both sites offer similar accommodations: studio, one-, and two-bedroom suites with kitchens, work areas, and flat-screen TVs. The main building in Georgetown also has several two-level, two-bedroom townhomes for larger groups and families. Nice touches include continental breakfast, 24-hour coffee in the dining room, and complimentary Wi-Fi.

HOTEL MONTICELLO $$
1075 Thomas Jefferson St. NW, 202/337-0900 or 800/388-2410, www.monticellohotel.com
Located steps from the C&O Canal and M Street, this small hotel with 47 studio and one-bedroom suites has a European feel, with small public spaces and larger guest quarters. Furnishings are traditional American style, such as Chippendale reproduction armchairs and Sheraton-style sofas. All guest rooms feature a wet bar with a refrigerator and a microwave, coffeemakers, plush terry robes, marble bathrooms with lighted makeup mirrors, and Hermès bath products. Breakfast and Wi-Fi are complimentary. As with many Georgetown hotels, the Monticello is not convenient to the Metro, so if you plan to stay in this popular neighborhood, prepare to walk or budget in taxi fare for your trips around town.

LATHAM HOTEL $$
3000 M St. NW, 202/726-5000, www.thelatham.com
An unassuming brick facade hides a hotel containing one of Washington's destination restaurants, Citronelle, along with 142 guest rooms geared mainly to business travelers. In-room amenities include oversize work desks, coffeemakers, morning newspapers, and in the bathrooms, heated towel racks and lighted makeup mirrors. The hotel has two two-story suites called carriage rooms that feature a living room, a half bath, and a refrigerator on the first floor and a master bedroom upstairs. Because of the hotel's design, some rooms have no windows; claustrophobics should inquire about room availability before booking. The rooftop sundeck and pool are a popular gathering place in the summer; leave time during your visit to enjoy this amenity.

THE RITZ-CARLTON
GEORGETOWN $$$

3100 South St. NW, 202/912-4100 or 800/241-3333,
www.ritzcarlton.com/hotels/georgetown

A small, intimate hotel housed in the neighborhood's former incinerator near the waterfront, the Ritz-Carlton has 86 guest rooms decorated in contemporary style, a direct contrast to the property's clubby Degrees Bar and wood-and-brick-trimmed restaurant. Many of the guest rooms offer river and sunset views but also unfortunately overlook (and are exposed to the noise from) the Whitehurst Freeway, an elevated roadway that has long been a target for demolition. The Ritz-Carlton's Boutique Spa features Prada products and exercise equipment, and the AMC Loews Georgetown 14-screen movie theater occupies the same block. The attractions of Georgetown lie just two blocks away.

Greater Washington DC   Map 9

Many of Washington's best lodgings aren't found within the tidy confines of map boxes. Others are located so close to DC in Virginia that they are actually closer to the Lincoln Memorial than the city's northernmost neighborhoods. Just because a hotel doesn't have a DC address doesn't mean it's inconvenient or unworthy of mention. After all, the Pentagon has a Virginia zip code and phone number and no one disparages it for being in "the suburbs." The outlying areas offer a wide selection of accommodations; choose one within a few blocks of a Metro station and you'll barely know that you're not staying "in the city."

GAYLORD NATIONAL RESORT AND
CONFERENCE CENTER $$

201 Waterfront St., Oxon Hill, Md., 301/965-2000,
www.gaylordnational.com

A Disney World of hotels, the Gaylord is a spectacle to behold, with a jaw-dropping 19-story atrium and center court that contains two full-sized reproduction colonial houses, shops, a cobblestone "street," and a restaurant that overlooks an artificial dock and wharf. The over-the-top design nearly overshadows the hotel's natural setting on the banks of the Potomac River just south of the Woodrow Wilson Bridge with views of area marinas and green spaces. The Gaylord is the cornerstone of the $2.1 billion National Harbor development, a mixed-use area opened in 2008 designed to capitalize on Oxon Hill's waterfront and its proximity to the city. Most guests who stay at the Gaylord have business here, either a conference or an event. The Gaylord has 2,000 guest rooms, a gargantuan fitness room, seven restaurants, an arcade, a 24-meter indoor pool, an outdoor pool in warmer months, and a full-service spa. The surrounding area has many new restaurants, shops, and nightspots and is a 20-minute (up to 40 minutes in traffic) drive to downtown Washington. The hotel offers shuttles to DC and is close to a water "taxi" stand (more like a tour boat than a real water taxi) to Old Town Alexandria across the river.

HOTEL PALOMAR ARLINGTON $$

1121 N. 19th St., Arlington, Va., 703/351-9170 or
866/505-1001, www.hotelpalomar-arlington.com

Why stay at the Kimpton-owned Palomar in Arlington when there is another Hotel Palomar just three miles away in the city, at Dupont Circle? The answer, of course, is money. Hotels in the "suburbs" tend to cost less, and this one does—a price difference of more than $60—but it's actually just as close to the Metro and even closer to the restaurants and nightlife of Georgetown than the downtown location. Another plus? Many guest rooms have views of the Potomac River. The Palomar Arlington is located in a development designed by architect James Freed of the renowned Pei Cobb Freed firm. Like its DC counterpart, its interiors celebrate the arts, showcasing original sculpture and decorative arts in the lobby, restaurants, and guest rooms. Guest suites are decorated with contemporary furnishings, with linens and accents in deep orange, grays, and zebra stripes, and all rooms come equipped with an oversized work desk with built-in electrical outlets and ergonomic chairs. Specialty rooms include several Motion Rooms, with in-room exercise equipment, and Waterview King Suites, with large soaking tubs and panoramas of the river and the striking Key Bridge.

HYATT ARLINGTON $$

1325 Wilson Blvd., Arlington, Va., 703/525-1234, www.arlington.hyatt.com

The recently renovated Hyatt Arlington, just across the Key Bridge from Georgetown, is popular for its prime location, a block from the Roslyn Metro and conveniently located near restaurants, an underground supermarket, and convenience stores. Often bustling with families and tour groups, the hotel satisfies customers with its friendly staff and spotless, if not huge, guest rooms, some with views of Georgetown and the National Cathedral. The Hyatt is just a short walk from Ray's Hell Burger, the cash-only burger joint made famous by the Food Channel and President Obama.

KALORAMA GUEST HOUSE $

2700 Cathedral Ave. NW, 202/588-8188, www.kaloramaguesthouse.com

Simple furnishings in a grouping of row houses, a TV and a telephone in the common areas, free Wi-Fi access, and a substantial continental breakfast bring repeat travelers back to Kalorama Guest House, one of the city's first B&B-style lodgings. Amenities include free afternoon cookies and lemonade and a glass of sherry in the evening. The houses are close to the National Zoo and Woodley Park Metro as well as Embassy Row and the sizzling nightlife of Adams Morgan.

OMNI SHOREHAM HOTEL $$

2500 Calvert St. NW, 202/234-0700 or 800/843-6664, www.omnishorehamhotel.com

The historic 834-room Omni Shoreham drips with 1930s elegance, greeting guests in the lobby with plush furniture, crystal chandeliers, fine fabrics, and classic style and service that somehow manages to be unpretentious, even though the place is a member in the Historic Hotels of America, a program overseen by the National Trust for Historic Preservation. The Omni Shoreham's guest rooms are large, the smallest being nearly 300 square feet, and its public areas are spacious as well, with wide hallways and huge arched windows that let in natural light. The hotel has an outdoor pool set amid its six manicured acres as well as an in-house restaurant and bar, and it is within walking distance of the Metro. Guests who believe in ghosts may want to steer clear of the aptly named "Ghost Suite." Two women—a housekeeper and a young resident—died in the rooms in the 1930s, and one or both of them reportedly haunt the spaces.

RESIDENCE INN COURTHOUSE $$

1401 N. Adams St., Arlington, Va., 703/312-2100

Optimal for families looking to save some money during a visit to Washington or business travelers on extended stays, the Residence Inn Courthouse is a sparkling new property featuring 176 suites with full kitchens, including granite counters, blond cabinetry, and stainless steel appliances, including dishwashers. Beds and linens are comfortable, if not top-of-the-line, but guest rooms feature flat-screen TVs and bathrooms with granite countertops. The hotel has a small fitness facility and an indoor pool and serves a delicious hot breakfast daily with eggs, sausages, and waffles. For the environmentally conscious, this property has met county LEED requirements, meaning it was designed with energy conservation and a reduced carbon footprint in mind. This location is a stone's throw from the Courthouse Metro stop as well as Ray's The Steaks and Five Guys, and it is just blocks from the area's premier dining district in Clarendon. Morning coffee is served in-house, but for an adventure, check out the friendly Java Shack two blocks away on North Franklin Street. A local hangout, owner Dale Roberts has created a coffeehouse version

HOTELS

of *Cheers* in this building that once served as headquarters to the American Nazi Party.

WASHINGTON MARRIOTT WARDMAN PARK $$

2660 Woodley Rd. NW, 202/328-2000 or 800/228-9290, www.marriotthotels.com/wasdt

The city's largest hotel is the Washington Marriott Wardman Park, a sprawling campus of multiple buildings on 16 leafy acres containing 1,316 guest rooms and suites and a number of ballrooms and event spaces. The original section, built in 1918, is a quiet historic tower of rooms with high ceilings and ornate interiors, including fanciful crown moldings, silk draperies, and French reproduction furniture. The other buildings—a 1953 addition and a 1964 tower—have been renovated and finished with Marriott's top-of-the-line furniture, including wooden headboards with built-in reading lights, flat-screen TVs, and comfortable upholstered chairs and desks. The property has a large fitness center and an outdoor pool, and it sits directly across Connecticut Avenue from the National Zoo, providing a convenient, free place to walk and run from dawn to dusk.

WOODLEY PARK GUEST HOUSE $$$

2647 Woodley Rd. NW, 202/667-0218 or 866/677-0218, www.dcinns.com/woodley.html

The upscale Woodley Park Guest House features 13 guest rooms in a 1920s-era home decorated with fine antiques and reproductions. All but two guest rooms have private baths; most

© PATRICIA KIME

The porch is inviting at Woodley Park Guest House.

have seating areas, desks, and beautiful beds decorated with coverlets, quilts, and throw pillows. Amenities include fresh continental breakfast, parking for a fee, access to a large library, and the chance to sit a spell on a large front porch, enjoying the quiet neighborhood with its towering trees and vast green spaces. The house is located a block from the Woodley Park Metro stop.

EXCURSIONS FROM WASHINGTON DC

Marble-clad Washington lies in the Mid-Atlantic, a region of geographic diversity and historical significance, where mountains and sandy beaches are within a morning's drive and the nation's history—political and military battles—played out across the area's fledgling cities, farmland, and wilderness. East of Washington, roughly three hours away, are the sprawling shores of the Atlantic: remote undeveloped beaches like Assateague, Maryland, where wild ponies roam free, along with small family beach towns in Delaware and the bustling boardwalks and high-rise developments of Ocean City, Maryland. To reach the beach, travelers must cross spectacular Chesapeake Bay and the vast Eastern Shore, an expanse of farmland also known as the Delmarva Peninsula. The bay is an historic waterway plied and mapped in 1607 by Capt. John Smith, 13 years before the Pilgrims landed at Plymouth, Massachusetts (which itself was named by Smith in 1615 when he explored the Massachusetts coast). The Chesapeake Bay remains a significant food source for the area and is a recreational treasure known worldwide for its sailing and boating activities. The Eastern Shore beyond consists of farms, marsh, rivers, and fishing villages that hold their own special charm, including a slower-paced lifestyle that draws Washingtonians for weekends of relaxation and peaceful respite. Traversing the bay to the Eastern Shore is the Chesapeake Bay Bridge, which carries U.S. 50 and U.S. 301 past Maryland's state capitol, Annapolis, a favorite day-trip for its waterfront scenery, charming bed-and-breakfasts,

HIGHLIGHTS

LOOK FOR ◖ TO FIND RECOMMENDED SIGHTS, ACTIVITIES, DINING, AND LODGING.

◖ **Most Impressive Home:** Built by brothers Augustine and Lawrence Washington and developed into an estate worthy of a president by their half-brother George Washington, **Mount Vernon** is the finest and most famous colonial farm still in existence, on 500 well-tended acres overlooking the Potomac River (page 242).

◖ **Best Off-the-Beaten-Path Site:** The home of the forgotten Founding Father George Mason is one of the area's most unsung colonial structures. **Gunston Hall** has many of the trimmings of Mount Vernon – waterfront, gorgeous grounds and trails, beautifully restored interiors and a gift shop – without the crowds (page 243).

◖ **Best Way to Enjoy the Sunset:** Climb aboard a 74-foot schooner and enjoy a **sailboat tour** at dusk on Chesapeake Bay near Annapolis. Sister ships *Woodwind* and *Woodwind II* set sail for two-hour excursions (page 251).

◖ **Most Impressive Church:** A 200-foot dome, seating for 2,500, impressive stained glass windows, and a crypt guarded by U.S. Marines make the chapel at the **U.S. Naval Academy** a must-see (page 252).

◖ **Nearest Civil War Battlefield:** Skirmishes and battles took place across the region between 1861 and 1865, but on July 21, 1861, the first major land battle of the Civil War occurred just a morning's ride from Washington at **Manassas National Battlefield,** otherwise known as the Battle of Bull Run (page 258).

◖ **Best Grown-Up Outing:** Hire a car, rent a limo, or find a designated driver, and head to **Virginia's vineyards:** Loudoun County has 28 wineries and tasting rooms (page 262).

© ISRAEL PABON/123RF.COM

Manassas National Battlefield

EXCURSIONS

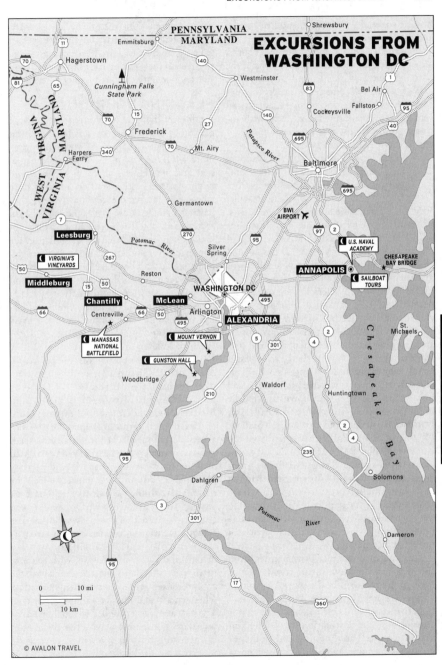

historic colonial architecture, and lively social and dining scene.

West of DC, beyond the immediate suburbs, are open fields, farms, and small towns of the Maryland and Virginia Piedmont, a geographic area of rolling hills and gentle creeks that has spawned a sizeable wine industry, equestrian ventures, and small towns that teem with antiques stores, shops, and fine restaurants. A trip to this area has been labeled as a "Journey through Hallowed Ground" by the National Trust for Historic Preservation for its historical significance: The 175-mile stretch from Gettysburg, Pennsylvania, to Charlottesville, Virginia, contains the homes of six presidents, 58 significant Civil War sites and numerous points of interest for African American and Native American history as well as the colonial period. In this area, a number of small towns and their nearby surroundings draw visitors, including historic Frederick, Maryland, and nearby Antietam Battlefield, site of the single bloodiest day of the Civil War; Leesburg, Virginia, a colonial-era town known for its antiques stores and outlet shopping; and tiny Middleburg, Virginia, in the heart of hunt country, romantic and relaxing, a posh village centrally located near wineries, state parks, and historic sites. Between these towns and DC lie important historic sites such as the Manassas National Battlefield and tiny Bristoe Station. Far to the west, roughly two hours from the city, rise the Blue Ridge Mountains, a segment of the Appalachian Range, with elevations between 2,000 and 3,000 feet, tall enough to sustain small ski resorts and host winter sports, and the Shenandoah Valley, cradling the Shenandoah River, providing opportunities for hiking, white-water rafting, horseback riding, and camping.

Due south of the city, seven miles from the Washington Monument, stands one of the nation's most historic towns, Alexandria, Virginia, home to George Washington and Robert E. Lee, a historic colonial port that is a major daytime destination for dining and nightlife as well as shopping and points of interest. Charming and alluring, Alexandria

has more than 4,000 historic buildings, many along cobblestone streets, and hundreds of art galleries, boutiques, pubs, historic taverns, and fine restaurants—a step back in time with cuisine and amenities planted firmly in the now.

PLANNING YOUR TIME

A bonus of living in Washington is the city's proximity to the country: less than 30 minutes away, you can immerse yourself in a remote wilderness, a place where bald eagles soar and blue herons vie for fish, where you might not see another soul on a hiking trail, where you can paddle down a river without passing a single house. Turn the opposite direction and you'll wind up in a historic colonial town like Alexandria, Virginia, on the Potomac River and chockablock with art galleries, stores, and boutiques as well as historic sites; or Annapolis, Maryland, the state capital, with magnificent universities, the U.S. Naval Academy and St. John's College, a historic statehouse, seafood restaurants, a lively waterfront, and quaint streets lined with colonial and Victorian homes. If you are visiting DC and plan on making any of these trips, Alexandria is a best bet, practically a requirement for history buffs and easily reached by Metro. George Washington's plantation, Mount Vernon, lies roughly 25 minutes south of Alexandria along a stunning scenic parkway, accessible by tour bus or car. A morning spent at Mount Vernon can be followed up with an afternoon and evening out in Alexandria, a city so compact you can park your car, stroll the streets, have dinner and drinks, and be back at your hotel in downtown DC before your coach turns into a pumpkin. Every other destination mentioned here lies an hour away by car. Annapolis, roughly 45 minutes away, is a delightful day trip destination, with room to roam, places to shop, and the chance for the adventurous to get out on the water on a sailing schooner, a boat cruise, or a simple water taxi. The city also has a number of small bed-and-breakfasts and chain hotels for those who want to linger longer. If you have a night or weekend to spare, consider heading west to the Virginia countryside for a mini break. Again, the destination is not far—an hour's drive—but a trip to hunt country is a step into a romantic world of wineries and bed-and-breakfasts, historic Civil War battlefields and plantations, point-to-point horseracing and equestrian farms, and the opportunity to hike miles of forest or fish along pristine rivers.

Alexandria

Older than Washington DC itself, Alexandria, Virginia, is a historic city that melds the charm of yesteryear with attractions desired most by visitors today, including top restaurants, chic boutiques, interesting art galleries, lively bars, and notable sights. Easily accessible from DC by Metro, car, or even bicycle, the city, in most Washingtonians' minds, is simply another neighborhood they travel to for top-shelf entertainment and nightlife, a place for relaxation, recreation, and absorbing the area's history without leaving the comfort of their own backyard. Founded in 1749 by Scots 50 years before the site for Washington was selected, Alexandria grew as a bustling and wealthy seaport, declared by the Duc de Liancourt in 1796 as "the handsomest town in Virginia—indeed it is among the finest in the United States." Today, that beauty continues to shine. Old Town Alexandria, as the historic center is called, is on the National Register of Historic Places, the third-oldest federal historic district in the country, a mix of preserved 18th- and 19th-century townhomes and commercial buildings mixed with World War II–era warehouses, reproduction row houses, and historic taverns, churches, and businesses.

Just eight miles south of Alexandria lies Mount Vernon, George Washington's plantation, restored to its glory and now home to a large visitors center that contains numerous artifacts from Washington's life and three forensically reconstructed wax figures of the first president at ages 19, 45, and 57—worth the price of admission alone. Mount Vernon is among the finest of Virginia's plantation homes, run by a foundation that refuses to rest on its laurels; each year, the Mount Vernon Ladies Association demonstrates its commitment to preservation, historical research, and outreach, sponsoring public events such as wine festivals and colonial days, refurbishing outbuildings that include Washington's grist mill, and loaning artifacts to museums around the country. Washington began his career as a surveyor; at age 17, before he moved to Mount Vernon, he surveyed the land that became Alexandria. Many of the buildings that Washington and wife, Martha, frequented still exist in Alexandria today and are open to the public, including Gadsby's Tavern, where Washington celebrated his 66th birthday, and the Stabler-Leadbeater Apothecary, where Mrs. Washington purchased remedies and medicinal ingredients, including, according to store

© PATRICIA KIME

Old Town Alexandria

records, a bottle of castor oil just days before her death. Alexandria also sat at the crossroads of the Civil War, occupied within the first month of the war and firmly rooted in its ties to the Confederacy. After the Civil War, the small city suffered few of the consequences of towns elsewhere in the vanquished South; its location, on the Potomac River near Washington, a major railroad hub, sheltered it from decline. In the 1930s, it again made history as the site of one of the first civil rights sit-ins: In 1939, five African Americans staged a protest in the whites-only city library. The act forced the city to open a separate library for African Americans—not integration, but a step toward that ultimate goal.

Alexandria is a compact city easily traversed by foot. King Street is its major artery, lined with shops, boutiques, restaurants, and bars, and similar businesses are found throughout Old Town, along Washington Street and quiet side streets. The King Street Metro Station, at the head of the bustling Old Town shopping district, lies roughly a mile west of the Alexandria waterfront. In addition to its historic area, the city has fun, funky neighborhoods like Del Ray, an early 1900s streetcar suburb popular with families and home to ice cream parlors, restaurants, and an arts community. Del Ray is reachable by car, taxi, or Alexandria city's DASH transit system.

SIGHTS
Boat Cruises
A number of boat tours and cruises leave from Alexandria City Marina, behind the Torpedo Factory on Union Street, including trips to Mount Vernon, tours of the waterfront to the Woodrow Wilson Bridge, and event cruises like pirate parties and puppy voyages.
Potomac River Boat Company (Cameron St. at the water, 703/684-0580, www.potomac riverboatco.com) runs tours from one of its seven vessels as well as a water-taxi service to National Harbor and Georgetown. Sightseeing cruises include a 40-minute trip along the Alexandria waterfront on the *Admiral Tilp,* a double-decker launch that plies the waters

of the Potomac along the city, motoring past sights like the gardens of Founders Park, the homes of Admiral's Row, and the tiny historic white clapboard lighthouse at Jones Point.

Carlyle House
The magnificent Carlyle House (121 N. Fairfax St., 703/549-2997, www.carlylehouse.org, Tues.–Sat. 10 A.M.–4 P.M., Sun. noon–4 P.M. $5 adults, $3 children, free under age 5) is a preserved Georgian Palladian manor home built in 1753 by city founder and Scottish merchant John Carlyle. The enormous home, with elegant public spaces and lovely family rooms, hosted meetings of colonial governors with General Edward Braddock to discuss financing for the French and Indian Wars. Sandwiched between the Potomac River and what was once the city's thriving market square, it was designed for both life and work: Carlyle ran his merchant export business from the grounds and lived in sumptuous finery in the manor house. Today, the home's stunning formal gardens draw Alexandrians for picnics and relaxation.

Christ Church
One of 10 Anglican churches built in Virginia in the 18th century, Christ Church (118 N. Washington St., 703/549-1450, www .historicchristchurch.org, tours Mon.–Sat. 9 A.M.–4 P.M., Sun. 2–4:30 P.M., donation) is a handsome colonial Georgian house of worship, little unchanged since George Washington, and later Civil War Gen. Robert E. Lee, worshipped here. It held services attended by President Franklin Roosevelt and Winston Churchill on the World Day of Prayer for Peace, January 1, 1942. Its cemetery and grounds feature headstones dating to the late 1700s. One ivy-covered hillock marks the mass grave of 15 Confederate prisoners of war.

Friendship Firehouse
For those with an interest in firefighting, or if you happen to be walking by, drop into Friendship Firehouse (107 S. Alfred St., 703/746-3891, www.historicalexandria.org,

Fri.–Sat. 10 A.M.–4 P.M., Sun. 1–4 P.M.), home to the first volunteer fire company in Alexandria, organized in 1774. It features historic equipment on the first floor, including a hand-drawn fire engine, leather water buckets, and early hoses and axes; the second floor contains photos and memorabilia from the late 1800s. The current structure was built in 1855. The firehouse has a small parking lot that can be used to visit another nearby Alexandria City–owned historic site, The Lyceum.

Gadsby's Tavern

George Washington celebrated his 66th birthday at Gadsby's Tavern (134 N. Royal St., 703/746-4242, www.gadsbystavern .com, Apr.–Oct. Sun.–Mon. 1–5 P.M., Tues.– Sat. 10 A.M.–5 P.M., Nov.–Mar. Wed.–Sat. 11–4 P.M., Sun. 1–4 P.M.), and today, you can do the same; the tavern is both a working restaurant and a museum, although the museum actually contains the rooms where George and Martha Washington danced the night away, and the restaurant is in the former City Hotel. Gadsby's was built in 1785 and hosted a number of VIPs in addition to Washington. Notable guests included Thomas Jefferson, John Adams, James Monroe, and James Madison. The museum is a lesson on colonial-era provisioning and dining, with artifacts from the era and exhibits on food, clothing, and social customs. The City Hotel, built in 1799, was considered a veritable skyscraper at the time of its construction. At three stories plus a dormered attic on an English basement, it towered over nearby homes and businesses.

George Washington Masonic Memorial

The George Washington Masonic Memorial (101 Callahan Dr., 703/683-2007, www .gwmemorial.org, Oct.–Mar. Mon.–Sat. 10 A.M.–4 P.M., Sun. noon–4 P.M., Apr.–Sept. Mon.–Sat. 9 A.M.–4 P.M., Sun. noon–4 P.M., first and second floor free, tower exhibits and observation deck $5 over age 11, $20 families of 5 or more) dominates the skyline of Alexandria on Shuter's Hill, the Freemasons'

temple to member George Washington, charter Worshipful Master of Alexandria Lodge No. 22. The cornerstone of this neoclassical lighthouse-style structure was laid in 1923; it wasn't completed until 1970, funded entirely by donations from Masons. In addition to serving as a repository for Washington memorabilia and belongings, it houses a 17-foot-tall bronze statue of Washington. An observatory on the ninth floor affords vast views of Old Town, the Potomac River, and nearby Washington.

The Lee-Fendall House

Commonly mistaken for Robert E. Lee's boyhood home, the Lee-Fendall House (614 Oronoco St., 703/548-1789, www.lee fendallhouse.org, Tues. and Thurs.–Sat. 10 A.M.–3 P.M., Wed. and Sun. 1–3 P.M., tours on the hour) is a 1785 colonial that was home to 37 members of Virginia's prominent Lee family, starting with Lee cousin Philip Richard Fendall, who built the house in 1787. (He purchased the property from Henry "Lighthorse Harry" Lee, Robert E. Lee's father). The home served as a Union hospital during the Civil War—Northerners were fond of singling out Lee family homes for such use—and is restored and furnished as a museum showcasing the period from 1850 to the 1870s, when members of the Lee family once again lived in it. Its gardens are Victorian in style as well. As for Robert E. Lee, as a child he lived in the house across the street, 607 Oronoco Street, forced to move to Alexandria when his father couldn't afford the upkeep of the family plantation, Stratford Hall, in Westmoreland County, Virginia.

The Lyceum

Set in an 1839 Greek Revival building, The Lyceum (201 S. Washington St., 703/746-4994, www.alexandriahistory.org, Mon.– Sat. 10 A.M.–5 P.M., Sun. 1–5 P.M., $2) is Alexandria's city history museum, with rotating and permanent exhibits on the city's development, from its start as a port through its significance during the civil rights era, including the story told in the movie *Remember The Titans*. Archaeological finds, old photos, historical maps, artworks, and decorative arts from the city's former businesses and residents complete a picture of Alexandria's 250 years.

◖ Mount Vernon

The elegant riverfront estate of George Washington, Mount Vernon (3200 Mount Vernon Memorial Hwy., 703/780-2000, www.mountvernon.org, Apr.–Aug. daily 8 A.M.–5 P.M., Mar. and Sept.–Oct. daily 9 A.M.–5 P.M., Nov.–Feb. daily 9 A.M.–4 P.M., $15 adults, $14 over age 61, $7 ages 6–11) includes Washington's 1735 manor, acres of manicured gardens and wooded grounds, the tomb of George Washington and wife Martha, and outbuildings such as a working blacksmith shop, kitchens, and stables. A new orientation center and the Donald W. Reynolds Museum and Education Center feature a well-scripted film overview of Washington's years as a soldier in the French and Indian Wars, interactive exhibits, immersive experiences, and 700 artifacts, including the first president's famous false teeth. Mount Vernon is one of the prettiest, most inspiring, and most relaxing places to visit in the region. Get there early to avoid the lines for the house, and be mindful of the sometimes snappish women who stand in the hallways to hurry you along. Yes, they own the place, but if this is your once-in-a-lifetime visit, take the time and enjoy this American treasure. The gift shop at Mount Vernon is a personal favorite for special purchases. Down the road from Mount Vernon lies George Washington's Distillery and Gristmill, recently rebuilt and open to the public to demonstrate a facet of Washington's business as a manufacturer of his original-recipe rye whiskey.

WOODLAWN

Two miles west of Mount Vernon, past George Washington's Grist Mill and Distillery, lies Woodlawn (9000 Richmond Hwy., Alexandria, Va., 703/780-4000, www.woodlawn1805.org, Thurs.–Mon. 10 A.M.–5 P.M., $8.50 adults, $4 children), an 1805 Federal plantation built as a wedding gift from Washington to his nephew Lawrence Lewis and wife Nelly Custis, Washington's adopted daughter. The property once covered 2,000 acres and was farmed by

Mount Vernon, George Washington's riverfront estate

more than 90 slaves; their story and the interesting follow-up—that in 1846 the property became a Quaker colony for free laborers and subsequently was subject to numerous attacks by Confederates during the Civil War—is told through tours of the location.

In a locale with numerous 18th- and 19th-century buildings, a home on the grounds of Woodlawn attracts more visitors than the plantation itself: The **Pope-Leighey House** (9000 Richmond Hwy., Alexandria, Va., 703/780-4000, www.popeleighey1940.org, Thurs.–Mon. 10 A.M.–5 P.M., Adults $8.50, Children $4), is the only Frank Lloyd Wright–designed home open to the public in Virginia. Built originally near Falls Church, Virginia, and moved to the grounds of Woodlawn by the National Trust for Historic Preservation when it was threatened with demolition to make room for an interstate highway, this small-scale treasure—all 1,200 square feet of it—is one of Wright's Usonian designs, a work of art for the masses containing original furnishings and architectural elements that include casement windows that open to extend the living spaces, a cantilevered car port, an open fireplace, and built-ins.

◖ GUNSTON HALL

Gunston Hall (10709 Gunston Rd., Mason Neck, Va., 703/550-9220, www.gunston hall.org, daily 9:30 A.M.–4:30 P.M., closed Thanksgiving, Christmas Day, and New Year's Day, $9 adults, $8 seniors, $5 ages 6–18), a contemporary of Mount Vernon, was built between 1755 and 1759 by George Mason, father of the Virginia Declaration of Rights, considered by most to be the architect of the Bill of Rights. Mason's magnificent brick Georgian manor home lies 11 miles from Mount Vernon on the Potomac River, close enough to Washington's home that the president's adopted children traveled to Gunston Hall by boat for dance lessons. The beauty of this magnificent property lies in its solitude; while tour buses and lines and crowds trample all over Mount Vernon's yards, gardens, and interiors, the 550 acres of manicured and wooded grounds, riverfront gardens, the boxwood allée, colonial

terraces, and the magnificent preserved home at Gunston Hall lie still and beautiful, well cared for by the Colonial Dames of America and carrying the spirit of the happy residents who lived there more than 250 years ago.

If you are planning a day of house tours, begin with Mount Vernon in the morning, dine at the Mount Vernon Inn, and head to Woodlawn. If you find yourself in a time crunch, skip the main manor home in favor of the Pope-Leighey House, and then head over to Gunston Hall to complete your day.

Stabler-Leadbeater Apothecary Museum

Visitors to the colonial apothecaries of Fredericksburg or Williamsburg, Virginia, likely have preconceived notions of what they'll find at Stabler-Leadbeater (105–107 S. Fairfax St., 703/746-3852, www.apothecarymuseum .org, Apr.–Oct. Tues.–Sat. 10 A.M.–5 P.M., Sun.–Mon. 1–5 P.M., Nov.–Mar. Wed.–Sat. 11 A.M.–4 P.M.), and it does have familiar glass jars of herbs and ointments for colonial poultices, but it spans more than the colonial period: It is a pharmacy that ran from 1792 to 1933, a perfectly preserved memorial to the evolution of pharmaceuticals. When the store closed, the family who owned it shut the doors and walked away. On the first floor is a full-service retail store; the second floor contains a mysterious storage room, complete with bins for hemp and powdered dragon's blood. One of the most interesting artifacts is Martha Washington's tab dating to April 1802; she requested medicine weeks before she died.

Torpedo Factory Arts Center

The Torpedo Factory Arts Center (105 N. Union St., 703/838-4565, www.torpedofac tory.org, Fri.–Wed. 10 A.M.–6 P.M., Thurs. 10 A.M.–9 P.M.) is an original guns-to-butter operation, an arts center opened in 1974 in a World War II–era torpedo factory. At its commissioning, the complex seemed straight out of the Summer of Love, a communal place where artists vied for studio space in the unheated, un-air-conditioned former warehouse.

EXCURSIONS

In the early years, artists dripped sweat over their work cooled by industrial-size floor fans, and they bundled up with coats and gloves to ward off the winter's chill while doing their work. Today, the Torpedo Factor is far more sophisticated, with the appearance of the original factory but with upgraded systems and new flooring, windows, and a spiral staircase. The factory is home to more than 160 professional artists, a place to watch the process of art and purchase paintings, prints, photography, sculpture, and decorative arts.

Walking Tours

So much of Alexandria's charm lies in its history and architecture, best seen on foot and often better understood by an organized tour. A number of outfits run walking tours in the city, with quite a few held at night to capture the colonial ambience and spookiness of the city along darkened alleyways and shadowy cobblestone streets. **Alexandria Colonial Tours** (703/519-1749, www.alexcolonialtours.com, Mar.–mid-June and Nov. Fri.–Sat. 7:30 P.M. and 9 P.M., Sun. 7:30 P.M., mid-June–Sept. Wed.–Thurs. and Sun. 7:30 P.M. and 9 P.M., Sun. 7:30 P.M., Oct. Fri.–Sat. 7:30 P.M. and 9 P.M., Sun.–Thurs. 7:30 P.M., $12 adults, $6 ages 7–17) coaxes visitors along with period-costumed guides leading their tours by lantern, telling the history of Alexandria through ghost stories, legends, and tales. **Alexandria's Footsteps to the Past** (703/683-3451, www .footstepsttothepast.com, May–Nov. Sun.–Thurs. 7 P.M., Fri.–Sat. 7 P.M. and 8:30 P.M., $10 adults, $5 ages 7–12) hosts historical haunts tours they say even a skeptic will enjoy, full of history and interesting stories of the past, like why a dummy occupies the cupola at 515 North Washington Avenue. All tours leave from the Alexandria Visitors Center (221 King St.) in Ramsay House, the oldest house in Alexandria, built in 1724.

RESTAURANTS

With an economy geared toward tourism, Alexandria is a restaurant town, boasting more than 200 eateries that suit nearly every taste, budget, and food craving. Some of the area's finest chefs have landed in Alexandria, drawn to its charming architecture easily converted to cozy eating rooms and private dining areas. A steady stream of well-heeled locals and visitors sustains these establishments, many which have been in business for years.

Two consistently excellent and popular restaurants in Alexandria are **Restaurant Eve** (110 S. Pitt St., 703/706-0450, www .restauranteve.com, bistro lunch Mon.–Fri. 11:30 A.M.–2:30 P.M., bistro dinner Mon.–Sat. 5:30–10:30 P.M., tasting room dinner Mon.–Sat. 5:30–9:30 P.M., bar and lounge 11:30 A.M.–9:30 P.M.) and **La Bergerie** (218 Lee St., 703/683-1007, www.labergerie.com, lunch Mon.–Sat. 11:30 A.M.–2:30 P.M., dinner Mon.–Sat. 5:30–10 P.M., Sun. 5–9 P.M.), both award-winning restaurants with fine cuisine and extensive wine lists. Restaurant Eve, under owner-chef Cathal Armstrong, earned *Food & Wine*'s Best Wine List award in 2005, and its chef was named to the magazine's Best New Chefs list in 2006. Cuisine is New American with touches of Europe and Ireland, Armstrong's native country, with an emphasis on locally harvested and farmed organic ingredients. The tasting room menu is an opportunity to experience the creativity of an award-winning chef; the bistro is only slightly less casual than the tasting room (jackets required but ties not necessary), serving perfectly prepared and artfully served mid-Atlantic specialties like rib-eye with mizuna and Yukon Gold croquettes, and freshly caught Chesapeake rockfish with spring garlic cream. La Bergerie dishes up classic French cuisine with rich sauces and fresh ingredients; its wine list has been lauded by national magazines and local publications as well, designed to enhance its Provençal main menu and chef's tasting menu. Typical dishes include Dover sole prepared table-side with clarified butter and fresh lemon and tournedos de boeuf accompanied by red-wine shallot sauce and a gratin of Swiss chard and foie gras.

Delicious and expertly prepared cuisine can be found in less formal settings across the city.

The Majestic (911 King St., 703/837-9117, www.majesticcafe.com, lunch Mon.–Sat. 11:30 A.M.–2:30 P.M., dinner Mon.–Thurs. 5:30–10 P.M., Fri.–Sat. 5:30–10:30 P.M., Sun. 1–9 P.M.) emphasizes local and fresh ingredients along with its house-made desserts in a noisy, bustling art deco space that has served as a café since 1949. In the past five years under the ownership of chef Cathal Armstrong from Restaurant Eve and managed by chef Shannon Overmiller, a veteran of several top Washington kitchens, it has gained a following of steady clients for its Southern and Mid-Atlantic dishes as well as a few Italian offerings that include creamy fresh gnocchi, puffs of morel mushroom, and asparagus ravioli. For seafood, the Alexandria offshoot of DC's **Hank's Oyster Bar** (1026 King St., 703/739-4265, www .hanksdc.com, Tues.–Thurs. 5:30–9:30 P.M., Fri. 11:30 A.M.–4 P.M. and 5:30 P.M.–midnight, Sat. 11 A.M.–midnight, Sun. 11 A.M.–9:30 P.M.) is known for its New England–style prepared catches, with steamers, chowders, popcorn shrimp, ribs, oysters, and sandwiches that include lobster rolls. Ribs and schnitzel round out the menu for those who don't care for shellfish. Reservations are advised; this tiny town house fills up quickly.

If the ambience of Old Town has you hankering for Virginia colonial cooking, one of the area's top two destinations for period fare and ambience is the **Mount Vernon Inn** (3200 Mount Vernon Memorial Hwy., 703/780-0011, www.mountvernon.org, lunch daily 11 A.M.–3:30 P.M., dinner Mon.–Thurs. 5–8:30 P.M., Fri.–Sat. 5–9 P.M.). Expectations of restaurants in tourist venues often don't run high, but if you can snag a table at the Mount Vernon Inn, you'll find a surprisingly affordable menu of decently prepared food served by colonial costumed waiters and waitresses. With an extensive menu, a few choices still stand out—the peanut soup (try a cup), the spinach salad, and the rosemary chicken. And maybe by the time you visit, they will have returned their delicious fried chicken, with honey-sweetened batter, to the menu. The dining room at **Gadsby's Tavern** (138 N. Royal St., 703/548-1288, www.gadsbystavernrestaurant.com, lunch Mon.–Sat. 11:30 A.M.–3 P.M., dinner Mon.–Sat. 5:30–10 P.M., brunch Sun. 11 A.M.–5 P.M.), the other top pick, is not the same place that Jefferson, Adams, and Washington quaffed a few (that is the museum next door), but this space, built in 1799, is equally charming, with sack-back Windsor chairs, candles in hurricane lanterns, tavern tables, and period dressed servers. Menu favorites include George Washington's pick, duck breast with scalloped potatoes and corn pudding, and gentlemen's pye, a combination shepherd's pie and cottage pie with a savory red wine sauce.

Alexandria was founded by Scots, but its current residents have a passion for Irish pubs. **Murphy's** (713 King St., 703/548-1717, www .murphyspub.com) is an Old Town institution, one of those American Irish pubs that serves nachos alongside a nightly regaling of the *Unicorn* song, but with enough traditional pub fare, tab brews, humor, police patches on the walls, and rounds of the Red Rover to keep it authentic. In terms of dining, the burgers are probably the best thing on the menu. Murphy's is primarily a bar, drawing boisterous crowds after dinner with nightly entertainment and 14 beverages available on tap, including the usual suspects, Guinness and Harp, along with an India pale ale, a cider, two house ales, and Mooney's Irish Stout. Going head-to-head with Murphy's is **Daniel O'Connell's** (112 King St., 703/739-1124, www.daniel oconnells.com), which opened in 2006 aiming to be slightly more upscale than its rival and place a larger emphasis on food. The decor is authentic Ireland, interiors salvaged from castles, old churches, and Irish monasteries. Top choices on the menu include a delicious rib-eye, lamb burgers, and, of course, fish-and-chips. The whiskey and bourbon menus are extensive.

Alexandria's Del Ray neighborhood, a turn-of-the-century suburb of Sears bungalows and American foursquare farmhouses, has a number of casual restaurants, great for grabbing a meal before a show at the Birchmere or heading back to Washington. A couple of

EXCURSIONS

counter stores stand out as great destinations for a quick bite in this neighborhood, including **Cheesetique** (2411 Mount Vernon Ave., 703/706-5300, www.cheesetique.com, Tues.– Sat. 11 A.M.–10 P.M., Sun. 11 A.M.–2:30 P.M.), a specialty shop that carries gourmet cheeses, wines, and beer from around the world. But behind the retail space is a tiny cheese and wine bar that's open from lunch on with a cheese-centric menu of sandwiches, small plates, delicious soups, and fresh salads and a complementary selection of wine from around the world. In good weather, a patio provides much-needed seating at this popular venue. **Dairy Godmother** (2310 Mount Vernon Ave., 703/683-7767, www.dairygodmother .com, Sun.–Mon. noon–9 P.M., Wed.–Sat. noon–10 P.M., closed Tues.) is a dessert destination that features Wisconsin-style frozen custard. Chocolate and vanilla are always on the menu, with sorbets and special flavors like Bordeaux cherry, pumpkin pie, and orange chocolate shortbread changed daily. In addition to its frozen desserts, the DG also bakes cookies and sells house-made marshmallows.

NIGHTLIFE

The crowd—and the performers—are roughly DC's median age and older at **The Birchmere** (3701 Mount Vernon Ave., 703/549-7500, www.birchmere.com), an intimate 500-seat live music venue, with performers like B. B. King, the Bacon Brothers, Aimee Mann, Joan Armatrading, and Mary Chapin Carpenter. Patrons sit at long tables covered with checkered cloth, and audience members are not allowed to stand unless the performance features a dance floor. This odd rule for a music venue ensures that no one blocks anyone's view, but it doesn't exactly cultivate an atmosphere for rocking out, hence the Birchmere's emphasis on booking acoustic, folk, and adult contemporary artists. Tickets are general admission and should be purchased beforehand, but early birds still get good seats: Patrons receive a second timed ticket when they arrive at the venue; the earlier you pick it up, the earlier you'll be allowed in.

SHOPS

As a colonial port city, mercantilism is a tradition in Alexandria, a place where longtime storefronts stand side-by-side with newcomers, mixing homegrown boutiques and name-brand stores with art galleries, antiques emporiums, and specialty shops. Once considered a top destination for antiques and art, the ongoing economic downturn has taken its toll, with a number of long-standing storefronts closing their doors in the past five years. But a few hardy remain with fine selections of 18th-century furniture, antique jewelry, silverware, and books. As for art, the city's galleries are thriving, carrying a range from small, affordable, locally made pieces to top artists that fetch top dollar. If you want to window-shop, stroll along King Street, where you'll find a panoply of stores.

Boutiques

An American in Paris Fashion & Couture (1225 King St., 703/519-8234, Mon.–Sat. 10:30 A.M.–7 P.M., Sun. 11 A.M.–6 P.M.) is the epitome of boutique perfection, owned by a Parisian and stocked with clothing, accessories, shoes, and handbags of hard-to-find European labels and domestic designers. There are fashion consultants on hand to help put together an outfit or a wardrobe.

For casual, flowing clothes from Eileen Fisher, Flax, and other natural-fiber lines, check out **Gossypia** (325 Cameron St., 703/836-6969, www.gossypia.com, Mon.–Sat. 10 A.M.–6 P.M., Thurs. 11 A.M.–7 P.M., Sun. 12:30–5 P.M.), a boutique for women's wear, jewelry, and accessories, including handmade sweaters from Latin America and a funky collection of Day of the Dead–themed handbags, necklaces, scarves, and earrings.

The bee motif of **Shoe Hive** (127 S. Fairfax St., 703/548-7105, www.store.theshoehive.com, Mon.–Sat. 11 A.M.–6 P.M., Sun. noon–5 P.M.), is a cheery showcase for shoes from the practical to the fanciful from top designers like Tory Burch, Diane von Fürstenberg, and Kate Spade. Two blocks away, **Treat** (103 S. Saint Asaph St., 703/535-3294, www.shoptreat.com,

Wed.–Sat. 11 A.M.–7 P.M., Sun. noon–6 P.M.) carries women's clothing to complete the look at discount prices. The store sells samples from designers like Theory, Cynthia Steffe, and Bettye Muller. Treat is a routine stop for local fashionistas since selection changes weekly and sizes sell out quickly.

Home Furnishings

Handmade housewares and gifts can be found at **Ten Thousand Villages** (915 King St., 703/684-1435, www.villagesofalexandria.com, Mon.–Fri. 11 A.M.–7 P.M., Sat. 10 A.M.–7 P.M., Sun. noon–6 P.M.), which carries goods made by artisans from nearly 30 nations, with hand-knotted Persian rugs from Pakistan, baskets from African countries, fabrics from India and Thailand, and fair-trade coffee and chocolates.

Local artisans work and sell their creations at the **Torpedo Factory Art Center** (105 N. Union St., 703/838-4565, www.torpedo factory.org, Fri.–Wed. 10 A.M.–6 P.M., Thurs. 10 A.M.–9 P.M.), three floors of studios and galleries in a World War II–era munitions factory on the waterfront. Nearly 140 artists use the spaces at the Torpedo Factory, producing paintings, photography, sculpture, jewelry, papier-mâché, and assemblage pieces.

For fine and decorative arts and antiques, **Studio Antiques** (524 N. Washington St., 703/548-5188, www.studioantiquesand fineart.com, Tues.–Sat. 11 A.M.–5 P.M., Sun. noon–5 P.M.) carries a selection of 19th- and 20th-century oil paintings and watercolors as well as 18th-century decorative arts and furniture, mainly English and American antiques. Antiques shoppers who enjoy browsing for "smalls" appreciate **The Antique Guild** (113 N. Fairfax St., 703/836-1048, www.theantique guild.net, Mon.–Sat. 11 A.M.–5 P.M.) for its jewelry, hollowware, rugs, flatware, and decorative selection, with something to suit nearly any budget. And if visiting this historic town leaves you wanting a bit of Virginia colonial history, Christopher Jones at **Early American Antiques, Folk & Fine Art** (210 N. Lee St., 703/622-9978, www.christopherhjones.com, by appointment) favors Southern furniture up through the Federal period with a focus on Alexandria.

HOTELS

Alexandria's proximity to Washington makes it a day trip for most locals and area visitors; hence it lacks the variety of bed-and-breakfasts and cozy inns usually found in cities of its historic stature like Williamsburg, Virginia, or Savannah, Georgia. A few hotel groups are trying to change this by scooping up interesting properties and renovating them with the aim of luring visitors out of Washington. But exclusivity comes at a price; expect to pay upward of $200 per night, slightly less if you stay on a weekend.

The **Morrison House** (116 S. Alfred St., 703/838-8000, www.morrisonhouse.com, $240–270), a Kimpton property, is one of these hotels, a Georgian-style manor "home" built in 1985 that fits perfectly amid Revolutionary-era row houses, Carlyle House, and Gadsby's Tavern just two blocks away. Named as one of *Travel + Leisure*'s top 500 hotels in the world, Morrison House drips with 18th-century elegance, from the elaborate crown moldings and chandeliers to the fine furnishings and fireplaces found in some guest rooms. The in-hotel restaurant is well-known and popular with locals for an impressive breakfast, and it serves high tea on Saturday. As a Kimpton property, pets are welcome and pampered with treats, dishes, and toys.

For years, the property that is now the **Hotel Monaco Alexandria** (480 King St., 703/549-6080, www.monaco-alexandria .com, $185–300) was a Holiday Inn, one of the chain's most popular outlets for its paramount location, on King Street in the heart of Old Town, steps from the waterfront, galleries, shopping, nightlife, and restaurants. A luxurious redesign has melded funk and tradition; exposed brick and 1920s-style furnishings are combined with a colorful paint palette, vibrant print fabrics, and decorative arts. Some guest rooms have outdoor balconies overlooking a central courtyard; suites

EXCURSIONS

have private bedrooms with a door separating it from the living space. Hotel Monaco also has an indoor pool and is pet-friendly, without size restrictions.

The chic **Lorien Hotel & Spa** (1600 King St., 703/894-3434, www.lorienhotelandspa .com, $200–400) is another Kimpton boutique hotel with the only hotel spa in Old Town. Located less than a mile from the Potomac River, closer to the King Street Metro stop than Kimpton's other hotels in Alexandria, the Lorien has 107 guest rooms and suites with contemporary furnishings in a color palette of soothing blues and pale grays. The full-service spa has treatment rooms, lockers, and a steam room. The hotel also has an on-site fitness center. Guest can linger in the courtyard with its pedestal clock and fire pit.

For convenient access to the Washington Metro as well as Old Town, the **Embassy Suites** (1900 Diagonal Rd., 703/684-5900, www.alexandriaoldtown.embassysuites.com, $220–240) delivers, just steps to the King Street Metro stop and blocks from the bustle of the historic district. This all-suites hotel suits families and is popular with business travelers, featuring an afternoon manager's reception, made-to-order breakfasts, suites with private bedrooms, a pool, and a fitness center.

INFORMATION
Visitors Center
The main Alexandria Visitors Center (221 King St., 703/746-3301, www.visitalexandria .com, Apr.–Dec. daily 10 A.M.–8 P.M., Jan.– Mar. daily 10 A.M.–5 P.M.) is located on busy King Street in one of the city's oldest buildings, Ramsay House, thought to have been built in 1724 in Dumfries, Virginia, and relocated to Alexandria in 1749 by owner William Ramsay. It has operated as a visitors center since 1956. Parking is available in nearby garages and on the street; the visitors center even hands out parking passes that allow out-of-towners to park free at metered spots. The center distributes guides, maps, and pamphlets and is staffed by people who can help plan an individual itinerary for your visit to Old Town.

Media
The **Washington Post** is the main daily newspaper in Alexandria, covering news that affects the region and publishing a local section on Thursday geared toward readers in Arlington and Alexandria as well as a daily Metro section that features news of the city. The **Washington Times** and **Washington Examiner** are also published daily and frequently contain news of interest to Alexandrians. But published in the shadow of these dailies is a weekly that holds a noteworthy distinction: The **Alexandria Gazette-Packet** is the oldest continuously published newspaper in the country, established in 1800, and because of its owner's link to a previous publication, it can trace its roots to 1784. Now a free weekly, it covers local government, education, school sports, and community arts. In terms of television and radio, Alexandrians watch and listen to DC-based stations. The only indigenous radio station is AM 730, WTNT, a talk radio station that broadcasts syndicated hosts like Laura Ingraham, Jerry Doyle, and Michael Savage.

GETTING THERE
Alexandria lies seven miles due south of Washington DC. To get there by car, cross the Memorial or 14th Street bridges and head south on the George Washington Memorial Parkway, which becomes Washington Street in Alexandria and bisects King Street in the center of town. To get to Mount Vernon, continue on the parkway an additional 15 miles; the road effectively ends at the plantation visitors' gates. Alexandria is accessible by Metro; the King Street Metro Station is served by both the Yellow and Blue lines; the station is roughly a mile from the Potomac River and 0.25 miles from the start of the shopping and historic district. Taxis also will carry passengers to Alexandria; expect to pay roughly $20 for a one-way trip.

GETTING AROUND
Old Town Alexandria is compact, with sights, shops, and restaurants within a square mile on the waterfront. Everything is reachable on foot

with the exception of outlying neighborhoods like Del Ray. Activities center around busy King Street, although shops, restaurants, and galleries are found on cross streets like Fairfax, Royal, Union, and St. Asaph Streets.

The city of Alexandria runs a bus system, the DASH bus, with routes that traverse Old Town every day, including routes AT 2 and AT 5, which travel through the city and make stops at the King Street and Braddock Road Metro Stations, and AT 10, which runs to the Del Ray neighborhood. The cost is $1.50 per ride.

There are sightseeing carriages for hire as well; horses and their drivers tend to congregate near the waterfront at the intersection of King and Strand Streets. Expect to pay $25–80 for a tour.

Annapolis

The City Dock in Annapolis is a water-bound town square, a bulkhead along Spa Creek that draws lingerers of all ages from boisterous teens and snuggling couples to locals with their coffee and newspapers, crews, yacht owners, and the bikini-clad beauties that adorn the luxurious motor craft that tie up here. Annapolis, Maryland's state capital, is one of the country's most scenic cities, with the largest concentration of 18th-century homes and buildings in the United States abutting miles of sparkling waterways. Brimming with restaurants, shops, and historic sites, it is a favorite destination for a day trip from Washington and Baltimore, both just 45 minutes away by car.

The state of Maryland was established by charter in 1629, bequeathed to a member of the Irish House of Lords who wanted to create a haven for Roman Catholics in the American colonies. Although many of its early settlers were Protestants, Maryland, named for the wife of England's Charles I, became known for its religious tolerance. When Virginia's Anglican-led government butted heads with a group of strict Puritans residing on Virginia's Eastern Shore, the group pulled up stakes and headed for Maryland, founding a town called Providence on the banks of the Severn River. The town was relocated across the river from its original site, where it thrived. With its protected harbor located close to the shipping lanes of Chesapeake Bay and the Atlantic, the town became a stepping-off point for tobacco exports to Europe; it also grew into a major entry

point for an even more lucrative business in the southern colonies, the slave trade. Within 50 years of its founding, the city was known as a center of wealth, with great townhomes and country estates lining its nearby creeks and rivers and a sophisticated, educated population. Near the end of the 17th century, Providence was renamed in honor of Princess Anne, later Queen Anne, who formally rechartered the town as the city of Annapolis in 1708.

Annapolis became Maryland's colonial capital and even briefly served as the capital of the United States after the Revolutionary War from 1783 to 1784. In its state house, George Washington resigned his commission as general in the Continental Army, and the treaty ending the war—the Treaty of Paris—was ratified. While the city eventually lost its shipping trade to the deeper harbor at the port of Baltimore, Annapolis continued to develop as a maritime destination, known for sailing and racing activities and its yacht-oriented maritime industry. In 1845 it became home to the U.S. Naval Academy, the country's military school for training naval officers. But the Academy wasn't the city's first university. That distinguished title goes to St. John's College, the third oldest in the United States, after Harvard and the College of William and Mary. The quads and trees of the campuses of St. John's and the U.S. Naval Academy, along with the city's design of circles, orderly streets, cobblestone alleyways, and historic buildings, including Maryland's State House, with their spires, rotundas, and widow's walks, create an incomparable ambience in the city. Along the waterfront, evidence of Annapolis's stature in the global sailing scene is evident as well. Spa Creek and the Severn River are home to numerous marinas housing some of the world's finest sailboats and yachts. Large homes line the city's inlets and smaller creeks, each with its own dock and usually a boat tied to it. Each Wednesday from April through September, members of the Annapolis Yacht Club hold a regatta; spectators enjoy watching the colorful scene from a drawbridge over Spa Creek or the restaurants and streets near City Dock. During the 2005–2006 racing season, the Volvo Ocean Race included this tiny city of 35,000 in its ambitious around-the-world itinerary.

SIGHTS
City Dock and
Kunta Kinte-Alex Haley Memorial

At the bottom of Main Street lies the City Dock, the heart of historic downtown Annapolis, a meet-up spot that draws visitors year-round. The dock is a popular spot for a picnic lunch or an after-dinner stroll, located near restaurants, shops, and lodgings. Sightseeing cruises and water taxis leave from the bulkhead regularly, and seafarers often pull their boats, yachts, and even ships up to its moorings. During the summer, bands and musical groups from the Naval Academy perform in the area, and the dock is often the site of town activities, including festivals and the Christmas boat parade. A collection of statues in the sidewalk marks the spot believed to be where the ancestor of Alex Haley, author of the book *Roots*, was brought ashore as a slave. The memorial is a sculpture of Haley reading to three young children; he is telling the story of his ancestry and of Annapolis's role in the slave trade during the 18th century. Haley's novel and its subsequent 1977 TV miniseries were groundbreaking, casting light on an often ignored chapter in U.S. history and the ancestry of millions of Americans. Although the accuracy of Haley's book was later questioned, *Roots* prompted historical sites and museums nationwide to widen

their scope to include African American and Native American history.

Charles Carroll House

One of only 15 residences left that belonged to a signer of the Declaration of Independence, the Charles Carroll House (107 Duke of Gloucester St., 410/269-1737, www.charlescarrollhouse .com, Jun.–Oct. Sat.–Sun. noon–4 P.M., donation) was home to Charles Carroll, grandson of Irish immigrant Charles Carroll, a Roman Catholic who moved to Maryland to escape persecution for his religious beliefs. Charles Carroll the grandson was the only Catholic to sign the Declaration of Independence; his former home is owned by the Congregation of the Most Holy Redeemer. He was also the last signer of the Declaration to die, in 1832 at age 95; he was also one of the founders of the B&O Railroad. Sited on Spa Creek, the house is a 1720s mansion that has been added onto over the years and is in the process of being restored, offering a glimpse into the home's architectural alterations and history as well as a look at building methods and styles of the past 300 years. For example, the original front door is on the second story, since the land was regraded for construction of St. Mary's Church, an 1860s Gothic structure that sits behind it. If you visit Charles Carroll House, take a moment to peek inside the church; the interior is breathtaking.

Maryland State House

The oldest state capitol building still in use by a state legislature, the wooden-domed Maryland State House (100 State Circle, 410/974-3400, open daily, guided tours hourly) was completed in 1797, the third building on State Circle to serve as the legislature. Construction began on the Georgian-style building in 1772; legislators have met in it since 1780. The State House's dome is the largest wooden dome in the United States. It contains no metal nails. The lightening rod—a large acorn skewered by a metal pole—is based on a design by Benjamin Franklin and is the largest built in Franklin's lifetime. It is a replica of the original,

© KUOSUMO/123RF.COM

the Maryland State House in Annapolis

removed in 1996 after protecting the building for more than 200 years (the original suffered dry rot and metal fatigue). The interior of the state house was updated and redesigned in 1905; it features marble-lined chambers and skylights made by Tiffany. Outside the northwest side of the statehouse is a statue of Supreme Court Justice Thurgood Marshall, a native of Baltimore who became the first black American to sit on the high court. The sculpture marks the former site of the Maryland Court of Appeals, where in 1935 Marshall argued *University v. Murray,* a case that contributed to the desegregation of Maryland state colleges. The other statues that make up the memorial are of Donald Murray, the plaintiff in that case, and two children representing the victors in the landmark 1954 *Brown v. Board of Education* decision, Marshall's most significant case.

◀ Sailboat Tours

Much of Annapolis's allure lies in its sparkling waterways: the Severn River, Spa Creek, and just around the bend, mighty Chesapeake Bay. If you've arrived at the city by land, take heart; you can experience the joys of the open waters by reserving a trip on a watercraft tour, which allows you to feel the sun on your face, the wind in the sails, and sea spray as it splashes over the bow. For an immersion into Annapolis's historic sailing culture, consider reserving a spot on the **Woodwind** or sister ship the **Woodwind II** (Pusser's Landing at the Marriott Waterfront, 80 Compromise St., 410/263-7837, www .schoonerwoodwind.com, 2-hour weekend sail $39 adults, $37 seniors, $25 children), 74-foot two-masted wooden schooners that take up to 48 guests for two-hour tours of the area. (If you saw the movie *Wedding Crashers,* you might recognize the *Woodwind II* as Christopher Walken's yacht.) On weekends and during the summer, the company offers sunset cruises and special Sunday champagne brunch tours.

    Watermark Cruises (City Dock, 410/268-7600, www.watermarkcruises.com) leads 40- and 90-minute tours of Annapolis harbor and the Naval Academy waterfront or the Spa Creek area aboard the motorized launches *Harbor Queen* and *Miss Anne* as well as special kid-friendly *Pirates of the Chesapeake* tours, trips out to Thomas Point Lighthouse, or day trips to scenic St. Michaels, Maryland, on the Eastern Shore. Tours run daily from Memorial Day through Labor Day and on a shorter schedule in spring and fall; prices range $13–70 adults, $5–30 children.

St. John's College

The third-oldest college in the United States, St. John's (60 College Ave.) was founded in 1696. It is a liberal-arts school of roughly 460 students who study a unique curriculum called a "Great Books" program, during which they read from an established list of source material, including classical Greek works—Homer, Sophocles, Aristotle, Plato, and others—in their freshman year and moving through history, with seniors exposed to the works of more contemporary writers like Virginia Woolf, Joseph Conrad, William Faulkner, and W. E. B. Du Bois. It's the ultimate liberal-arts education, without majors or formal lectures. A school that bucks conformity by refusing to provide information to *U.S. News & World Report*'s widely distributed college ranking list, St. John's develops highly qualified students, most of whom go on to graduate school. The college's striking Georgian-style campus lies directly across the wall from its antithesis, the disciplined, science-oriented United States Naval Academy. In the spring, the two schools go head-to-head in what is one of the city's most well-attended spectator events, an intercollegiate croquet match. Spectators dress in finery—bow ties, suspenders, and coats for the men, sundresses and hats for the women—for the festivities. St. John's inevitably comes out the winner; croquet is only one of three sports offered at the school.

◖ U.S. Naval Academy

Go Navy; beat Army. Thousands of men and women have launched their naval or Marine Corps careers from the U.S. Naval Academy, the nation's military college for naval officers,

a public institution founded in 1845 that currently has a student body of roughly 4,400. The Naval Academy is the second oldest of the country's five service academies, behind its rival the U.S. Military Academy at West Point, New York, established in 1802. *Annapolis* is a term used nearly synonymously with the Academy; the town and the university are intertwined historically and socially, with the students, called midshipmen, seen out and about on weekends enjoying the city's historic district and major regional events and activities taking place frequently on the Yard, as the school's grounds are known. The Academy occupies 340 acres on the Severn River and Spa Creek, its architecture a mix of beaux arts and Second Empire. Notable buildings include Bancroft Hall, the largest dormitory in the world, home to the entire Brigade of Midshipmen and encompassing Memorial Hall, a stirring space containing the names of all Academy graduates who have been killed in action. **The Chapel** is a beaux arts masterpiece designed by Ernest Flagg and crowned with a 225-foot copper-clad dome. It contains the elaborate crypt of John Paul Jones of "Don't Give up the Ship" fame, the father of the American Navy.

Visitors can take a formal tour of the school from the **Armel-Leftwich Visitors Center** (52 King George St., 410/293-8687, www .usna.edu/nafprodv/vc, summer Mon.–Sat. 9:30 A.M.–3 P.M., Sun. 12:30–3 P.M., winter reduced hours). The visitors center is free; tours cost $9.50 adults, $8.50 seniors, $7.50 children. On the tour, you'll learn about the history of the grounds as well as the stories of famous graduates, including astronaut Alan Shepard, President Jimmy Carter, Sen. John McCain, and others. If formal tours aren't your style, you can still enter the grounds (everyone 16 and older must present a picture ID) and explore it on your own; the **U.S. Naval Academy Museum** (118 Maryland Ave., 410/293-2108, www.usna.edu/Museum, Mon.–Sat. 9 A.M.–5 P.M., Sun. 11 A.M.–3 P.M., free), contains a collection of uniforms, artifacts, ship models, maritime maps, prints, and paintings.

William Paca House

The William Paca House (186 Prince George St., 410/990-4543, summer Mon.–Sat. 10 A.M.–5 P.M., Sun. noon–5 P.M., winter reduced hours, guided tours on the hour, admission $8 adults, $7 seniors, $5 children) is one of the best-preserved 18th-century buildings in Annapolis, a 1765 Georgian-style home designed by its owner, planter William Paca (pronounced PAY-ka), signer of the Declaration of Independence who later served as a state legislator and governor. The house and gardens have been restored to their original appearance at the height of Paca's career, with antique furniture, decorative arts, and silverware as well as a paint scheme and layout designed by Paca to personalize the home, including a dark robin's-egg blue on the walls of the second floor and a "lying-in" room where his wife, Mary Paca, would have received guests during the weeks following childbirth. The splendorous gardens with colonial terraces and a fish pond have taken great commitment from dedicated preservationists: At one time the gardens were covered by a hotel that had been built on the site. When the entire property, then known as Carvel Hall Hotel, was slated for demolition in 1965, the Historic Annapolis Foundation stepped in to save the home and restore the gardens. It was opened to the public for tours in 1973.

RESTAURANTS

Historically, Annapolis has served as a home to the rich and powerful; it continues to draw a steady stream of wealthy visitors and boaters, and as the state capital, a regular menu of politicians, lobbyists, and residents who have the money to purchase homes in this charming town. As such, numerous fine and upscale eateries cater to this clientele and feature a range of dining options, with many focusing on fresh offerings from Chesapeake Bay, including oysters and Maryland's state catch, rockfish.

For seafood and Maryland's signature dish, the crab cake, few restaurants can be topped by **O'Leary's Seafood** (310 3rd St., 410/263-0884, www.olearyseafood.com, Mon.–Sat.

5–11 P.M., Sun. 5–10 P.M.), an upscale eatery with a range of fresh choices on the menu prepared New American style, including a lobster "cappuccino" that's a bisque treated like a beverage, tuna sashimi, duck, and, of course, jumbo lump crab cakes. **Carrol's Creek Café** (410 Severn Ave., 410/263-8102, www.carrols creek.com, Mon.–Sat. 11:30 A.M.–4 P.M. and 5–10 P.M., Sun. 10:30 A.M.–1:30 P.M. and 3–9 P.M.) is popular with locals for its cream of crab soup and waterfront dining.

To dine in historic ambience and enjoy a range of pub fare, seafood, and even high tea, check out two historic way stations that served the colonists. **Middleton Tavern** (2 Market Space, 410/263-3323, www.middelton tavern.com, Mon.–Fri. 11:30 A.M.–1:30 A.M., Sat.–Sun. 10 A.M.–1:30 A.M.) played host to Washington, Jefferson, and Franklin; today, its location adjacent to the City Dock, outdoor dining areas, and dark traditional spaces are continuously packed with diners and revelers. If you're an oyster fan, try the oyster shooter, an oyster served in a shot glass with cocktail sauce and vodka and served with a beer chaser. For more genteel entertainment, consider tea and scones or High Colonial Tea at **Reynold's Tavern** (7 Church Circle, 410/295-9555, www .reynoldstavern.org, lunch and afternoon tea daily 11 A.M.–5 P.M., dinner Wed.–Sun. 5:30–9:30 P.M.), which contains the **Sly Fox Pub** (Sun.–Thurs. 11 A.M.–midnight, Fri.–Sat. 11 A.M.–2 A.M.). It is the oldest "ordinary" in the city, an early Tidewater-style tavern built in 1747 that also has a full restaurant and basement bar that serves lunch and pub fare in the evenings.

A trip to Annapolis or anywhere in the vicinity is not complete, at least for my family, without a visit to **Chick & Ruths Delly** (165 Main St., 410/269-6737, www.chickandruths.com, Sun.–Thurs. 6:30 A.M.–11:30 P.M., Fri.–Sat. 6:30 A.M.–12:30 A.M.), a venerable institution that draws customers with its stacked sandwiches, burgers, and ginormous milk shakes that taste like they're made purely from a gallon of ice cream. The menu features a range of sandwiches named for Maryland state figures, military heroes, and international stars, many of whom have eaten in this narrow, bustling circa-1950s lunch counter. Staffers are friendly and chatty, regardless of how packed the place gets, and it stays busy throughout the day, with local lawmakers popping in for breakfast and lunch, visitors getting an afternoon snack, and midshipmen looking for a break from King Hall. The milk shakes are a must-try.

If you have a car or access to one, consider heading to **Cantler's Riverside Inn** (458 Forest Beach Rd., 410/757-1311, www.cantlers.com, Sun.–Thurs. 11 A.M.–11 P.M., Fri.–Sat. 11 A.M.–midnight) for a taste of pure Chesapeake Bay—steamed crabs, rockfish bites, slaw, french fries, and cold beer served in cans. This remote waterside spot is accessible by road or by boat, with plenty of draft for a sailboat (14 feet MLW and 15 slips). Patient servers will instruct you on how to eat a blue crab if you're not familiar with the process; New Englanders accustomed to the ease and reward of eating a steamed lobster tend to get the most frustrated by the labor-intensive effort.

SHOPS

Historic Annapolis is geared mainly to window-shoppers and weekenders, featuring a number of stores selling apparel, arts and crafts, jewelry, and souvenirs as well as nautical and maritime-themed items. A stroll up Main Street, around Church Circle and State Circle, over to Maryland Avenue, and then down Prince George Street back to the northern side of City Dock will give you a sense of Annapolis's history while exposing you to most of the historic area's shopping opportunities. If Naval Academy logo merchandise and crab-themed memorabilia rank high on your list, check out **A. L. Goodies** (112 Main St., 410/269-0071, Sun.–Thurs. 9 A.M.–10 P.M., Fri.–Sat. 9 A.M.–midnight) for all things related to Annapolis, Maryland, and the Navy goat mascot. For a sophisticated reminder of your visit, **McBride Gallery** (15 Main St., 410/267-7077, www.mcbridegallery.com, Mon.–Wed. and Fri.–Sat. 10 A.M.–5:30 P.M.,

Thurs. 10 A.M.–9 P.M., Sun. noon–5:30 P.M.) includes fine oil paintings, photography, etchings, and prints by local artists of Annapolis and the local region in addition to landscapes, portraits, and sculpture. **Easy Street Gallery** (8 Francis St., 410/263-5556, www.easystreetgallery.com, daily from 10 A.M., closing time varies), is a colorful, happy space featured handblown glassware and artwork such as light catchers, bowls, vases, and sculptures made with creative flair and humor.

For antiques, including furniture, costume jewelry, china, crystal, and historic Naval Academy plates, drop by **Evergreen Antiques** (69 Maryland Ave., 410/216-9067, Sun.–Fri. 11 A.M.–5 P.M., Sat. 10 A.M.–5 P.M.), a reasonably priced store with a collection of unusual items. Another unusual place to spend some time is **Stevens True Value Hardware** (142 Dock St., 410/263-3390, Mon.–Fri. 8:30 A.M.–5:30 P.M., Sat. 10 A.M.–5 P.M., Sun. noon–5 P.M.), a throwback that is crammed full of tools, screws, nails—just about any fix-it item you'd ever need—as well as an interesting assortment of souvenirs and home items like brass nameplates for doors, oil lanterns, nautical clocks, ships bells, and door knockers. The place has been in business since 1960. **Annapolis Bookstore** (35 Maryland Ave., 410/280-2339, www.annapolisbookstore.com,, Mon.–Thurs. 7 A.M.–6 P.M., Fri.–Sat. 10 A.M.–9 P.M., Sun. 10 A.M.–6 P.M.) is an independent shop for new, rare, and used books, each carefully selected by the owners. A coffee shop in the back entices customers to linger.

HOTELS

While Annapolis is the perfect size for a day trip, it is also a favorite getaway for a quick break or a romantic weekend, revered by Baltimoreans and Washingtonians for its ambiance and character. Budget-conscious visitors or those who need space may want to consider staying at one of the larger hotel chain properties near the newly developed Annapolis Towne Center or by the Annapolis Mall, where prices tend to be lower than downtown.

If you plan to stay in the historic district, be ready to spend from $170 on a weekday up to $280 and beyond on a weekend in this popular resort town. Many of the hotels listed here offer breakfast with their lodgings; if yours doesn't, consider trotting over to Chick and Ruths Delly for an inexpensive rib-sticking breakfast.

The location can't be beat at the **Marriott Annapolis Waterfront** (80 Compromise St., 410/268-7555, www.annapolismarriott.com, $269–379), although guest rooms that overlook the parking lot, Dumpsters, and rowdy Pusser's Bar next door are less than ideal—if you're going to spend the money to stay here, pay for an upgrade to a water view, with spectacular scenery of Spa Creek, marinas, and the City Dock. Close to shopping, restaurants, the Naval Academy, and nearly all of the city's historic sights, a recent renovation has freshened the interiors, with a beige and blue color palette, rooms with flat-screen TVs, and comfortable bedding and linens.

For a historic view and feel, the **State House Inn** (25 State Circle, 410/990-0024, www.statehouseinn.com, $149–179) on State Circle directly across from the State House was built in 1786 and now contains eight guest rooms furnished in period and reproduction furniture. Most have views of downtown and the water; some have fireplaces. The front porch is an ideal place to rest after a day of sightseeing. This is an inn, not a bed-and-breakfast, although its coziness and charm bear all the markings of a B&B, including the sitting room where guests can enjoy a good book. All guest rooms have private baths and free wireless Internet access.

Another intimate lodging is the William Page Inn (8 Martin St., 410/626-1506, www.williampageinn.com, $175–235), a 1908 cedar-shake American foursquare home near the Naval Academy gates with five guest rooms and period furnishings, including the Fern Room, with direct access to the wraparound porch, or the Marilyn Suite, under the dormers, which occupies the entire third level. A front porch, common room, and patio with Adirondack chairs provide public spaces for guests to mingle and relax.

The **Governor Calvert House** (58 State Circle, 410/263-2641, www.historicinnsofannapolis.com, $159–184), with 51 guest rooms, is among the larger inns downtown, a 1727 building once home to Benedict Leonard Calvert, who served as governor from 1727 to 1731. The upscale boutique lodgings feature elegantly appointed guest rooms and offer full-service amenities like a cardio workout room and Internet access along with proximity to the State House and colonial gardens. It is operated by the Historic Inns of Annapolis, a group that has two other downtown properties, the Maryland Inn and Robert Johnson House.

Adrift from the bustle of downtown, the **Inn at Horn Point** (100 Chesapeake Ave., Eastport, 410/268-1126, www.innathornpoint.com, $159–269) lies across Spa Creek from historic downtown, accessible by water taxi and just a 15-minute walk to the City Dock through a neighborhood and across a drawbridge. This quirky Victorian home contains five guest rooms, each named for a famous yacht made by a neighborhood yacht company and dressed in cottage style. Breakfast is served at this B&B; according to *Coastal Living* magazine, it is one not to miss.

INFORMATION
Visitors Center
The main Visitors Center (26 West St., daily 9 A.M.–5 P.M., closed Thanksgiving Day, Christmas Day, and New Year's Day), run by the Annapolis and Anne Arundel County Conference and Visitors Bureau, is just off Church Circle. To get to it by car, you must still briefly suffer Annapolis's traffic congestion, but once you've arrived, you'll find parking in the adjacent Gotts Court Garage, where you'll be able to leave your car and walk if you are visiting the city for the day. The center is staffed by volunteer specialists who can distribute pamphlets and brochures and share their insiders' view of special events and happenings in the city. At City Dock, the bureau also runs

a seasonal **Information Booth** (Apr.–early Oct. daily 9 A.M.–5 P.M.), staffed by the same helpful volunteers.

Media

The *Capital* is Annapolis's daily newspaper, covering local and regional events as well as goings-on at the State House. Many Annapolitans also receive the *Baltimore Sun* or *Washington Post* for news of state and world interest. The tabloid *Bay Weekly*, a free publication, focuses on arts and entertainment and feature news that keeps residents abreast of activities, business openings and closings, gallery news, and more. On the radio, Navy sports and talk can be heard on WNAV 1430 AM; modern rock is broadcast by WRNR, 103.1 FM, and Latin American music now reverberates from 99.1 WLZL FM El Sol. The station was once the beloved WHFS, an alternative music station. The times, they are a changing, but many area residents, from Washington to Baltimore, haven't forgiven the suits at CBS for the switch.

GETTING THERE

Annapolis is 33 miles due east of Washington DC, accessible from the District's New York Avenue, which becomes U.S. 50. Head east on U.S. 50 and turn right on Rowe Boulevard, bear right or turn a hard right on College Avenue, and you'll find yourself between State Circle and Church Circle. The City Dock is on the water at the end of Main Street, which is a one-way heading away from the water. It takes roughly 45 minutes by car to reach Annapolis from DC; in traffic it can take much longer. A car is really the only dependable and viable option for getting from Washington to Annapolis; Greyhound's bus option is untenable, a trip that requires two transfers and takes more than three hours. There is no rail service.

THE BAY BRIDGE

The Eastern Shore of Maryland and the Atlantic beaches lie east of Annapolis on U.S. 50, and to reach these popular destinations for fun in the sun, you must cross Chesapeake Bay via the massive William Preston Lane Jr. Bay Bridge, twin spans that rise 190 feet over the water, affording stunning, if not slightly intimidating, views of the water, cargo ships, sailboats, and tiny fishing vessels far below. Before the spans were built, travelers between the eastern and western Maryland shores took ferries; approval for bridge funds came in 1938 with the promise of cutting travel time between Washington DC and Ocean City, Maryland by nearly two hours.

It wasn't until after World War II that construction on a bridge began in earnest. When the first two-lane bridge opened in 1952, it was the longest steel structure built over water and the third-longest bridge in the world at 4.3 miles. The bridge proved so popular that within a decade, state officials realized they needed another span to relieve congestion and ensure the continued flow of commerce. In 1973, a wider three-lane bridge span opened north of the existing bridge. Today, it carries westbound traffic, but during peak hours, one of its lanes is often used for eastbound traffic, which is often a bit confusing but is readily marked with traffic cones and directional lights. While the bridge often is subject to high winds, it has only been closed once in its nearly 60-year history, in 2003 during Hurricane Isabel.

During the summer months and at rush hour, the bridge remains a source of traffic congestion. The **Maryland Transportation Authority** (877/229-7726, www.baybridge. com) operates a website and phone number to check traffic updates. The Bay Bridge is a toll bridge; a one-way car trip costs $2.50. Given its height and length, this bridge is exceptionally terrifying to gephyrophobics (those who fear bridges); **Kent Island Express** (410/604-0486, www.kentislandexpress.com) offers a service to shuttle sufferers and their cars across for a fee.

GETTING AROUND

Annapolis is compact, with nearly all major sites accessible on foot, the preferred way to tour the city, since traffic frequently snarls along its tight colonial streets and parking is difficult to find. Most attractions are five to 10 minutes' walk apart, and if you tire, **Annapolis Transit** (410/263-7964, www .annapolis.gov/government/departments/ Transportation/ShuttleService.aspx) runs two shuttle buses, the Navy Blue and State Shuttles, during daylight hours. The lines cover most of the historic area as well as the U.S. Navy–Marine Corps Memorial Stadium. Shuttles run more frequently on football game days.

Sightseeing buggies can often be hired at City Dock for $25–80—negotiate your fare.

You can usually catch a taxi in the City Dock area or call a taxi from your hotel.

The Virginia Countryside

In the suburbs surrounding Washington, the National Park Service has preserved large tracts of land, great swaths of wilderness that protect the Potomac River watershed, historic battlefields, and shadowy woods. Farther afield, the suburbs give way to a genteel land where horse farms and vineyards fill gaps between small towns, where great plantations rise above winding creeks and small rivers, where foothills give way to the ancient Blue Ridge Mountains.

The history of the present-day United States starts in 1607 when 100 men and boys landed at Jamestown, Virginia, in search of riches in the New World. Spanish explorers had found great wealth in South America and had already established a settlement in St. Augustine, Florida; English settlers had attempted to colonize North Carolina in the late 1500s but had failed, with two separate parties disappearing. In 1607, however, Capt. John Smith arrived and navigated the hostile environment, establishing a foothold for England to colonize the Mid-Atlantic. Smith traveled the Chesapeake Bay and up the Potomac River, eventually exploring much of the Atlantic coastline. Farther north and 13 years later, the *Mayflower* arrived with its group of Puritans seeking a place to openly practice their religion; the rest is history. Smith's settlement eventually grew beyond Jamestown to Williamsburg and much of southeastern Virginia. The crown distributed numerous land grants to its subjects, and through this method of land distribution, most of what is now the Virginia countryside outside Washington became great farms, fields, and plantations, with rich earth to grow tobacco and raise horses, named for their proprietors: Lord Thomas Fairfax; John Campbell, Fourth Earl of Loudon; and governor of the Virginia Colony, Lord Francis Fauquier, who allegedly won the land that makes up the present day Fauquier County in a poker game. But even before the British divvied up the land, Virginia was home to great Indian nations—Monocan, Powhatan, Chickahominy, and Dogue. During the Revolutionary War, the colony was the site of several battles, including the one that ended the war, at Yorktown, a three-hour drive from DC. Northern Virginia became disputed territory during the Civil War; present-day Arlington and Alexandria were occupied by Union soldiers within weeks of the declaration of hostilities and remained so for the remainder of the war, while the outlying areas became passageways for Southern and Northern troops as they crossed disputed territory into the realm of the opposing forces. Today, the war-torn towns of Leesburg, Warrenton, and Fredericksburg are small cities, DC exurbs with histories unique and separate from Washington, with Southern charm, abundant antiques stores, boutiques, restaurants, small-town culture, and close proximity to famous battle sights such as the Battle of Manassas (Bull Run), Chancellorsville, Balls Bluff, the Wilderness, and Brandy Station. Tiny

EXCURSIONS

Middleburg, Virginia, in Loudoun County south of Leesburg, has become the center of Virginia hunt country, so named since the colonial era when lords on horseback chased foxes with great packs of hounds. Today, it remains home to the wealthy, with great horse centers and farms. The area is so rich in history that the National Trust for Historic Preservation has named a trip through it "A Journey through Hallowed Ground," a nearly 180-mile route that runs from Gettysburg, Pennsylvania (90 minutes from DC by car), to Charlottesville, Virginia (2.5 hours away). A trip to any of the small towns or sights mentioned here requires a car. Pick your interest—following in the footsteps of Founding Fathers or Civil War troops, antiques shopping in charming towns like Leesburg or Middleburg, or visiting wineries—and plot your route. But as close as 30 minutes away, in Great Falls, Virginia, you can discover a region far removed from the busy type A personality of Washington DC, a place to sample the Virginia countryside while barely off the Beltway.

McLEAN
Claude Moore Colonial Farm

Many settlers in Virginia weren't landed gentry; their farms were more like the homestead at Claude Moore Colonial Park (6310 Georgetown Pike, McLean, Va., 703/442-7557, www.1771 .org, Wed.–Sun. 10 A.M.–4:30 P.M., $3 adults, $2 children) than the beautiful plantations of Mount Vernon or Gunston Hall. Nine miles from downtown Washington, Claude Moore is a popular destination for families, a living history museum where staffers farm the land and conduct the daily routine of a typical low-income settler in 1771. Depending on the season, visitors will see workers in colonial garb tilling, planting, weeding, cooking, harvesting, putting up crops, and tending to the animals. Young visitors are often asked to pitch in with the chores; the family's buildings, including the home, barn, and tobacco sheds, are open to the public. The park holds several special events, including spring and fall market fairs, where youngsters can bob for apples, learn to

handle a sword, watch spinners and weavers, and, of course, work.

Great Falls National Park

An 800-acre park 15 miles northwest of Washington, Great Falls National Park (9200 Old Dominion Dr., McLean, Va., 703/285-2965, www.nps.gov/GRFA, daily 7 A.M.–dark, visitors center daily 10 A.M.–5 P.M., $5 per car) abuts the Mather Gorge, where the Potomac River barrels over boulders and rocks and flows downstream toward Washington. The park has miles of hiking trails, most of them wide, mulched pathways along the remnants of the old Patowmack Canal appropriate for beginner hikers and families with small children. The more adventurous can boulder down along the falls near Difficult Run, finding hidden outcrops to enjoy the scenery. The park has grills and picnic areas as well. On hot days, no matter how tempting the water looks, don't wade; the eddies and currents caused by the falls can knock the most steadfast off their feet and into the dangerous river.

MANASSUS
◖ Manassas National Battlefield

On a hazy, hot Sunday, July 21, 1861, many Washingtonians packed up their picnic blankets and lunches and headed to Virginia, to bluffs overlooking a creek known as Bull Run to watch what they believed would be the opening and closing battle of the Civil War. Their surety of an early Union victory was dashed, however, when the evenly matched forces—18,572 for the Union and 18,053 for the Confederacy—clashed along the river, resulting in a victory for the South. Roughly 4,700 Americans died in that first battle, marked today as Manassas National Battlefield (intersection of Sudley Rd./Rte. 234 and Lee Hwy./U.S. 29, Manassas, Va., 703/361-1339, www.nps.gov/mana, daily 8:30 A.M.–5 P.M., $3 adults, free under age 17). This site of the first major land battle of the Civil War is among the most endangered of Virginia's battlefields; located amid the urban sprawl of Manassas, park officials and local preservationists have fought hard to maintain

© PATRICIA KIME

Manassas National Battlefield

the views from the visitors center, a tree-lined horizon similar to the rural landscape of 1861. The park has miles of easy walking trails that pass through rolling farmland and forest and follows an unfinished railroad used repeatedly by Stonewall Jackson and his troops.

CHANTILLY
National Air and Space Museum
Steven F. Udvar-Hazy Center

Building on the enormous popularity of the Air and Space Museum and needing more room to showcase its largest aircraft, including a Space Shuttle, the Smithsonian opened the National Air and Space Museum Steven F. Udvar-Hazy Center (14390 Air & Space Museum Parkway, Chantilly, Va., 703/572-4118, www .nasm.si.edu, daily 10 A.M.–5 P.M., admission free, parking $15) in 2003, adjacent to Dulles International Airport. The holdings at the main National Air and Space Museum in DC and the Udvar-Hazy Center represent the largest collection of aviation and space artifacts in the world. In addition to housing some of the world's most important historic and groundbreaking aircraft, including the *Enola Gay,* a Concorde, and an SR-71 Blackbird, the three-story center has an IMAX theater, a mock aircraft control tower featuring the real-time voices of Dulles controllers, and in late 2011, a hangar where visitors can watch the work of museum restorers.

Sully Historic Site

Directly across historic Route 28 from the Udvar-Hazy Center is the **Sully Plantation** (3650 Historic Sully Way, Chantilly, Va., 703/437-1794, www.fairfaxcounty.gov/parks/ sully/, Wed.–Mon. 11 A.M.–P.M., closed federal holidays, tours $7 adults, $6 students, $5 over age 64, $5 ages 5–15), built in 1799 by Richard Bland Lee, Virginia's first member of Congress. The Federal- and Georgian-style manor home and its grounds have been preserved by Fairfax County to showcase early-19th-century life in Virginia. Preservationists will enjoy learning about how the site was spared during the construction of Dulles airport, and the grounds, with preserved outbuildings and a representational slave quarters, indicate how the Lee family lived during the early days of the nation. While not exactly a must-see home like Mount Vernon or Gunston Hall, Sully is exemplary of a modest-income Virginian family at the time of the country's birth.

LEESBURG AREA
Leesburg Historic District

When Dolley Madison fled the marauding British in 1814, she headed to Leesburg, where many Washingtonians now go for a day of antiquing, shopping, and dining. Leesburg traces its roots to the 1722 Treaty of Albany, when the Iroquois abandoned all lands east of the Blue Ridge Mountains to the colony of Virginia. The town originated as an outfitting post for the French and Indian Wars and was later named the site of the Loudoun County courthouse. It is where President James Madison spirited the Declaration of Independence and the Constitution during the War of 1812 and where James Monroe kept a house and drafted the Monroe Doctrine. During the Civil War, its location, close to the division between North and South, put it at the center of combat action. The nearby Battle of Balls Bluff marked an early Confederate victory; Col. John Mosby later used the city as a base of operation for his raiders. Leesburg became a boomtown in the 1980s as tech business sprung up along the Dulles Airport corridor, pushing the suburbs farther west. Today, much of its downtown area is preserved, featuring an abundance of antiques shops, boutiques, and cafés. A vast outlet mall on Route 7 on the city's eastern boundary draws bargain shoppers from around the region.

Oatlands Plantation Historic Houses and Gardens

The magnificent Oatlands Plantation (20850 Oatlands Plantation Lane, Leesburg, Va., 703/777-3174, www.oatlands.org, Mar. 28–Dec. 30 Mon.–Sat. 10 A.M.–5 P.M., tours on the hour 10 A.M.–4 P.M., $10 adults, $9 over age 59, $7 ages 6–16, free under age 6) appeals to fans of plantation homes. Oatlands is a massive Greek Revival mansion built in the 1820s by a Carter, one of the state's founding families. Its 360 acres contain a number of houses as well as formal gardens, with terraces and plantings harking back to the period when Carter first began work on the home in 1803. Prior to the Civil War, Oatlands housed the largest slave population in Loudoun County, numbering 128 people. The home later became a girls school, a summer boardinghouse, and a weekend property for a prominent Washington couple who preserved the property and restored the gardens. A favorite activity at Oatlands is afternoon tea; the calendar varies, but on special weekends and throughout the fall, Oatlands hosts high tea and speakers on subjects ranging from gardening to the Civil War and the history of tea.

Balls Bluff Battlefield Regional Park

To get to Balls Bluff Battlefield (Balls Bluff Rd., Leesburg, Va., 703/737-7800, www.nvrpa .org, daily dawn–dusk, tours Apr.–Oct. Sat.–Sun. 11 A.M. and 1 P.M., free), you pass through a subdivision of McMansions—a landscape that belies the Civil War skirmish, the Battle of Ball's Bluff, that happened here on October 21, 1861. The result of miscommunication between Maj. Gen. George McClellan and his men, Union forces crossed the Potomac River at an unknown steep spot in the river, and believing they had found a line of Confederates, began preparing for battle. A lack of reinforcements and poor communications among the Union soldiers gave the Confederates time to organize their forces, and by mid-afternoon, the battle was practically over, with one U.S. senator, Col. Evan Baker, dead and 553 Union prisoners taken. The tiny battle was significant in that it led Union commanders to continue second-guessing their decisions throughout the rest of the war. Today, the small regional park has a number of trails, none longer than two miles, and is home to the third-smallest national cemetery, containing the graves of 54 Union soldiers.

White's Ferry

Of the hundreds of ferries that crisscrossed the Potomac River between Virginia and Maryland, only White's Ferry (24801 Whites Ferry Rd., Dickerson, Md., 301/349-5200) remains, a cable-towed barge that carries cars, cyclists, and hikers traveling between Leesburg and Poolesville, Maryland. While it's not worth driving out of the way for, there's something enchanting about waiting in line for a five-minute crossing on a flat ferry named the *Gen. Jubal Early,* especially if you happen to be traveling between rural Maryland and northern Virginia. A store on the Maryland side sells T-shirts and refreshments and rents canoes and bikes. White's Ferry is popular with commuters and is at its most crowded during rush hour. It is also subject to the whims of the Potomac River; if you plan to go, call ahead to check the ferry's status. The store is normally open from mid-April through October, although don't be surprised if you find it closed, with operators posting Facebook status updates such as: "Sorry, no way. There's about three feet of the Potomac River in it."

SOUTHERN LOUDOUN COUNTY AND MIDDLEBURG
Middleburg

At the heart of Virginia's hunt country lies Middleburg, a one-stoplight town that has changed little since it was founded in 1787, a picture postcard village for spending a quiet afternoon walking the streets. A central gathering place for the wealthy owners of nearby farms and equestrian operations and students from the region's private schools, Middleburg contains tack shops, antiques stores, and boutiques as well as a number of restaurants, including the Red Fox Inn, which began as Mr. Chinn's Ordinary in 1728 and continues to operate as a tavern and inn today, making it one of the country's oldest, visited in 1748 by a young George Washington. In late May, farms throw open their barn doors for the Hunt Country Stable Tour (www.middleburgonline.com), revealing the pampered lives of the Loudoun County's thoroughbreds and point-to-point steeds. The first weekend of October is time for the Virginia Fall Races (www.vafallraces .com)—exciting steeplechase races that have participants taking on huge jumps and water obstacles as well as racing on the flat.

Aldie Mill

On the drive to Middleburg along U.S. 50, visitors pass Aldie Mill (39401 John Mosby Hwy.,

© PATRICIA KIME

the Aldie Mill

Aldie, Va., 703/327-9777, www.nvrpa.org/park/aldie_mill_historic_park, mid Apr.–late Nov. Sat.–Sun. afternoon, free), Virginia's only tandem-waterwheel mill. Restored in 2010, the mill complex consists of the mill, a granary, and a storehouse. During the Civil War, miller John Moore (only one of five men in Aldie to vote against secession) provided grain to the Union; his son, a Southern sympathizer, sold grain to Confederate troops. Now owned by a regional park authority, the mill hosts an art show each weekend in September to benefit restoration of the facility.

C Virginia's Vineyards

Virginia's efforts to become a world-renowned wine region can be traced to the failed effort by Jamestown settlers to cultivate grapes and Thomas Jefferson's more vigorous effort—growing grapes for 30 years at Monticello—that never produced a single bottle of wine. In the 1870s the state finally received recognition at the Vienna World's Fair for a vintage made from Virginia's only fine native grape, Norton, and finally, in the 1970s, a number of wineries began to take root. Today, the state has 140 wineries, several of which are within minutes of Middleburg and Leesburg. The state's most notable wines are its viognier, cabernet franc, and Norton.

Among the award-winning wineries are **Chrysalis Vineyards** (23878 Champe Ford Rd., Middleburg, Va., 540/687-8222, www.chrysaliswine.com, daily 10 A.M.–5:30 P.M., tasting $5), known for its Norton, viognier, and albarino varietals; **Piedmont Vineyards** (2546D Halfway Rd., The Plains, Va., 540/687-5528, www.piedmontwines.com, daily 11 A.M.–6 P.M., tasting $5), one of the pioneers established in 1973 and known for its chardonnay, white wines, and fruit wines, including peach; **Boxwood Winery** (2042 Burrland Rd., Middleburg, Va., 540/687-8778, www.boxwoodwinery.com), which offers tours and tastings by appointment at the winery and has a tasting room in Middleburg, and is hailed for respectable reds; and **Willowcroft** (38906 Mount Gilead Rd., Leesburg, Va., 703/777-8161, www.willowcroftwine.com), closer to

Leesburg with beautiful views and a variety of white and red wines.

Sky Meadows State Park

In the fall, Sky Meadows State Park (111012 Edmonds Lane, Delaplane, Va., 540/592-3556, www.dcr.virginia.gov/state_parks/sky.shtml, Apr.–Oct. Mon.–Fri. 11 A.M.–5 P.M., Sat.–Sun. 10 A.M.–6 P.M., Nov.–Mar. Mon.–Fri. 11 A.M.–4:30 P.M., Sat.–Sun. 10 A.M.–4:30 P.M.) burns in golds, reds, and browns, with views of wooded hills and rolling farmland. In the spring the trees burst forth in new green and wildflowers and shrubs bloom alongside the Appalachian Trail, which crosses the park at roughly 2,000 feet in elevation. If all the driving around the Virginia countryside has you itching to get out and walk, Sky Meadows has 12 miles of hiking trails ranging from moderate to difficult. Located not far from the charming villages of Paris and Delaplane, Sky Meadows also has a one-acre pond for fishing and offers numerous nature-oriented tours and activities on weekends.

RESTAURANTS

Located in the county with the highest median income in the United States, Leesburg and Middleburg have a plethora of good restaurants to feed the discriminating locals as well as visitors who expect much from a region that specializes in organic and sustainable agriculture. Middleburg's **Red Fox Inn** (2 East Washington St., Middleburg, Va., 540/687-6301, www.redfoxinn.com, breakfast daily 8–10:30 A.M., lunch daily 11:30 A.M.–3 P.M., dinner Mon.–Sat. 5–9 P.M., Sun. 4:30–8 P.M., brunch Sun. 10 A.M.–3 P.M.) is a historic restaurant and inn of cozy fireplaces, farm tables, and an ages-old stuffed fox in the dining room, with a menu of seasonal and colonial fare that includes peanut soup and prime rib along with lighter fare like crab cakes, gazpacho, and salads stacked with tomatoes and mozzarella. **The French Hound** (101 Madison St., Middleburg, Va., 540/687-3018, www.thefrenchhound.com, lunch Wed.–Sun. 11:30 A.M.–2:30 P.M., dinner Tues.–Thurs. 5:30–9:30 P.M., limited menu until 10:30 P.M., Fri.–Sat. 5:30–10 P.M., limited menu until 11 P.M.) has quickly won the hearts of Middleburgians as one of the few places to relax after dark. The French-inspired bistro, whose kitchen is led by local John Gustin-Burkitt, who earned his strips at Napa Valley, California's Domaine Chandon and Brix, hits the high notes for its snacks, including spicy peanuts and house-marinated olives, and French standards like goat-cheese puffs and steak frites. For casual dining, try **Julien's Café** (3 West Washington St., Middleburg, Va., 540/687-3123, Fri.–Wed. 11 A.M.–9 P.M.) for *croque-monsieur,* soups, pâté, and sandwiches like the tasty smoked salmon BLT. For a sweet treat to eat or take home, check out the **Little Apple Pastry Shop** (23217 Meetinghouse Lane, Aldie, Va., 703/327-2500, www.hotapple pie.com) in tiny Aldie. You'll miss it if you drive even a mile per hour over the speed limit. In addition to mouthwatering fruit pies, the shop makes sandwiches and ham biscuits, meat pies, and homemade candy.

During a day of antiquing in Leesburg, a few restaurants can meet the need for sustenance, including the **Green Tree** (15 S. King St., Leesburg, Va., 703/777-7246), which serves colonial-themed fare in a casual setting conveniently located in the middle of the historic district. It's a go-to place for a rib-sticking meatloaf or basic chicken Caesar and a draft beer. The city's **Wine Kitchen** (7 S. King St., Leesburg, Va., 703/777-9463, www.thewinekitchen.com, Tues.–Thurs. and Sun. 11:30 A.M.–9 P.M., Fri.– Sat. 11:30 A.M.–10 P.M.) serves small plates, salads, and charcuterie prepared with ingredients from local producers as well as wines by the glass in a tiny storefront restaurant of white wood, exposed brick, and warm cherry finishes. **Lightfoot** (11 N. King St., Leesburg, Va., 703/771-2233, www.lightfootrestaurant .com, Mon.–Thurs. 11:30 A.M.–2:30 P.M. and 5:30–11 P.M., Fri.–Sat. 11:30 A.M.–2:30 P.M. and 5:30 P.M.–midnight, Sun. 11:30 A.M.–10 P.M.), in a former bank, has an eclectic international menu that features dishes ranging from pad thai and Baja fish tacos to Cajun spaghetti and meatloaf. Southern dishes fare well here, such as the crab bisque and fried green tomatoes at lunch.

A block and a half from the center of Leesburg (intersection of U.S. 15 and Rte. 7) is Market Station, with **Tuscarora Mill** (203 Harrison St., Leesburg, Va., 703/771-9300, www.tuskies .com, Mon.–Thurs. 11 A.M.–11 P.M., Fri.–Sat. 11 A.M.–midnight, Sun. 11 A.M.–9 P.M., brunch 11 A.M.–2:30 P.M.), one of those restaurants that looks like it was built exclusively to gouge visitors but is a real crowd-pleaser with locals and visitors alike, with 22 beers on tap, an extensive wine menu, and ambitious, well-prepared selections such as duck and waffles, grilled bison, and shrimp and grits, made with Virginia ham and truffled grits.

SHOPS

Browsers and serious antiques lovers alike enjoy **Middleburg Antique Emporium** (107 W. Washington St., Middleburg, Va., 540/687-8680, daily 10 A.M.–5 P.M.), which has 24 dealers selling fine arts, silverware and hollowware, fine furniture, clocks, prints, oil paintings, vintage linens, and china with very few "dustables" and tchotchkes. An extensive selection of antiques, from Louis XIV and Directoire to Louis Philippe, are displayed alongside farm tables and garden ornaments at **JML French Antiques** (17 E. Washington St., Middleburg, Va., 540/687-6323, www.jml-french-antiques.com, Mon.–Sat. 11 A.M.–5 P.M., Sun. 1–5 P.M.). For decorative and fine arts, check out the **Shaggy Ram** (3 Washington St., Middleburg, Va., 540/687-3546, www.shaggyram.com), with a mix of antiques and new merchandise as well as sporting art. Need a dog? Owner Joanne Swift runs her own pet adoption agency out of the shop.

I've been poking my nose into **The Fun Shop** (117 W. Washington St., Middleburg, Va., 540/687-6590, www.thefunshop.com, Mon.–Sat. 9 A.M.–5 P.M., Sun. 1–5 P.M.) since attending school near Middleburg, back when I shopped for grosgrain ribbon and all manner of accessories from *The Preppy Handbook.* A miniature department store, the Fun Shop carries housewares, home-decor items, bedding, fox-hunting and horse-themed accessories and gifts, toys, greeting cards, and more.

Even if you don't have a need for a new

EXCURSIONS

saddle, it is fun to drop into the **Tack Box** (7 West Federal St., Middleburg, Va., 540/687-3231, www.thetackboxinc.com, Mon.–Sat. 9 A.M.–6 P.M.), a store redolent with the rich fragrance of leather and carrying equipment and items needed or desired by the horsey set. The shop has some clothing items, like jeans and T-shirts, as well as horse-themed accessories for your barn or a favorite teenage horse-lover on your list.

Leesburg's storefronts combine the old and new, with many of the antique stores carrying goods at prices more affordable than in Middleburg but also more hunt-and-peck, geared to those who find joy in gleaning in boxes of collectibles and merchandise. The **Black Shutter Antiques Center** (1 Loudoun St., Leesburg, Va., 703/443-9579, www.blackshutterantiques.com, Mon.–Sat. 10:30 A.M.–5:30 P.M., Sun. noon–5 P.M.), in a 19th-century row house, contains an eclectic assortment from a multitude of dealers, from vintage clothes and comic books to dishes, 1950s housewares, 1930s and 1940s mahogany furniture, and a backroom filled with a disturbing but fascinating collection of Nazi memorabilia and Japanese World War II weapons and combat artifacts. Across the street is the **Leesburg Antiques Emporium** (32 S. King St., Leesburg, Va., 703/777-3553, www.leesburgantiqueemporium.com, Mon.–Sat. 10 A.M.–6 P.M., Sun. noon–6 P.M.), with two floors of collectibles and many flea market finds, record albums, Depression glass, linens, clothing, and collectibles. One notable booth carries an assortment of political memorabilia, including hard-to-find campaign buttons.

Rows of beautiful French linens, placemats, china, cutlery, and toiletries can be found at **Crème de la Crème** (127 S. King St., Leesburg, Va., 703/737-7702, www.shopcremedelacreme.com), an upscale shop that also carries an assortment of colorful ceramics from Italy and France. For humorous cards, gag gifts, candies, jewelry, and funny hats, the **Pink Shop** (109 S. King St., Leesburg, Va., 703/669-1800, Mon.–Sat. 11 A.M.–6 P.M., Sun. noon–5 P.M.) is full of items you don't need but might want.

The **Leesburg Corner Premium Outlets** (241 Fort Evans Rd. NE, Leesburg, Va., 703/737-3071, Mon.–Sat. 10 A.M.–9 P.M., Sun. 10 A.M.–7 P.M.) is a manageable mall with more than 90 stores of designer cast-offs and sale clothing, shoes, accessories, handbags, and housewares. Stores include Theory, Restoration Hardware, Pottery Barn, Kate Spade, Michael Kors, and Juicy Couture.

HOTELS

Life slows down in the small towns of central northern Virginia, at luxury bed-and-breakfasts and inns, in their cozy rooms and gardens amid pastures and fenced fields. Couples and history buffs can enjoy a weekend escape, with days filled with outdoor activities and sightseeing or spent simply in a hammock under a towering oak or on a porch swing with views of the Blue Ridge Mountains.

The guest rooms at the stone **Red Fox Inn** (2 East Washington St., Middleburg, Va., 540/687-6301, www.redfoxinn.com, $175–245) have canopy or four-poster beds, luxury linens, and country furnishings; some guest rooms have fireplaces. Rates include a hearty Hunt Country breakfast and evening turn-down service. If you've yearned to own a country "hunt box" but don't have the cash for another mortgage, the **Goodstone Inn** (36205 Snake Hill Rd., Middleburg, Va., 877/219-4663, www.goodstone.com, $385–630), a 265-acre working estate next door to former socialite Pamela Harrington's farm, fits the bill, with a carriage house and outbuildings turned into luxury accommodations. Guests can bring their own horses or borrow bikes to tour the area; hiking and wineries are not far. Unique accommodations include the Bull Barn, a cottage with a library, a king bed, a jetted tub, and a private fenced garden; and the French Farm Cottage, a home to complete the country-house fantasy with stone exteriors and plaster walls, a great room, floor-to-ceiling fireplaces, and hammocks.

In tiny Paris, the **Ashby Inn and Restaurant** (692 Federal St., Paris, Va., 540/592-3200 or 866/336-0099, www.ashbyinn.com,

$165–295) coddles guests in a 19th-century colonial home and schoolhouse, with 10 guest rooms furnished in country-antique reproductions. A full-service, award-winning restaurant serves new American cuisine crafted from seasonal ingredients.

John and Jackie Kennedy helped put Middleburg on the map by spending weekends in the cozy hamlet; Ronald Reagan enjoyed retreating to the cattle farm belonging to J. W. Marriott, now home to the **Inn at Fairfield Farm** (5305 Marriott Lane, Hume, Va., 877/324-7344, www.marriottranch.com, $139–219), otherwise known as the 4,200-acre Marriott Ranch. Guests can stay at the historic main home, built in 1814 by James Marshall, brother of Supreme Court Chief Justice John Marshall, with its bed-and-breakfast feel; the carriage house rooms, more akin to Marriott corporate style; or the Baroness's cottage, decorated in a Western theme, a nod to J. W. Marriott's roots in Utah. Although Marriott's budget hotel chain, Fairfield Inn, is named for the property, the experience here is anything but bargain-basement: wine and cheese in the afternoon, hearty breakfasts, in the morning and the chance to ride horses and hunt.

INFORMATION
Visitors Center

Loudoun County operates a visitors center (112-G South St., Leesburg, Va., 800/752-6118, ext. 11, www.visitloudoun.org, daily 9 A.M.–5 P.M., closed Thanksgiving Day, Christmas Day, and New Year's Day) in Leesburg's Market Station complex that contains a small exhibit about the county as well as maps and information about hotels, restaurants, tours, festivals, and wineries in Loudoun's myriad small towns and hunt country villages.

Media

Residents of Loudoun County get their news from several dailies, including the *Washington Post,* the *Washington Times,* and the *Washington Examiner* as well as a plethora of weekly newspapers with blanket coverage of local news,

schools, high school sports, and events, including the venerable *Loudoun Times Mirror,* owned by local publishing family the Arundels, and *Leesburg Today* and *Middleburg Life,* both published alongside other northern Virginia weeklies by a Texas-based company. Most of what is on Loudoun's radio and television airwaves comes from outside the county; its one local radio station, WCRW AM 1190, focuses on Asian news and entertainment, and there are no publicly broadcasted television stations.

GETTING THERE

Leesburg is 40 miles northwest of Washington DC, and Middleburg is 40 miles due west of the capital. The best way to travel to either area is by car; take I-66 to the Dulles Toll Road (Virginia Rte. 267) and continue on the Dulles Greenway to reach Leesburg. To get to Middleburg, take I-66 to U.S. 50 north, which runs straight through the center of the village. If you are exploring the area, a number of scenic byways connect Leesburg and Middleburg, the largest being U.S. 15. For a day trip to Leesburg on weekdays only, visitors can catch a "reverse commute" shuttle (703/777-0100, www.loudoun.gov/Default.aspx?tabid=3093, $2.50 cash one-way) from the West Falls Church Metro Station, on the Orange Line, in the morning and a bus home in the afternoon. Manassas National Battlefield is 30 miles from Washington DC, and is reached by taking I-66 to Exit 52, and then U.S. 29 south.

If you want to take a trip outside DC, consider planning to leave after 9 A.M., once traffic has cleared, or before 2:30 P.M., to avoid the evening rush hour. You can also leave after 6:30 P.M., catching the tail-end of traffic and avoiding restricted carpool-lane closures.

GETTING AROUND

Both Leesburg and Middleburg are easily traversed by foot. Leesburg has a dense downtown historic district of shops, restaurants, and cafés; Middleburg is a one-stoplight town with all the activity along the two roads that intersect, Washington and Madison Streets. But to travel around the entire area, car trips are necessary.

BACKGROUND

The Setting

The waters of the Potomac River tumble over falls great and small just northwest of Washington before fanning out under the city's broad bridges, forming the U.S. capital's western boundary. To the northeast, the Anacostia River—more a wide creek than a great tributary—enters from the Maryland suburbs, cleaving the city in two before converging with the Potomac, which pours into mighty Chesapeake Bay 100 miles downstream. Washington sits at the confluence of these two rivers, a city straddling the mid-Atlantic geographic fall line that separates the region called the Piedmont Plateau, a raised area of rolling hills and valleys that slopes steadily to the Blue Ridge Mountains to the west and the Coastal Plain, a wide, flat region formed from eons of fluvial deposits that stretches to the Atlantic Ocean. The site for the city was selected largely in part for its location about midway among the 13 original colonies. Today, this city of 650,000 and its sprawling suburbs of nearly 5 million rests in the middle of the Eastern Seaboard, in an area that is largely agrarian outside the suburbs to the west, south, and east,, with small cities such as Annapolis and Frederick, Maryland, and Fredericksburg and Leesburg, Virginia, each within an hour's

© PATRICIA KIME

drive. To the north is the industrial northeast, with Baltimore, Philadelphia, and New York City 1, 3, and 4 hours, respectively, by car. To the south, 90 miles away, is the former capital of the Confederacy, Richmond, home to Virginia's statehouse.

GEOGRAPHY AND CLIMATE

Washington is bordered on three sides—west, north, and east—by the state of Maryland and to the south by Virginia. The Potomac River, where it runs along the city, lies entirely within the District of Columbia, which means the DC border runs directly to the Virginia shoreline, and some city landmarks, reachable only from Virginia, including Roosevelt Island and the land that contains Lady Byrd Johnson Memorial Grove, are actually considered to be in DC and not in Virginia, as they appear. Washington covers an area of 68.3 square miles, 61 of which are land, with nearly seven square miles of water. The geography of the northern and northwestern portions, visible in and around Rock Creek Park, is rough and rugged, a reflection of its placement in the Piedmont Plateau, an area created by the erosion and upheaval of ancient mountains. Rocks and boulders in this area are largely metamorphic and igneous, with the predominant minerals being boulder gneiss, granite gneiss, mica schist, and quartzite. The city's eastern and southern portions belong in the Coastal Plain, referred to as the Tidewater region in Virginia, a flat area of light soils and sediments that encompasses marshes and broad waterways. The highest point in Washington is 410 feet above sea level in the Tenleytown neighborhood at Fort Reno, a neighborhood park and former Civil War fort. The lowest geographic point is sea level, at the shorelines of the Anacostia and Potomac Rivers from just south of Little Falls, near Chain Bridge to the city's southernmost point. The city is divided into quadrants that meet at the U.S. Capitol, although the city's actual geographic center is near the intersection of 4th Street, L Street, and New York Avenue NW. Nearly 20 percent of the District's land is parkland, second only to New York City in terms of preserved acres as a percent of land area in the United States.

Washington has four distinct seasons, but with a relatively mild climate that offers a taste of the best—and worst—of each. Spring and autumns are the city's most glorious, often with crystal-clear deep-blue skies and warming, moderate, or slightly cool temperatures (although early spring can sometimes be unseasonably cool and wet, and winter occasionally comes early in the fall). Summers are decidedly Southern in nature; the region is classified as subtropical humid, and days are hot and exceedingly sticky, with average high temperatures of 88°F in July and 85°F in August. Humidity is often upward of 55 percent late in the day. As a result, late-afternoon thunderstorms are commonplace from late June through Labor Day, although their occurrence isn't quite as dependable as they are in tropical regions like Florida. Winters are mild, although an errant arctic air mass can force the mercury down to the single digits. Snowfall is hit or miss—in some years the area receives none; at other times, major snowstorms have paralyzed the city for up to a week. The average is roughly 14 inches of snow per year. Because of this ambiguity, the city departments that handle snow removal and oversight do not have the large budgets or capabilities for performing their tasks that Chicago, Boston, and any place north of New York have, a situation that often leads to mass closings of the federal government and schools and opens Washington to great ridicule. Still, the surprise closings lead to a few of those fun, unexpected joys of childhood—the snow day.

Average rainfall in DC is nearly 40 inches per year, with much of it coming in rain that lasts for days but also comes in thunderstorms. If you find yourself on the National Mall or in an open space when a thunderstorm is approaching, head indoors and remain there until the storm passes. They usually move on quickly.

ENVIRONMENTAL ISSUES

The Washington of today is very different than it was 40 years ago. In the 1960s and early 1970s, the pollution in the Potomac

River was so objectionable that President Lyndon Johnson cited its filth as a reason to urge passage of the Water Quality Act of 1965. Georgetown housed great factories, including a flour mill and a rendering plant that emitted a smell so putrid the flour mill posted a sign along the Whitehurst Freeway: "The Objectionable Odors You May Notice in This Area Do Not Originate in This Plant." Even today, an aging power plant on Benning Road in the city's eastern half is blamed for releasing unhealthy amounts of particulates into the air. Still, Washington never quite developed as an industrial city, so it has far fewer problems with health concerns caused by tainted water, air, and land than major industrial cities. But it does have at least one unique issue, a problem that came to light in northwest DC in the neighborhood of multimillion-dollar homes around American University, that might indicate further hidden health concerns: In 1992 Rick Feeney, who lived in Spring Hill near American University, was cutting his lawn when he heard his dog whining nearby. Responding to the dog in a nearby construction site, Feeney was overcome with watering eyes, stinging skin, and a bitter taste in his mouth. His dog had stumbled on a canister containing chemical weapons, left by soldiers in the 1920s when the area contained the U.S. Army's chemical warfare research center. When the Army shut down its program, service members buried many of the leftovers and walked away. Since 1993, the Army has worked to test and clean up the area that spans the Spring Valley and American University neighborhoods.

With restrictions and cleanup of the area's sewer plants and water treatment facilities as well as renovations and restrictions on existing factories and businesses, Washington on the whole is much cleaner than it was two decades ago. The Potomac River is now used for recreational boating and fishing, and families gather at the banks of the Anacostia River and the Potomac for picnics. Even swimmers venture into the water—unheard of just 10 years ago, but still not recommended because the seemingly placid river has treacherous hidden currents.

Hot, stifling summer days can sometimes put a strain on people prone to heat, humidity, and high ozone levels. The city often has Code Red and Code Orange air quality days, meaning that on Orange days, people susceptible to respiratory distress should avoid being outside from mid-morning through evening, and on Red days, everyone should limit outdoor activity. There is also apparently a Code Purple designation that urges everyone to stay indoors, but I've never experienced one. To check the daily air quality for the region and the forecast, visit www.mwcog.org/environment/air/forecast/.

Regarding the city's efforts to become greener, many of Washington's new buildings are being designed to meet Leadership in Energy and Environmental Design (LEED) standards, with some older structures being renovated to improve their green practices. The first LEED-certified building in the city was the National Association of Realtors building on New Jersey Avenue NW. Other platinum- and gold-certified buildings include the Hermann Miller National Design Center and Nusta Spa.

One more environmentally conscious thing to note: If you grocery shop in DC, expect to pay a $0.05 surcharge for plastic bags. The tax was added to reduce the number of unsightly nonbiodegradable bags that end up in the waterways around the nation's capital.

History

17TH AND 18TH CENTURIES

When Capt. John Smith—English adventurer, colonist, mapmaker, and yes, the same John Smith whose life was saved by the legendary Pocahontas—explored the Potomac River in 1608, he traveled all the way to the falls north of what is now Washington, encountering Native American villages lining the great waterway's shores. Groups with names like Anacostin, Dogue, Tauxenent, Piscataway, and Nacotchtank were affiliated with great Native American confederacies like the Conoy, Iroquois, and Powhatan. Native Americans had, in fact, occupied the region for more than 13,000 years. European settlement of the region would come slowly as Europeans clashed with local Native Americans until the latter eventually moved west. Seventy years later, land grants were awarded by the British crown, traded and sold, and English colonists began to settle the area, mainly in Alexandria, Virginia, and the area round Georgetown. The two cities flourished as ports where crops like tobacco, wheat, and corn left America for Europe and supplies, including provisions for the French and Indian War, troops, and slaves entered the growing colony. In 1762, George Washington inherited his brother's farm southeast of Alexandria, Virginia, but he was long familiar with the entire region, having surveyed much of it starting at the age of 17. At the end of the Revolutionary War, leaders from the large Northern cities lobbied for one of their established cities to become the capital, while the Southern states wanted it closer to their region to ensure that the politicians in Washington would look out for their agrarian interests and economy, whose success depended largely on the controversial slave trade. In a compromise among James Madison, Thomas Jefferson, and Alexander Hamilton, the Founding Fathers decided to place the capital near the South—between two slave states, in fact—if the South would help pay off Northern debt from the war. The city's exact site was chosen by George

WHAT'S WITH THE NAME?

The capital city is called many things: Washington; the District; Washington DC; or simply DC. The unwieldy name came about during the two decades following the British surrender at Yorktown that ended the Revolutionary War. In 1791, three commissioners, appointed by George Washington to establish the city, named the selected area the Territory of Columbia. At the time, "Columbia" was a nickname and sentimental term for the United States. The area became known as the District of Columbia by 1801 and included the original federal city and the city of Georgetown and Alexandria, Virginia, inside the 100-square-mile city. The federal portion, the capital city, was named the City of Washington in honor of the first president. In 1871 Congress passed the District of Columbia Organic Act, revoking the charters of the cities of Washington and Georgetown as well as the County of Washington (the city of Alexandria had been returned to the state of Virginia, breaking up the perfect square), and placed them under one city government, with all three areas joined as the city of Washington in the District of Columbia. Thus Washington is known as Washington DC.

Washington. The new capital district stretched from northwest of Georgetown to Jones Point just south of Alexandria, Virginia, and included stipulations that all federal buildings be built on the Maryland side of the Potomac. A survey team placed boundary markers, some of which still exist, in 10 square miles on each side, based on calculations by self-taught mathematician and surveyor Benjamin Banneker. In 1791, Washington chose French engineer and Revolutionary War hero Pierre L'Enfant to design the future city. Taking inspiration from his native Paris, he drafted plans for a federal town of broad streets built on a grid with great parks, city squares, and grandiose public buildings. Although he came into conflict with the city's oversight board and eventually was removed, many of L'Enfant's design elements form what is recognized as Washington today. On June 11, 1800, the city officially became the seat of power for the new country.

19TH CENTURY

In the 19th century's first decade, the city developed within its borders: Construction began on a canal designed to improve transportation and drainage for the city, and buildings sprung up alongside the U.S. Capitol and the White House. But an unexpected war destroyed much of the work: In August 1814, the British dealt a devastating blow to the United States during the War of 1812, invading and burning Washington and setting afire buildings such as the Capitol, the White House, the Navy Yard, the Arsenal on the point between the Anacostia and the Potomac Rivers, the Treasury Office, and the Long Bridge, located not far from the present-day 14th Street Bridge. During this famous raid, First Lady Dolley Madison instructed members of the White House staff, including slaves, to save important artifacts, while her husband James Madison had already spirited the Charters of Freedom to a private home in the Virginia countryside near Leesburg. The British spared the Marine Barracks, leaving the Commandant's home untouched, and today, it remains the oldest occupied public building in the city. After the 1814 peace treaty that ended the war, Washington began to rebuild. In 1835 the railroad arrived; in 1848 construction began on the Washington Monument. In 1847 the city underwent a permanent change in its boundaries: Tensions regarding the inclusion of Georgetown's port in the city as well as the stipulation that no federal buildings be built on the Virginia side of the river proved detrimental to Alexandria's economy. Tension also existed with Virginia's involvement in the slave trade and rising antislavery sentiment

in the nation's capital, leading the city to return the area to the state in a move known as retrocession. In 1861, when Fort Sumter fell in Charleston, South Carolina, and Virginia seceded in April, troops poured in to protect the capital and government offices. The population of the city doubled, and the city managed to stay relatively removed from the war, with the notable exception, the Battle of Fort Stephens in 1864, when Confederate Gen. Jubal Early attacked the fort near 13th Street and Military Road NW. President Lincoln rode out to survey the skirmish, and he came under fire while standing on a parapet. A year later the war ended, and a week after the Confederacy's surrender in Appomattox, Virginia, Lincoln was shot, assassinated in Ford's Theatre by Confederate sympathizer John Wilkes Booth. The president died on April 15, 1865, in Petersen House, across the street from the theater. War has often served as the impetus for growth and change in DC, and the post–Civil War era proved to be no different; city roads were paved, sewer improvements were made, Georgetown was absorbed into the city proper, and entire neighborhoods fell under the governance of Washington. The Washington Monument was completed in 1888, a great spire overlooking new streetcar lines, city neighborhoods, suburbs, and grand public and private buildings like the Renwick Gallery, the Smithsonian Castle, the Corcoran Gallery, and fanciful but long-gone buildings like the original Department of Agriculture offices, a massive Victorian–Second Empire building near the National Mall.

20TH CENTURY TO THE PRESENT

The 20th century brought sweeping improvements to the city's design, with a commission led by Michigan senator James McMillan, inspired by the City Beautiful movement, to create a capital that encouraged civic pride through monumental architecture. McMillan sought to fulfill the vision of original designer Pierre L'Enfant for the city to be on par with Paris, London, and Rome. Hiring the geniuses behind the designs for the 1893 World's Columbian Exposition—famed architects like Daniel Burnham and Charles McKim, sculptors Augustus Saint-Gaudens and younger brother Louis St. Gaudens, and landscape architect Frederick Law Olmsted—the McMillan Commission permanently altered the landscape of Washington, dredging the Potomac River and using the reclaimed soil to build up the riverbanks for great memorials, including the Lincoln Memorial, finishing the National Mall, overseeing completion of the Tidal Basin, creating landscapes that enhanced the city's monumental buildings, erecting the Memorial Bridge, and constructing Union Station. While the efforts halted briefly during World War I, they neared completion with the construction of the Lincoln Memorial in 1922. Projects continued throughout the city during the Great Depression, when Franklin Delano Roosevelt put people to work, including artists, through the Works Progress Administration. Today, the most notable evidence of FDR's New Deal program is the Department of the Interior Building, built in 1936 and painted inside with extensive murals and decorated with photographs by Ansel Adams taken expressly as part of a WPA project.

World War II brought a building boom to the city, whose population had been increasing steadily as a result of New Deal programs and the war effort. Construction began in the suburbs to help alleviate housing shortages, and the Pentagon was constructed in Arlington, Virginia, to consolidate the War Department under one roof. National Airport, also across the river in Arlington, opened in 1941, replacing an inadequate Hoover Field and further linking the city with the rest of the world. Embassies opened across the city, bringing in international residents. The city's African American culture also flourished. U Street became the center of music, theater, and entertainment, with jazz greats Duke Ellington and Shirley Horn appearing often alongside stars like Ella Fitzgerald, Cab Calloway, and Louis Armstrong. The city was a "majority-minority" region by 1950, with African Americans

making up 60 percent of the total population. Howard University attracted the young and ambitious; the city became known for cultivating a learned African American population, even as segregation continued in federal buildings and private businesses and clubs throughout the city.

Two hundred thousand people stood on the Mall near the Reflecting Pool on August 28, 1963, to hear Martin Luther King Jr. deliver his "I Have a Dream" speech at the Lincoln Memorial. The civil rights movement grew momentum; in 1964, Congress passed the Civil Rights Act outlawing segregation; the Voting Rights Act followed a year later. Despite the successes, however, a civil rights–related murder set the city back for decades: In 1968, following the assassination of King, entire city blocks were burned and destroyed in five days of rioting. Nearly 14,000 U.S. troops, including Marines and the Army, were called in to guard the city's federal buildings. The National Guard assisted the police force with quelling the unrest, but by the end of the week, some 1,200 building had been burned, including 900 stores, many of them African American–owned, and 12 people had been killed. Washington became the city I knew as a child, with a devastated inner-city economy where once-grand showcases like the Warner Theatre showed X-rated movies just to survive economically. Whites and middle-class African Americans fled the city for the suburbs, with many African Americans heading to nearby Prince George's County, Maryland, now the wealthiest African American county in the country. Crime surged, and Washington was not a place to spend time after dark. The great Bicentennial Celebration in 1976 helped demonstrate that the city was not going to collapse under its enormous challenges, and the opening of the Metro, also in 1976, helped revitalize entire city blocks. Visionaries built entertainment venues, including Kennedy Center and the MCI (now Verizon) Center. Businesses reopened in riot-torn neighborhoods, and an influx of immigrants, particularly in Adams Morgan and areas north such as

Mount Pleasant as well as in the northeastern and eastern parts of the city, helped repopulate. The city's leadership extended breaks to businesses to entice them to build in the city while passing legislation and approving development to encourage young people to live within the city's boundaries.

At the same time, changes were afoot in Congress to allow Washington more self-governance. Until 1973, when the District of Columbia Home Rule Act was passed, management of the city's municipal services were overseen by a three-member board of commissioners appointed by the president. The Home Rule Act allowed for an elected mayor and city council comprising a chairman elected at large, four at-large members, and one from each of the city's wards. Under Home Rule, Congress reviews all legislation passed by the council before it can become law and also reviews and is responsible for the city's budget. The District of Columbia, like many U.S. territories, has a non-voting representative in Congress. The first popularly elected mayor of Washington was Walter Washington, a Howard University graduate who served as appointed mayor-commissioner before winning the popular vote. Mayor from 1975 to 1979, Washington attempted to bridge the gap between the white congressional committee that oversaw the city and its African American residents, but his consensus-building style proved to be his undoing, since he was largely perceived by city voters as not understanding their needs. He was replaced by the headline-grabbing Marion Barry, a popular yet divisive leader who continues to serve on the city council. Barry, a civil rights activist, school board member, and city council member before he was elected, was seen as a hero by African American residents, a man who had been shot during a siege of the District Building in 1977 and who stood for the poor and underprivileged. He spent his first term solving the city's sanitation problems and solidifying his office's place in the governing system, but he began running into trouble, with his administration often implicated in questionable contracting and hiring tactics, by his second term. Trouble continued to follow Barry,

and he continued to be reelected despite rising crime rates, personal scandals, and increased unemployment. In 1990 he was arrested for crack cocaine possession during an FBI sting. He stepped down in 1991 and subsequently served six months in prison but was reelected mayor in 1994, when he lost control of the city to Congress, which created a Financial Control Board to manage Washington. The city's chief financial officer at the time, Anthony Williams, later succeeded Barry as mayor. Under the leadership of Williams and successor Adrian Fenty, the city has surpassed its previous successes, attracting residents and young families back to city neighborhoods with a vibrant arts community, attractive housing, lively nightlife and restaurants, and quality entertainment and recreation venues, with more planned to include often overlooked neighborhoods.

At the start of the 21st century, the city had firmly established itself as a major metropolitan destination, an approachable town with all the trimmings of sophisticated urban life. The turn of the new century was not without its painful moments, however. For two consecutive autumns, DC residents faced horrific events, including the September 11, 2001, attack on the Pentagon, during which numerous area residents died, both inside the buildings and on American Airlines Flight 77; the anthrax attacks on the U.S. Capitol that killed two postal workers and caused thousands to take precautionary antibiotics; and a year later, a sniper and an accomplice who terrorized the city for three weeks, killing 10 people and injuring three more in random attacks. These events prompted changes in security at buildings across the city and alterations to landscaping as well as increased hidden security measures, but they also reaffirmed many Washingtonians' commitment to living in their city. Washington today remains a youthful, ambitious place where anything is possible.

Washington Today

The Washington you see today—the vibrant neighborhoods, clean streets, a sparkling convention center, new hotel and office towers—is as much a reflection of a nationwide interest in urban renewal as it is a monument to its business and city leaders who had the gumption and ambition to continue on a path set by planner Pierre L'Enfant more than 200 years ago. Washington is a lively city with a diverse ethnic population, including diplomats and embassy staffers; a burgeoning Latino population mainly from Central and South America, especially El Salvador; a large Ethiopian population; and in predominantly white, prosperous north Arlington just across the Key Bridge, a large Mongolian population. Ethnic groups are changing the way Washington eats and shops, with new restaurants and stores. And the influx of new blood is attracting the young and wealthy who want to live at the heart of it all.

There's a downside, of course, to the redevelopment—a rise in property values and assessments that has forced longtime businesses and residents to head for less expensive areas and suburbs. Gentrification of many of the city's neighborhoods has ensured that only the wealthiest individuals can live in many parts of the city. Washington DC remained the hottest real estate markets in the country through the recent recession. When real estate values crashed nationwide in 2007, they only dipped in DC, and during the recovery, while other cities' values remained low, Washington's recovered and increased, the only city in the country to do so from 2010 to 2011. The average price of a home in the 20003 zip code, which includes Capitol Hill, is nearly $500,000.

The upside of gentrification is the revival of areas long overlooked by city planners and residents. The neighborhoods of Anacostia, to the east of the Anacostia River, and Trinidad, in northeast DC, classified for years as hopeless for their high crime rates, drug problems, and burned-out housing stock, are starting to see renewed interest. In the past year, young entrepreneurs in Anacostia have opened an organic grocery store, shops, and a neighborhood tavern, and artists are scooping up buildings at the edge of Trinidad near H Street for galleries and showcase venues. The city's renewed optimism permeates the neighborhoods across its three corners.

Government and Economy

As the capital of the most powerful democracy in the world, Washington is home to the U.S. government, housed in buildings across the cityscape, with the executive branch headquartered at the White House, the legislative branch at the U.S. Capitol and the judicial branch in the U.S. Supreme Court. The federal government plays a prominent role in day-to-day DC housekeeping as well. The city is governed by a mayor and a 13-member city council, but Congress has authority over the city's budget, approving it as part of the federal appropriations process, as well as the city's laws. City residents pay federal and local income taxes but have no voting representation in Congress. Until 1961 and passage of the 23rd Amendment, city residents couldn't even vote for the president of the United States. The reason Washington residents do not have congressional representation dates to 1801, when Congress enacted the District of Columbia Organic Act, declaring the city independent of any state. The writers of the Constitution sought to establish the nation's capital with the federal government in a place with its own sovereign jurisdiction.

While Washington's economy is tied largely to the federal government and the many businesses and agencies associated with it, the region actually has a fairly diverse economy, with nongovernmental industries centered largely on higher education, finance, public policy, scientific research, and technology. The unemployment rate in the city proper is roughly 6 percent, with the same rate across the region in adjacent Maryland and Virginia. It ranks third in the amount of office space among U.S. cities, behind New York and Chicago.

GOVERNMENT

Washington's government structure has changed throughout history, tied to the desires and whims of Congress as well as the U.S. Constitution and numerous acts, including the Organic Act of 1801, which stipulates that the city is an independent entity ruled by the federal government and doesn't belong to any state. As a result, Congress has the ultimate authority over Washington, although the system of governance has fluctuated over the years. In the beginning, a mayor was appointed by the president. From 1812 to 1820, mayors were elected by a city council. From 1820 to 1871, the mayor was popularly elected, although only for the city of Washington: Georgetown and an unincorporated area had their own councils. After 1871 the municipalities were merged into a single District of Columbia government with a territorial governor. From 1874 a three-member Board of Commissioners, appointed by the president, oversaw the city's governance until 1975, when the city was granted permission to elect its own mayor, who is elected to four-year terms without term limits. The city also has a 13-member council; representatives hail from the city's eight wards and occupy five at-large seats, including the council chair's seat.

DC still very much heeds to Congress's oversight, however. In 1995, when the city was on the verge of insolvency under then-mayor Marion Barry, Congress formed the District of Columbia Financial Control Board, which seized the duties of the mayor, overseeing all municipal spending. By September 2001, with Mayor Anthony Williams at the helm, Congress again gave control of the city's finances to the mayor,

SCANDALS

The combination of power, money, and constant attention from staff, constituents, and equally powerful people proves to be the downfall of some people in Washington, and yes, it's nearly always men who believe they'll get away with impropriety, ranging from the forgivable, such as the randy encounter Rep. John Jenrette had with his wife on the steps of the U.S. Capitol, to the unlawful, the same John Jenrette convicted of taking a $50,000 bribe from the FBI in the 1980 Abscam sting.

One scandal was so huge in DC that it continues to prompt journalists and Washington-watchers to tack the word *gate* on the end of nearly every scandal, at least while the scandal is hot (recall the use of "Contra-gate" to describe the Iran-Contra affair or "Weiner-gate" in 2011). But the original was a scandal that brought down a president. On June 17, 1972, five men were arrested for breaking into the Democratic National Committee Headquarters at the Watergate office complex on the banks of the Potomac River next door to Kennedy Center; an investigation revealed that the men were paid by a Nixon campaign committee, and secret tapes, made by President Nixon in the White House of conversations that took place between him and others, implicated Nixon in the cover-up. Facing impeachment, Nixon resigned on August 9, 1974.

Before Watergate, there was Teapot Dome, a scandal that sullied the reputation of the Harding Administration, involving oil leases and vast sums of money. Warren Harding's Interior Secretary, Albert B. Fall, leased the Navy's petroleum reserves at Teapot Dome, Wyoming, and elsewhere to private companies without competitive bidding. The lease wasn't unlawful, but he received kickbacks and gifts totaling more than $5 million in today's dollars for the arrangement. Fall was convicted of conspiracy and bribery and sent to prison.

With the nation still reeling from Nixon's resignation, Arkansas representative Wilbur Mills, considered one of the most powerful Democrats in Congress, gave the country something to talk about. The married chairman of the Ways and Means Committee began seeing Argentinean stripper Fanne Foxe, and one evening while riding in the car with Foxe, Mills was pulled over by police. Foxe jumped out of the car and careened into the Tidal Basin, to be rescued by law enforcement. The incident and suspending the control board's operations. Congress retains the right to review and overturn the city's laws and can control the city's budget as well. The mayor and council adopt a local budget that is then approved as part of the appropriations process by Congress. Income, sales, and property taxes provide roughly two-thirds of the city's revenues, with Congress making up the remainder through federal grants and direct funding. The federal government pays for the city's courts, public defenders, and prison system, and its agencies operate a vast police force within the city's borders, including the U.S. Park Police, Secret Service, U.S. Marshals, and others.

The city has one representative in Congress, Eleanor Holmes Norton, who has served since 1990. She has limited voting rights: She is able to vote at committee level but cannot vote on final passage of laws. She is also allowed to speak in committee and on the House floor. She has been a tireless advocate for earning DC full voting rights in Congress. The city has no Senate representation, although it does have three votes in the Electoral College and its citizens can vote in presidential elections, due to the passage of the 23rd Amendment to the Constitution in 1961.

The congressional Financial Control Board and the city's chief financial officer at the time, future mayor Anthony Williams, are largely credited for the city's recovery from massive deficits and real estate development. Williams served as CFO and made a number of changes to the city financial structure and the system's human resources, backed by the board, which drew power away from then-mayor Marion Barry. Williams was able to take the city from

---

subsequent appearances in public by Mills with Foxe prompted the House's Democratic leadership to revoke Mills's chairmanship.

The line Marion Barry uttered when he was nabbed by the FBI for smoking crack in a Washington DC hotel room has become part of the nation's slang lexicon: "Bitch set me up." Law enforcement had investigated Barry, the mayor of Washington, for six years, suspecting illicit drug possession and use. He was convicted of one possession charge and spent six months in jail; he went on to win the mayoral race again three years later.

The name of a starstruck White House staffer surfaced during legal proceedings brought against Bill Clinton by Arkansas state employee Paula Jones and led to the impeachment of a president: The young lady's name was Monica Lewinsky. She had left a job at the White House and was working at the Pentagon when she submitted an affidavit in the Jones case denying a physical relationship with the president. But she had been telling Pentagon coworker, Linda Tripp, another story, and Tripp had secretly recorded those conversations. When word of the relationship broke, Clinton denied it, wife Hillary defended him,

and the Clinton Administration went into full attack mode, smearing Lewinsky as a liar and tool of the Republicans. But the besmirched gal had an ace in the hole, a blue dress containing evidence of a sexual encounter with Clinton. The president was impeached for perjury and obstruction of justice in the House but was cleared by the Senate. He finished out his term.

Bad behavior often brings down politicians – cases in point, New York governor Elliot Spitzer, Sen. John Ensign, Rep. Anthony Weiner, Sen. Larry Craig – but some recover resoundingly, as in the case of Sen. Edward Kennedy, who survived numerous scandals, including one that killed a 28-year-old woman at Chappaquiddick Island, Massachusetts; reports of alcohol-fueled antics; and a 1985 incident with best buddy senator Chris Dodd at a Washington restaurant, where the two formed a "waitress sandwich" with their server while their dates were in the restroom. Kennedy survived it all to outlive his famous siblings and become the revered the "Lion of the Senate," passing vast amounts of legislation, including major health care reform laws.

a $355 million deficit in 1995 to a $185 million surplus just two years later. He ran for mayor and won resoundingly, continuing his efforts to bring economic development to the city, bringing in more than $40 billion worth of investments and bringing Major League Baseball back to the city. Still, despite his successes that put DC on the path to where it is today, Williams was criticized for ignoring those who live in poverty and supporting gentrification, which forced many longtime residents out of their neighborhoods.

If Williams was known for putting the city back on solid financial footing, Mayor Adrian Fenty was known for carrying the mantle, focusing on attracting young people and families to the city, improving schools, reducing crime, and renovating city structures. To fix the city's broken public school system, Fenty restructured it, hiring a chancellor, controversial reformer Michelle Rhee, who reported directly to him. Together, Rhee and Fenty closed schools, fired teachers, repaired aging infrastructure, and demanded accountability, resulting in an unprecedented rise in test scores, although analysts debate whether Rhee's reforms can be directly linked to the increase. Widely praised by many city residents, Rhee's methodology, manner, and ruthlessness was widely opposed by longtime teachers, administrators, and teachers unions. Rhee's contract was not renewed by the mayor who defeated Fenty, Vincent C. Gray, a former council member. Fenty also beefed up the city's police presence, rehabilitated and built playgrounds and recreation areas, and created additional affordable housing spaces.

ECONOMY

According to a Gallup poll, 38 percent of DC workers are employed by the government, the highest percentage of any jurisdiction on the country. Not surprisingly, the states of Virginia and Maryland rank 3rd and 4th in the nation for government workers, at 27 and 26 percent of their populations, respectively. (Alaska comes in second, with 31 percent working either for the state, federal, or local government). The city's reputation as a "government town" is thought to shield Washington from fluctuations in the economy, as the federal government continues to run regardless of booms or busts. Still, with the government facing possible cuts and downsizing to reduce deficits, the possibility exists that the city's federal employees may not be so secure in their jobs. This uncertainty, however, doesn't deter job seekers and newcomers from traveling to Washington with the expectation of landing a position either with the federal government or one of the many organizations whose work supports or contracts with the government. In addition to direct government jobs, the city is rife with positions relevant to government service, including those in law, contracting, defense support, nonprofits, lobbying, trade unions, industry groups, and professional associations that have their headquarters in the city, close to where they can try to influence lawmakers on their interests.

Outside government, the largest industries are education, health care, and public policy, with several universities and their medical hospitals ranking in the top 10 of nongovernmental employers in the city in 2010. The city is also home to four Fortune 500 companies, including mortgage backer Fannie Mae, manufacturing and technology company Danaher, energy titan Pepco, and media powerhouse The Washington Post. An additional four Fortune 500 companies are in adjacent Bethesda, Maryland, including hospitality corporations Marriott and Host Hotels and Resorts and defense powerhouse Lockheed Martin. Nine Fortune 500 companies are located in the Virginia suburbs within 10 miles of the city in industries as varied as media, defense, banking, mortgages, and consulting.

The city is also regarded as a global real estate investment opportunity, recognized as a top area that favors business expansion, drawing foreign investors to capitalize on its real estate boom. In 2009, Forbes ranked it a top real estate investment destination over London and New York. In terms of the residential market, the city has remained fairly isolated from the housing crash; while prices dropped precipitously in the outer suburbs when the bubble burst, they only dipped in many areas inside the Beltway, the name for I-95 and I-495, the expressways that circle the city, and have regained strength in the past couple of years. In 2009, Washington reported a higher annual income per capita than any state, $63,492, beating out Connecticut's $60,310. The nationwide personal income per capita is $42,539. Despite the preponderance of wealth, nearly 19 percent of Washington's population lives below the poverty line.

The Government

More than one-third of Washington's residents work for the government, including the federal government, the city, and DC's transportation arm, the Washington Area Metro Transit Authority. Unemployment in early 2011 hovered at 5.9 percent and never got much higher than 7 percent at the height of the recession. Most Americans would attribute this to the growth of bureaucracy, and it's true: Washington remains isolated from economic dips because its economy is supported largely by government employment. Federal employment increased by nearly 20,000 jobs, many of them related to helping save, bail out, or manage the ailing private sector, during the first years of the economic downturn. Notably, though, as the federal government moved to hire more people, state governments in the region cut jobs. And with the federal deficit rising and Congress looking to tighten its belt, the public sector forecast might not be as rosy as it has in the past two decades. Historically, Washington's economy has benefited from upheavals such as wars and economic calamities. But public calls for cuts and efforts to eliminate the deficit may sway Congress to cut programs and trim the workforce, currently at 246,000 people, with neighboring Virginia and Maryland carrying an additional 1.2 million public-sector employees statewide, including and local municipal workers, according to the Bureau of Labor Statistics.

Health Care, Medical Research, and Sciences

Americans spend roughly $2.3 trillion on health care each year, and the Washington region is home to several of the top medical facilities handling the research that supports much of the medical care nationwide. The city has 16 medical centers and hospitals, with the National Institutes of Health in Bethesda, Maryland, serving as the federal government's research arm, with 27 institutes and centers of its own that focus on specific diseases or body systems. In addition, NIH is the world's largest source of funding for medical research, providing grants and money for thousands of scientists at universities and research centers worldwide. Washington Hospital Center is the largest nonprofit hospital in the region, located in north Washington with Children's National Medical Center, one of the country's top pediatric hospitals. Across the road from Washington Hospital Center and Children's is the Veterans Administration's Washington VA Medical Center, a busy hospital that serves aging veterans as well as the recently wounded. The area's major universities all have hospitals, research facilities, and associated medical schools, including Georgetown, George Washington, and Howard. The National Naval Medical Center in Bethesda consolidated with the Army's Walter Reed Army Medical Center to become the Walter Reed National Military Medical Center Bethesda, the military's flagship hospital, responsible for treating wounded warriors as well as members of Congress. Other hospitals include popular neighborhood facilities such as Sibley, Providence, and Suburban Hospital, also in Bethesda, affiliated with Johns Hopkins in Baltimore.

Education

DC is home to 11 major colleges and universities, mostly private institutions that employ thousands of workers in the Metro area, not counting the medical centers affiliated with the universities. Five of the top 10 private employers by the number of employees in DC are universities, with Georgetown ranking first and George Washington second with 7,466 employees. Also in the top 10 are Howard

University (5th), American University (7th), and Catholic University (9th).

Washington's universities are among the most elite in the nation, drawing students from across the country and around the world to their undergraduate programs as well as their renowned law and medical schools. The DC area has about 140,000 students and was ranked fourth most desirable metropolitan area in the country to attend school, according to the College Destinations Index put out by the American Institute for Economic Research. The largest university by student population is George Washington University, with 10,370 undergraduates. It has a law school and medical schools as well as world-renowned programs on public policy and government. Georgetown University is considered one of the country's top universities, vying for students who apply to the Ivy League and the nation's other top schools. Its undergraduate student population is second in size, with 7,433 students, and it boasts a highly regarded law school as well as one of the country's most prestigious medical schools. Other historic and unique schools in the area include Howard University, a historically African American college and university, and American University, which draws students from around the world as well as from across the United States. Other notable schools include Catholic University; Gallaudet, the nation's only institution of higher learning for the deaf; and the small and highly competitive Corcoran College of Art and Design. The only public university in the city is the University of the District of Columbia, a school with 4,779 undergraduates that serves primarily low-income and nontraditional students.

Tourism

As the nation's capital, Washington is one of the top tourist destinations in the United States, with the National Mall and its monuments ranking third behind Times Square in New York City and the Las Vegas Strip as the most popular, according to Forbes. Slow economy be damned: Tourists spent $5.5 billion in Washington in 2008 and 2009. About

Washington DC is one of the top tourist destinations in the U.S.

16.6 million arrive each year to visit the sights for a vacation; 1.6 million come from overseas, making the city the seventh most visited U.S. destination for international travelers in 2009. International travelers are especially welcome in Washington; although they account for only 10 percent of the visitors to the capital, they are responsible for 22 percent of all the spending, according to Destination DC. This robust industry shows no signs of declining; new meeting spaces like the Walter E. Washington Convention Center and National Harbor are attracting convention and event planners, and new hotels are rising alongside them as this book goes to press. This business, which reaches its peak yearly from March to July, is one of the city's most profitable sectors, although many of the jobs created by tourism are low-paying and often seasonal—perfect for the area's teenagers and part-timers. Destination DC estimates that the travel and tourism industry supports 66,000 full-time jobs in the city, generating $2.6 billion in wages.

People and Culture

DEMOGRAPHICS

Reversing a population slide that began 60 years ago, Washington experienced an increase in population in 2010, surging past 600,000 residents for the first time since 1990. The city gained 30,000 residents since the 2000 census, according to the U.S. Census Bureau. The newcomers, according to the Census, were predominantly white and Hispanic, a fact that has left the historically African American city hovering at the edge of losing its status as a majority African American city (50.7 percent). Seven in 10 Washingtonians were African American in 1970; according to the 2010 census, the African American population dropped by more than 39,000 in the previous decade while the white population soared, from 50,000 to 209,000 residents. City analysts attribute much of the change to gentrification—middle-class blacks have left the city in search of more affordable housing as their neighborhoods have become transformed into upscale housing areas with posh retail stores, boutiques, and services that cater to the upper-middle and upper classes. But an influx of residents following the September 11, 2001, terrorist attacks—the result of a larger government—also contributed to the population change. The city had 601,723 residents in 2010, with roughly 12 percent born overseas and 15 percent speaking a language other than English at home. The median age is 35, and the population is well-educated—nearly half the city's residents have bachelor's degrees and 21 percent have advanced degrees. Females also outnumber males in the city, 53 percent to 47 percent.

RELIGION

A multicultural city founded as a sectarian seat of government, Washington shows little evidence of a predominant religion, although it has a multitude of Protestant and Catholic churches, including two of the largest in the United States. Other houses of worship include a mosque, several Buddhist meditation centers and temples, synagogues, and others. The city's oldest congregation—and oldest church structure as well—reflects the religion of many colonists, the Church of England: St. Paul's Episcopal Church in Northwest Washington was founded in 1712, and its building was constructed in 1775, incorporating parts of the original church. St. Patrick's is the oldest Roman Catholic congregation within the original boundaries of Washington, established in 1794 to serve the Irish stonemasons who built the White House and the U.S. Capitol. Its current building dates to the late 1800s. Holy Trinity Catholic Church in Georgetown was also founded in 1794 and remains one of the oldest churches in continuous operation in the city. The current sanctuary dates to 1829, although the original church is in use as a chapel. The Pew Forum on Religion and Public Life lumps Washington and Maryland together in their surveys of area religions: 20 percent report practicing in mainline Protestant sects; 15 percent worship as evangelical Protestants; 18 percent report being Roman Catholic; and an additional 18 percent attend churches that serve the African American community, such as Baptist or African Methodist Episcopal. Five percent of the population is Jewish.

ARTS AND CULTURE

Washington is a smorgasbord for the arts and culture, a city whose sophisticated tastes began emerging in the late 1800s and benefited from the wealth of great philanthropists like Briton James Smithson, whose money established the Smithsonian Institution, and native son and successful banker William Corcoran, whose art collection became the basis for the city's first art museum in 1874. While many of the city's museums and galleries are devoted to showcasing some of the world's greatest works and collections, Washington also has fostered a community of artists, nurturing creativity in small galleries in nontraditional neighborhoods and hosting events that draw in the city's young population to experience and appreciate the city's more affordable, offbeat, and hidden talent. The city is known for nurturing talent in many forms: The Corcoran College of Art and Design is a small institution of under 700 students who can earn a variety of bachelor's or master's degrees in the fine arts and education; Catholic University is widely recognized for its music programs as well as its musical theater programs—who can forget Susan Sarandon's singing in *The Rocky Horror Picture Show*—and its music programs. Even stalwart Georgetown, known more for its schools of law, foreign service, and medicine, has nurtured great talent, with graduates like actor Bradley Cooper, director and funnyman Carl Reiner, and Pulitzer Prize–winning writers Mary Jordan and Margaret Edson.

Washington is emerging as a major theater city, named in the top 10 nationwide by *Travel + Leisure* magazine for its visiting productions and venues that house them, as well as its homegrown creations, especially productions by the Shakespeare Theatre Company; Arena Stage, which nurtures new playwrights; Woolly Mammoth Theatre Company and Studio Theatre, for their avant-garde productions; and Signature Theatre, for supporting the development of new musicals. In the past year, two Broadway shows were launched from Kennedy Center, including *Ragtime* and Stephen Sondheim's *Follies*, with an all-star cast that included Bernadette Peters, Jan Maxwell, Ellen Paige, Linda Lavin, Régine Zylberberg, Ron Raines, and Danny Burstein. Washington audiences are devoted to the stage; shows often sell out, and those who can't afford the pricey admission to the top venues can find quality, thought-provoking, or edgy entertainment at small regional showcases or often in performance-art spaces.

Classical music is treasured in Washington, home of the National Symphony Orchestra, Washington National Opera, the Washington Chorus, and many other smaller companies and groups that perform the classics. The city also has clubs and bars that host every type of music, from punk and rock to rap, techno, and rhythm and blues. On a national level, the city played a significant role in the development of jazz music. Duke Ellington, considered one of the finest jazz composers, was born in Washington, and he lived near U Street, which, at its prime, was the largest social and urban African American community before Harlem took the spotlight. Theaters such as the elegant Lincoln, an all-African American venue with top-quality entertainment, and the Howard Theatre thrived, as did clubs like Crystal Caverns, now Bohemian Caverns, hosting performers such as Duke Ellington and his Washingtonians, Cab Calloway, Billie Holiday, and Pearl Bailey, who named the U Street area "Black Broadway." The cultural mecca of U Street has rebounded in the past 15 years, now accessible by Metro and home to many clubs and music venues, including the indie and rock forum the 9:30 Club and the Black Cat, an alternative and punk venue, as well as jazz and blues bars. Beyond U Street, which is now frequented by Washingtonians of all ethnicities, lie primarily African American neighborhoods with their own low-key dance halls and clubs, venues that host events featuring the city's own version of funk, called go-go, and halls where young and old practice a unique form of swing called hand dancing or, sometimes, DC swing. As with other areas that have their own unique styles of swing—West Coast swing, Carolina shag—hand dancing developed in the 1920s and 1930s. It is characterized by gliding footwork, continuous hand connection between the partners, and expressive movement with the hands.

ARTS, CRAFTS, AND FOLK TRADITIONS

The city's struggling Historical Society of Washington DC (www.historydc.org) houses several collections of DC artifacts in the former Carnegie Library at Mount Vernon Square as well as a research library that contains a large collection of historical photographs and memorabilia. The Cultural Alliance of Greater Washington (www.cultural-alliance.org) is a popular organization that helps artists, residents, acting troupes, and musicians flourish, helping support, develop, and promote the region as a major arts and culture destination. The website www.culturecapital.org offers an extensive listing of cultural happenings in the city, including shows, openings, events, artisans fairs, and more.

LITERATURE

Most of the writing that goes on in Washington is journalism, requiring the talent to distill complex and often dull bureaucratese and events, paring it into something palatable and comprehensible. Still, Washington often appears in nonfiction works on politics, people, and governance and remains a popular backdrop for fiction novels, although it inspired few to write about its own individual quirks and peculiarities, except for those writers who need the city's alleyways and parks as dead-drops for a great spy caper or dangerous mission. Mark Twain satirized the greed and corruption of the city's upper class in *The Gilded Age,* and Henry Adams explored the same themes—power, greed, and corruption—among politicians in his novel *Democracy.*

In fact, it seems that if an author needs a setting for evil spies, backstabbing politicians, corrupt people, and the do-gooders who battle them, Washington is the perfect setting. Mystery writer Margaret Truman set entire series in Washington, including her most famous work, *Murder at the Smithsonian,* and writers David Baldacci, James Patterson, and Tom Clancy have put their children through college many times over for their mysteries and spy thrillers based in Washington.

But Washington has long nurtured literary talent. New York-born Walt Whitman arrived in Washington in 1862 to help injured soldiers, having already published one version of *Leaves of Grass.* He worked various jobs and as a volunteer Army nurse, inspiring him to pen works on the experience, including *Memoranda During the War, Drum-Taps,* and the often quoted "O Captain! My Captain!" about Abraham Lincoln's death.

Sixty years later in Washington, a former Columbia University student working as a busboy at the Woodley Hotel thrust copies of his poetry at famed poet and customer Vachel Lindsay, who took an interest in the writer. Langston Hughes, who often cited Walt Whitman as inspiration, graduated from Lincoln University in 1929 and went on to publish numerous volumes and inspire generations of writers himself as well as contribute to the efforts of the growing civil rights movement.

The Washington setting, or at least the historic brick quads at Howard University, taught and developed Nobel Prize–winning author Toni Morrison, a student and later a teacher at Howard, who created, honed, and nurtured a short story into her first novel, *The Bluest Eye,* about a young black girl who dreamed of having blue eyes.

And although most of her writing took place in Florida, inspired by the country surroundings and Cracker residents, the Pulitzer Prize–winning Marjorie Kinnan Rawlings, who penned the three-hankie coming-of-age saga *The Yearling,* got her start as a child in Washington, where she jotted stories in notebooks and submitted articles to area newspapers for publication.

Washington is home to the largest collection of Shakespeare materials in the world, the **Folger Shakespeare Library,** a trove of the Bard's printed works assembled by Standard Oil Executive Henry Clay Folger that includes more than one-third of the First Folios—the first collected edition of Shakespeare's writings, printed in 1623—in existence. The collection contains more than 100 Second, Third, and Fourth Folios as well as Shakespeare collections owned by famous temporary residents of Washington, including John Adams and Abraham Lincoln as well as George Washington. The library is considered the foremost research center on Shakespearean works, with 280,000 books and manuscripts and 27,000 rarely seen paintings, drawings, and prints. When library director Gail Kern Paster retired after nine years in 2011, Queen Elizabeth II, via her son Prince Charles, presented her with an award for distinguished service to the arts.

Frederick Douglass, born a slave on Maryland's Eastern Shore and who, after the Civil War, was among the first African Americans to purchase property in the all-white section of DC known as Anacostia, wrote throughout his life, penning *Narrative of the Life of Frederick Douglass, an American Slave,* in 1845.

And several contemporary writers call Washington home, most notably Laura Hillenbrand, author of *Seabiscuit: An American Legend* and *Unbroken.* Hillenbrand has done most of her writing and research from her Glover Park townhome, overlooking the forest and a cemetery in the city; she suffers from chronic fatigue syndrome and rarely leaves her house.

MUSIC

For the title of most famous musician from Washington, it's a toss-up between march king John Philip Sousa and jazz master Duke Ellington, both born in Washington roughly 40 years apart. Sousa penned the country's most recognized march, "Stars and Stripes Forever," while Ellington gained fame worldwide for his compositions, arrangements, and contributions to what he called "American music," jazz. Sousa, born in a row house on G Street SE, two blocks from the Marine Barracks where he spent about one-third of his life, was born to a musical family; his father served as a trombonist with the Marine Band and persuaded his son to apprentice with the group, joining at age 13. Sousa studied all the band's wind instruments as well as the violin and eventually learned to conduct. In 1880 he became the head of the Marine Band and led it for 12 years, a period in which he wrote several famous marches, including the "Semper Fidelis" march (the official march of the Marine Corps) and "The Washington Post" march. His most famous work, the piccolo-imbued national march of the United States, "Stars and Stripes Forever," was written in 1896 after Sousa formed his own band. Marching bands across the world owe much to Sousa, the idea man behind the sousaphone, invented in 1893. Although Sousa moved to New York in later years, he was buried with family members in Washington at Congressional Cemetery.

The city's other famous son is Edward Kennedy "Duke" Ellington, the jazz great who wrote more than 1,000 works that stretched beyond jazz to blues, gospel, popular music, and classical. His talent and leadership in the big band era helped elevate jazz music to level of acceptance in high society on par with classical music. Ellington was born in Washington and lived in the West End not far from Georgetown. As a child he was encouraged to take piano lessons, although he wasn't devoted to them until he became old enough to sneak into pool halls and hear pianists in the bars. He began composing in his head and playing his own music; eventually, under the tutelage of a high school teacher, he received formal training. But Ellington's success was not just attributable to his talent; he was a tireless entrepreneur, a self-promoter who often landed musical gigs as a result of his daytime job as a sign painter. Small gigs turned to larger, and Ellington outgrew Washington. In Harlem, after landing a long-running job at the Cotton Club, fame followed. Ellington is best known for such works as *Such Sweet Thunder* and the *Far East Suite.*

Washington in the mid-20th century was a haven for jazz musicians, with legends like Cab Calloway, Billie Holiday, Shirley Horn, and Leo Parker making appearances. Other notable African American musicians include soprano Lillian Evans Tibbs, the first African American woman to sing opera with a company in Europe; Jelly Roll Morton, who moved to DC in 1935 to perform and enjoy the thriving jazz scene on U Street; and Washington native Charlie Rouse, saxophonist for the Thelonious Monk Quartet. The great Al Jolson, whose appearances in blackface, including the first talking movie *The Jazz Singer,* introduced traditionally African American music to white audiences, spent his childhood in Washington, singing on street corners for coins. Years later, guitarist Charlie Byrd would launch his career from the city, collaborating with others to create a unique sound of bossa nova and jazz.

Several Motown and easy-listening artists called Washington home as well, including Marvin Gaye, Roberta Flack, Herb Fame (of Peaches and Herb, who still performs today with the same Herb and a younger Peaches), and Toni Braxton. Pop singers also called the area home in the 1970s, like the members of the Starland Vocal Band (creators of the impossible-to-forget "Afternoon Delight") and Peter Tork of the Monkees, although he moved away at a young age.

The city's proximity to the South reveals itself in the folk, country, and acoustic shows popular in venues like the Birchmere in Alexandria and Iota in Arlington. Half of the Mamas and the Papas attended George Washington High School in Alexandria (Mama Cass and John Phillips), and more recently, singers like Mary Chapin Carpenter and the late Eva Cassidy developed their talents in the bars and coffeehouses around the region. But DC isn't just about jazz, easy listening, or folksy rock. Two clubs—the 9:30 Club and the Black Cat—have made a name for themselves hosting headlining artists and offering stages to post–hard-core groups like Washington's own Fugazi and Black Flag vocalist Henry Rollins. The Foo Fighters' Dave Grohl is a product of the Washington suburbs; his mother still lives near Springfield, Virginia.

The city is widely known for its underground go-go—the music, not the scantily clad dancers in boots—a blend of funk and sing-talk that features a highly syncopated nonstop backbeat. While the genre never reached a nationwide audience, its riffs feature prominently on Beyoncé Knowles' "Crazy In Love." Homegrown go-go artists include Chuck Brown, Experience Unlimited, Rare Essence, and Trouble Funk.

FILM AND TELEVISION

What cinematographer can resist the lure of Washington's dreamy backdrops? The city has played a role in motion pictures and television since the technology was invented. The 1915 silent masterpiece *The Birth of a Nation,* a highly controversial movie about the Ku Klux Klan and segregation, features horrific images of Klansmen marching down Constitution Avenue. The film explores themes of racism and stereotypes in post–Civil War America more than it focuses on Washington, but it was among the first motion pictures to be shot on location in DC. As the center of government, Washington finds itself in just about any movie about politics, government, U.S. wars, or world affairs. *Mr. Smith Goes to Washington,* the tale of an accidental congressman whose beliefs in honesty and integrity nearly kill him in a battle with a corrupt lawmaker, remains a favorite for many current and wannabe legislators. Naturally, movies about spies, political scandals, and corruption are set in Washington. Some with great shots of the nation's capital include *No Way Out;* Russell Crowe and Ben Affleck's *State of Play; Fair Game,* the Hollywood version of the story behind the outing of CIA officer Valerie Plame; *Salt,* another CIA spy flick about a vixen accused of being a double agent; *In the Line of Fire,* with Clint Eastwood; and Tom Clancy's *Clear and Present Danger.*

Not every movie filmed in DC is a thriller or serious political statement. The raunchy, hilarious *Wedding Crashers* reveals the exploits of two Washingtonians trying to hook up with young wedding guests and bridesmaids; *Burn After Reading* is a black comedy from the Coen brothers with an all-star cast that, in typical Coen brothers fashion, revels in the idiocy of its characters; *Charlie Wilson's War* offers a fairly accurate portrayal of the late representative Wilson's conduct and efforts in the 1970s, according to my sources; *National Treasure* and *National Treasure 2: Book of Secrets* sends Nicolas Cage scurrying all over town and the Eastern Seaboard; and *Night at the Museum: Battle at the Smithsonian* was the first major film ever done inside the Smithsonian.

Washingtonians are often amused by the pains filmmakers take to make other cities look like Washington. While the city is film-friendly, it is difficult to get permission to shut down city streets, and some areas, like the National Mall, require local and federal approval for use. Thus many filmmakers simply rely on other areas to serve as stand-ins. For example, *Transformers: Revenge of the Fallen* features a scene where its star leaves the Stephen F. Udvar-Hazy Center (definitely in the film), but when he steps outside, he's in the desert, with the Arizona or California mountains in the background. For the latest *Transformers* movie, however, director Michael Bay did jump through the necessary hoops to get permission to film on the Mall. The fourth installment of the *Die Hard* series, *Live Free or Die Hard,* didn't even bother; the outdoor shots were filmed in Baltimore and Philadelphia, with some token stock footage of Washington tossed in.

As for television, Aaron Sorkin's *The West Wing,* which ran from 1999 to 2006, was widely hailed as capturing the "feel" of working in the White House, although it was filmed mainly on sound stages in California and sometimes on location in DC and Virginia. The show made the city's commonplace "walk with me" meetings seem fascinating, full of brilliant observations, wittiness, and glib retorts. Other current television shows set in DC but not necessarily filmed in the city include *Bones,* about FBI forensic anthropologists and written by an American University graduate; *NCIS,* a crime show centered on the Naval Criminal Investigative Service; and *Cory in the House,* a Disney Channel sitcom now in reruns about a boy whose father is a White House chef. Classic television shows set in DC include *Get Smart, Murphy Brown, The X-Files,* and *Wonder Woman.* (Linda Carter, for reasons unrelated to playing a superhero in the 1970s, lives in the region).

Washington is home to *It's Academic,* the longest-running quiz show in the world, started in 1961 and airing on local NBC station WRC-TV 4. The show features teams from 171 high schools from across the region competing for the title of champion.

ESSENTIALS

Getting There

Washington DC is nearly the midpoint on the U.S. East Coast, just slightly north of the halfway mark of I-95 if you were to travel its length from Miami to Houlton, Maine. With the exception of the immense traffic that builds up daily along the I-95 corridor south of Washington, starting around Fredericksburg, Virginia, and running north of the city to Baltimore, DC is fairly easy to reach from points north or south by car. Points west and east are a little trickier; no major east–west interstate highway runs through Washington. Historic U.S. 50 is the main thoroughfare from points east, including the Atlantic beaches, and I-66 and I-270 connect the city to Front Royal, Virginia, and Frederick, Maryland, where other highways carry travelers west. Bus service to DC is frequent and often inexpensive; the city is served by Greyhound and a number of other private companies that shuttle travelers between New York City and DC at rock-bottom fares. Train travel is a popular option too—Washington is the southern terminus for Amtrak's *Acela* as well as many of Amtrak's northeast regional trains. And in terms of air travel, DC is connected to the world by three major airports, including Dulles and Reagan National, a quick Metro ride to downtown.

© PATRICIA KIME

BY AIR

Located just three miles south of the Washington Monument with gorgeous views of the capital's landmarks on takeoff and landing, **Ronald Reagan Washington National Airport** (DCA, 703/417-8000, www.met washairports.com/reagan/reagan.htm) is a short-haul airport used for flights within 1,250 miles, with a few notable exceptions passed by Congress to include Denver, Las Vegas, Los Angeles, Phoenix, Salt Lake City, and Seattle. The reasons for such flight restrictions include runway length—Reagan National's runways, built on reclaimed land in the Potomac River, are relatively short—and population density. The airport was built at the edge of Washington halfway between Alexandria and DC in an area well inhabited by the time the main terminal opened in 1941; noise abatement and aircraft mandates are in place that limit the number of flight and the size of aircraft used. The property consists largely of two primary terminals: a historic one that just celebrated its 70th birthday and is set to be renovated to preserve its original grandeur; and a new terminal that opened in 1997 with 35 gates, hundreds of ticket counters, shops, restaurants, and direct access to the Metro and covered parking garages. The historic building currently houses Terminal A, which serves several of the airport's budget carriers. Carriers at Reagan National include American (www.aa.com), United (www.united.com), Continental (www.continental.com), and one foreign airline, Air Canada, as well as a low-cost airlines like U.S. Airways, Spirit, and Air Tran. JetBlue (www.jetblue.com) has also started running a number of flights. Reagan National is a short trip by car in nonrush-hour traffic and by Metro, 15 minutes from the Smithsonian Metro stop, making it a popular choice for business travelers and vacationers who don't want to rent a car. The main terminal has a number of clothing stores, souvenir shops, newsstands, and restaurants, including a Five Guys hamburger stand near one of the main concourses. Reagan National also offers free wireless Internet access throughout its main terminal.

The region's largest airport, **Dulles International Airport** (IAD, 703/417-8000, www.metwashairports.com/dulles), is 26 miles west of the city near Chantilly, Virginia, a nearly 12,000-acre facility that handles more than 23 million passengers per year on 336,500 flights. Dulles's main terminal is an architectural masterpiece, a stunning visual design created by Eero Saarinen in 1962 that's impressive by day, breathtaking at night, and a must-see for students and fans of architecture. The facility has four lengthy runways with a planned fifth that serve long-haul flights, including nonstop trips to Tokyo, Johannesburg, and other major international cities. Dulles, named for Eisenhower's secretary of state John Foster Dulles, has 139 airline gates spread over five concourses, many of them reachable by a new underground electric train system that carries passengers from security to the gates. But passengers heading to Gate D still enjoy a bit of retro airport travel to reach their flight—the gate is still serviced by Dulles's vintage "mobile lounges," 18- by 54-foot wheeled boxes invented by Chrysler in the 1960s that carry people across busy runways and the tarmac to reach their destination. Concourses at Dulles have bars, restaurants, and fast-food stores as well as acceptable, if uninspired, stores. The airport also offers wireless Internet access in most locations. Dulles is roughly a 35-minute car ride from downtown; Metro is currently building a train line to the airport, but an estimated time for construction and completion has yet to be established. Passengers leaving from Dulles should plan to arrive early; a new security plan implemented in 2011 along with the opening of its underground aerotrain seems to have slowed the security checkpoint lines enormously. During peak travel times, you can expect to spend at least 30 minutes in the security line. It is recommended that travelers on domestic flights arrive no later than an hour before their flight; international passengers should consider arriving 2–2.5 hours early.

Dulles is a gateway to the world: 32 airlines fly into the airport, including domestic carriers United, U.S. Airways, Delta, American,

Dulles International Airport

Continental, and Southwest as well as major international airlines like British Airways, Air France, Lufthansa, KLM, South African Airways, and Aeroflot. Smaller international carriers include Cayman Airways and Aer Lingus.

Travelers looking for a deal to Washington often turn to **Baltimore-Washington International Thurgood Marshall Airport** (BWI, 410/859-7111, www.bwiairport.com), a busy regional airport just 45 minutes north of Washington by car or train that is a main hub for Southwest Airlines, responsible for more than half of BWI's load. BWI is served by 14 airlines, flying to 65 domestic destinations and five foreign countries. Travel between BWI and Washington is possible by Amtrak and Maryland's commuter train, MARC, during the week as well as by cab, shuttle bus, and rental car.

BY TRAIN

Washington's main train station is **Union Station** (50 Massachusetts Ave. NE, 202/908-3260, www.unionstationdc.com), the beaux arts–style railway hub designed by Daniel Burnham that's one of the busiest crossroads in the city. Union Station is a major terminus for many trains in the Amtrak system; regional trains arrive from New York and Boston nearly hourly. The high-speed Amtrak *Acela* serves Union Station 15 times per day during the week and a dozen times each weekend day. During the week, Maryland's commuter rail line, **MARC** (www.mta.maryland.gov), runs from Baltimore and makes stops along the way. Also during the week, **Virginia Railway Express** (www.vre.org) carries commuters from Fredericksburg and Manassas, Virginia, to Union Station. Washington's local subway system, the Metro, also has a stop at Union Station for its Red Line trains. Travelers arriving to Washington by train can easily traverse the city by Metro or catch a cab directly outside Union Station to get to their destination.

For regular regional trains, Amtrak runs to Baltimore (40 minutes, $15), Philadelphia (2 hours 10 minutes, $68), New York City

(3 hours 15 minutes, $78), and Richmond, Virginia (3 hours, $31). The *Acela* runs from Boston to DC; a trip on this high-speed railway from New York City takes two hours and 50 minutes and costs $162.

BY BUS

The city's main **Greyhound Station** (1005 1st St. NE, 202/289-5160, www.greyhound.com) is located two long city blocks behind Union Station. Up until a few years ago, this was a sketchy neighborhood, and it's still in the process of transformation, with construction cranes a common sight in the lots surrounding the bus depot along with a large number of vagrants and the homeless who hang around the safe but dirty station. During the daytime, it's OK to walk to Union Station and its Metro stop from the bus station; at night, call a taxi and don't be taken in by drivers who pull up to the station offering rides for a fee. Taxis rarely stop here, so it is best to call for one. Greyhound is an inexpensive but not fast way to travel to other cities like New York. But if you're heading for a destination not served by a train or are on a budget, it can be a wallet-friendly way to travel.

Currently, the most popular method for the budget-conscious of all ages to travel between New York City and DC are independent bus companies often referred to generically as "Chinatown" buses, which make round-trips from locations in Arlington, Virginia, downtown Washington, and Maryland to New York City for relatively inexpensive fares, ranging from $25 one-way and $40 round-trip. They are a viable alternative to Greyhound, although a ticket purchased for one doesn't offer the flexibility of date changes or catching an earlier or later bus that Greyhound has. A couple of the most referred bus companies include **Vamoose** (301/718-0036, www.vamoose.com), with stops in Arlington, Virginia; Bethesda, Maryland; and New York City's Penn Station; **Bolt Bus** (877/265-8287, www.boltbus.com), which now runs from Union Station rather than Chinatown to New York City; and **Dragon Deluxe** (800/475-1160, www.dragondeluxe.com), which picks up in the downtown Chinatown neighborhood. **Megabus** (877/462-6342, www.megabus.com) is another low-cost option that offers trips from a number of destinations besides New York City, including Philadelphia; Pittsburgh; Richmond, Virginia; Charlotte and Raleigh-Durham, North Carolina; and Toronto.

BY CAR

Washington can be accessed by several interstate highways, including I-95, which carries drivers along the entire Eastern Seaboard; I-270, which begins at the Beltway encircling the city (I-495) and ferries vehicles to Frederick, Maryland, where it connects with I-70 and heads west to its endpoint in Utah; and I-66, which also begins (or ends) in DC, running west to Front Royal, Virginia, where it intersects with I-81 for points north, including Canada, or south through America's heartland. U.S. 50 is the primary thoroughfare for travel from the Atlantic Coast to Washington; U.S. 301 runs roughly parallel to I-95 between the city and the coast, an alternate for bypassing Washington's traffic.

By car, Baltimore is about 45 minutes away, Philadelphia is roughly a three-hour drive, and New York City is four hours. Richmond, Virginia, is about two hours south of Washington on a good traffic day.

Getting Around

Washington DC is easily navigable without a car. It is foot-traffic friendly with an extensive public transit system, including inexpensive bus options and numerous opportunities to catch taxis. In fact, for a short stay in the city, a car is somewhat of a financial burden since many hotels and all parking garages charge high rates to keep your car. If you plan to take day trips, including drives to the area's Civil War battlefields and George Washington's Mount Vernon, having a car makes life easier, although your hotel concierge can easily track down a car and driver for a day trip if you didn't come by car. Most visitors and even a lot of locals don't like driving in DC: Traffic lights abound, pedestrians are often unaware of their surroundings, and the system of one-way streets can frustrate drivers unfamiliar with them. Washington is also divided into quadrants that intersect at the U.S. Capitol, so knowing an address's designation—Northwest, Northeast, Southwest, Southeast—is a requirement for finding a location. For example, 900 Pennsylvania Avenue SE lies southeast of the Capitol near Eastern Market in the Capitol Hill neighborhood; 900 Pennsylvania Avenue NW is downtown, northwest of the Capitol.

Washington's public transit system is extensive. Its Metro trains have convenient stops in nearly all city neighborhoods or within half a mile of top destinations. The bus system can get passengers within a couple of blocks of nearly anywhere they want to go, although the routes and schedules are confusing, making this option less suitable for visitors and used mainly by locals. The easy-to-understand and inexpensive DC Circulator bus is used by both visitors and commuters alike to reach destinations along five transit loops.

AIRPORTS

Travel to and from all three airports is easy by car: Reagan National Airport is located in Arlington, Virginia, just off the George Washington Parkway; Dulles International Airport is at the end of the Dulles Airport Access Road on Virginia Route 267; and BWI Marshall Airport is located on Maryland Route 295, the Baltimore-Washington Parkway. Reagan National is the easiest to access by public transportation: A Metro station is located directly across from the main concourse. The Blue and Yellow Lines travel through the station and cost $1.60–2.55 from downtown Metro Center, depending on the time of day. Metro opens Monday–Friday at 5 A.M. and Saturday–Sunday at 7 A.M., and it closes Sunday–Thursday at midnight and Friday–Saturday at 3 A.M. The MARC commuter train and Amtrak run trains to and from BWI and DC's Union Station; MARC, which only runs on weekdays, costs $6; Amtrak costs $14.

All three airports have taxi service: Expect to pay $15–20 for the 15-minute ride from Reagan National to downtown. Washington Flyer is the sole proprietor of taxis at Dulles—a ride from the airport to downtown costs $50–60. A taxi ride from BWI, 45 minutes away, to downtown DC costs about $90.

The three airports are also served by SuperShuttle (800/258-3826, www.super shuttle.com), vans that offer door-to-door service between the airport and major hotels or an agreed-on destination or pickup point. This service bases its prices on zip code; expect to pay about $14 for a trip from National, $29 from Dulles, and $37 from BWI, with charges ranging $10–12 for additional people.

Washington Flyer also runs a shuttle bus service to and from the West Falls Church Metro rail station from Dulles (Mon.–Fri. about 6 A.M.–10:30 P.M., Sat.–Sun. 8 A.M.–10:30 P.M., $10 one-way). A cheaper option is Metrobus's Route 5A (hourly, $4.10), which runs from Dulles to the L'Enfant Plaza Metro station not far from the National Mall.

All three airports have car rental desks with vehicles on-site. The companies at the three airports are **Alamo** (888/215-0010, www.alamo .com), **Avis** (800/331-1212, www.avis.com),

Budget (800/527-0700, www.budget.com), **Dollar** (800/800-4000, www.dollar.com), **Hertz** (800/654-3131, www.hertz.com), **National** (877/222-9058, www.nationalcar.com), and **Thrifty** (877/283-0898, www.thrifty.com). The **Enterprise** (800/261-7331, www.enterprise.com) site at National Airport is located off-site; a shuttle bus transports renters to their offices. The Dulles and BWI locations are on-site.

PUBLIC TRANSPORTATION

The city's public transportation system is overseen by the Washington Metropolitan Area Transit Authority (WMATA, 202/962-1195, www.wmata.org). **Metro** is the most popular, efficient, and easy-to-use way to get around the city, with five color-coded lines that run through the city center and out to the Maryland and Virginia suburbs. Metro has a variable cost schedule depending on the time of day; rush hour is Monday–Friday 5–9:30 A.M. and 3–7 P.M. The system is fairly straightforward; riders purchase fare cards at vending machines at station entrances and exits, first consulting a guide to determine cost based on the time of travel and distance. Fees range $1.60–2.75 during nonpeak hours and $1.95–5 during peak hours. Metro also sells a seven-day Rail Fast Pass, a money-saving deal good for seven consecutive days for those who plan to use Metro extensively during their stay. See the WMATA website for details. Using Metro is easy: Fare cards are inserted into the gate to enter the station and then returned to the passenger, who need it to exit the station at the destination. At the end of a trip, if a rider has spent the exact fare, the gate will keep the ticket. Riders can load varying amounts of money onto their cards when purchasing them, ensuring they don't have to buy a ticket every time they travel. Up to two children age four and under can ride with a fare-paying adult; children over age five must have a standard ticket. The system has eight transfer hubs; riders do not need to leave the station to switch trains. A bit of trivia—the longest escalator in the western hemisphere, 230 feet long, is at the Wheaton Station on the Red Line.

Metro also operates an expansive **bus system** (202/737-7000, www.wmata.org) that

DC's Metro is fast and efficient.

© PATRICIA KIME

travels 340 routes operating in 1,500 square miles. The bus system is not intuitive; check out WMATA's website to determine which bus you need and the schedule. Bus fares start at $1.45 and can cost upward of $3.20 for express buses. Many bus stops (designated by red, white, and blue Metro signs) have the bus designations posted at stops; the system is also placing signage containing the routes and schedules throughout the system.

Visitors find the **DC Circulator** (202/962-1423, www.dccirculator.com) bus to be a convenient and understandable mode of transportation to reach places not accessible by Metro. The result of a public-private partnership between WMATA, the city, and a private company, DC Circulator operates five routes that carry passengers to Georgetown, the Washington Navy Yard, Adams Morgan, and the Southwest Waterfront. Circulator also operates on extended hours to Nationals Park on game days. Bus stops are designated by red and gold signs that resemble the colors of the distinctive red buses. Fares are $1.

DRIVING

Driving around DC isn't hard; it's just a hassle. Honestly, you can get around town quicker by foot, Metro, Circulator bus, or cab as fast as you can in a car. Most visitors to DC do arrive by car, and while it's handy to have one for day trips outside Washington, it's not necessary. Overnight parking rates can add a hefty cost to your vacation, running $25–45 per night at hotels and flat rates of $20 in many parking garages. DC has many metered spaces, but pay close attention to the signs; some parking lanes become travel lanes during rush hour (especially along the National Mall), and your car will be towed. DC has both coin-operated meters that run on quarters and credit-card meters. Sunday parking is usually free.

Washington is laid out in a fairly straightforward grid pattern with numbered and alphabetical streets in order. With a compass, it's nearly impossible to get lost, since most streets run north–south or east–west. The exception is streets named after states, many of which seem to run higgledy-piggledy across the city. Remember that the city is laid out in quadrants; you can determine the location of your destination by paying attention to the "NW, NE, SW, SE" designation at the end of the address. If it is missing, ask for it. You need it to determine where to go. The best local maps are made by ADC (www.adcmap.com) and can be purchased at area book stores. For updates on traffic, check out the websites of the *Washington Post* (www.washingtonpost .com/local/traffic-commuting) and radio station **WTOP** (103.5 FM, www.wtop.com), both know for staying on top of road closings, accidents, police activity, motorcades, and other events.

TAXIS

Taxi cabs in DC operate on time- and distance-based meters, with fares starting at $3 plus $0.25 for each additional one-sixth of a mile, $0.25 per minute for wait time, and $1.50 for each additional passenger. Other rates might apply for taking a cab to the airport, carrying additional luggage, and a dispatch fee if you call for a cab by phone. Top cab companies include: **Yellow Cab** (202/544-1212), **Diamond Cab Company** (202/387-6200), and if you traveling to or from Virginia, **Arlington's Red Top Cab** (703/522-3333).

BICYCLING

Washington is fairly bike-friendly, with numerous off-road trails, bike lanes along main thoroughfares, and bicycle-sharing kiosks located across the metropolitan area. Former mayor Adrian Fenty was an avid cyclist; he set out to make the city more friendly for two-wheelers by embarking on a number of initiatives, including **Capital Bikeshare** (www.capital bikeshare.com), which now has 114 stations and 1,100 bicycles on the streets for borrowing (for a fee). The city has several local groups geared toward encouraging bicycle travel and commuting, including the **Washington Area Bicyclist Association** (202/518-0524, www .waba.com) and **Potomac Pedalers** (202/363-8687, www.potomacpedalers.org), geared to recreational cycling. While DC is making progress on being more bike-friendly, cycling on city streets remains dangerous, and serious accidents occur nearly monthly. Many cyclists stick to the extensive trail system that lines the city's edges along the Potomac River or traverse Rock Creek Park.

DISABLED ACCESS

Nearly all of Washington's museums and major sights comply with the Americans with Disabilities Act, meaning they have been retrofitted with ramps or lifts that may not be near the front entrance but do exist. Some businesses in historic row houses and many streets and sidewalks in historic neighborhoods are difficult to traverse in a wheelchair. Call ahead if you think your destination is in one of these locales. Metro operates elevators at all Metro rail stations; WMATA also operates the **MetroAccess** (301/562-5360, www .wmata.com) program, a shared-ride, door-to-door service for those whose disability prevents them from riding buses or rail; fees vary.

Tips for Travelers

TRAVELING WITH CHILDREN

Washington is a veritable smorgasbord of activities for children; few cities in the United States can best it for its variety of free kid-friendly attractions. The Smithsonian alone has 17 free museums along with the National Zoo—and that's not counting all the monuments, free shows, and government buildings. And when factoring in fun activities for youngsters, don't forget Metro, which children seem to find as fascinating and fun as any major attraction. Washington is well-planned and easily navigated; families and groups with children just need to make sure that youngsters stick with their groups, mind traffic signals, and stay to the right on sidewalks. Among the biggest complaints children have in DC is the heat and the amount of walking they have to do. Be sure your group members stay well hydrated and wear comfortable shoes. Area podiatrists report an uptick each spring of foot injuries from visitors wearing flip-flops, open-toed shoes, or shoes without arch support. Dress children accordingly for what could end up being miles of walking. An ice cream break every afternoon is well worth the investment.

For information on activities and events geared to children, check out the *Washington Post's* "Weekend" guide, available in Friday papers, or www.washingtonpost.com, which has a kids section under the tab "Going Out Guide."

You can also consult the city's official tourism website (www.washington.org), which has an entire section for families under its "Experience DC" tab.

WOMEN TRAVELERS

Washington is an exciting city for those traveling alone, and women can feel safe in the nation's capital nearly all day and night if they stick to the well-populated areas. Some neighborhoods get a little more rowdy late in the evening, and single women travelers should take care not to put themselves in harm's way in areas like U Street and Adams Morgan as the night—and the crowds—become more intoxicated. Most people are friendly and willing to give their opinion on great, safe places to eat and go out at night, so ask if you have concerns. Stick to the main roads and avoid side streets alone at night, even in upscale neighborhoods like Georgetown and Capitol Hill, which are relatively safe—but you don't want to become the exception to the rule. Stay alert. When exercising, stick to main trails that run along the National Mall, major roadways, and the Potomac River, where you will always be in clear view of passers-by, and avoid remote areas such as the wooded trails of Rock Creek Park or Theodore Roosevelt Island, especially during weekdays when the parks are less visited.

SENIOR TRAVELERS

Washington has a great deal to offer seniors, many of whom flock to the city to see its memorials and monuments, especially the National World War II Memorial and the U.S. Holocaust Memorial Museum. The city is very senior-friendly: Its free museums and monuments are soft on the budget, and many other venues offer seniors discounts, including Metro, and some theaters and museums such as the Phillips Collection and the Corcoran. The age definition of "senior" varies with each venue: Some are age 60 and older; others are 62 and even 65 and older. Carry an ID and ask about requirements.

The city has its share of vibrant after-hours neighborhoods, but for the most part, Washington is quiet after about 10 P.M., especially during the week. Noise will not be an issue at your hotel if you stay near the National Mall, in the Penn Quarter section of downtown, in Foggy Bottom, or in the Georgetown hotels described in this book (with the exception of the Georgetown Suites property on the Whitehurst Freeway). Safety is rarely an issue in the popular neighborhoods, even at night.

GAY AND LESBIAN TRAVELERS

Travel safety for LGBT types is not an issue in DC. The city is a popular place for gays to visit and live in, and since March 2010, a destination to get married. Whole swaths of DC owe much to its gay population: The entire Dupont Circle neighborhood was revitalized by gays in the early 1970s and wouldn't be what it is today without their influence. Dupont Circle continues to be known for its diversity, but gay clubs and bars are now no longer centered around this neighborhood; they can be found in all sections of the city and the suburbs.

The *Washington Blade* is the oldest newspaper in the country for the gay community, published weekly on Friday and available at kiosks throughout the metro area. Founded in 1969 as a one-sheet newsletter, it ceased publication in November 2009 when its parent company folded but was revived by staffers who purchased the paper's name, furniture, computers, and archives lock, stock, and barrel and kept the presses rolling. Today, it is the city's primary source for gay-oriented news. In addition to featuring news and information on its website (www.washingtonblade.com), the *Blade* offers an extensive arts and leisure section on gay-oriented activities in the city. Capital Pride is the city's annual gay festival, held during the first full week of June and featuring a parade, a street festival on Pennsylvania Avenue, special events, a gala fund-raiser, dances, parties, and activities. For information on getting hitched or for general information on LGBT events and gay-friendly restaurants, bars, and sights, consult Washington's official tourism guide, www.washington.org, which features an in-depth guide labeled "For LGBT" under its "Experience DC" tab.

TRAVELERS WITH DISABILITIES

The Americans with Disabilities Act was passed by Congress in 1990, and the federal government has put its money where its mouth is, ensuring that Washington has adapted nearly all its federal structures—even the hard-to-alter historic ones—to accommodate disabled and wheelchair-bound visitors. This means that structures like the U.S. Capitol, the White House, the Washington Monument, and all the memorials are accessible to individuals with special needs. Most hotels also are disabled accessible; travelers with disabilities are more likely to encounter issues of access at restaurants and private stores. Information and reviews are available online from **Access Information** (301/528-8664, www.disability guide.org), a nonprofit established by local resident Russ Holt, whose group disseminates critical information to wheelchair users. A hard copy of the guide can be ordered as well.

Metro is wheelchair accessible, with elevators at each station, wide gates for entry and exit, and accessible rail cars. WMATA also operates a transportation system for travelers with disabilities and provides discounts to people with severe disabilities (although it can take up to three weeks to process a request for a discount card). To arrange transportation by MetroAccess, call 301/562-5360. For additional information, call 202/962-1212.

WEATHER

Washington's weather is mercurial, a four-season climate that swings yearly from 100°F-plus days in July to blizzards and wind chills below 0°F in January. Change often comes within 24 hours: You may wake up to fair skies and experience torrential downpours, hail, and high winds by afternoon. The city is technically categorized as "subtropical humid," meaning it has four distinct seasons and summers that are sticky without the cooling breeze you'd find in a tropical paradise near the ocean. The average precipitation is nearly 40 inches a year, including an average of 15 inches of snow, which can fall anytime between early December and the end of March.

July is the warmest month of the year with an average high of 88°F and humidity levels at roughly 55 percent in the afternoon. August isn't much better, with an average of 86°F and the same levels of average humidity. The coldest month is January, with an average high of 42°F, which actually sounds fairly mild, but the average is reached by often wild swings, like the odd 80°F day in December or the below-zero temperatures in February when the occasional arctic air mass dips into the region. Winter is DC's most unpredictable season. Some years, the area receives no snowfall; in December 2009, a storm dropped 20 inches of snow on the city, and a month later, back-to-back storms slammed it with an additional two feet. Ice storms are another frequent event that often shuts down city roads, operations, and businesses. Be prepared for nearly any scenario if you plan to visit Washington in the winter.

WHAT TO TAKE

The weather is going to be the determining factor in what you bring. If you are visiting in the spring, bring a wide selection of warm and light clothes, including a rain jacket, especially in early spring, when the climate is often cool and damp. Late spring tends to be sunny and mild; sunscreen is a necessity. For summer, pack the lightest clothes you own if you plan to spend a lot of time outside. Also, if you think you'll be outside at dusk and in the early evening, carry insect repellent to deter mosquitoes and gnats. Temperatures begin to drop by October, so a light jacket is recommended; by the end of November, the weather becomes unpredictable, and it's wise to bring a heavy winter coat. An umbrella is also recommended. You don't have to carry one around every day, but you'll find one handy if you plan to spend more than a few days here. Runners—don't forget your gear; you'll be disappointed if you leave it at home, given the incredible sights and miles of easy flat trails around the region.

Visitors in DC tend to dress extremely casually—maybe that's the case everywhere—but in the museums you'll also encounter people wearing professional attire (usually on their lunch break from a nearby office). If you wear shorts or succumb to the current fad of wearing pajama bottoms when out sightseeing during the day, you might want to change for dinner, at least into jeans for casual restaurants. The majority of restaurants aren't "coat and tie" fancy but many nicer ones prefer a "casual" or "business casual" dress code. A few restaurants are "jacket required;" those listed in this book are designated as such. Patrons tend to dress in all ways at Kennedy Center, Arena Stage, and other theater venues, from casual to fabulous; Friday and Saturday nights at the symphony or in the opera house tend to be dressier, but still, no need for a tuxedo. Finally, some clubs have and enforce strict dress codes. Do some research before you head out for a night on the town, because often the codes forbid sneakers, chinos, and polo shirts.

CONDUCT AND CUSTOMS
Smoking

In Washington smoking is prohibited indoors at all public workplaces, including museums and federal buildings as well as restaurants and bars. In addition, offices are allowed to post "No Smoking" signs in front of their doorways to keep secondhand smoke from entering building, the result of smokers congregating around entryways. Smoking is allowed at a few establishments, mainly those that sell tobacco such as cigar stores and tobacco "bars," including lounges that have hookahs or on-site humidors. Smoking also is allowed in outdoor areas of restaurants, clubs, and bars, an exception that has turned many of these areas into de facto smoking sections for many establishments. Some hotels still have guest rooms set aside for smokers; if you are one, ask when making reservations whether your hotel is smoke-free to avoid any problems on arrival.

Hours

Washington is in the eastern time zone, five hours earlier than Greenwich Mean Time (GMT), from the first Sunday in November to the second Sunday in March. From mid-March to the first Saturday in November, it operates on Eastern Daylight Time, four hours earlier than GMT.

Early in the week, much of Washington rolls up the sidewalks fairly early, with most restaurants closing by 9 or 10 P.M. and bars shutting down by 2 A.M. On weekends, bars stay open later, with last call before 2:30 A.M. to ensure for complete shutdown by 3 A.M., when all alcohol must be closed or disposed of on premises. Be aware that if you are out enjoying a drink or two from Sunday through Thursday, Metro stops running at midnight, so be prepared to take a cab back to your hotel if plan to stay until last call. Metro stays open later—3 A.M.—on Friday and Saturday to accommodate late-night revelers and the workers who serve them, but as of press time, the transit authority was considering cutting those hours back to midnight as a cost-saving measure. Also, be aware that some establishments have agreements with their residential neighbors to limit their hours; this means that during the week, you'll be shooed inside if you are on a patio after midnight, or the bar might close as early as 1 A.M.

Tipping

Tipping is greatly appreciated in DC and often yields better and friendlier service. In restaurants and bars, 15 to 20 percent is normal for waitstaff and bartenders, and $1 per coat is the norm at checkrooms. Tip the valet $1–3 when you pick up your car.

At your hotel, tip the bellhop who carries your bags at least $1 per bag; tip the concierge at your discretion if they acquire tickets for you, rent a car, call a cab, or perform some other service; tip the housekeeping staff at least a couple of dollars per day, and the valet parking attendant on pickup. Other odd places Americans tip include the hairdresser, hair salons, spas, and barbers, 15–20 percent of the cost of services.

HEALTH AND SAFETY
Hospitals and Pharmacies

Washington has several world-class medical facilities, including **Georgetown University Hospital** (www.georgetownuniversityhospital.org), affiliated with the world-renowned Georgetown University Medical Center, the research and educational arm of the legendary university, and **George Washington University Hospital** (www.gwhospital.com), where Ronald Reagan was rushed after he was shot in 1981 and notables such as former attorney general John Ashcroft, Chief Justice William Rehnquist, and others have been treated. Other hospitals with emergency rooms include **Children's National Medical Center** (www.childrensnational.org), **Washington Hospital Center** (www.whcenter.org), and **Howard University Hospital** (www.huhealthcare.org). Large chain pharmacies such as **CVS** (www.cvs.com) and **Rite Aid** (www.riteaid.com) are located throughout the city, stocking analgesics, cold and asthma remedies, vitamins, health and beauty products, and remedies for mild ailments. Many drugs that are available over-the-counter in other countries are restricted in the United States and available only by prescription.

Emergency Services

In a serious emergency, call **911** for police, fire, and rescue; the call is free from any public phone. Dial **311** for nonemergency services like reporting a theft or property crime that is no longer in progress, minor vehicular accidents, a stray dog, or other issue. To report a power outage or downed power line, contact **Potomac Electric Power Company** (PEPCO, 877/737-2662, www.pepco.com). For travel emergencies and help during a vacation or short-term stay, contact **Travelers Aid Society International** (202/546-1127, www.travelersaid.org), an international nonprofit that helps travelers in financial straits or binds. The society has booths at both Reagan National and Dulles International Airports.

Safety
Violent crime has dropped significantly in the city, down by two-thirds from its highs in the early 1990s, due mainly to a larger police and security presence as well as economic revitalization of once-depressed areas. The events of September 11, 2001, also transformed the city's security; most government buildings, visitor attractions, Metro, and airports have increased their security measures, most noticeable to visitors in the form of electronic scanners and bag checks at entry points. This increased vigilance translates into long lines to enter some buildings, memorials, and monuments. To avoid the long lines, leave backpacks and purses at home and carry what you need for the day in your pockets.

Don't allow the enhanced police presence and frequent checks to lull you into a sense of complacency. Washington is still a major metropolitan area where out-of-towners often make easy targets. In general, the areas that visitors frequent are safe and highly patrolled. But stay alert and keep your belongings and bags close to your body. If you are traveling to a specific destination and have concerns about the neighborhood, ask for an honest assessment from your hotel staff before heading out. In general, much of what is mentioned in this book is in relatively safe areas.

Take extra care after dark. While the main visitor areas often remain populated, there are places that are unlit and secluded. Main stretches in Adams Morgan and U Street, such as 18th Street and U Street themselves, are relatively safe; avoid straying into the surrounding neighborhoods, however, unless you are with someone familiar with them. The same goes for Dupont Circle and Georgetown. Violent crime is a rarity in these areas, but again, you don't want to become the exception.

Information and Services

MAPS AND VISITOR INFORMATION
Destination DC (901 7th St. NW, 202/789-7000, www.washington.org), formerly the Washington DC Convention and Tourism Corp., is the city's primary tourism organization. While it doesn't have a one-stop visitors center, it does distribute maps and brochures and dispense information from its fourth-floor offices in a redbrick building in the Downtown neighborhood at the corner of 7th and I Streets. Pamphlets, information, and tour tickets can also be found at Union Station, with company-run kiosks in the station's Main Hall and hospitality desks to answer questions. Concierges at most large hotels also have maps and brochures and can dispense advice as well as arrange for tickets and services.

MEDIA AND COMMUNICATION
Phones and Area Codes
The main area code for Washington is 202. Much of northern Virginia, including neighboring Arlington and Alexandria, falls under the 703 area code, with area code 571 now used mainly by cell phones but also newer companies and businesses in the region. Area code 301, once the area code for all of Maryland, now covers most of Maryland surrounding metropolitan DC, with 240 used for cell

RELOCATING TO WASHINGTON

Washington, with its mild climate, steady source of jobs, and vibrant community, is a desirable place to live, but the city is also one of the most expensive in the country, according to global consulting company Mercer. A general rule of thumb is the closer residents are to the city center or to a Metro stop, the higher the prices for housing and consumer goods. The high cost of living has forced many to choose to live in outer suburbs – exurbs – but the trade-off comes at a high price; commuters who live in Fredericksburg or Leesburg, Virginia, or Frederick, Maryland, face a 90-minute commute by car one-way each day. Commuting options are plentiful, including commuter trains, buses, Metro, and an organized hitch-hiking movement called "slugging" that allows drivers to pick up passengers heading to the same destination in an effort to increase use of commuting lanes on major highways. Still, residents are often reluctant to abandon their cars, and traffic in DC also remains some of the worst in the country. Despite the drawbacks, residents are willing to pay a premium for the DC lifestyle. If you are planning a move, a number of resources can help.

HOUSING

The *Washington Post*'s real estate section and its apartment guide, as well as the paper's accompanying website, offer a wealth of information about neighborhoods and apartment complexes, including details such as cost, proximity to Metro, information on services and schools, as well as an area's personality. A new website, www.buydccondos.com, gives information on area condominiums, including reviews and information about buildings where condos aren't for sale but may be coming on the market. Washington's Craigslist (http://washingtondc.craigslist.org) is the most popular listing area for condominiums and apartments as well as homes for sale by owner. If you are looking to buy a home, DC has branches of major real estate companies, including Long & Foster, Coldwell Banker, and Weichert, as well as quite a few Web options for low-cost realtor fees and direct transactions, including Franklymls.com and Redfin.

FINDING A JOB

The area's largest employer, the federal government, advertises all its openings at www.usajobs.gov, but the civil service isn't the only game in town. Employment sites like www.dcjobs.com and listing sites, including www.washingtonpost.com/wl/jobs/home, list numerous professional jobs. The newspaper also sponsors quarterly job fairs and publishes special classified sections for the tech, medical, and education sectors. Again, Craigslist has a fair number of job listings, although many of its listings are entry-level or hourly wage positions.

---

phones and many new numbers since 1997. Area code 410 covers Annapolis and its surrounding county, Anne Arundel; Baltimore; and Maryland's Eastern Shore.

Internet Services

If you have your own computer, free wireless Internet access is available in numerous hot spots throughout the city, including all three area airports. For a directory of free and paid wireless hotspots in the city, check out www.jiwire.com. Nearly all DC hotels listed in this book have Internet access, although in some cases, hotels charge a daily fee for access. If the wireless connection in your room is spotty or nonexistent, ask the front desk whether they have a spare Ethernet cable; they often do.

If you don't have a computer and want to access the Internet, many hotels have business centers that provide a computer and access for a fee. FedEx office locations often have computers and printers available for use, again for a fee. The **DC Public Library System** (www.dclibrary.org) offers free Internet access to all library patrons. The library has 24 branches in addition to the Martin Luther King Jr.

Memorial Library (901 G St. NW, 202/727-0321), the central location.

Mail and Messenger Services

The city has numerous post offices managed by the **U.S. Postal Service;** check www.usps.gov or call 800/275-8777 for locations. The main post office is in an off-the-beaten-path neighborhood called Brentwood; the facility is now called the Curseen-Morris Processing Facility in tribute to the unfortunate mail handlers who died in 2001 as a result of processing anthrax-laden envelopes destined for the U.S. Capitol. An especially convenient post office is located at the National Postal Museum next door to Union Station. There are several **FedEx** (www.fedex.com/us/office) locations throughout the city as well as 15 **UPS Stores** (www.theupsstore.com).

Reliable messenger services include **Quick Messenger Service** (240/223-2233, www.qmsdc.com) and **Washington DC Courier Service** (202/986-0100, www.bestmessenger.net).

Magazines and Newspapers

The **Washington Post** is the city's largest-circulation newspaper, with roughly 545,000 daily subscribers. A multiple Pulitzer Prize–winning publication, it is best known for its role in obtaining information linking President Nixon to the break-in at the Democratic National Headquarters in the Watergate hotel and condominium complex, eventually leading to his resignation. Today, it continues to be among the top five newspapers in the country in terms of circulation and the second most popular U.S. newspaper on the Internet. The **Washington Times** began publishing in 1982, an antidote to the perceived liberal leanings of the *Post,* with a commitment to reporting against communism. It is a conservative-leaning newspaper that covers both international and local news and has had financial troubles during the past decade, but in 2011 was repurchased by a group affiliated with its founders, the Unification Church; it is rebuilding under the management of Ed Kelley, former editor of *The Oklahoman.*

The **Washington Examiner** is a tabloid publication delivered free to suburban homes and distributed at kiosks throughout the region; it concentrates primarily on news of local interest. The **City Paper** is an alternative free weekly paper that publishes feature news stories and serves as a resource for happenings about town, including concerts, gallery openings, theater, and events.

Other publications include the **Washington Business Journal,** covering regional business news, and **Washington Jewish Week.** The **Washington Blade** is the main weekly for the gay, lesbian, bisexual, and transgender communities.

The **Washingtonian** is the most widely read lifestyle magazine in the region and for many residents is considered a monthly must-read. Its yearly "100 Best Restaurants" and "Cheap Eats" issues are often kept as reference guides. **Washington Life** and **Capitol File** are two other glossy lifestyle magazines that cover the region.

Radio and TV

The city has six major television stations: **WRC-TV 4** (NBC), **WTTG 5** (Fox), **WJLA-TV 7** (ABC), **WUSA 9** (CBS), **WDCA 20, WETA 26** (PBS), and **WHUT-TV 32** (PBS).

Washington has a variety of radio stations, a thorough listing of which can be found at www.ontheradio.net. Fans of alternative and college radio stations will be disappointed at this major area's surprising lack of a decent radio station. The most popular stations are **WAMU** (88.5 FM, American University Radio, playing National Public Radio and talk), **WKYS** (93.9 FM, hip-hop and urban contemporary), **WPGC** (95.5 FM, hip-hop and urban contemporary), **WMZQ** (98.7 FM, country), **WIHT** (99.5 FM, pop), **WWDC** (101.1 FM, rock), and **WRQX** (107.3 FM, adult contemporary).

Traffic and weather reports can be heard "on the 8s" on news station **WTOP** (103.5 FM). **WMAL** (630 AM) is a popular conservative talk radio station; **WJFK** (103.5 FM) is DC's all-sports station.

PUBLIC LIBRARIES

The main branch of Washington's public library system is **Martin Luther King Jr. Memorial Library** (901 G. St. NW, 202/727-0321, www.dclibrary.org), a Mies van der Rohe–designed building (the only one in the city). In addition to housing thousands of books, it contains more than 1 million photographs from the archives of the *Washington Star*, a newspaper whose editor, Theodore Noyes, served on the library board of trustees for more than 50 years. Funds for its previous building were donated in 1899 by philanthropist Andrew Carnegie. The library has 24 branches.

PLACES OF WORSHIP

Washington's houses of worship are as diverse as the city's population. Protestant and Catholic churches abound, including the second-largest cathedral in the United States by size, the Episcopalian **Washington National Cathedral** (Wisconsin Ave. and Massachusetts Ave. NW, 202/537-6200, www.cathedral.org), and the largest Roman Catholic church in North America, the **Basilica of the National Shrine of the Immaculate Conception** (400 Michigan Ave. NE, 202/526-8300, www.nationalshrine.org). The Roman Catholic Archdiocese of Washington is based at the **Cathedral of St. Matthew the Apostle** (1725 Rhode Island Ave. NW, 202/347-3215, www.stmatthews cathedral.com). Other large churches include the **National Presbyterian Church** (4101 Nebraska Ave. NW, 202/537-0800, www.nat presch.com) and the historic **Metropolitan AME Church** (1518 M St. NW, 202/331-1426, www.metropolitaname.org).

DC has a large Jewish population. *Washington Jewish Week* (washingtonjewish week.com) is an excellent resource for the Jewish community, as is the vibrant staff at **Sixth & I Historic Synagogue** (600 I St. NW, 202/408-3100, www.sixthandi.org), a Jewish center that serves all Jewish denominations.

The massive **Washington DC Temple of Jesus Christ of Latter Day Saints** (9900 Stoneybrook Dr., Kensington, Md., 301/588-0560, www.lds.org) is a sight to behold, an otherworldly blinding-white marble structure visible from I-495 in suburban Maryland. Its interior is not open to the public, but it does have a visitors center. LDS members are admitted in accordance with the tenets of their faith.

The **Islamic Center** (2551 Massachusetts Ave., 202/332-8343, www.islamiccenter.org) in northwestern DC welcomes visitors as well as worshippers to its mosque on Massachusetts Avenue near Embassy Row.

Buddhists can consult the website of the **International Buddhist Committee of DC** (www.ibcdc.org) to help decide which of Washington's meditation centers and temples they want to visit.

MAJOR BANKS

Once home to a number of powerful homegrown banks, including Riggs, American Security, and the National Bank of Washington, the city now resembles nearly every other branch city, with a few notable exceptions, such as **Capital One** (www.capitalone.com), headquartered in nearby McLean, Virginia, and the **National Capital Bank** (www.nationalcapitalbank.com). Several large and small banking companies have branches and ATMs throughout the city, including **Bank of America, BB&T, Wells Fargo,** and **SunTrust.** Expect to pay $2–3 to use an ATM if it is not owned by your bank.

RESOURCES

Suggested Reading

HISTORY, NONFICTION, AND GENERAL INFORMATION

Berg, Scott W. *Grand Avenues: The Story of the French Visionary Who Designed Washington, DC.* New York: Pantheon, 2008. The tale of a brilliant but obstreperous Pierre Charles L'Enfant reads like a novel; *Grand Avenues* captures Washington at its birth, when the Founding Fathers debated, quarreled, and mused over the city's potential, handing responsibility for its design to a Revolutionary War volunteer who hoped to build the world's most stunning capital. L'Enfant died poor and unfulfilled, having been forced to step down from his post as lead designer mainly because of his personality. His vision was largely fulfilled 100 years later by the McMillan Commission. Buckley, Christopher. *Washington Schlepped Here.* Washington DC: Crown, 2003. Political humorist and oldest son of conservative columnist William F. Buckley, Christopher Buckley brings his sass, satire, and vast knowledge of the city to three walking tours of Washington. The book turns readers into Washington insiders, carrying them along the streets of D.C. as it unveils the rich history through anecdotes, factoids, and historic details.

Cordery, Stacy A. *Alice: Alice Roosevelt Longworth, from White House Princess to Washington Power Broker.* New York: Viking Adult, 2007. The glamour, style, politics, and society of beaux arts–era Washington serves as the backdrop for this biography of Theodore Roosevelt's oldest daughter. While much of official Washington, including Alice's father, focused on the business of the times, Alice, with her acerbic tongue and independent streak, enjoyed the glamorous life of a political princess. This biography traces one of America's most popular public figures of the time from childhood to her role as political doyenne and counselor to members of both parties.

Furgurson, Ernest B. *Freedom Rising: Washington in the Civil War.* New York: Knopf, 2004. A readable portrait of Civil War Washington written by a longtime journalist for the *Baltimore Sun,* this book captures the essence of war-torn Washington, of a city rife with Southern sympathizers and abundant with abolitionists at the border of a determined set of breakaway states. *Freedom Rising* traces the history of the city during this tumultuous period, revealing a city's transformation that helped heal a troubled nation.

Moeller, Gerard Martin Jr. *AIA Guide to the Architecture of Washington, DC.* Baltimore: Johns Hopkins University Press, 2006. Washington's architecture spans more than 200 years, and while the city is most noted for its neoclassical buildings, it has a breadth of other styles and treasures revealed in this guide. An excellent read for its historical anecdotes and essays as well as its photographs.

Peck, Garrett. *Prohibition in Washington, DC: How Dry We Weren't.* Charleston, SC: The History Press, 2011. A romp through the city's 3,000 backrooms and speakeasies during the 16 years of Prohibition (in DC; in the rest of the country it was 14 years), this entertaining tour of a book includes photos, recipes, and an overview of the model city for the Temperance movement as it partied its way through the national dry spell.

Woodward, Bob, and Bernstein, Carl. *All the President's Men.* New York: Simon & Schuster, 1974. The meticulous gumshoe investigation of a third-rate burglary by two journalists for the *Washington Post*'s Metro section brings down a president. From an early-morning phone call about a break-in at the Democratic National Headquarters to clandestine meetings in underground parking lots, document drops, and wiretaps, the story of the Watergate scandal remains riveting 40 years later.

LITERATURE AND FICTION

Adams, Henry Brooks. *Democracy: An American Novel.* New York: Henry Holt & Co., 1880. A best seller in its day and still considered the quintessential political novel, *Democracy* traces the discoveries and disappointments of Madeleine Lee, a widow who travels to the city to understand the business of power. Through a presidential election, befriended by the elite and pursued by an influential senator, Lee learns the lessons of her predecessors and successors: that power can corrupt even the most sincere. Buckley, Christopher. No one is safe from Buckley's withering satire splayed over the course of 14 novels, including *Thank You for Smoking* (New York: Random House, 1994), *No Way to Treat A First Lady* (New York: Random House, 2003), and *Little Green Men* (New York: Random House, 1999). Buckley's humorous look at self-absorbed Washington will have you laughing out loud, regardless of your political leanings.

Pelecanos, George. *The Night Gardener.* New York: Little, Brown and Co., 2006. Brooklyn-born George Pelecanos has discovered gold in the streets, bars, and neighborhoods of Washington DC, the backdrop for crime novels that tear at the seamy underbelly of the "real" DC. *The Night Gardener* follows two detectives as they investigate the murder of a 14-year-old girl, digging into the motivation of the murderers, the investigators, and everyone in between.

Vidal, Gore. *Washington DC: A Novel.* New York: Little, Brown and Co., 1967. In the same vein as *Democracy,* Vidal's novel, the sixth in his *Narratives of an Empire* series, traces two political families from the late 1930s through the Cold War, examining their rise to power and efforts to remain at the top. The characters' stories can be recognized today with each report of political scandals, horse-trading, and political grandstanding.

Suggested Viewing

The American President. Before he created *The West Wing,* Aaron Sorkin tested the waters for an intimate portrayal of a White House president with this romantic political drama directed by Rob Reiner. Reiner's love for the city pervades the entire movie, with numerous shots of the White House, the Capitol, the Washington Monument, the Willard Hotel, and the Cato Institute, a libertarian think tank, representing the company where environmental lobbyist Sydney Ellen Wade, the president's love interest, played by Annette Bening, worked.

Get Smart. For five season in the late 1960s, Agents 86 and 99 (Don Adams and Barbara Feldon) amused and entertained the nation, spoofing the James Bond series and diverging from the standard comedy shows of the day by focusing on work rather than families. The series, created by Mel Brooks, showcased physical comedy, brilliant satire, and a stunning parade of guest stars.

Mr. Smith Goes to Washington. The 1939 Frank Capra film remains a favorite for many current representatives, senators, and idealistic young staffers. A sentimental story about a naive young senator going toe-to-toe with a corrupt politician continues to win fans and educate them about the odd but useful tool called the filibuster.

St. Elmo's Fire. Probably the worst of the brat pack–genre films, this 1985 movie elevates the obnoxious and self-absorption to a new level, but since the setting is Washington, it makes so much *sense.* Worth watching for the great '80s styles of its stars, including Emilio Estevez, Rob Lowe, Andrew McCarthy, Demi Moore, Judd Nelson, and Ally Sheedy, the portrayal and film shots of Washington, and for some a two-hour trip down memory lane, when the Sign of the Whale, Mr. Days, and Third Edition bars packed the house nightly. The Tombs—the inspiration for this movie of disillusionment and angst—continues to be a favorite hangout of Georgetown University students and new alums, just like the ones in the movie.

The Stone Carvers. This Oscar-winning 1984 short film portrays a few of the last stone carvers working in the United States, those sculpting the decorative touches and ornamentation of the Washington National Cathedral. The stonemasons take the audience through a tour of the cathedral for a glimpse into its history.

The West Wing. Loved by many critics from both sides of the aisle and often derided as "The Left Wing," this television show, which aired on NBC from 1999 to 2006, captured the essence of a presidential administration, albeit one protected, it seems, from mundane daily routines. Brilliant writing from Aaron Sorkin explored the humanity behind the difficult decisions made daily at the White House.

Internet Resources

GENERAL INFORMATION
Destination DC
www.washington.org
Operated by Destination DC, formerly the Washington, DC Convention and Tourism Corporation, this comprehensive user-friendly site features listings of attractions, restaurants, hotels, and events, with suggested itineraries for special groups and seasonal advice as well as discounts and package deals.

District of Columbia
www.dc.gov
The city's official website includes links to the Washington Metro website, attractions, history, and libraries as well as the websites for the mayor, city council, and agencies. A great resource for new Washington residents, it includes information on city laws and regulations as well as links to the Department of Motor Vehicles and parking registration offices.

Cultural Tourism DC
www.culturaltourismdc.com
A 230-member organization geared toward advancing the arts, history, and culture in Washington, this site features listings, recommendations, and ideas for experiencing the city's vast cultural offerings. The website features

tours and attractions and serves as the source for Passport DC, the international festival in May whose highlights include embassy tours.

National Park Service
www.nps.gov

According to Destination DC, 70 percent of the land in the city is controlled by the National Park Service, including the National Mall and its landmarks, Rock Creek Park, East and West Potomac Parks, and a host of neighborhood parks, monuments, and memorials. The National Park Service website holds numerous keys to enjoying these vast spaces as well as itineraries and information on places of interest.

Smithsonian Institution
www.si.edu

A helpful guide before visiting any Smithsonian museum or an ongoing resource for the thousands of events and special exhibits that take place yearly at the Smithsonian, this website features information on special events and opportunities, tours, attractions, hours, and more. It also has tips for families with children, groups, and those needing special accommodations.

Washington Metro Area Transit Authority
www.wmata.com

Featuring timetables, maps, and an interactive capability that helps riders determine how to travel between points, this site include bus and subway information as well as fares and advance ticket purchasing.

WTOP
www.wtop.com

For weather, traffic, or local news, WTOP maintains a handy interactive traffic website, perfect for planning around construction delays and heavily traveled roads. It is also one of the best sites to go for weather updates. For local news it is also unmatched, but sometimes the station's rush to be first leads to eating humble pie later.

EVENTS LISTINGS
Washington City Paper
www.washingtoncitypaper.com

Information on the city's offbeat, hip, alternative, and unusual events as well as standard fare can be found at the site of the city's independent alternative weekly.

Washingtonian
www.washingtonian.com

The magazine read widely by Washingtonians maintains a site for those who want to find out about events attended and enjoyed by insiders, from gallery openings and shows to concerts and galas held throughout the city.

Washington Post Going Out Guide
www.washingtonpost.com/gog

A comprehensive overview of what seems to be everything to do in Washington can be found in this easily navigable website, with helpful guidance from the *Post* staff ("editors' picks"), reviews, advice, and links to an entertaining blog with suggestions and opinions on current offerings from the *Post*'s Going Out Gurus.

WASHINGTON'S BEST BLOGS
Capital Weather Gang
www.washingtonpost.com/blogs/capital-weather-gang

For an understanding of why Washington weather is capricious, check out this blog, entertainingly written by several folks who have their heads in the clouds. From whiteout blizzards to dangerous heat and humidity, the Capital Weather Gang has it covered.

DCIST.com
www.dcist.com

Dedicated to providing residents hyperlocal news, commentary, and events listings, DCist gives up-to-the-minute information on the bus accident down the road or the latest review of the hottest new local band.

Prince of Petworth
www.princeofpetworth.com

A look at the DC neighborhoods that aren't Georgetown or Capitol Hill, this blog focuses on the news and information of DC in areas such as Adams Morgan, U Street, and Petworth, with posts on restaurant and business openings and closings, real estate transactions, and area events.

Wonkette
www.wonkette.com

The left-leaning Wonkette focuses on political discourse, trashing the mainstream media and simply being snarky, although the sarcasm is usually accompanied by a hefty dose of well-thought-out political discourse.

Index

Restaurants Index

Nightlife Index

Shops Index

Hotels Index

www.moon.com

DESTINATIONS | ACTIVITIES | BLOGS | MAPS | BOOKS

MOON.COM is ready to help plan your next trip! Filled with fresh trip ideas and strategies, author interviews, informative travel blogs, a detailed map library, and descriptions of all the Moon guidebooks, Moon.com is all you need to get out and explore the world—or even places in your own backyard. While at Moon.com, sign up for our monthly e-newsletter for updates on new releases, travel tips, and expert advice from our on-the-go Moon authors. As always, when you travel with Moon, expect an experience that is uncommon and truly unique.

MOON IS ON FACEBOOK—BECOME A FAN!

JOIN THE MOON PHOTO GROUP ON FLICKR

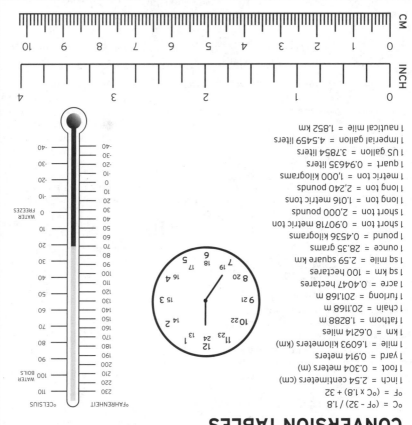

CONVERSION TABLES

°C = (°F - 32) / 1.8
°F = (°C x 1.8) + 32
1 inch = 2.54 centimeters (cm)
1 foot = 0.304 meters (m)
1 yard = 0.914 meters
1 mile = 1.6093 kilometers (km)
1 km = 0.6214 miles
1 fathom = 1.8288 m
1 chain = 20.168 m
1 furlong = 201.168 m
1 acre = 0.4047 hectares
1 sq km = 100 hectares
1 sq mile = 2.59 square km
1 ounce = 28.35 grams
1 pound = 0.4536 kilograms
1 short ton = 0.90718 metric ton
1 short ton = 2,000 pounds
1 long ton = 1.016 metric tons
1 long ton = 2,240 pounds
1 metric ton = 1,000 kilograms
1 quart = 0.94635 liters
1 US gallon = 3.7854 liters
1 Imperial gallon = 4.5459 liters
1 nautical mile = 1.852 km

MAP SYMBOLS

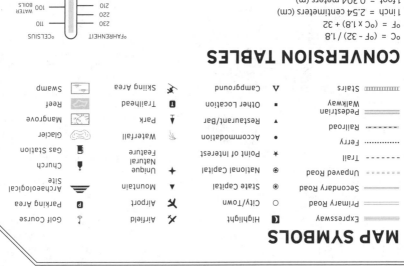

- Expressway
- Primary Road
- Secondary Road
- Unpaved Road
- Trail
- Ferry
- Railroad
- Pedestrian Walkway
- Stairs

- Highlight
- City/Town
- State Capital
- National Capital
- Point of Interest
- Accommodation
- Restaurant/Bar
- Other Location
- Campground

- Airfield
- Airport
- Mountain
- Unique Natural Feature
- Waterfall
- Park
- Trailhead
- Skiing Area

- Golf Course
- Parking Area
- Archaeological Site
- Church
- Gas Station
- Glacier
- Mangrove
- Reef
- Swamp

MOON WASHINGTON DC
Avalon Travel
a member of the Perseus Books Group
1700 Fourth Street
Berkeley, CA 94710, USA
www.moon.com

Editors: Shari Husain, Erin Raber, Jamie Andrade
Series Manager: Erin Raber
Copy Editor: Christopher Church
Production Coordinator: Elizabeth Jang
Graphics Coordinator: Elizabeth Jang
Cover Designer: Elizabeth Jang
Map Editor: Albert Angulo
Proofreader: Elizabeth Hui
Cartographers: Albert Angulo, Kaitlin Jaffe, Heather Sparks

ISBN-13: 978-1-61238-038-4
ISSN: 2160-8385

Printing History
1st Edition – February 2012
5 4 3 2 1

Front cover photo: Looking upwards at the columns of the Supreme Court building © Amalia Ferreira-Espinoza/www.4femimages.ca

Title Page: Mama Ayesha's Presidential Mural, 1967 Calvert Street NW Washington DC 20009, USA. Artist name: Karlisima Rodas. Karlisima Fine Art, Murals & Graphic Design. www.Karlisima.com Art Studio Tel. 202-483-3630. Mural funded in part by the D.C. Commission on the Arts and Humanities and by Mama Ayesha's Restaurant – www.mamaayeshas.com. Photo courtesy of Daniel Lobo – Daquellamanera.org.

Interior color photos: p. 2 (left) the Supreme Court building, (center) Vietnam Veterans Memorial, (right) Winged Victory, 1st Division American Expeditionary Forces Memorial, all © Patricia Kime; p. 23 (inset) the White House © Ritu Jethani/123rf.com, (bottom left) Arlington National Cemetery © Patricia Kime, (bottom right) cherry blossoms near the U.S. Capitol building © Emanuel Kaplinsky/123rf.com; p. 24 © Patricia Kime; p. 25 © Yevgenia Gorbulsky; p. 26 © Patricia Kime; p. 27 © Brandon Bourdages/123rf. com; p. 29, 30, 31 © Patricia Kime; p. 32 © Gary Blakeley/123rf.com

Printed in Canada by Friesens

All recommendations, including those for sights, activities, hotels, restaurants, and shops, are based on each author's individual judgment. We do not accept payment for inclusion in our travel guides, and our authors don't accept free goods or services in exchange for positive coverage.

Although every effort was made to ensure that the information was correct at the time of going to press, the author and publisher do not assume and hereby disclaim any liability to any party for any loss or damage caused by errors, omissions, or any potential travel disruption due to labor or financial difficulty, whether such errors or omissions result from negligence, accident, or any other cause.

KEEPING CURRENT

If you have a favorite gem you'd like to see included in the next edition, or see anything that needs updating, clarification, or correction, please drop us a line. Send your comments via email to feedback@moon.com, or use the address above.